REFERENCE

Encyclopedia of American Holidays and National Days

REFERENCE

ENCYCLOPEDIA OF AMERICAN HOLIDAYS AND NATIONAL DAYS

Volume 1

Edited by Len Travers

GREENWOOD PRESS
WESTPORT, CONNECTICUT • LONDON

Library of Congress Cataloging-in-Publication Data

Encyclopedia of American holidays and national days / edited by Len Travers.
p. cm.
Includes bibliographical references and index.
ISBN 0–313–33130–8 (set) — ISBN 0–313–33131–6 (vol. 1) — ISBN 0–313–33132–4 (vol. 2) 1. Holidays—United States—Encyclopedias. 2. United States—Social life and customs—Encyclopedias. I. Travers, Len, 1952–
GT4803.A2E63 2006
394.26973—dc22   2005036319

British Library Cataloguing in Publication Data is available.

Library of Congress Catalog Card Number: 2005036319

ISBN: 0–313–33130–8 (set)
0–313–33131–6 (vol. 1)
0–313–33132–4 (vol. 2)

First published in 2006

Greenwood Press, 88 Post Road West, Westport, CT 06881
An imprint of Greenwood Publishing Group, Inc.
www.greenwood.com

Printed in the United States of America

The paper used in this book complies with the Permanent Paper Standard issued by the National Information Standards Organization (Z39.48–1984).

10 9 8 7 6 5 4 3 2 1

CONTENTS

VOLUME 1

VOLUME 2

PREFACE

The entries in this volume trace the origins and development of some of most significant civic and religious observances in America today. In addition to the officially recognized, federally mandated holidays currently observed, we have chosen to include ceremonial and festive occasions from the nation's past, as well as new holidays emerging from contemporary American life. As the following essays reveal, public holidays and festive days are manufactured "organic" entities, created and shaped to serve the needs of the people observing them. Some have outlived their usefulness and have disappeared from the American calendar—or nearly so. Others are of recent coinage, vying for official approval, or achieving near-holiday status by popular acclaim, regardless of official endorsement. All tell us a great deal about the shared, and contested, values Americans hold and have held.

The contributors to this volume are scholars in the fields of American history, folklore, politics, and popular culture. They have researched and published, some extensively, on their subjects in recent years. Together they bring the most current scholarship on American festive culture to these pages for the academic and lay reader alike. Presented in a chronological framework from Martin Luther King Jr.'s Birthday to New Year's Eve, each article traces the origins, development, and maturation of a holiday, paying particular attention to changes in its forms of celebration, and its purpose, popular perception, and significance.

In order to treat the holidays featured in this volume in appropriate depth, the editors have had to impose restraints in breadth. This collection is not and cannot be exhaustive; we have for example excluded the nearly innumerable state and local holidays that now make up (or once did) so much of Americans' cultural experience. To determine the entries for this book, we first looked for rites and holidays with significance of regional or national scope, eschewing those of strictly local consequence. We determined to include treatments of both civic and major religious holidays, rather than to impose distinctions, on the understanding that Christmas and Easter as practiced in the United States might be as American as Memorial Day. The editors also desired to address festive and ceremonial occasions derived from major ethnic and cultural groups within the present United States. Hence the reader will find in this book treatments of Kwanzaa, Native American Powwow, and Passover, as well as the more universally familiar Mother's Day, Thanksgiving, and Independence Day. Last, we sought out scholars whose work has focused on the holidays and festive occasions meeting the above criteria. Thus, while not comprehensive, our collection comprises most of America's premier holidays, while hinting at the rich variety of commemorative activity that exists beyond this volume's bounds.

INTRODUCTION

Over the last several decades especially, American historians have emphasized the usefulness of public holidays for comprehending the formation of political culture in the United States. They have been guided, to a greater or lesser degree, by two complementary models borrowed from social science. The first, that of "imagined communities," comes from the work of Benedict Anderson, who explains the formation of modern nationalism as mental leaps on the parts of people willing to subordinate parochial beliefs and practices to larger, "master narratives" of belonging that embrace people with different beliefs and practices.[1] "America," for example, is a nation comprised of Jews and Gentiles, Anglo-Saxons and African Americans, conservatives and progressives, native-born and immigrant, all of whom claim "Americanness" despite their racial, ethnic, and political diversity. The second model employs the concept of "invented traditions" described by Eric Hobsbawm.[2] This model describes the often self-conscious creation of cultural memory through appropriate rituals, symbols, apparel, speech, art and musical forms, customs, and beliefs—in a word, heritage. As the reader will discover, American festive culture owes much to a great number of invented traditions, the regular celebration of which, at carefully prescribed times, forges American identity, even while many of these (such as St. Patrick's Day) ostensibly celebrate distinctiveness.

American public observances, like those anywhere, are often distinguished by their style, that is, by the demeanor and behavior expected of those taking part. Sociologist Ronald L. Grimes made pertinent distinctions between *ceremonial* and *celebratory* occasions.[3] Ceremonial events tend to be rigidly structured affairs, demanding a relatively high level of decorum. In the course of the ceremony the participants signify their respect for the causes, values, offices, or traditions represented in the performances. Ceremony is thus clearly a structuring activity, reinforcing and validating the identities and convictions of those participating. Veterans Day and Passover are examples of observances marked primarily by ceremonial style. Celebration, on the other hand, is not (intentionally) structuring, largely dispenses with decorum, and permits, indeed encourages, recreation tending to exuberance. Merriment and fun is the whole point, or at least it seems to be. There is no apparent message in celebration, no necessary result, and, unlike ceremony, spontaneity is perfectly acceptable—within prescribed limits. Into this category readers may easily place Mardi Gras and New Year's Eve.

Most commonly however, holidays combine both observance styles to varying degrees. Independence Day, for example, has always been marked, as John Adams predicted, by "solemn acts of devotion to God almighty . . . solemnized with pomp and parade" but also "with shows, games, sports, guns, bells, bonfires, and illuminations, from one end of this continent to the other, from this time forward, forevermore."[4] Christmas has become very much a mix of these two styles, with sincere Christian devotion coexisting (uneasily) with crass consumerism. And even Memorial Day, that solemn day of remembrance and veneration, has its Indianapolis 500 and its modern status as the unofficial beginning of the summer recreation season.

Thus the modern American festive calendar is a polyglot of occasions religious and secular, family- and community-centered, serious and silly. Virtually all have had to fight for their place in the calendar and for their acceptance by the American people, for prior to 1776 there were few red-letter days in the English calendar, and no regular days off except the Sabbath. In the sparsely populated Spanish colonies there were the numerous saints' days, but these were not grafted onto the national festive calendar once these regions became part of the United States. After the creation of the American republic, nationally recognized holidays or festive occasions were adopted slowly, sometimes grudgingly, by people commonly accustomed to uninterrupted work patterns. In the last decades of the nineteenth century, the number of holidays increased markedly, responding to a growing middle class's demand for leisure, labor and veterans' groups' demands for justice, and immigrants' demands for acceptance. As this collection makes clear, the list of holidays now competing for Americans' attention is the result of more than two centuries of cultural negotiation and political pressure.

Some of the observances included in this book did not stand the test of time. Arbor Day is but a distant memory for most Americans, and Congress has not declared a fasting day in a long time. America's most traumatic wars inspired patriotic observances, most of which are now defunct, or nearly so. The War of Independence produced Evacuation Day in Boston and New York, commemorating the withdrawal of British troops from those cities, but these observances rarely extended beyond the municipal locale. Even Patriots Day, marking the opening shots of the war that began on April 19, 1775, is a holiday only in Massachusetts. The Civil War gave rise to the modern Thanksgiving, of course, and to Memorial Day, but also to distinctively Southern red-letter days. Robert E. Lee's birthday and Thomas "Stonewall" Jackson's birthday contributed to the elevation of these generals to the pantheon of American heroes, and to the romanticizing of the South's "Lost Cause," but were primarily observed in the generals' native state of Virginia. For the World War II generation, VE Day and VJ Day recalled the euphoria of ending the century's most devastating war, but public appreciation for these days too has lapsed. American holidays do not generally commemorate or celebrate wars; Veterans Day, which grew out of World War I's Armistice Day, is perhaps closest to the exception in that regard.

The above examples demonstrate a vital point: successful commemorations must meet the spiritual and intellectual needs of those who create and observe them, but to remain relevant and retain broad appeal, their vital directives must be capable of adapting to succeeding generations and shifting concerns. Armistice Day, originally dedicated to remembering the American dead of World War I, was soon overshadowed by a decade-long depression; another, bigger, world war; the Cold War; and the Korean War. Rechristened Veterans Day in 1954, November 11 now honors the living veterans of all wars—especially significant in an era of officially undeclared but still lethal conflicts. Christmas provides a more cheerful example of adaptation. Greatly shunned in predominantly Protestant early America, the now indispensable holiday gained visibility in the nineteenth century with the new wave of European immigrants, and respectability via the British royal family. Assaulted in the twentieth century by shameless commercialism, and faced with an increasingly multicultural population, Christmas nevertheless maintains its place in the first rank of American holidays by mingling rites of homecoming, family, and generosity with the original Christian directive to honor the birth of Christ. As with natural selection, it seems, so with holidays: a certain flexibility is the key to survival.

This adaptive requirement raises the issue of the functional character of commemorative days, and in this regard historians are greatly indebted to social scientists such as Victor Turner and Claude Levi-Strauss. These and other scholars remind us that holiday observances are based on ritual processes, and that these rituals are chiefly meant to express beliefs, assert identity, and strengthen solidarity. The political application of this principle should be obvious, as it was to a French observer of an Independence Day celebration in the midst of the Revolutionary War against Britain. He noted that with the war not yet won, patriotic celebrations were "usual and frequent with the Americans, probably because they need to maintain their spirits at a high degree of enthusiasm."[5] The urgent, immediate function of Independence Day has faded, but since that time, politicians of every stripe have delivered orations, manipulated symbols (such as flags), and marched in parades each year in efforts to marshal the unifying message of the day for particular agendas.

As often as not, however, what they find is division rather than unity. The recognition that public commemorations are essentially persuasive exercises, usually endorsing and reinforcing the status quo, fairly invites alternative or competing expressions. Realizing the capacity of holiday rituals to validate and authenticate, to foster inclusion, "outsider" groups often attempt to become "insiders" by winning acceptance as participants in those rites. Thus, holidays often prove moments of conflict, as formerly shunned or ignored groups struggle for recognition and legitimacy. In the early republic, Democratic-Republicans clawed their way to national prominence in part by reinventing Independence Day as an occasion on which to castigate Federalist policies, while their Federalist rivals championed the celebration of George Washington's birthday to mark their own distinctiveness. During the nineteenth century, labor organizations agitated for acceptance, eventually winning a nationwide Labor Day.

Recognition (often grudging) of America's multicultural character has added variety as well as conflict to the American festive calendar. In a manner similar to that described above, immigrant organizations more than a century ago fought back against nativist efforts to marginalize or exclude them from full American membership. The results of these efforts produced new holidays, widely or even nationally recognized, such as Columbus Day, St Patrick's Day, Hanukkah, and Cinco de Mayo. African Americans, combating the heritage of slavery and the lingering effects of a century of Jim Crow legislation, have also been successful, to varying degrees, in registering dissent or securing recognition via the commemorative process. Frederick Douglass challenged white Americans to live up to the promise of the republic with his famous Independence Day address, "What to the Slave is the Fourth of July?" It took the assassination of civil rights leader Martin Luther King in 1968, however, to win a federally approved place in the calendar for American blacks. With the "culture wars" of the late twentieth and early twenty-first centuries far from over, however, the potential for American holidays to serve as occasions for political posturing, protest, and negotiation of "Americanness" remains strong. Consequently, modern Americans should not be surprised to see Kwanzaa so pointedly juxtaposed with Christmas, Irish American gay rights activists demanding a place in South Boston's St. Patrick's Day parade, or Native Americans observing a "Day of Mourning" on Thanksgiving.

Perhaps it is because of the inherent potential for conflict in existing holidays that some of the "holidays" gaining currency in modern America are so emphatically apolitical. Super Bowl Sunday, Mardi Gras, and even the weeklong, hedonistic festival known as Spring Break, are semirecognized "antiholidays" seemingly dedicated to pure fun. On these occasions there is no apparent patriotic message, no strictly religious import, no desired result beyond having a good time. Recalling the characterizations made earlier, we might say that these new observances are virtually devoid of the ceremonial and are strictly celebratory. It would be a mistake, however, to dismiss these occasions as trivial, or as functionless. All attract huge numbers of Americans from all walks of political and social life, and all demand that divisive intrusions such as religion and politics be temporarily forgotten in the name of family, friends, and fellowship. Super Bowl Sunday is the new quintessential American holiday of homecoming, featuring communal feasting and gathering together around the "hearth"—in this case, the largest television in the "family." If Super Bowl Sunday is the new Thanksgiving, then perhaps Mardi Gras is the new rite of spring, with its spiritual center in a warm locale, where extraneous clothing and inhibitions may be shed—again, temporarily—to welcome a season universally associated with the renewal of life. And for college students similarly inclined, Spring Break has risen to the level of an academic rite of passage. Despite their seemingly chaotic cachet, each of the above occasions promotes, in its own way, a communion of the faithful.

Some Americans fear that the proliferation of holidays, and government manipulation of their observances, has already diluted the American ceremonial calendar, never mind whatever new holidays, official or unofficial, wait in the wings. With the passage of the Monday Holiday Act in 1968, the federal government relegated the observance of several formerly "floating" holidays, such as Columbus Day and Memorial Day, to the first day of the traditional working week. In doing so, knowingly or otherwise, they sacrificed a degree of meaning intrinsic to these days to corporate expediency and the American culture of leisure—the three-day weekend. But while some see civil declension in the disparate ways in which American holidays are observed, abused, or ignored, others remain optimistic. In the sincerity with which many still regard American holidays, the optimists see the continuing potential for these occasions to educate, inspire, and unite. This is so not only for already well-established holidays. In contrast to the mostly frivolous emergent holidays described above, Earth Day, a grass-roots production first observed in 1970, combines festivity with a message of serious concern that crosses religious, ethnic, and political lines. Despite an undoubted loosening of decorum in the American celebratory style, despite the bitterness and discord often attending even our most entrenched civic and religious holidays, despite the rampant commercialism, multiplicity of messages, and widespread apathy, holidays have always *mattered* to the great majority of Americans. They still do, and for that reason alone this volume is necessary.

NOTES

1. Benedict Anderson, *Imagined Communities: Reflections on the Origins and Spread of Nationalism* (London: Verso, 1991).

2. Eric Hobsbawm, "Introduction: Inventing Traditions," in *The Invention of Tradition,* ed. Eric Hobsbawm and Terrence Ranger (Cambridge: University of Cambridge Press, 1983), 1–14.

3. See Ronald L. Grimes, *Beginnings in Ritual Studies* (Lanham, Md.: University Press of America, 1982), 41–49.

4. John Adams to Abigail Adams, July 3, 1776.

5. Quoted in Elmer Douglas Johnson, "A Frenchman Visits Charleston in 1777," *South Carolina Historical and Genealogical Magazine* 52, no. 2 (April 1951), 89.

MARTIN LUTHER KING JR.'S BIRTHDAY

The establishment of a national holiday honoring Martin Luther King grew out of the numerous localized efforts to honor King in the aftermath of his assassination. During the months following King's death on April 4, 1968, many communities reacted by naming streets, schools, and other public landmarks after the slain leader. In Chicago, the major avenue on the city's south side became Martin Luther King, Jr. Drive. At colleges and universities throughout the nation, campus buildings and new programs were named in King's honor.

Supplementing these efforts, Coretta Scott King began to play an increasingly important role in mobilizing popular support for a holiday honoring her slain husband. On June 26, 1968, she founded the Martin Luther King, Jr. Memorial Center (later renamed the Martin Luther King, Jr., Center for Nonviolent Social Change, Inc., and then simply The King Center). The King Center soon became an important repository of King's papers and attracted growing numbers of researchers studying his life and the movements with which he was associated. In addition, the Center's staff soon began to play a significant role in organizing nationally visible commemorations of King's birth. On January 15, 1969, The King Center held an ecumenical service and other events to observe the date of Dr. King's birth 40 years earlier.

During the 1970s, these efforts gained momentum as African Americans acquired increased political power, and popular interest in African American history became more evident. In 1971 Atlanta, Georgia, the city where King was born on January 15, 1929, designated King's birthday a paid holiday for city employees. In 1973 the first state King Holiday bill (sponsored by then

MARTIN LUTHER KING JR. DAY

- ☐ Martin Luther King Jr. Day is a federal holiday, observed on the third Monday of every January (King was born on January 15, 1929).

- ☐ The holiday honors famed 1950s and 1960s African American civil rights leader Martin Luther King Jr., who was assassinated on April 4, 1968 in Memphis, Tennessee.

- ☐ It was signed into law by President Ronald Reagan on November 3, 1983.

- ☐ The first national celebration of the holiday was held on January 20, 1986.

- ☐ Illinois was the first state to declare Martin Luther King Jr. Day a state holiday, in 1973.

- ☐ New Hampshire was the last state to officially observe Martin Luther King Jr. Day, doing so for the first time in 1999.

- ☐ Atlanta, Georgia was first city to declare Martin Luther King Jr. Day a holiday, in 1971.

- ☐ Federal Martin Luther Jr. King Day observation was strongly opposed by North Carolina Senators Jesse Helms and John P. East, based on FBI reports of King's association with communists and adulterous activities.

Assemblyman Harold Washington) was signed into law in Illinois, and in 1974 similar legislation was passed in Massachusetts and Connecticut. Most other states followed suit during the following decade.

TOWARD A NATIONAL HOLIDAY

Congressman John Conyers (D-MI) had initially introduced national holiday legislation just four days after King's assassination, and he continued to push this legislation in subsequent sessions of Congress. But Conyers's proposal garnered little support until the numbers of African Americans elected to Congress increased and led to the establishment of the Congressional Black Caucus (CBC) in 1969. As the CBC's ranks expanded from the 13 members who founded it in 1969, the idea of establishing a national King holiday gained substantial political backing. The Southern Christian Leadership Conference (SCLC), which King had led since its founding in 1957, supported the CBC's attempt to pass King holiday legislation; in 1971 the SCLC gathered petitions bearing three million signatures in support of a King Holiday and presented them to Congress.

These efforts at the local and national levels sparked resistance, however, as opponents voiced objections to renaming plans, citing cost and inconvenience. Some opponents also insisted that King was unworthy of such public commemoration, noting his controversial views and the allegations disseminated by the Federal Bureau of Investigation (FBI) that King had Communist ties and had engaged in adultery. Still others argued that Americans such as Abraham Lincoln and John F. Kennedy were more deserving of a day of national recognition. For nearly a decade these objections, sincere or otherwise, helped to check progress toward a national King holiday.

The movement to pass national King holiday legislation gained momentum in the late 1970s, during the presidency of Jimmy Carter, who had won election with strong black support (including an endorsement by Martin Luther King Sr.). The King Center's efforts on behalf of the King holiday expanded and intensified after it moved in 1979 to its permanent home on Atlanta's Auburn Avenue, a block from King's birth home in Atlanta. Subsequent birthday celebrations at The King Center often featured ceremonies at King's crypt, which was relocated to the center. The center also began to encourage and provide educational materials for King holiday commemorations throughout the nation. In November 1978, the National Council of Churches had called on Congress to pass a King Holiday bill. The following February, Coretta Scott King urged passage of the bill when she testified during hearings before the Senate Judiciary Committee; in March she again testified before joint hearings of Congress. Meanwhile, she had directed King Center staff to begin intensive organizing of a nationwide citizens' lobby for a national Martin Luther King Jr. Holiday. The King Center's nationwide King Holiday petition campaign garnered more than 300,000 signatures before the end of the year. With support from the Carter administration, a King Holiday bill emerged for the first time from congressional committees, but in November 1979 the bill was defeated in a floor vote in the House of Representatives, by only five votes.

The setback did not end the national campaign, however, and on January 15, 1981, more than 100,000 people rallied at the Washington Monument to express support for the King holiday movement. Singer Stevie Wonder performed a song celebrating King's birth, and his hit recording of the birthday song further increased popular support for the holiday. Coretta Scott King testified before congressional committees in support of legislation establishing a national historic site in honor of Martin Luther King Jr. In 1981 she wrote to governors, mayors, and chairpersons of city councils across the United States, requesting them to pass resolutions and proclamations as well as organize celebrations commemorating Martin Luther King Jr.'s birthday and send the materials to The King Center's archives. She further urged them to organize local and statewide celebrations and programs of observance.

During 1982 The King Center began working with Wonder to organize an observance of the twentieth anniversary of the 1963 March on Washington for Jobs and Freedom. This effort proved effective in increasing popular interest in the stalled King holiday legislation. With financial support from Wonder, a lobbying office opened in Washington, D.C. Mrs. King and Stevie Wonder presented petitions bearing more than six million signatures in support of the King holiday to Massachusetts Democrat Tip O'Neil, Speaker of the U.S. House of Representatives.

As the anniversary of the march approached during the summer of 1983, support for the legislation increased. On August 2, the House passed a bill creating the King holiday by an overwhelming vote of 338–90. The bill received bipartisan support, and President Ronald Reagan indicated that he would not veto the legislation if it came before him. But the Senate debate concerning the bill was nonetheless contentious. Opponents such as North Carolina Senators Jesse Helms and John P. East strongly opposed the legislation, calling attention to FBI reports based on its surveillance of King. East also condemned the holiday as elevating King "to the same level as the father of our country and above the many other Americans whose achievements approach Washington's." Helms also unsuccessfully filed suit to obtain the release of FBI surveillance tapes on King that had been sealed by court order until the year 2027. Supporters of the legislation countered by denouncing the use of FBI documents that were based on illegal surveillance of King. And to critics who disingenuously balked at the financial costs involved with creating a new national holiday and the resultant loss of productivity, Republican Senator Bob Dole famously retorted, "I suggest they hurry back to their pocket calculators and estimate the cost of 300 years of slavery, followed by a century or more of economic, political and social exclusion and discrimination." To maintain public pressure on the Senate, on August 27, 1983 The King Center convened the "Twentieth Anniversary March on Washington," supported by more than 750 organizations. More than half a million people attended the march and the rally at the Lincoln Memorial, and all of the speakers called upon the Senate and President Reagan to enact the King holiday.

When the Senate considered the House bill in October, opponents continued to complain that the legislation would be too costly, given that federal workers would receive another paid holiday (the Congressional Budget Office estimated the federal cost at about $18 million for the first year of the holiday). Helms doggedly attacked King's character, insisting that while "there was no record that Dr. King himself ever joined the Communist Party," the civil rights leader "kept around him as his principal advisers and associates certain individuals who were taking their orders and directions from a foreign power." Helms's effort to derail the legislation through a filibuster was unsuccessful, however, as Senate Republican and Democratic leaders agreed to schedule a final vote after two additional days of debate. Democratic Senator Edward M. Kennedy of Massachusetts vigorously defended King against the allegations of Helms and other heirs of "arch-segregationists" who were engaged in a "last-ditch stand against equal justice." Kennedy noted that King's political affiliations had been thoroughly examined during the Senate investigations of intelligence agencies following the Watergate scandal and that no evidence of ties between King and the Communist Party had been uncovered. Prominent Republicans such as Robert Dole of Kansas and Howard H. Baker Jr. of Tennessee also lauded King, defended him against Helms's accusations, and agreed to back the bill. President Reagan, however, indicated a degree of support for Helms's charge that King was a Communist sympathizer when he told a reporter, "We'll know in about 35 years, won't we?" This was a reference to Helms's effort to gain the release of FBI surveillance tapes on King that had been sealed under a 1977 court order until 2027.

When the Senate finally voted on the bill on October 19, the packed galleries included numerous prominent proponents of the holiday, including Coretta Scott King, SCLC President Joseph E. Lowery, and Representative John Conyers. Ending a campaign for the King holiday that had lasted more than a decade, the bill was approved by a vote of 78 to 22 (37 Republicans and 41 Democrats voted in favor; 18 Republicans and 4 Democrats voted against).

After Senate passage of the legislation, President Reagan promised that he would sign the legislation, though with some reluctance: "Since [supporters] seem bent on making it a national holiday, I believe the symbolism of that day is important enough that I would—I'll sign that legislation when it reaches my desk." On November 2, 1983, with Coretta King in attendance at a morning White House ceremony, Reagan signed H. R. 3706, Public Law 98-144, establishing the third Monday of every January as the Martin Luther King Jr. National Holiday, beginning in 1986.

CELEBRATING THE HOLIDAY

The first official King holiday on January 20, 1986, was widely observed throughout the United States. In Atlanta, King family members and The King Center organized a major event at Ebenezer Baptist Church, the institution on Auburn Avenue where King had once served as co-pastor with his father. Even before the passage of national legislation, annual commemorations of King's birth had been held at Ebenezer since the civil rights leader's assassination in 1968. In addition to Coretta King and her four children, those in attendance included Rosa Parks, whose 1955 protest against segregated bus seating had been the stimulus for a year-long boycott movement led by King; Vice President George H. W. Bush, representing the president; Senator Kennedy; and numerous other political and religious leaders. South African Anglican bishop Desmond Tutu, who like King was a Nobel Peace Prize laureate, was awarded the King Peace Prize. Commenting in his acceptance address that he trembled while standing "in the shadow of so great a person," he used the occasion to urge the United States and other nations to support the continuing struggle against apartheid in South Africa.

In many other cities and towns, the King holiday was also celebrated, but the controversies associated with the campaign for the federal holiday continued to simmer during the years after the holiday legislation became law. There was little agreement regarding how the holiday should be celebrated, with some King supporters insisting that he should be honored for his controversial views—such as his opposition to the war in Vietnam and his call for a Poor Peoples Campaign—rather than simply as a civil rights advocate and inspirational orator. Many who had celebrated King even before the establishment of the federal holiday resisted efforts to turn holiday events into occasions for posturing by political leaders who would not have supported King when he was alive. As with other national holidays, those who favor it have also had to resist the tendency of many Americans to see it merely as a three-day holiday rather than a time for reflection on King's principles and ideals.

Moreover, as with other federal holidays, the observance of the national King holiday applied only to federal workers rather than employees of state and local governments or of private institutions. Not all educational institutions recognized the holiday, and some had no official commemoration ceremony to mark the holiday. When the first federal holiday was observed, only 17 states officially recognized the occasion. During the 1980s and 1990s, advocates for a truly nationwide observance sought to broaden popular support for the holiday and to convince the remaining states to pass holiday legislation. This effort would achieve considerable success during the late 1980s, but resistance to the King holiday remained strong in a few states, such as New Hampshire and Arizona.

In the spring of 1984, The King Center developed a legislative proposal to establish the Martin Luther King, Jr. Federal Holiday Commission. With Coretta Scott King making personal appeals to leaders and members of the House and Senate, Congress passed by a voice vote legislation to create the commission, which President Reagan signed on August 27, 1984. The commission was to last for a term of five years, with an option to renew for another five years. At the first meeting of the commission in November of 1984, Mrs. King was unanimously elected chairperson, and the commissioners were officially sworn in by federal district judge Horace Ward on the day of first national observance. The commission got busy, lobbying state legislatures and sponsoring educational programs to promote public awareness and support for adoption of the holiday in states not yet observing it. Their efforts, and those of other agencies, bore fruit: by the time the King holiday was observed in 1989, the number of states that had enacted King holiday observances had grown to 44.

Labor unions did their part to make sure that the King holiday would enjoy the same status as other recognized holidays in one crucial respect. The *Wall Street Journal* reported on January 15, 1990 that according to a survey taken by the Bureau of National Affairs, only 18 percent of 317 corporate employers provided a *paid* King holiday. The United Auto Workers set out to help rectify that situation; in that same year the powerful union negotiated contracts with the big three auto companies requiring a paid holiday for all their employees. Eight years later the bureau's survey indicated significant improvement, discovering that out of 458 employers surveyed, 26 percent provided a paid holiday for their workers on the King holiday. Significantly, the survey found that 33 percent of firms with union contracts provided the paid King holiday, while only 22 percent of nonunion shops did so.

Resistance in the last holdout states ended in the 1990s. After a coalition of citizens for a King holiday in Arizona launched successful protests and boycott campaigns, the people of Arizona passed a referendum in November of 1992 establishing Martin Luther King Jr.'s birthday as a state holiday. With that state's first observance of the King holiday in 1993, only New Hampshire remained without a state holiday in honor of Dr. King, but on June 7, 1999 the state ended its distinction when Governor Jean Shaheen signed her state's King holiday legislation into law, finally completing enactment of the holiday in all of the states.

Since the mid-1990s, Coretta Scott King and The King Center have sought to broaden the appeal and purpose of the King holiday. Citing Dr. King's statement that "Everybody can be great because everybody can serve," Mrs. King in 1994 testified before Congress in support of making the King holiday an official national day of humanitarian service. In August of that year President Clinton signed the Martin Luther King, Jr. Federal Holiday and Service Act, expanding the mission of the holiday as a day of community service, interracial cooperation, and youth antiviolence initiatives. Having used up its optional five-year extension, the Martin Luther King, Jr. Federal Holiday Commission in 1996 concluded its mission, transferring responsibility for coordinating nationwide holiday programs and activities to The King Center in Atlanta. Today, the King holiday is celebrated in U.S. installations and observed by local groups in more than 100 other nations. Trinidad and other nations have also established a holiday in honor of Dr. King.

FURTHER READING

Dyson, Michael Eric. *I May Not Get There With You: The True Martin Luther King, Jr.* New York: Free Press, 2000.
Williams, Clarence G., ed., *Reflections of the Dream, 1975–1994: Twenty Years of Celebrating the Life of Dr. Martin Luther King, Jr. at the Massachusetts Institute of Technology.* Cambridge, Mass.: MIT Press, 1996.

Clayborne Carson

The Monday Holidays Act, and other "Saint Mondays"

Among the many issues facing Congress in the tumultuous year 1968 was a piece of legislation called the Uniform Holidays Bill. The bill sought to regularize federal holidays, keeping them to a prescribed number and having more of them fall at the end or beginning of the work week, rather than on their actual dates. Additionally, Congress needed to respond to agitation for a new holiday for the recently slain civil rights leader Martin Luther King Jr. As originally passed (as the Monday Holidays Act), and put into practice in 1971, the bill moved four federal holidays—Washington's Birthday, Memorial Day, Columbus Day, and Veterans Day (formerly Armistice Day)—to their closest Monday dates each year. New Year's Day, Independence Day, and Christmas were left to "float" throughout the week as before, and Thanksgiving retained its traditional place on the fourth Thursday of November. Labor Day had traditionally been observed on the first Monday in September anyway, and the new Martin Luther King's Birthday holiday joined the list of "Saint Mondays" in 1971. One Monday holiday was dropped: after vigorous protests from veterans' groups, Veterans Day was returned to its November 11 date in 1978.

Federal holidays apply only to federal workers and agencies, and state governments are not required to adopt them. Most do, however, if only eventually and sometimes under great pressure—witness the recent holdouts against Martin Luther King Jr.'s Birthday. States also have some latitude in adapting federal holidays within their borders—12 states celebrate Washington's Birthday as Presidents' Day.

The creation of predictable three-day weekends has been welcomed by most Americans, especially retailers and those connected with the tourist and recreation industries (the president of the National Association of Travel Organizations dubbed the Monday Holidays Act "the greatest thing that has happened to the travel industry since the invention of the automobile"). For Matthew Dennis, author of *Red, White, and Blue Letter Days: An American Calendar* (2002), this easy acceptance is a convincing, and disturbing, sign of Americans' growing disinterest in their past. In passing the Monday Holidays Act, Congress in effect recognized, and approved, "the modern economic and social imperatives of leisure and consumption" over the distinctly edifying messages of the now moveable holidays.

HOLIDAYS FOR HEROES OF THE LOST CAUSE: LEE, JACKSON, AND DAVIS

Confederate holidays were a response to loss, acts of defiance, and celebrations of the values of southern nationalism. Confederate Memorial Day emerged unofficially as a southern spring ritual of bereavement at the close of the Civil War and by the late nineteenth century became an official holiday in all states of the former Confederacy. By the 1890s, during the South's decade of black disfranchisement and racial violence, southerners pushed for a celebration of their white heroes, primarily Robert E. Lee and Jefferson Davis. For decades, southern states officially and unofficially marked the birthdays of Lee and Davis with ceremony and tribute to their lives in the region's public schools. Then, over the course of the twentieth century, Confederate holidays evolved from well-attended and honored celebrations to days of diminished crowds and recognition.

During times of racial discord, Confederate holidays took on added significance among white southerners, and what began as commemoration influenced by southern women is today more likely to be part of a predominantly white male ritual. White male reactionaries who feel dispossessed by political gains for women and minorities find in the old holidays not only a means of honoring their Confederate ancestors, but a restoration of their symbolic role as manly protectors of the virtues of honor and chivalry.

Many southern states still officially recognize Confederate Memorial Day—the most celebrated of the Confederate holidays—as paid holidays for state employees or by closing state offices. In many ways, the holiday is a relic of the "Lost Cause" myth and is no longer significant to the vast majority of white southerners.

CONFEDERATE HOLIDAYS: CONFEDERATE MEMORIAL DAY, JEFFERSON DAVIS DAY, ROBERT E. LEE DAY, STONEWALL JACKSON DAY

- Because these are not federal holidays, observances vary by state and are only observed in former Confederate States.

- They emerged as a commemoration of Confederate war dead in several southern states in the years immediately following defeat in the Civil War.

- Confederate Memorial Day originated at the local level by Ladies' Memorial Associations, which were formed to care for the graves of southern war veterans and honor their memory through the springtime ritual of placing flowers on their graves.

- Date of observation varied by region, depending on when flowers blossomed.

- After the end of Reconstruction in 1877 Confederate Memorial Day became a rallying point for celebrations of white southern regionalism during the Jim Crow era and spawned state observations of Jefferson Davis's (June 3) and Robert E. Lee's (January 19) birthdays, and the day of Stonewall Jackson's death (May 10).

- It inspired the creation of Memorial, or Decoration, Day in the North to commemorate Union war dead.

- The Confederate holidays became vehicles to celebrate the "Lost Cause," southern manhood, and southern (and later national) patriotism.

- In 1903 the first Confederate Memorial Day ceremony was held at Arlington National Cemetery.

THE CREATION OF CONFEDERATE MEMORIAL DAY

The first postwar holiday to be established in the South was Memorial Day, sometimes referred to as Decoration Day, the term more generally applied to the same commemoration in the North. It was an outgrowth of the activities of ladies' memorial associations (LMAs) that emerged in the region immediately after the Civil War. Women who formerly belonged to soldiers' aid societies formed LMAs to care for the graves of deceased veterans and to honor their memory through the springtime ritual of placing flowers on their graves, a ritual that evolved into Confederate Memorial Day.

Many communities lay claim to being the first to have begun Confederate Memorial Day, but clearly the ritual developed simultaneously in several places throughout the South, as memorial associations emerged in various communities. What is more significant to understand is the way the holiday developed, the rituals that were observed, the differences between the South's memorial day and Decoration Day in the North, and its place in the context of a national memorial day, which remains an official U.S. holiday.

It was important to white southerners that the South receive credit for the national celebration. Articles in the *Confederate Veteran,* the official organ of southern heritage organizations like the United Confederate Veterans (UCV) and the United Daughters of the Confederacy (UDC), went to great pains to document the development of Memorial Day, explaining that it was only after General John A. Logan of the Grand Army of the Republic (GAR) witnessed southern women in Richmond and its environs decorating the graves of Confederate soldiers, that the idea of a national holiday emerged. Logan's "tender heart was deeply touched . . . by seeing the graves of the Confederate dead all marked by little white flags, faded wreaths of laurel, and such tributes to their memory that had been placed there by their friends."

Having witnessed the way in which the South honored its dead, Logan, also a congressman from Illinois, proposed the resolution to set aside May 30 for decorating the graves of the Civil War dead. That resolution, passed on May 5, 1868, established Decoration Day to specifically honor Union war dead. While engaging in rituals similar to those in the South, it marked a divergence from Confederate Memorial Day, and the two evolved along different trajectories.

Rhetorically, Decoration Day was intended to be a time for sectional reconciliation by honoring all the dead. In 1876, *Harper's Weekly* described the holiday as a "feast of reconciliation," though by no means did it concede the "essential justice" of the Union cause. Separate commemorations, however, offered proof that white southerners were unwilling to relinquish what they regarded as a holiday they originated to become a symbol of reconciliation.

Thus, while May 30 was commemorated in the North, southerners observed memorial days on different days in different states. The dates differed depending

Festooning a Civil War memorial statue on Decoration Day in New York, 1902. Courtesy of North Wind Picture Archives.

on when that state's flowers were in bloom but might also mark days that an individual state imbued with some significance. The two most common were April 26 and May 10, the day of Joseph E. Johnston's surrender and the anniversary of General Thomas "Stonewall" Jackson's death, respectively. June 3 was chosen as Memorial Day in Louisiana in honor of Jefferson Davis's birthday. Regardless of the day, North or South, what both sections could agree upon was that Memorial Day was intended to honor the common soldier.

HOLIDAYS FOR HEROES

If Memorial Day began during a period of bereavement in the South, then holidays for Confederate heroes grew out of the celebratory phase of the Lost Cause that emerged in the late 1870s and continued into the early twentieth century. Once federal troops had left the South and with the return of former Confederate leaders to power in state governments, the tone of the Confederate tradition changed drastically. Monuments and their unveiling ceremonies met enthusiastic responses. During the 1890s, southern hereditary societies were formed to preserve and honor Confederate memory as well as Anglo-Saxon supremacy. It was during this decade that the region witnessed the creation of holidays for Confederate icons, primarily General Robert E. Lee and Jefferson Davis, the former Confederate president. Other states honored different heroes, the most popular being General Thomas "Stonewall" Jackson.

Calls for honoring the birthday of Robert E. Lee were being made in the pages of the *Confederate Veteran* beginning in 1896, although communities throughout the South had independently commemorated the day prior to then. This call, however, was for establishing an official holiday. "Every Southern State could well enough and most appropriately make January 19th a holiday," editor Sumner Cunningham wrote, adding "whether they had Confederate men in the Virginia army or not." The article noted that only Georgia and North Carolina observed the general's birth. Yet by 1901, the *Confederate Veteran* provided extensive coverage of Lee's birthday in its article "The Celebration of Lee's Natal Day." According to Cunningham, the observance of Lee's birthday had "become almost universal throughout the South." In fact, the magazine boasted that it could have issued a "Lee Number" devoting all its space to the many celebrations in "Northern and Southern cities of the Union."

As of 1904, only four of the former Confederate states had made Lee's birthday a legal holiday—Virginia, North Carolina, Georgia, and South Carolina. Yet according to Kate Mason Rowland, a UDC member and descendent of George Mason, the holiday was commemorated in other southern states by "common consent." Indeed, many southern towns and cities officially honored Lee each January 19, often led by members of the UCV and UDC. Nine years after its first appeal in 1905, the *Confederate Veteran* again called on all southern states to make the date a legal holiday.

The celebration of white manhood in the South during the 1890s extended to its most unrepentant hero, Jefferson Davis, also known as the "martyr of the Lost Cause." At the end of the war, Davis's reputation suffered even in the South as he was blamed for the Confederacy's loss. In the North, national magazines such as *Harper's Weekly* disseminated the account of Davis's capture while allegedly disguised as a woman. Yet his capture and imprisonment at Fort Monroe in Virginia became the material for southern legend, and in his later years Davis came to represent the South in her loss and defiance. Davis himself

An engraving of Robert E. Lee after a photograph by Matthew Brady, 1867. Courtesy of the Library of Congress.

lived up to the legend, remaining unrepentant until his death, perpetuating the story of his imprisonment, and always denying the story of his capture in feminine attire. Indeed, northern fascination with the tale only served to reinforce Davis's role as martyr, since attacking Davis's masculinity was considered an attack on the manhood of all southern men. Thus, a holiday for Davis had significant meaning for white southern manhood. It necessitated the reinvention of Davis as a hero of a just cause and a defender of Anglo-Saxon supremacy, which in the 1890s was an ideal southerners shared with the rest of the nation's white men. One writer supported the legalization of the Davis holiday for that

An engraving of Jefferson Davis after a photograph by Matthew Brady, 1861. Courtesy of the Library of Congress.

very reason, noting that Davis represented the "heroic fortitude characteristic of Southern manhood," a description that had eluded the Confederate president at war's end.

The call to make Davis's birthday a legal holiday was initiated in 1897 by Virginian Kate Mason Rowland at the UDC convention in Baltimore, Maryland. It was part of a larger effort to honor the Confederate president that included raising money for a large monument to be erected in Davis's honor in Richmond, a project to which the Daughters of the Confederacy were fully committed. In 1900, Rowland made another motion to make June 3 a legal holiday in all southern states. And in that year, it became legal in Florida, Georgia, and Virginia. Just as the Lee holiday was deemed an appropriate day for children to learn of the general's heroic exploits, it was considered equally meritorious for southern youth to study Davis's life. A Virginia state congressman offered a resolution to that effect, asking that the state general assembly "declare the birthday of Jefferson Davis a day of recreation in the public schools" to teach them about Davis's deeds so that "out of the mouths of babes men may learn wisdom." Indeed, the UDC believed that instilling in children a reverence for the Confederacy and its heroes was important to the development of the region's next generation of leaders. By 1904, half a dozen Confederate states, including Virginia and Louisiana, where Davis died, had legalized the holiday. In Louisiana, Davis's birthday also served as Confederate Memorial Day.

WOMEN'S INFLUENCE

All three holidays—Confederate Memorial Day, Robert E. Lee's birthday, and Jefferson Davis's birthday—were made legal due to the dogged persistence of women, first organized as ladies' memorial associations, then later as the United Daughters of the Confederacy. As women's public role evolved from wartime helpmeet to postwar memorializers, southern women became more political. They used their power and influence to build monuments, promote pro-Confederate history in the public schools, and eventually create Confederate holidays.

Ladies' memorial associations were the keepers of Memorial Day traditions from its beginning. These organizations, transformed from wartime soldiers' aid societies into postwar memorial societies, immediately assumed a leadership role in the Lost Cause tradition by helping to designate Confederate cemeteries, raise money for headstones, and erect monuments. These women remained leaders of the tradition until the end of the nineteenth century when they were joined by a new generation of women, those in the UDC, who also took as their goal the memorialization of the Confederate dead.

Southern women's involvement in the movement to establish Memorial Day was culturally significant in the South, since the holiday centered on honoring their dead. It devolved upon women to create these cemeteries, as the federal government had created a system of cemeteries for the burial of Union soldiers only. Federal cemeteries existed in the South, but the Confederate dead were not welcome in these.

As the new generation of women in the UDC became involved in the 1890s, they added the celebration of heroes to the solemn occasion of Memorial Day. It is no coincidence that the movement to legalize Confederate holidays was spurred on by the UDC. From its founding in 1894, it had quickly become an important and influential women's organization, and the Daughters were known to use their influence with men of power to assist them in their agenda to preserve Confederate culture for future generations. Holidays were important

Dr. Katherine Allen, president of the local chapter of the United Daughters of the Confederacy, puts a Confederate battle flag on the gravesite of a Confederate soldier in preparation for Confederate Memorial Day on April 26, 2000. © AP / Wide World Photos.

to that goal. In fact, when the bill to legalize Davis's birthday went before the general assembly of Virginia, Congressman Wayne Anderson began his remarks by stating that he "offered the resolution at the request of the devoted women of the Confederacy," later adding, "let us grant it because our women ask it."

In addition to leading public celebrations of Confederate holidays, the Daughters resolved at their annual and state conventions to petition their state legislatures for individual holidays for both Lee and Davis. Despite their claims of being nonpolitical, UDC members proved to be astute politicians when it suited their needs. Indeed, when the *Confederate Veteran* announced the legalization of a holiday in a southern state, it was often accompanied by the pronouncement, as it was in Texas when the Davis holiday was legalized, that it was due to the "dedicated commitment" of a UDC leader that the holiday had become became legalized. General C. Irvine Walker agreed, noting that it was "largely by their [the UDC] influence that Mr. Davis's birthday has become a legal holiday in most of the states which were in the Confederacy."

Whether or not they were legalized, Confederate holidays were ritually commemorated throughout the South by the turn of the twentieth century. Since the end of the Civil War, women organized and led these commemorations, although men also had an important role to play as patriarchal figureheads and as the object of the celebrations. Women, however, were primarily responsible for the development of holiday rituals, choosing who would participate in solemn ceremonies or be tapped as speakers, as well as deciding the roles to be played by children and by themselves.

THE ROLE OF CHILDREN

Children had been involved in the rituals of Memorial Day since the end of the Civil War. Mrs. Charles J. Williams of Columbus, Georgia, the self-proclaimed founder of the holiday, stated that while regularly visiting her husband's grave to lay flowers, her daughter covered the flowers of unmarked graves of Confederate soldiers. When the little girl died, Mrs. Williams claimed to take charge of the unknown graves and called on all southern women to engage in the ritual and involve children so that it would become a "religious custom" in the South.

The birthdays of Confederate heroes were less solemn occasions, and children were usually engaged more directly in the celebration of their lives. Because Lee's birthday fell in January, superintendents, principals, and teachers guided public school children in the study of Lee's life, and since it was also the month of Thomas "Stonewall" Jackson's birth, students honored his life as well. Through such activity the public school curriculum in the South had, by the 1920s, set aside January for the study of the Confederacy and its most notable generals. This study was made more meaningful with the publication of two primers written by Mary L. Williamson on the lives of Lee and Jackson. These books, along with the portraits of Lee that adorned many southern public schools, gave import to his role in preserving Confederate values. According to Francis Thornton Smith, a student in Hattiesburg, Mississippi, in the 1920s, her classroom had portraits of "all the generals we studied."

Children observed Lee's birthday in Charlotte, North Carolina, in 1901 when Anna Jackson, wife of Stonewall Jackson, pinned the Cross of Honor on the coats of veterans—medals that were the gifts of the children of Charlotte. A few years later in Atlanta, Georgia, all exercises commemorating Lee's birthday, including "recitations, readings and songs suitable to the occasion," were performed in the public schools. In response, the *Confederate Veteran* argued that Lee's birthday should be made legal to "annually impress upon our children the justness of the South and heroism of our people in the War Between the States."

Fewer children commemorated Jefferson Davis's birthday, though only because his June 3 birthday fell on the cusp of summer vacations from public school. This did not prevent members of the UDC from petitioning their states to make the date a legal holiday on behalf of school children. In 1900, the Virginia Daughters called upon their general assembly to declare Davis's birthday a school holiday, so that southern youth would be free to learn about Davis, and through lessons on his life be inspired to emulate him.

During the centennial of Davis's birth in 1908, the UDC proved quite successful in influencing several states to declare June 3 a legal holiday. Although many schools were closed on the actual centennial, those that were open "celebrated the day and loyally installed portraits of the great Confederate chieftain." Additionally, the Daughters petitioned to have the names of public schools renamed for Davis. In fact, it was during the first two decades of the twentieth century that many public schools in the South were renamed for Confederate heroes.

Celebrations involving schoolchildren were instrumental to the development of a southern citizenry dedicated to Confederate principles during the period of the New South. While these celebrations mirrored those for George Washington and Abraham Lincoln, celebrations of southern heroes were less about national identity and more about regional identity. Furthermore, these days were an expression of patriotism, as the spokespersons of the Lost Cause, especially the UDC and UCV, felt that Confederate heroes typified American patriotism better than most as they had fought to defend Constitutional principles, namely states' rights—even when it meant a defense of white supremacy.

MEN AND MANHOOD

While women were instrumental in the establishment of Confederate holidays, men were always integral to these occasions whether as the honored subjects or as speakers. Moreover, each significant holiday—Confederate Memorial Day, Lee's birthday, and later, Jefferson Davis's birthday—was a celebration of heroism and white southern manhood. Holiday rituals included marking the graves of men not only with flowers, but with speeches by men who paid homage to their male ancestors. Similarly, speeches given during the commemoration of birthdays also included themes of valor, heroism, and patriotism.

Memorial Day was the most sacred of Confederate holidays as it honored men who had died in behalf of the South. Women's involvement was important to this holiday, as it was a day that could not have been created by the generation of men who fought on the losing side of the war. However, women always made sure that men played a highly visible role during the actual event, especially as keynote speakers frequently dwelt on the themes of heroism and the manhood of all Confederate soldiers. As one speaker put it, "This ceremony is not, and ought not to be, in honor of any one man."

Men of the Confederate generation, those who belonged to the UCV, held the holiday as sacred as did women. In 1904, the commanding general of the UCV in Georgia asked that the organization pass a resolution to protest the use of Memorial Day as a day of leisure. Specifically, they protested the fact that the South Atlantic Baseball League had scheduled the beginning of its season on April 26—Confederate Memorial Day. Veterans were upset that this legal holiday intended to honor the Civil War dead would be used for sports and insisted that it would "lessen the interest and loyalty of our young people," if they did not honor Confederate heroes. As the commander of the Georgia veterans remarked, the day was "set apart for the decoration of the graves of our honored dead comrades" and should not be "desecrated by unseemly amusements."

Manhood was always a significant theme on the birthdays of heroes. Robert E. Lee, whose birthday was likely the first to be legalized, was the white South's symbol of heroic manhood. Despite the South's loss, Lee remained a hero and was never criticized as was Jefferson Davis. While Davis initially bore the brunt of southerners' anger and blame for the Confederacy's loss, Lee was invariably worshiped by white southerners who considered him the ideal Christian, southern gentleman. Georgia was one of the first states to make January 19, Lee's birthday, a legal holiday. As early as 1896, the event was observed in the state capitol, Atlanta, where speeches were given on Lee's career and sacrifices. North Carolina also honored Lee's memory that year in its state capitol of Raleigh. A legal holiday there, the day was observed by closing banks, state offices, and displaying Confederate flags on the capitol building. Several pastors gave sermons that upheld Lee's life as one worth emulating.

Jefferson Davis represented a different type of manhood to the white South. Following the return to home rule in the South, during the 1870s, the Lost Cause eventually began to focus on celebration rather than bereavement, and Davis emerged as a reinvented man. No longer was he the emasculated Jeff Davis, pilloried in the North for his alleged cross-dressing escape attempt and in the South as the man who lost the war. The new Jefferson Davis was a martyr for the southern people. Less heroic than Lee, Davis nonetheless earned the respect of white southerners for the way he suffered in prison following the war. Women especially regarded his sacrifices as similar to that of Jesus Christ—and were explicit when making such analogies. Yet men, too, developed a new-found respect for the Confederate president who remained unrepentant and unreconstructed until his death in 1889.

By 1904, June 3—Davis's birthday—had become a legal holiday in Louisiana (where it served as Confederate Memorial Day), Florida, Georgia, South Carolina, Tennessee, and Virginia. That same year, Texas veterans successfully petitioned their state legislature to legalize the holiday. The Texas petition reveals

The First National flag of the Confederate States of America flies over the state capitol in Raleigh, North Carolina to commemorate Confederate Memorial Day, May 10, 2000. © AP / Wide World Photos.

how the movement to honor Davis had evolved. J. D. Haw, a veteran and editor of a Waco newspaper, was inspired to react to the resolution in his revealing editorial. "For many years after the war the name of Jefferson Davis was seldom mentioned in public," he wrote, "not even in the South." Even at Confederate reunions, Haw recalled, as speakers mentioned many of the South's heroes, they never mentioned Davis. Haw suspected that it could have been fear of "Northern criticism or in deference to Northern prejudice." While he believed that Lee and other southern military leaders deserved praise, Davis above all represented "the heroic fortitude characteristic of Southern manhood."

During the centennial year of his birth in 1908, a regional celebration of Davis's life ensued. Speeches and ceremonies marked the complete reinvention of Davis in southern memory. No longer was he blamed for Confederate defeat. According to General C. Irvine Walker, Davis ought to be remembered as someone who willingly accepted the responsibility that the South "forced upon him." No longer the unmanly "Jeff in Petticoats," Walker suggested that Davis was "almost superhuman" and "one of the greatest of the Anglo Saxon Race."

Women also had an interest in upholding Davis as representative of white southern manhood as they led the centennial celebration of the Confederate chieftain. Under the auspices of the Confederated Southern Memorial Association (CSMA) led by Katie Behan of New Orleans, women secured the publication of a "true portrait" of Davis for placement in southern public schools. That true portrait, according to Behan, was one that depicted Davis in the "vigor of his strong intellectual manhood and not in the decrepitude of old age."

In Mississippi and Louisiana, the states of Davis's birth and death respectively, state newspapers donated several of these portraits to their public schools. Moreover, the Parish superintendents of education in Louisiana, as well as the Director of Archives and History in Mississippi, helped distribute a pamphlet on the life of Davis produced by the *Times-Democrat* of New Orleans.

The celebration of white manhood in the 1890s and early years of the twentieth century through the observance of Confederate holidays mirrored the celebration of Anglo-Saxon supremacy across the nation. Even though men of the Confederate generation had lost the war, holidays and their rituals gave those same men an opportunity to recast themselves as Anglo Saxon heroes. Simultaneously, it allowed women to participate in the reinvention of southern society as they returned, if only symbolically, to the role of helpmeet requiring male leadership. Thus, while women were clearly responsible for pressing for the legalization of Confederate holidays, and assumed roles as "New Women," the spotlight was on men and the rhetoric of manhood and racial superiority.

SOUTHERN NATIONALISM AND CITIZENSHIP

Regardless of their origins, Confederate holidays were, like the celebrations of national holidays, often about nationalism and citizenship. In the South, however, nationalism assumed a decidedly regional form: being citizens of the South was just as important as being citizens of the nation. White southerners regarded Memorial Day as the day *their* women had created, and they did not necessarily acknowledge the day in the same way as did the North. Mildred Rutherford, a Daughter of the Confederacy from Georgia, even protested against the term "Decoration Day" (used in the North) in favor of "Memorial Day," as she believed it was a day for southerners to teach their children "to honor and revere the memory of the heroes of the Confederacy." What she called for, and what many white southerners preferred, was a separate memorial day for the South, the day that became Confederate Memorial Day.

Confederate holidays, especially Confederate Memorial Day, were used as occasions to instill a new sense of duty to the principles of southern nationalism, especially states' rights. Indeed, as part of the ritual of Confederate Memorial Day in Texas, passages from the Texas declaration of secession were read aloud. While southerners remained wedded to the idea that theirs was the purest form of American patriotism, it did not, in their estimation, conflict with the concept of being good citizens of the South. In other words, to be southern *was* American.

For the Confederate generation and subsequent generations, the dual nature of southern and American citizenship was significant to the concept of sectional reconciliation. To have lost the war was enough; southerners were not about to concede that they were lesser citizens of the nation. In fact, much of the Lost Cause rhetoric in the 1890s and beyond was about defending southerners as patriotic Americans. They did so by clinging to their own interpretation of why the South went to war, which was to uphold the principles of the United States Constitution, specifically the Tenth Amendment protecting states' rights.

DECLINE

Confederate holidays continued to serve the purpose of defending the South's role in the Civil War as white southerners sought recognition for their patriotic contributions to the nation. The need for this recognition became less important after World War I, as Confederate holidays entered a period of decline. The reason for this decline is linked to both sectional reconciliation and generational change. World War I helped to unify the nation in a way that reunions of the Blue and Gray, and even the Spanish-American War, never had done. Confederate holidays had been as much an assertion of southerners' genuine American patriotism as they were about honoring the dead. Widespread southern participation in World War I rendered the question of authentic patriotism moot.

A second reason for the decline in participation in Confederate holiday celebrations is that by World War I, white southerners were three and four generations removed from the actual events of the Civil War, and that conflict did not hold the same emotional sway as it did for the first and second generations after the war. Most of the Confederate generation—the veterans who could tell their stories of glory and suffering—were now dead. In their absence, the region's connection to its past became less tangible.

Confederate holidays, however, were already established rituals within southern communities and continued to be celebrated over the course of the twentieth century. The study of heroes, moreover, had been institutionalized in the region's public schools and remained so in some southern states until the 1970s.

Additionally, the tradition of involving children in the holiday rituals remained steadfast, despite decreased participation over time.

During the 1950s and 1960s, such celebrations took on significant meaning as the white South waged war against desegregation, regarding federal intervention on this matter as the second invasion of the South. Confederate Memorial Day, an official state holiday in most southern states of the time, still served as a reminder that Confederate memory was alive and well. A review of such celebrations in Charlotte, North Carolina, is illustrative.

Celebration of Confederate Memorial Day in the spring of 1953 was marked by students at nearby Davidson College when members of the Kappa Alpha fraternity staged a mock battle dressed as Confederate soldiers. They "lay siege" to the Student Union Building, accepted the surrender of Union forces (students dressed in khaki pants) and "hoisted the Confederate [battle] flag" on the school flagpole. Marching to the tune of "Dixie," the "rebels" then captured the town of Davidson, having first been inspired by a series of "damnyankee" speeches.

In 1955, the year the Supreme Court decision *Brown v. Board of Education* ruled that school segregation was inherently unequal, Memorial Day was celebrated in Charlotte's Elmwood Cemetery where Confederate soldiers are buried. In addition to comments on the valor of those Confederates, the Reverend Russell M. Kerr's speech suggested that the Brown decision was not far from his mind when he said, "we should not live only in the past . . . but live in the present and not lose faith in *our ideals.*" Commemorations of Memorial Day in the 1950s and 1960s benefited from the fact that state offices closed to observe the holiday. Thus, southern states continued their official acknowledgement of the Confederacy and its principles of states' rights and white supremacy in the face of racial discord.

RACE

From the earliest observances to the present day, race has been an undercurrent in the commemoration of Confederate holidays, with the focus on whiteness and the disavowal of the meaning of the Civil War for African Americans. Indeed, as David Blight has demonstrated in his book *Race and Reunion: The Civil War in American Memory,* North and South alike left African Americans out of the national memory of the war. In the South, Confederate holidays in particular have long served as statements about the superiority of the white race.

Responding to a 1907 editorial from an Indianapolis newspaper that called on the South to adopt May 30 as its "Decoration Day," editor Sumner Cunningham of the *Confederate Veteran* explained that the commemoration of a day shared with the North brought back a "painful memory in the minds of the Southern people." It reminded them of Reconstruction, when "crowds of negroes [he also referred to the crowds as a "rabble"] attended these decorations." This magazine, the official organ for all Confederate organizations, made it clear that any celebration of the Confederacy must first be a celebration of the Anglo-Saxon race.

With the movement, after 1968, to establish the Martin Luther King Jr. holiday, the topic of race and race relations came to the forefront of public discussion of Confederate holidays. For years, African Americans were marginalized in their communities as celebrations of Confederate heroes took place. The push for a national holiday for King meant that the underlying racism of Confederate organizations, which celebrated white heroes, came bubbling to the surface. Confederate organizations did not exhibit the active racism present during the 1950s and 1960s; rather they exhibited what one scholar has described as "symbolic racism," by condemning a symbol—in this case a holiday—that represented a group of people, African Americans.

The struggle to establish the King holiday echoed sentiments expressed by Frederick Douglass a century earlier about the marginalization of African Americans as citizens, whose own collective memory of the Civil War held that it was chiefly concerned with the emancipation of their race. Those sentiments were again expressed in the effort to establish the King holiday, as African Americans pointed out that honoring King was only part of what they sought. In fact, legalizing the holiday also begged the question as to whether blacks would "share equally in the social and cultural life of the community."

After the legalization of the King holiday in 1986, southern states sought ways to both achieve compromise by accepting the holiday, and to compromise the holiday by linking it with the holiday honoring Confederate hero Robert E. Lee, since both King and Lee shared January birthdays—on the 15th and 19th, respectively. In Virginia, what had been the Lee-Jackson holiday (commemorating both Lee and Stonewall Jackson's birthdays) became in 1989 the Lee-Jackson-King holiday—upsetting both southern heritage organizations and African Americans.

The Lee-Jackson-King holiday remained in place in Virginia until the year 2000, when the holidays were officially separated. Amazingly, the UDC urged the Virginia legislature to keep the combined holidays as a "unique opportunity to honor the memories of three Christian gentlemen." They further suggested that Generals Lee and Jackson "would both be pleased and proud to be honored along with Dr. King." Incredibly, the Daughters believed that to separate the holidays would "widen the existing divide between blacks and whites in the Old Dominion." Theirs was a unique opinion and suggested that the Daughters misunderstood both current events and the historic role their organization had played in the establishment of the Lee holiday.

The response to combining the Lee and King holidays met with a different response in Alabama when Governor Bob Riley sought to do so in 2004. The Sons of Confederate Veterans (SCV) attacked the governor, stating that the combination of holidays was an assault on Confederate heritage. Benjamin Hestley, chief of heritage defense for the Alabama SCV, said the Riley proposal was "in line with the 'cultural genocide' waged by the NAACP and other groups that want to erase Confederate symbols throughout the South." While the governor sought to combine the holidays to save the state money, he bowed to the pressure of Confederate organizations and withdrew the legislation—evidence that even today, Confederate memory has a powerful hold on the region.

CONTEMPORARY OBSERVANCES

Southern states independently decided how to commemorate the King and Lee holidays, yet Confederate Memorial Day remains the most important of the holidays for the current generation of Confederate organizations as it is the one holiday most universally observed throughout the region. Despite dwindling numbers of observers, Confederate Memorial Day both resembles and differs from the original commemorations.

In 2004, as in 1866, commemorations of Confederate Memorial Day included speeches and sermons from men in the community, decorating the graves of soldiers in Confederate cemeteries with wreaths of flowers, and flying the Confederate battle flag. New traditions welcome and honor veterans who served during World War II, Vietnam, the Gulf War, and the Iraq War. Reenactors are also likely to be present.

Significantly, these occasions now adopt a defensive tone, which just 40 years before was not deemed necessary. "This is not about wanting to bring back slavery or to restore the old Confederacy," SCV Chief of Staff Ron Casteel stressed in 2004. In his remarks during the commemoration of Confederate Memorial Day in Alabama, Reverend Harry Reeder of Birmingham said that the battle flag that flew that day was not an emblem of hate. Alabama governor Bob Riley defended the Confederate dead by stating that they fought for honor, adding "I don't think it [the Civil War] was all about slavery." These statements offer evidence that while Confederate memory still plays out in southern communities, participants are compelled to justify their celebration in a region that is no longer dominated by a tradition that ignores the contributions of nonwhites to the South's history.

Confederate holidays, as symbols of southern memory, will likely remain in place for several generations, even though they are observed by a comparative few. It is those few who see these days, like the battle flag that is flown for the occasion, as symbols of their southern identity. Like their forbears, they will celebrate and defend their right to celebrate Confederate holidays, as they did in Georgia in 2004, when Confederate Memorial Day was used to honor soldiers in the "War for Southern Independence."

As of this writing, Confederate Memorial Day is an official state holiday (meaning state offices are closed) in Florida, Georgia, Alabama, Mississippi, South Carolina, and Louisiana. Robert E. Lee's birthday is an official state holiday in Florida, Georgia, Louisiana, Alabama, Virginia, and Mississippi. Jefferson Davis's birthday is an official state holiday in Alabama, Florida, and South Carolina; in Louisiana Davis's birthday is regarded as Confederate Memorial Day. Robert E. Lee and Martin Luther King Jr. holidays are jointly commemorated in Mississippi and Arkansas. Alabama is the only state to have three official state holidays linked to the Confederacy.

FURTHER READING

Cooper, William J. *Jefferson Davis, American.* New York: Vintage Books, 2000.
Cox, Karen L. *Dixie's Daughters: The United Daughters of the Confederacy and the Preservation of Confederate Culture.* Gainesville: University Press of Florida, 2003.
Gallagher, Gary L. *Lee and His Generals in War and Memory.* Baton Rouge: Louisiana State University Press, 1998.
Litwicki, Ellen. *America's Public Holidays, 1865–1920.* Washington, D.C.: Smithsonian Institution Press, 2000.

Karen L. Cox

SUPER BOWL SUNDAY

- This is not an official holiday that is recognized as such by any state or federal entity.

- The first Super Bowl (Super Bowl I, of course) was held on January 15, 1967 at Memorial Coliseum in Los Angeles, California. Final score: Green Bay 35, Kansas City 10.

- It has been staged between January 9 (XI) and February 6 (XXXIX).

- Commentators see the Super Bowl as a holiday that celebrates the ascendancy of consumer society and leisure in modern America.

- It is estimated that about 200 million viewers watched the 2005 Super Bowl—or roughly two-thirds of the population of the United States.

- 37 of 39 Super Bowls have been held in the South or West.

- It is estimated that fans attending recent Super Bowls spent at least $350 per person per day bringing in upwards of $300 million in revenue for the host city.

- About 30,000 non-ticket-holding fans travel to the city where the Super Bowl is held.

- The NFL stripped Phoenix, Arizona of hosting Super Bowl XXVII (scheduled for 1993) in 1991 because the state refused to officially recognize Martin Luther King Jr. Day. The state duly recognized MLK as a state holiday shortly thereafter and hosted Super Bowl XXX in 1996.

- More money is legally gambled on the Super Bowl than any other sporting event—an estimated $40 million in 1985.

- In 1985, President Ronald Reagan postponed his second-term inauguration by one day when it fell on the same day as Super Bowl XIX, January 20.

SUPER BOWL SUNDAY: AN AMERICAN HOLIDAY?

Once a year on a Sunday, when outside of a few bright pockets in the Sunbelt the bleak midwinter blankets the nation, vast numbers of Americans gather to eat, drink, and make merry. This celebration combines Thanksgiving-like feasting, Fourth of July–like Americanism, and Christmas-like commercialism into a spectacle that draws the largest audience for any event in modern national life. Ironically, while scholars of American culture would search government lists of national celebrations without finding any mention of it, the average citizen of the contemporary republic would undoubtedly recognize that Super Bowl Sunday reigns as a significant holiday.

Indeed, irony abounds in the rise of Super Bowl Sunday to popular if not official status as a holiday. The newest of American holidays, dating only to 1967, Super Bowl Sunday has neither a connection to religious festivals nor origins in a memorial to a great event in the national experience. It does not mark a modern revision of the celebration of a particular ethnic or racial heritage. If, as so commonly lamented, other American holidays have become too commercialized, Super Bowl Sunday originated through the designs of powerful American commercial interests. If sporting traditions once adorned holidays, as the football games of medieval England festooned Christmas Day or Shrove Tuesday (the day before Ash Wednesday in the traditional Christian calendar), then Super Bowl Sunday has inverted the traditional holiday paradigm and driven modern American football to the center of a festival experience on a day that has historically been set aside as the most important weekly event in the Christian tradition, Sunday.

In spite of its novelty and its lack of connection to venerable historical traditions, Super Bowl Sunday has since the mid-1970s garnered popular recognition as a national holiday. In 1977 *New York Times* columnist Jon Nordheimer declared that the Super Bowl brunch had become "as much of an institution in American suburbs as eggnog parties at Christmas or picnics on the Fourth of July." In 1982, Los Angeles Rams' defensive end Fred Dryer proclaimed Super Bowl Sunday the "first holiday of the year"—apparently forgetting New Year's Day and its football traditions. That same year nationally syndicated columnist Russell Baker compared watching the Super Bowl to Thanksgiving turkey and other uniquely American holiday traditions. "If eating turkey is what you have to do to qualify for fellowship in the American community, I'll force myself to do it, just as I force myself to watch . . . the Super Bowl on television." In response to calls for a postponement of Super Bowl XXV due to the start of the Gulf War in 1991, National Football League (NFL) Commissioner Paul Tagliabue asserted that the event had become the "winter version of the Fourth of July." In 1995, National Broadcasting Corporation (NBC) Sports President Dick Ebersol anointed Super Bowl Sunday "our ninth national holiday." A *Washington Post* columnist in 2002 insisted that Super Bowl Sunday belonged to the list of days that "define us as Americans" with Independence Day, Thanksgiving Day, and Mother's Day. Of course, as another scribe pointed out in narrowing the list of American holidays, Pakistanis and Norwegians love their mothers too, but Super Bowl Sunday, like Independence Day and Thanksgiving Day, represents a "quintessential American creation."

At the beginning of the twenty-first century this quintessential American creation provides more than 200 million Americans with an annual, day-long time-out from their normal Sunday obligations to attend a variety of festive parties celebrating professional football's national championship game. Two-thirds of the televisions switched on during the Super Bowl are tuned in to the game. More than half of the nation's population huddles around television screens at home while millions more watch at bars, churches, or other public gathering places. In the rankings of the largest audiences in American television history, Super Bowls hold the top 10 spots. Super Bowls routinely draw some of the highest television ratings ever recorded.

The power of television in contemporary American culture has catapulted the Super Bowl into the realm of national holidays. Super Bowl Sunday manifests the same collective changes in daily routines as other national holidays. Super Bowl Sunday requires the adoption of holiday schedules. Shopping malls and retail stores empty. Religious services adjust to provide parishioners opportunities to fulfill their sacred obligations without missing the kick-off. Automotive, airline, and telephone traffic diminishes sharply during the game. Other forms of recreation, from golf courses to amusement parks to movie theaters, experience huge drops in attendance. Just as at Thanksgiving, Christmas, New Year's Day, and the Fourth of July, Americans gather for a common purpose. The vast majority of the nation participates in a "national social spectacle" on Super Bowl Sunday. Unlike other holidays, however, in which patriotic pageants or religious celebrations form the core of the common experience, Super Bowl Sunday's powerful populism concentrates the nation's passions on an American professional football game.

A BRIEF HISTORY OF FOOTBALL AND HOLIDAY TRADITIONS

Super Bowl Sunday certainly qualifies as an American creation, but football and holiday celebrations have an older history in Western civilization. The traditional versions of the games that gave birth in nineteenth-century Great Britain to modern varieties of football (including association, rugby, and American versions of football) have an ancient lineage in Europe, dating at least to the era of the Roman Empire. For a millennium in medieval European peasant cultures, football games provided rough-and-tumble celebrations that enlivened the holiday festivals of the Christian calendar.

In the late nineteenth century, when the American strain of football evolved from rugby into a distinctive sport first played primarily on college campuses, the game quickly developed a connection with a uniquely American holiday, Thanksgiving Day. Thanksgiving, originally an amalgam of American patriotism and Protestant sentimentalism, became an important national festival in the decades after the Civil War. By the 1880s and 1890s intercollegiate and interscholastic football matches had become Thanksgiving staples, along with turkey and cranberry sauce. American churches initially protested the incursion of football into the Thanksgiving Day calendar but eventually moved their services to accommodate kick-off times for major games. "Thanksgiving Day is no longer a solemn festival to God for mercies given," observed the prominent American journalist Richard Harding Davis in 1893. "It is a holiday granted by the State and the nation to see a game of football."

Thanksgiving Day football placed the game firmly in the currents of American national pageantry and holiday traditions. In the first half of the twentieth century football also became enmeshed in a less patriotic and less religious national holiday—New Year's Day. Ironically, New Year's Day football games had also been popular in medieval Europe. The modern version began when ambitious civic boosters in cities with mild climates seeking increased winter tourism began to stage New Year's Day bowl games in order to cash in on the national fascination with college football. The practice began in 1916, when Pasadena, California, staged the first Rose Bowl. During the 1930s the Orange Bowl in Miami, the Sugar Bowl in New Orleans, the Cotton Bowl in Dallas, and the Sun Bowl in El Paso expanded the New Year's Day intercollegiate football tradition.

For much of the first century of American football, from the 1870s through the 1950s, the professional version of that game served as a sporting sideshow to the intercollegiate and interscholastic versions of the spectacle. Professional football attempted to emulate the college game's marriage to the Thanksgiving holiday, with little success. In 1902 and 1903 professional teams also faced off on Christmas in an indoor national tournament—an event that quickly evaporated due to lack of interest. The professional game's early incursions into traditional American celebrations did not bear any lucrative fruit.

Until the 1950s, professional football trailed intercollegiate and interscholastic versions of the game in popularity. Generally relegated to Sundays, the least desirable day of the nation's weekly leisure calendar given historic commitments to Christian Sabbatarianism, professional football drew fans mainly from working-class enclaves in a handful of American cities. The press outside of large urban centers rarely covered professional contests. Saturday intercollegiate gridiron spectaculars represented the most popular and lucrative brand of American football. Professional football's ownership marketed their product relentlessly but made little gain against their college rivals until television altered the American social landscape.

During the 1950s and 1960s professional football developed into one of the new electronic media's most valuable franchises. While intercollegiate football programs initially failed to appreciate the enormous power of television and responded to broadcast possibilities in a haphazard fashion, professional franchises took advantage of the new social and economic demographics. The popularity of professional football exploded in the decade culminated by the inaugural Super Bowl I in 1967. The 1958 NFL championship game, a dazzling sudden-death overtime clash between the Baltimore Colts and the New York Giants, lit the fuse, attracting a television audience of over 30 million fans. Those numbers did not escape the attention of professional football's ownership class. Led by league officials who recognized that television made it possible for professional football to challenge not only college football but even major league baseball for market shares in the booming American sports marketplace, the well-established NFL and its new rival, the American Football League (AFL), which appeared in 1960, built lucrative partnerships with the nation's television networks. Football fit television's parameters better than the nation's old national pastime, baseball. By the end of the 1960s professional football became the most popular spectator sport in the United States. At that moment professional football replaced, according to many commentators, baseball as the American national pastime.

THE ORIGINS OF THE SUPER BOWL

Ending an expensive turf war between the two professional leagues by engineering a 1966 merger of the NFL and the AFL, NFL commissioner Alvin "Pete" Rozelle created a championship game between the former rivals to determine the "world champion" of American football. Rozelle thought the game would garner strong interest from television. Television networks snapped up the new game. Both NBC and the Columbia Broadcasting System (CBS) broadcast the first Super Bowl, drawing a respectable audience although not as many viewers as had watched the earlier NFL championship.

The public reception of the first few Super Bowl Sundays resembled the enthusiasm generated at a tree planting ceremony during an Arbor Day celebration rather than a fireworks display at the Fourth of July. League officials promoted the game during its first two years as "The AFL-NFL World Championship Game." The moniker of "Super Bowl" did not appear on the covers of the game's program until its third year, although the media dubbed the game the "Super Bowl" from the very beginning. Unexpectedly meager attendance at Super Bowl I left 30,000 empty seats at the Los Angeles Memorial Coliseum. The NFL fell roughly $250,000 short of their projected million-dollar gate. The first game also left no mark in the annals of historically high (or low) television ratings in spite of the fact it appeared on two major networks. The original Super Bowl did not particularly impress the media. In a typical assessment *New York Times* columnist Jack Gould offered a scathing critique of the production. "The Super Bowl yesterday was a representative example of most television dramas coming out of Los Angeles," Gould opined, comparing the game to a mediocre Hollywood production. "The advance build-up was more impressive than the show." The show left "a million-dollar dud in everyone's closet."

If media critics did not warm to the game, however, fans took it seriously. The home cities of the two teams playing for the championship, Kansas City and Green Bay, came to a standstill. Traffic disappeared from normally busy thoroughfares and telephone use plummeted as fans gazed anxiously at their flickering televisions. The game also appealed to fans far removed from the loyal bastions of the Chiefs and Packers. Another *New York Times* commentator, Bernard Weinraub, offered an alternative view to Gould's caustic assessment. Weinraub described New York City as "gripped by a giddy fever," consumed by a "vague madness," and overcome by a never-before-seen excitement characterized by a "rapt, hypnotic stare" at television sets throughout the city. Weinraub's diagnosis, while perhaps exaggerating the national passion for the first game, proved prescient about future Super Bowls.

The Super Bowl's creators faced an initial problem in the general conception that NFL teams were vastly superior in talent and skill to any of the newly merged AFL teams. The easy victory by the NFL's Green Bay Packers over the AFL's Kansas City Chiefs in Super Bowl I and a repeat Packer title over the AFL's Oakland Raiders in Super Bowl II confirmed that notion. Audiences would not have continued to tune into broadcasts in large numbers if the outcome continued to be such a foregone conclusion. In 1968, after the Packer's second victory, Super Bowl Sunday did not seem destined for holiday status.

Super Bowl III, in 1969, changed everything. When a flamboyant young quarterback from the New York Jets, "Broadway" Joe Namath, brazenly predicted and

Green Bay Packers play Kansas City Chiefs in Super Bowl I at the Los Angeles Memorial Coliseum, 1967. © AP/Wide World Photos.

then delivered victory for his upstart AFL team over the NFL's Baltimore Colts, the Super Bowl landscape altered dramatically. Namath's accomplishment immediately swayed much of the media. One commentator declared that "pro football would never be the same again" and that Namath had elevated the Super Bowl's status equal to the World Series, the Kentucky Derby, and the Masters golf tournament. "Namath," *New York Times* columnist William N. Wallace announced, "put competition, anticipation, and equality into an extravaganza that needed a justification for its continued existence." Television ratings confirmed that Super Bowl III had cemented the game's place in the nation's consciousness. For Super Bowl IV, advertising rates increased by more than 40 percent, evidence that the networks were convinced of the game's enduring popularity. The AFL's Kansas City Chiefs victory over the NFL's heavily favored Minnesota Vikings in Super Bowl IV tied the Super Bowl series with two victories for each league and convinced the nation that the game was worth watching. By the 1970s Super Bowl "fever" had infected not only the hometowns of the competing teams but the entire United States.

New York Jets quarterback Joe Namath hands off the football to Matt Snell during Super Bowl III in Miami, 1969. © AP / Wide World Photos.

CONSPICUOUS CONSUMPTION AND THE SUPER BOWL

In creating this season-ending clash for professional football, the NFL and the television networks laid the groundwork for the creation of the nation's most recent national holiday, Super Bowl Sunday. The game has become, as sports commentator Tony Kornheiser observes, "corporate America's annual holiday," a monument "built to honor conspicuous consumption." Kornheiser's employment of the popular phrase "conspicuous consumption" drives to the heart of the Super Bowl's appeal as an American holiday.

Designed by two of the nation's leading entertainment industries, professional football and television, Super Bowl Sunday symbolizes the conspicuous power of consumption in contemporary American culture. The hundreds of millions who watch the Super Bowl consume not only a televised football spectacle but also variety of other products. On Super Bowl Sunday Americans eat more chips, popcorn, pretzels, and snack nuts than on any other day of the year. The day ranks at or near the top of the lists for consumption of soda, beer, chicken wings, and a host of other items that litter the menu of affluent diets.

Advertising, the mother's milk of the consumer economy, reaches a fever pitch during the Super Bowl broadcast. The Super Bowl sells the priciest advertising slots available. The advertisements themselves have become one of the central features of the experience. Hundreds of millions of consumers tune in not only for the football but for the premiere of a slew of new ads in which the world's leading corporations hawk everything from automobiles to sexual dysfunction remedies. Beer-guzzling lizards and beer-swilling dogs have become pop icons through these advertisements. Indeed, the "ad bowl," as the annual parade of consumer desires has been dubbed, has become as important as the football game itself. This is certainly the grand American holiday of conspicuous consumption.

An analysis of Super Bowl statistics on attendance, ticket prices, television advertising rates, and television ratings and shares reveals the dynamics of the holiday's patterns of conspicuous consumption. The history of ticket prices reveals that the game rapidly evolved from an event accessible to common fans into a spectacle open mainly to the comparatively wealthy. Ticket prices for Super Bowl I in 1967 averaged $8, although even at that relatively moderate price, the NFL could not give enough of them away to fill the Los Angeles Coliseum. The NFL actually decreased the ticket prices for Super Bowl II in order to attract a larger crowd at the game. The ploy worked. The Super Bowl has enjoyed sell-out crowds ever after. Historically, increases in ticket prices have far outstripped the rate of inflation. By 1984 tickets averaged $60, much more expensive than earlier rates but still within the reach of the common fan's income. By the mid-1980s, however, very few tickets remained available to the general public. League officials made sure the majority of seats went to corporate sponsors who used them as business perks. Scalpers resold tickets for exorbitant sums. The rising costs and lack of accessibility led a *Newsday* journalist to lament that the Super Bowl had become a festival "for the royalty to attend and for the peasants to watch on TV, a situation that does not cause the NFL any guilty feelings." By 1988, the face value of tickets rose to $100. In 1999 tickets had climbed to $325. By 2004, a seat at the Super Bowl cost $500 and was generally available only if the consumer had close connections to the NFL.

TELEVISION, CONSUMERS, AND THE SUPER BOWL

Television ratings and shares grew even more quickly than ticket prices. After attracting respectable if not astounding numbers of viewers for the first three Super Bowls, television ratings exploded in the 1970s. Since Super Bowl VI (1972), the NFL has enjoyed a television rating of over 40, indicating that of all televisions in the United States (including those turned off), 40 percent were tuned to the station broadcasting the Super Bowl. By another measuring stick, television share—an indication of the percentage of households using televisions (those turned on) tuned to a specific channel at a specific time—the television take-off began even earlier. Television shares have consistently run in the sixties and seventies for the NFL since Super Bowl II. Taken together, the ratings and share numbers reveal that on Super Bowl Sundays in the United States since the beginning of the 1970s almost half of all existing televisions and almost three-quarters of all televisions switched on have been tuned to the game.

The popularity of Super Bowl telecasts has remained remarkably stable over time. Super Bowls regularly rank among the most-watched television programs of all time as well as dominating the lists of most-watched sporting events in U.S. history. As the nation's population grows, the size of the audience increases correspondingly. By the mid-1980s the broadcast began drawing 100 million viewers. In 1981 the NFL began broadcasting the game live to foreign markets as well as to the domestic audience. Globally, the Super Bowl stands as the most popular single-day sporting event in the world. Only multiday events, the World Cup soccer tournament and the Olympic Games, outnumber the Super Bowl's worldwide audience.

In the twenty-first century, Super Bowl television ratings reveal that audiences in the United States consistently exceed 140 million viewers. Representing a "conservative estimate" of viewers, these Nielsen ratings underestimate the total audience since the measurements do not reflect the estimated 20 to 25 percent of fans who watch the games away from their homes, consuming the televised spectacle in bars, in churches, or at gatherings in front of someone else's television. The addition of these uncounted viewers to the actual Nielsen ratings uncovers an audience that approaches 200 million. Those numbers make Super Bowl Sunday the national holiday of television-watching—a pastime that resides at the core of contemporary American conspicuous consumption.

ADVERTISING, CONSUMERS, AND THE SUPER BOWL

The gargantuan television audiences created by Super Bowl Sunday provide unparalleled opportunities for the purveyors of consumer goods. For the corporations that profit from conspicuous consumption, Super Bowl Sunday reigns as the most important day of the year. The tremendous rise in televising advertising rates during Super Bowls demonstrates the power of the holiday for connecting with American consumers. As with ticket prices, the advertising growth rates far exceed inflation indicators. In 1966, with Super Bowl I on the horizon, NFL Commissioner Rozelle fretted that the league could not expect much more for a Super Bowl commercial minute than the current rate for the NFL championship game—roughly $42,500 for a 30-second spot. After "Broadway" Joe Namath's infamous "guarantee" at the 1969 Super

Bowl, rates jumped from $55,000 to $78,000 for a 30-second ad. The cost of advertising steadily increased thereafter. Thirty-second opportunities to reach consumers went for $103,000 in 1974, $368,000 in 1984, $900,000 in 1994, and $2,250,000 in 2004. Overall, television advertising rates have increased an average of more than 11.65 percent annually.

The rapid increases in sponsorship costs have not lessened corporate interest in promoting conspicuous consumption through the game. Since the 1990s, advertising agencies have snatched up the spots by purchasing billion-dollar packages years in advance. Like other holidays, the Super Bowl has become an advertiser's goldmine. Unlike other holidays, advertisers, in concert with television and the NFL, invented Super Bowl Sunday. The unprecedented size of the television audience for the game made the Super Bowl the most coveted advertising space in contemporary consumer culture. "There are few opportunities for marketers to appeal to an audience as broad as the Super Bowl's," noted one observer of the modern advertising business. "Every year, the championship football game is by far the most-watched television show, gathering 130 million to 140 million viewers before the electronic hearth for what has become a midwinter orgy of commercial culture."

In 1984, a new company in a new industry cemented the Super Bowl's place at the pinnacle of American consumer culture. Apple's debut of its Macintosh Computer through a $1 million, 60-second commercial spot during Super Bowl XVIII became the most publicized moment in advertising history. Apple's hugely successful television spot revolutionized the "midwinter orgy." The clever advertisement kicked off an intense competition among corporations to reach Super Bowl consumers known thereafter as the "Ad Bowl." Unable to dismiss the demographic desirability of enormous Super Bowl audiences, companies since 1984 have used the "Ad Bowl" within the Super Bowl to sell their products and shape their brands for the nation's consumers. Indeed, viewers often report that they watch as much for the new and innovative advertisements as for the game itself, an unprecedented development in American consumer culture.

Since its creation by corporate entertainment interests in 1967, Super Bowl Sunday has evolved into a national celebration of consumption. The tradition of watching the game, in person or on television, exploded after Super Bowl III. While attendance at the game could not grow beyond the capacities of the selected stadiums (between 70,000 and 105,000 seats), the demography of fans attending the games changed from predominantly middle-class crowds who happily grilled hot dogs and guzzled beer at tailgates to leisure-class audiences whose appetites for luxury tended more to caviar and champagne. However, on television, the Super Bowl remained hugely popular with the common folk. Corporations recognized the mass appeal of the Super Bowl and sought to associate their products with the game, spending huge amounts of marketing dollars with the hopes that their products and services would stick in the minds of one the largest television audiences of the year. Indeed, according to market research by Master Lock, a company famous for its Super Bowl ads, "people are twice as apt to remember the commercial if it's aired during the Super Bowl." Just as high ticket costs restricted attendance at the game to the wealthy, so too did the enormous cost for advertising spots during Super Bowl contests limit the list of corporate sponsors to mainly the wealthy to tier of "Fortune 500" companies. As one advertising journalist observed, "Being on the game is being in the game."

CONSPICUOUS CONSUMPTION AND CIVIC BOOSTERISM

Hosting the game has become another way of "being in the game." The development of the Super Bowl in the late 1960s coincided with the emergence of the Sunbelt, the southern and southwestern regions of the United States stretching from Florida to California, as the center of the American economy and polity. As millions of Americans migrated from the decaying "Rustbelt" of the industrial East Coast and Great Lakes regions to the balmy climates and the sprawling suburbs of the new national power center, Sunbelt cities began to compete for the right to advertise their civic wares by hosting Super Bowls. American interests in conspicuous consumption extended to climate and geography. Sunbelt cities have dominated the Super Bowl venue selection process, driven largely by the NFL's basic criteria that a site "had to be warm and it had to be big." Sunbelt metropolises continue to reap the economic and public relation benefits surrounding the spectacles.

The use of Super Bowls to market cities and regions dates to the beginnings of the game. Immediately after Super Bowl I in Los Angeles, travel agencies began attracting vacationers to Miami, host of Super Bowls II and III, by adding game tickets to vacation packages. After Super Bowl III in Miami other cities began to flood the NFL with proposals to host games. The travel industry began using the game as a marketing tool to give a "powerful shot in the arm" to the January tourism slump that normally occurred after New Year's Day. By the 1970s the travel industry viewed the game as a "springboard for winter vacations." Initially, the NFL awarded the honor to a city only one year in advance. Given the vigorous demand, the league quickly began bestowing hosting privileges two, three, and finally four years in the future. Drawing on their experience in hosting major college bowl games, South Florida, Southern California, and New Orleans have dominated the bidding wars. Through 2005, New Orleans played host to nine Super Bowls, Miami to eight, Pasadena to five, San Diego to three, Tampa to three, and Los Angeles to two. The Super Bowl has appeared in other major Sunbelt cities including twice each in Atlanta and Houston and once in Phoenix, Stanford, and Jacksonville. Only twice between 1967 and 2005 has a Super Bowl been staged in a cold-weather climate—Detroit in 1982 and Minneapolis in 1992. Neither "Frostbelt" city earned glowing reviews for their Super Bowl efforts.

Super Bowls generate considerable revenues for cities and tourist businesses. In 1980, Pasadena, California, reported the influx of 75,000 out-of-towners who spent $14 million on round-trip airline tickets and roughly $11 million a day in town. During the same era a Miami Chamber of Commerce executive identified the Super Bowl as "the biggest single event a community can have economically," estimating that fans attending the game spent between $40 and $50 million. New Orleans officials concurred with those figures. By the mid-1980s economic analyses indicated considerable growth in the financial power of the game, estimating that Super Bowl XIX (1985) generated more than $113 million for the San Francisco Bay area and predicted that Super Bowl XX (1986) would produce at least $90 million for New Orleans. City leaders in San Diego estimated that Super Bowl XXII (1988) generated a $150 million impact.

In the 1990s, predictions of Super Bowl windfalls became even rosier. Originally, civic leaders generally projected only the direct impact of the Super Bowl—hotel rooms, rental cars, restaurant meals, bar tabs, souvenirs, and so on. Beginning in 1990 Super Bowl promoters began to add to their calculations of direct impact the estimated indirect economic benefits of the game. This latter category included such items as caterers buying food from local stores or hiring extra workers to handle the Super Bowl event. According to boosters, such activity created economic ripples that some optimistic economists estimated as an additional $1 to $2 for each direct dollar spent. Predictably, the "economic impact" numbers presented after 1990 grew dramatically, provoking even NFL officials to issue cautions about the validity of such revenue projections.

Warnings aside, host cities claimed that bounteous rewards flowed from Super Bowls. Promoters of Super Bowl XXV (1991) in Tampa Bay estimated a $123 million impact as well as an increased ability to steer new convention business to the area. Southern California disclosed $182 million in economic gain from Super Bowl XXVII (1993) in Pasadena. In 1995 metropolitan Phoenix area boosters estimated that more than $200 million in Super Bowl treasure flowed into the area. New Orleans officials assessed the economic impact of Super Bowl XXX (1997) as $250 million—equaling that from the city's famous Mardi Gras celebrations that year. By the end of the century, Miami looked forward to a $300 million profit from Super Bowl XXXIII (1999). Looking to get into the lucrative Super Bowl business, New York City boosters proposed the construction of an indoor-outdoor domed arena in Manhattan to guarantee the city its first Super Bowl. According to Baltimore Ravens owner Art Modell, the city's planned coliseum guaranteed "a chance that the Super Bowl would come to New York every few years or so."

At the beginning of the twenty-first century the Super Bowl attracts 25,000 to 35,000 extra fans to the host cities, in spite of the fact that they know they have no opportunity to get into the stadium. They come for a week of associated festivities, spending as copiously as their comrades with tickets. Certainly

Super Bowl fans spend. Georgia State University economists estimated that the average visitor in Atlanta for Super Bowl XXXIV (2000) spent at least $350 per day. Five years later the NFL awarded Super Bowl XXXIX (2005) to Jacksonville, Florida, the smallest city yet granted that opportunity. When Jacksonville fell 3,000 rooms short of the NFL's requirements for hotel rooms, city officials brought cruise ships into port to meet the accommodations target and keep their lucrative Super Bowl Sunday payday.

Sunbelt cities host the Super Bowl to attract tourists and to lure new residents and businesses. The home cities of Super Bowl teams have also used the game to market their urban identities in the national arena. The Super Bowl success of the Dallas Cowboys from the 1970s through the 1990s earned that Sunbelt expansion franchise the title of "America's team." For more than two decades the Cowboys reigned as the new national pastime's most beloved (and most hated) team—football's equivalent of baseball's New York Yankees. The Miami Dolphins of the 1970s and the San Francisco 49ers of the 1980s and 1990s briefly earned similar acclaim. Those teams seemed to link the thriving economies of their regions with the glamour of their victories, providing more evidence that the future of the nation resided in the booming new cities of the South and West.

For cities in the declining Rustbelt that had no real chance of hosting a Super Bowl, victories by the home team temporarily salved the wounds of lost manufacturing jobs and faltering national prestige. No team better represented the power of Super Bowl championships in revitalizing civic pride in the midst of long-term urban decay than the Pittsburgh Steelers of the 1970s. Super Bowl losses sometimes signified Frostbelt fatalism, as hometown reactions to the four-time losers from Minneapolis and Buffalo demonstrated. A Super Bowl triumph could overcome a legacy of big game losses and polish a city's image, as the back-to-back victories in the late 1990s of the Denver Broncos restored metropolitan confidence after four earlier lopsided losses in the nation's most important spectacle. Super Bowl victories by the nation's leading urban areas, New York, Los Angeles, and Chicago, although less frequent than their triumphs in major league baseball's World Series, confirmed those cities' places at the top of the nation's urban hierarchy.

THE MIDWINTER ORGY OF COMMERCIAL CULTURE AND AMERICAN POLITICS

The Super Bowl holiday serves as a site not only for promoting urban identities and selling consumer goods but also for marketing politicians. Campaign operatives see an opportunity to connect their candidates with the common folk during this festival centered on the nation's most popular sport. Political opportunism at the Super Bowl dates to the original game. In 1967, the staffs of

Senators Robert F. Kennedy and Jacob Javits of New York managed to get the press to report that the two politicians "hardly moved away from the television set" during Super Bowl I. Vice President-elect and former Maryland governor Spiro Agnew sat on the Baltimore Colts' bench before the kickoff of Super Bowl III. When the game began, NFL officials asked Agnew to leave the field since his presence violated league policies. After the completion of Super Bowl IV, Agnew's boss, President Richard Nixon, instituted the tradition of the republic's "quarterback" phoning congratulations to the quarterback of the winning team. In 1982, Vice President George H. W. Bush created monstrous traffic problems with his motorcade when he attended Super Bowl XVI. Chief executives, and those who aspired to the office, clearly saw connections to the Super Bowl as good politics.

The 1985 controversy surrounding the inauguration and the Super Bowl cemented the connections between the game and the executive branch of the federal government. As early as 1983, concerns arose regarding the possibility that Super Bowl XIX might fall on Inauguration Day, Sunday, January 20, 1985. When that conflict did in fact transpire, the government promptly delayed the public inauguration ceremony to the Monday after the Super Bowl. The press howled that football had become more important than the nation's civic pageants. In fact, an old historical precedent of moving Sunday inaugurations to Monday accounted for the switch rather than any concession by President Ronald Reagan's staff to the NFL. James Monroe (1817), Zachary Taylor (1849), Rutherford B. Hayes (1877), Woodrow Wilson (1917) and Dwight D. Eisenhower (1953) moved their inaugurals from Sunday to Monday without fanfare. The press, however, consistently misreported the reasons for moving the inauguration. "It reads well and it tells well," observed John Chambers, the Capitol's expert on inaugurations, of the misrepresentations that the Super Bowl forced the inaugural switch, "but it just ain't true." Chambers's attempts to correct the record were mainly ignored.

Complicating the move of Reagan's 1985 inaugural, however, was the fact that he had agreed to toss the coin to begin the game. He performed that duty in Washington with the result beamed via satellite to the Stanford Stadium in California. Reagan's public relations ploy, along with the fact that the Super Bowl's television audience dwarfed the inauguration's constituency, proved too rich an irony for the pundits to ignore. One columnist quipped that "the swearing-in will probably get single-digit TV ratings. The toss for America's kickoff will probably set viewer records. The difference should tell us something about what's really important around here."

In the *New York Times* Richard Reeves opined that "The coin in the air—and on the air—could serve as the symbol of the partnership of sports and politics in our time." Reeves asserted that the Super Bowl had become "such a national holiday now that the President has to be a part of the game to prove he really is the President." Reeves proposed a constitutional amendment recognizing that supremacy of football. "Congress shall make no law respecting an establishment of events, institutions or encumbrances of any kind interfering with the play of the Super Bowl," he suggested. "No business shall be conducted by any Federal official, specifically including the President of the United States on the day of America's game." Reeves insisted that the republic needed the amendment since "we now know [the Super Bowl] is a higher holiday than the day when we crown our king." Waxing serious at the conclusion of his diatribe, Reeves declared that the Super Bowl "actually replaced a political event as the symbolic holiday of America's civic religion." In a "Letter to the Editor," following Reeves' satire, one *New York Times* reader suggested that the inauguration ceremony should take place during the Super Bowl halftime. That would guarantee "the largest live and television audiences ever for a Presidential inauguration."

Friction between Super Bowl Sunday and other important political issues continued in the wake of the inaugural flap. One year later, NFL officials issued 2,400 media credentials for Super Bowl XX—roughly 1,400 more than the number requested for the Geneva Summit between President Reagan and Soviet Premier Mikhail S. Gorbachev. At the end of the 1980s, the NFL thrust itself into the political spotlight by relocating Super Bowl XXVII from Arizona to California due to Arizona's refusal to institute a Martin Luther King Jr. holiday. In 1996, with a King holiday firmly on the state calendar, Arizona hosted Super Bowl XXX.

In 1991, with the United States embroiled in the Gulf War and debates raging about whether or not to cancel, postpone, or play Super Bowl XXV, the NFL staged a patriotic spectacular. A decade later, the nation and the NFL faced a similar challenge in the wake of the 9/11 terrorist attacks. Once again, the NFL decided to play the game and turned the 2002 Super Bowl into a patriotic extravaganza. Becoming the first president to follow Ronald Reagan's precedent and appear in the Super Bowl's coin-toss ceremony, President George W. Bush flipped the coin in New Orleans' Superdome for Super Bowl XXXVI. Taking place only a few months after the 9/11 terrorist attacks in New York City and Washington, the NFL and television devoted a great deal of attention to patriotic themes at that game. Such sentiments neatly fit President Bush's political agenda in the War on Terror.

Two years later President Bush misplayed Super Bowl XXXVIII when he admitted to falling asleep during the first half of the game. Questioned about the scandalous halftime incident during which an alleged "wardrobe malfunction" revealed one of singer Janet Jackson's breasts on national television, President Bush claimed he had been napping. "Gonzo journalist" Hunter S. Thompson, long a Super Bowl aficionado, decried Bush's error in judgment. "What kind of all-American boy would say a stupid thing like that while he's running for re-election?" Thompson ranted. "Only a fool would deliberately insult the whole Football Nation, at a nervous time when polls show his Job Approval Rating plunging below 50 percent for the first time since he took office."

Justin Timberlake and Janet Jackson perform during halftime of Super Bowl XXXVIII in Houston, 2004. © AP / Wide World Photos.

THE SUPER BOWL AND CONSPICUOUS PATRIOTISM

Presidential phone calls to winning quarterbacks and presidential participation in Super Bowl coin-flips reveal that in addition to conspicuous consumption, the Super Bowl has also become a holiday devoted to conspicuous patriotism. Long before Hunter Thompson scored against a sleepy George W. Bush for his Super Bowl slumber or the nation turned Super Bowl XXXVI into a pep rally for the War on Terror, patriotism played a conspicuous role in Super Bowls.

American patriotism has been a consistent theme throughout the Super Bowl's history. Super Bowl III appealed to patriotic sentiment when all three Apollo 8 astronauts led the pregame Pledge of Allegiance. Anita Bryant, a former Miss Oklahoma and an icon of conservative patriotism, sang the "Battle Hymn of the Republic" at halftime of Super Bowl V. Super Bowl X in 1976 provided a national kickoff for American bicentennial celebrations. In 1981, for Super Bowl XV, the NFL swathed the Superdome in New Orleans with a mammoth yellow ribbon and anointed the Philadelphia Eagles and Oakland Raiders with yellow tape on their helmets to support the return of the American hostages from Iran. In 1991, President George H. W. Bush, commander-in-chief for the impending Persian Gulf War, ordered a "breathtaking display of military might" at the Super Bowl. Bush allowed Air Force jets to fly over Tampa Stadium to punctuate Whitney Houston's seismic performance of the national anthem. In 2002, the NFL wrapped Super Bowl XXXVI in red, white, and blue symbolism, patriotic songs, and more overtly nationalistic displays than any other previous football championship in response to the terrorist attacks of 9/11. The 2002 display of patriotism led a *Washington Post* pundit to contend that "with the helium steadily leaking out of Memorial Day, a holiday few Americans observe by actually attending events that honor the sacrifices of war, and Labor Day devolving into little more than cookouts and mattress sales, the Super Bowl is filling the void."

The patriotic strands running though Super Bowls developed most clearly in the pageantry of the halftime shows. Evolving from simple, college-like performances by marching bands, the Disney Corporation in 1976 pitched a Radio City Music Hall–style extravaganza involving large casts of performers and crowd participation. These productions revolved around common themes, which became the guiding characteristics of the Super Bowl festivities from pregame promotion to postgame analysis. The 1976 theme, for example, paid tribute to America's bicentennial. Over the next few years halftime shows honored American music, time periods in American culture, American movie and film stars, and the XVI Olympic Winter Games. In 1993, singer Michael Jackson's performance of "Heal the World" marked the first in a long list of headliner performers to grace halftime shows. The nationalistic themes continued with the added star power of pop-music icons, including a 2000 ode to American hegemony entitled "A Tapestry of Nations" and a 2002 memorial to the victims of the 9/11 terrorist attacks.

The comfortably packaged patriotism presented at halftimes did not completely escape criticism. In 1990 columnist Robert Klein scolded the American public for utilizing the Super Bowl as a "patriotic substitute for increasingly esoteric national holidays." Klein complained that Fourth of July is now only associated with firecracker and injury statistics, Veterans Day with no alternate-side-of-the-street parking, and Presidents' Day with mattress sales. Hunter S. Thompson, two years before his diatribe about President Bush's Super Bowl

Former President George Bush and former President Bill Clinton greet fans and reporters prior to the coin toss at the beginning of Super Bowl XXXIX between the New England Patriots and the Philadelphia Eagles, 2005. © AP / Wide World Photos.

sleeping habits, groused about the patriotic messages the White House pumped into post-9/11 Super Bowl XXXVI. "Has the NFL been drafted into the 'war effort' now?" Thompson snarled. Scholars have waded into the football and patriotism fray. The leading historian of football in American culture, Michael Oriard, warns that nationalism might obscure the game itself. While Oriard admits the strong desire to honor fallen Americans and national causes, he cautions that making patriotism a calculated Super Bowl marketing strategy "risks cheapening the very thing that [we] are celebrating."

The NFL, the networks, and politicians see the situation somewhat differently. At Super Bowl XXXIX (2005) in Jacksonville, President George W. Bush dispatched his father, former President George H. W. Bush, and his family's political nemesis, former President William J. Clinton, in a show of patriotic force for the coin-toss ceremony. Fox Television and the NFL staged a dramatic reading of the Declaration of Independence by former NFL stars as a highlight of the pregame show. As the former presidents watched, veterans of World War II marched to the center of the stadium in honor of the past glories of the "greatest generation," while the network cut to feeds of American soldiers standing at attention from bases in Afghanistan, Iraq, and Germany during the build-up to the "Star-Spangled Banner." Patriotism seems destined to continue at the center of Super Bowl pageantry.

Perhaps the clearest indication that the Super Bowl has become a holiday site for patriotic display as well as a celebration of conspicuous consumption appears in the rise of Super Bowl protests designed to challenge the status quo. The campaign to move the Super Bowl out of Arizona if the state did not recognize a Martin Luther King Jr. Day represents one example of the counterculture uses of the games. The demonstrations by the American Indian Movement against the misrepresentation of indigenous peoples during Super Bowl XXVI, a game in which the Washington Redskins played the Buffalo Bills, exemplifies the role of the Super Bowl in modern American political discourse. So, too, does the cranky radicalism of Hunter Thompson, who claimed to have been "physically ejected from the Redskins press box when [I] forgot to take [my] hat off for the National Anthem."

SUPER BOWL SUNDAY AND AMERICAN SOCIAL PATTERNS

The Super Bowl Sunday holiday provides forums for patriotism and protest. Super Bowl Sunday also impacts a variety of social practices. Gambling, both legal and illegal, has historically been associated with sporting events. The Super Bowl has become the most important gambling event in modern American culture. Some fans take a gambling pilgrimage during the Super Bowl holiday, traveling to Las Vegas for the weekend to make last-second bets. Others engage in illicit betting, risking money in office pools or turning to bookmakers to make wagers.

Americans gamble huge amounts of money on the Super Bowl. In 1985, bookmakers reported that Super Bowl XIX had set records. Legal betting action in excess of $40 million exceeded the amount gambled on any other event in American history. The next year an investigative journalist labeled the Super Bowl "the single biggest betting event in the country." Several factors account for the heavy betting action. First, the Super Bowl falls shortly after Christmas and New Year's Day—a time dominated by post-holiday blues and bills. Gamblers looking for midwinter excitement or a big score to climb out of debt find the game too attractive to resist. Second, the Super Bowl, a one-day event, caps a season's worth of gambling on other NFL games. "If you've had a losing season, this is the chance to win everything back," explains Keith Whyte of the National Council on Problem Gambling. "And if you've had a winning season, why not risk it all?" For the compulsive gambler, Super Bowl Sunday can be a dangerous day. "We expect to get a lot of suicide calls," on Super Bowl holidays, observes Dr. Valerie Lorenze of the National Center for Pathological Gambling. "We've gotten people who say they're going to rob a bank to pay their bookies."

While suicide may be on the minds of some unfortunate gamblers shortly after the Super Bowl, a study in the *Sociology of Sport Journal* suggests that suicidal patterns associated with the game mimic those of other American holidays. Comparing the "suicide-dip" effect on the Fourth of July and Thanksgiving Day with the rates for the last day of the World Series and Super Bowl Sunday, the study found similar patterns. Significantly fewer suicides occur during the days before and on the day of these holidays and events. Suicide rates jump after these holidays and events. The study argues that the communal bonding that holidays, including the Super Bowl, produce shrinks suicide rates during these celebrations.

Traveling further down this dark demographic highway, researchers reported in the *New England Journal of Medicine* that driving fatalities increased to a greater degree after the telecast of the Super Bowl than on New Year's Eve. While they found no significant difference in rates of traffic mortalities before the telecast and only a marginal increase during the telecast, the researchers discovered an average of about seven more deaths in the aftermath of Super Bowl Sunday when compared to other Sundays. The home states of the losing team incurred more fatalities than those of the winning states.

Gambling, suicide, and driving fatalities may not be the topics that the NFL likes to highlight, but their association with the Super Bowl demonstrates that Americans behave on Super Bowl Sunday in ways they behave on other American holidays. Researchers of social patterns recognize the Super Bowl functions as a holiday.

Super Bowl Sunday has also produced unfounded sociological claims. In 1992, a study performed by sociologist Garland F. White of Old Dominion University reported a link between domestic violence and holidays, especially Super Bowl Sunday. At press conferences and in television and newspaper interviews, domestic violence experts complained that spousal battery spiraled to unprecedented levels on Super Bowl Sunday. A few years later, however, a *Washington Post* reporter discovered that no hard evidence existed to support that widely touted assertion. The allegations sprang from the assumption that "a day of testosterone-fueled football, alcohol consumption and togetherness is a combustible mix that could erupt in violence" rather than reliable data. Professionals in the field acknowledged that no solid evidence to support the theory existed but were "understandably eager to seize on any opportunity to spotlight the problem." Ironically, female spectatorship has risen consistently throughout the Super Bowl's history. By the twenty-first century women constituted 40 percent of the Super Bowl television audience.

The Super Bowl has created more esoteric social ripples. By the 1990s, economists began to refer to the "Super Bowl Indicator," a concept that allegedly forecasts how the stock market will perform based on which team wins the game. According to the Super Bowl Indicator, if an original NFL team or an NFC team wins, the Dow Jones Industrial Average supposedly rises. If an AFC or original AFL team wins, the Dow allegedly drops. As far-fetched as the concept appears, only six years between 1967 and 2002 contradict this "theory." The Super Bowl has wedged itself even into the sooth-saying of stock market forecasters.

RELIGION AND THE SUPER BOWL

The construction of a clearly secular holiday on the Christian Sabbath reveals the waning power of religion over the calendar in contemporary American culture. Since the Reformation some Protestant groups have waged a long war against sporting competitions on the Christian Sabbath or on Christian holidays. In the United States until the beginning of the twentieth century the Sabbatarians generally won the conflicts. Outright legal bans on Sunday sport existed in some places, while cultural disdain for Sunday recreations pushed them to the margins of acceptable social practices, in cases where legal prohibitions were not as rigorous. Indeed, professional football's marginality at the beginning of the twentieth century earned the game its Sunday slot while the high school and college versions of the game enjoyed Friday and Saturday schedules. Sabbatarianism has declined markedly since the beginning of the twentieth century. Professional football on Sundays has not been a controversial issue in mainstream culture since the 1960s. Religious groups have adapted to the new realities and sought to connect sacred practices to the Super Bowl's secular ceremonies. Indeed, as one major religious leader, the Reverend Dr. Norman Vincent Peale, opined, "If Jesus were alive today, he would be at the Super Bowl."

In the wake of Peale's hyperbole, the Sunday placement of the Super Bowl holiday has led commentators to seek links between sporting fever and religious fervor. A *New York Times* story that ran on the Sunday of Super Bowl I proclaimed the game had supplanted the *Book of Genesis* in American life. On the seventh day "God rested, which would have made it a pretty humdrum Sunday," concluded the reporter, giving thanks for the creation of the Super Bowl. In a 1972 essay entitled "The Super Bowl Society," English professor Ronald Cummings lamented that "religious pageantry has waned" while sporting rituals had captured modern imaginations. Cummings claimed that in the new national culture centered on sport rather than Christian sacraments, "Super Sunday may soon be our most gala affair of all." Contemporary theologian Michael Novak concurred, describing the Super Bowl as a "therapeutic ritual, perhaps a religion, of modern high-speed society."

Theologians as well as secularists have read the apparent inability of traditional religion to generate the same enthusiasm among large masses of people as Super Bowl Sunday as more evidence of the decline faith in modern society. Such claims have produced a thriving debate. After a controversial 1986 article in the *Houston Chronicle,* the author apologized to his readers after making the blanket statement that the Super Bowl had replaced Easter as America's primary religious holiday. "What are 80 million American's [sic] doing on the day that the two conference champions play for the National Football League title on a Sunday in January?" the author observed in his original story, "Attending Mass?" In actuality, many American religious groups adapted their patterns to include the Super Bowl in Sunday schedules. Catholics attended Mass and Protestants went to Sunday services at modified times. Many religious groups sponsored Super Bowl parties or offered Super Bowl–related sermons, accepting the Reverend Peale's contention that if Jesus were about in the late twentieth-century United States he would be at the game.

Some churches, rather than fight the powerful influence of Super Bowl Sunday, embraced the game as a mechanism for promoting fellowship through football. As early as 1967, in response to Super Bowl I, St. Thomas Episcopal Church in Mamaroneck, New York scheduled its interfaith performance to end in time for the game's kickoff. In 1982, a Super Bowl spectator from Rye, New York claimed that all the churches in his area but one had the Super Bowl listed as the topic of that day's sermon. In 1986, Rabbi Arnold Kaiman, a Chicago Bears fan, scheduled a wedding ceremony to end before the start of Super Bowl XX's second half. The following year, a church in Boulder, Colorado, ended a 10:00 A.M. service with a prayer for the Denver Broncos and a toast of Orange Crush. The ritual did not prevent the New York Giants from crushing the Broncos.

In 1992, the Basilica of St. Mary's in Minneapolis draped huge banners outside its doors welcoming fans to Super Bowl XXVI while the local First Baptist Church held a Super Bowl Party. In 1995, in St. Louis, Missouri, the First Baptist Church of St. Peter combined their Christian obligations with watching the Super Bowl. Utilizing two 10-foot television monitors and a banquet of pizza, sandwiches and desserts, the Reverend David Spriggs used Super Bowl Sunday as "an opportunity to take something happening in society and share our faith." The viewing of the game, cheered "rather restrainedly," featured the replacement of beer commercials with clips from other football games. Half-time featured the singing of religious hymns and Christian videos by All-Pro Green Bay Packer defensive end Reggie White and several members of the San Diego Chargers and San Francisco 49ers. After he retired from football White continued as a prominent Christian evangelist, creating "Souper Sunday" parties at which church groups gathered to watch the Super Bowl and collect cans of soup to distribute to the needy. While religious groups fought fiercely to keep football and other nonreligious activities from intruding on Sundays and holidays from the sixteenth century through the mid-twentieth century, by the late twentieth century, religious institutions limited their suffering from Super Bowl fever by eagerly embracing the new national holiday.

A NEW SET OF RULES FOR CONSTRUCTING AMERICAN HOLIDAYS?

The emergence of Super Bowl Sunday as an American holiday raises questions about the contemporary dimensions of national celebrations. During the Super Bowl's short lifespan many of the nation's traditional holidays have been trivialized as brief escapes from work, which provide opportunities for retail sales and backyard barbecues. George Washington and Abraham Lincoln's birthdays, awkwardly amalgamated as Presidents' Day, have certainly lost much of their earlier luster in the veneration of American heritage. Memorial Day, Labor Day, Columbus Day, and Veterans Day have undergone similar if not as precipitous declines. Rarely in the twenty-first century do these holidays evoke the historical, ethnic, or religious sentiments that they once inspired.

By most measures Super Bowl Sunday has transcended these older holidays in the national imagination. Super Bowl Sunday began in 1967 as a mere football game. By 1969 it had captured massive public interest. In the 1970s it emerged as a national holiday. Since that time it has become a major site for patriotic display and has also ranked as the nation's most watched television spectacle. For more than three decades the Super Bowl has been the most popular event in the annual American calendar. In the first decade of the twenty-first century it shows no signs of declining.

The rapid rise and enduring appeal of Super Bowl Sunday raises questions about how Americans currently construct holidays. In many ways, Super Bowl Sunday represents the appearance of an entirely new type of holiday in American culture. Unlike many of the older festivals in the national calendar, Super Bowl Sunday did not evolve from a religious holiday. Nor did it originate to commemorate a significant event or person in American history. Super Bowl Sunday does not have ties to tradition or heritage. Created by secular commercial interests entirely for secular and commercial purposes, Super Bowl Sunday represents the triumph of consumer culture over older social patterns. Criticism that the Super Bowl has been corrupted by the forces of modern commerce, so common in regard to other national holidays, does not emerge from the throats of outraged football fanatics. Indeed, such criticism would be absurd since Super Bowl Sunday was created by the modern entertainment industry to celebrate the national appetite for conspicuous consumption. Nearly four decades after the first Super Bowl, the Sunday extravaganza has clearly become an enormously popular national event. If government agencies have not yet listed the Super Bowl among the nation's official holidays, the public has clearly embraced the spectacle. Consumers have voted with their pocketbooks, their television remotes, and their leisure time. The Super Bowl has been elected to holiday status.

While the forces of corporate capitalism certainly designed Super Bowl Sunday, it would be too facile to assume that they forced this new holiday on a passive, sports-addled proletariat. At the turn of the twentieth century the iconoclastic economist Thorstein Veblen incorrectly characterized football as an atavistic practice clearly bound for quick extinction by the forces of modernity. He accurately forecast, however, that consumers would play a dynamic role in the modern economy, that consumer choice as well as producer design would warp the contours of the next century's social life. In Super Bowl Sunday professional football, television, and advertisers have discovered an event that resonates deeply with enormous segments of the nation's consuming masses. The Super Bowl Sunday holiday emerged from this intersection of design and desire. In the process Super Bowl Sunday may have provided the blueprint for the way in which holidays are constructed in an age of conspicuous consumption.

FURTHER READING

Davies, Richard O. *America's Obsession: Sports and Society Since 1945*. Belmont, Calif.: Wadsworth Publishing, 1994.

Kanner, Bernice. *The Super Bowl of Advertising: How the Commercials Won the Game*. Princeton, N.J.: Bloomberg Press, 2004.

Rader, Benjamin, *In Its Own Image: How Television Has Transformed Sports*. New York: Free Press, 1984.

Schwartz, Dona. *Contesting the Super Bowl*. New York: Routledge, 1998.

Weiss, Don, with Chuck Day, *The Making of the Super Bowl: The Inside Story of the World's Greatest Sporting Event*. New York: McGraw-Hill, 2003.

Peter Hopsicker and Mark S. Dyreson

Hearts and Flowers

Before Valentine's Day in 2005, the National Retail Federation estimated that

- 92.8 percent of adult Americans with spouses or romantic interests intended to buy at least one gift for them
- 69.1 percent of Americans planned to buy gifts for other family members, such as children or parents
- 28.4 percent expected to buy something for friends
- 26.0 percent planned to buy something for classmates and teachers

Of these, an estimated 73.3 percent would buy cards, 53.2 percent would purchase candy, and 44.4 percent would go out for the evening. Additionally, 64.9 percent of men and 16.29 percent of women would buy flowers.

The estimates could not have been far off. In 2005, adult consumers on average spent $97.27 each for the occasion—down somewhat from $99.24 in 2004, but considerably more than 2003's $80.44. Overall, Americans spent approximately $12.79 billion for Valentine's Day in 2004, and only slightly less in 2005. Clearly, Americans, and American retailers, are in love with Valentine's Day, a day ostensibly honoring a Catholic saint's martyrdom, but in fact devoted to playful expressions of idealized romantic love, coquetry, and friendship.

Just who St. Valentine was is unclear. No fewer than three men of that name, all from different parts of the Christian world, appeared in early texts as having been martyred sometime in the third century, on February 14. But neither at that time, nor for the next thousand years, did St. Valentine have anything apparent to do with romantic lovers; he was simply one of many medieval saints upon whom the faithful might call. The first English evidence of a popular association of St. Valentine's Day with love is in Chaucer's "Parliament of Fowls" (1382):

> For this was sent on Seynt Valentyne's day
> Whan every foul cometh ther to choose his mate.

Thus it appears that the saint's feast day, associated in time with a well-known sign of approaching spring, became connected with stylized expressions of love in the chivalric age. February 14 became a day for stylized courting and romantic poetry, and St. Valentine was invoked to aid lovers in removing barriers to their happiness. There is evidence that people betrothed about that time of year referred to each other as "Valentines."

The religious aspects of Valentine's Day were all but lost in English North America; the Protestant reformers who dominated in most of the early colonies condemned saints' days. But popular associations of the day with romantic love persisted. Before leaving England in 1629, John Winthrop, soon to become governor of Massachusetts Bay Colony, assured his wife in a letter dated February 14 that "thou must be my valentine for none hath challenged me." For some, especially courting folk, Valentine's Day was an appropriate time for divination to discover future spouses. The day's traditions were recalled in many American almanacs. Nevertheless, until the nineteenth century, Valentine's Day in America had been an "often forgotten, easily neglected Old World saint's day."

All that changed during the 1840s. As is so often the case, Americans were captivated by a fad from overseas, in this case the English fashion of exchanging Valentine notes. All the vogue in London especially, the practice caught on quickly in the United States, to the point where a writer in 1849 remarked that Valentine's Day "is becoming, nay, it has become, a national holiday."

Why did Valentine's Day become such a sensation, and so quickly? Perhaps, as Leigh Schmidt argues in *Consumer Rites: The Buying and Selling of American Holidays* (1995), Americans were just ready for it. Already caught up in what historians call the "market revolution" of Jacksonian America, busy people needed a late-winter occasion for innocent fun. "We all calculate too much," argued an 1845 newspaper editor, and need "more soul-play and less head-work." Valentine notes, usually sent anonymously, provided safe outlets for "soul-play," and for feelings perhaps too awkward to express in other ways. People delighted in the "half serious, half-comic love-making, and humbug amorous declarations, made on paper and through the post."

Retailers were not slow to improve the commercial possibilities of the phenomenon. Obviously, Valentine's Day benefited printers, booksellers, and stationers. These began to offer commercially produced greeting cards (called "valentines") especially for the occasion, to aid those insufficiently creative or too busy to write their own. Critics of Valentine's Day denounced the store-bought cards as an assault on authentic self-expression, but in vain. Card makers, now taking a hand in actively promoting the "holiday," were rewarded with ever-increasing sales. Customers could soon purchase cards with satirical as well as sentimental messages, poking fun, often savagely, at the unfortunate, the unsuitable, or the rejected. Even enemies could be sent comic or mock valentines. During the

Civil War, the applications of Valentine's Day expanded, making it a day of special remembrance for parted lovers, spouses, and family. Card makers created valentines for these needs also.

To a great degree, Valentine's Day as we know it today is a story of commercial innovation and success. The expansion of the advertising industry after the Civil War helped promote the occasion through efforts to generate midwinter sales. Colorful shop displays fostered distinctive decorating motifs, such as the ubiquitous red hearts, often edged with lace. The recent war had helped to expand the range of suitable valentine recipients, and vendors worked to maintain and even expand this pool of buyers. Even children were encouraged to get involved, presaging the now-common practice of exchanging cards or treats in schools. Helping to justify this juvenile participation was the commercial elevation of the cherubic Cupid, the mythical agent of the love goddess Venus. Joining the card salesmen (such as traveling salesman Joyce C. Hall, who in 1910 began the business that became Hallmark Cards), jewelers, florists, and confectioners soon got into the act, also. This last group developed "systematic and aggressive" retailing strategies toward the end of the nineteenth century and created that other icon of Valentine's Day, the heart-shaped box.

By the end of the nineteenth century, merchants and consumers had created virtually all the popular customs and trappings of Valentine's Day familiar to people of the twenty-first century. What has followed since that time has been refinement in marketing and the scale of public participation, which today approaches 100 percent. The success of Valentine's Day lies chiefly in its playfulness: in the 1840s it "teasingly subverted the middle-class preoccupation with social transparency and sincerity." Today, "from co-workers to classmates," as a modern executive expressed it, "Valentine's Day has become a holiday to express appreciation for a variety of people." As with other carnivalesque occasions, appreciation can be expressed anonymously. Secrecy, surprise, and mystery are still a large part of the fun, with secret Valentines sent through the mail or delivered to the door or office. The near-universal participation may also be largely due to Valentine's Day's relative lack of potentially divisive political or religious messages—although in 2005, protesters objecting to the environmental effects of gold-mining demonstrated outside jewelry stores in some cities.

Make no mistake: Valentine's Day is big business, now ranked just behind Christmas and Mother's Day in terms of dollars spent on gifts. Florists sell in excess of 70 million roses each February. The Greeting Card Association reports that Valentine's Day is the second-most popular card-sending holiday in America. More than 36 million heart-shaped candy boxes were sold in 2005, helping to make February 14 fourth in candy sales, behind Halloween, Easter, and the Thanksgiving to New Year season. The modern ability to shop via the Internet has enhanced sales on this, as on other gift-giving occasions. Americans in 2005 made two and a half million at-home orders for gifts and flowers. Online florist services have seen phenomenal sales increases: FTD's Valentine's Day sales were up 106 percent over 2004, while business for Proflowers increased by 156 percent. Thanks to aggressive marketing and broad consumer responsiveness, Valentine's Day, in the words of National Retail Federation chief executive Tracy Mullin, "has become a very big business for retailers in what is traditionally one of the slowest shopping months of the year."

Washington, Lincoln, and Presidents' Day

Even before his death, many Americans celebrated the birthday of George Washington, hero of the Revolution and first president of the United States under the Constitution. Americans had been accustomed to honoring their sovereign's birthday only shortly before, so Washington may have served as a safe, transitional king-substitute in the uncertain first years of the republic. The Federalists especially, for whom Washington was their champion, during the 1790s turned each February 22 into a virtual rally for the party faithful. Ultimately, however, they were unable to monopolize so colossal a symbol. Evoking a figure of mythic moral strength and integrity, Washington's memory, and Washington's birthday, became potent forces for national unity and accord.

But in the antebellum years his name and reputation were summoned up for many other causes. Striking workers and social reformers invoked his name to promote their causes: advocates of temperance formed the Washington Temperance Society in 1840; the shoemakers of Lynn, Massachusetts purposely began their famous strike of 1860 on February 22nd; and antislavery groups held Washington's birthday orations. The great man, of course, had been a slave owner, but antislavery groups referred to his written sentiments expressing hope that slavery might end in America (Washington was in fact a cautious gradualist) and his example of manumitting his slaves after his death. Despite the liberal use of his name in often divisive causes, however, before the Civil War Washington's memory was generally a force for unity. The "nation's patriarch," the "virtual patron saint of the United States," in Matthew Dennis's words, could not be used for mere partisan purposes. And even when war came, even as North and South both claimed the blessing of America's greatest hero,

Washington could not be made to take sides unequivocally. Many southerners regarded him as the model for their cause, the original rebel, and a Virginian at that. Northerners, on the other hand, saw him as the "emblem of the Union" (considering the unmistakably unionist sentiments expressed in his Farewell Address, the North probably had the better argument). Washington's image, at least, emerged untarnished from the conflict. In 1885, President Chester A. Arthur signed a bill making Washington's birthday a federal holiday, reflecting the reality that already existed in virtually all states and territories.

Meanwhile, another president had achieved heroic status in much of the nation. Abraham Lincoln's assassination at the end of the Civil War, and on Good Friday at that, brought him an almost Christ-like status as martyr and savior of the republic. Within two years of his death some Americans celebrated his birthday (February 12), and by the end of the century five states officially recognized the day. Predictably, southern states resisted the notion of Lincoln as hero; only after the failure of Reconstruction and abandonment of southern blacks by the Republican Party after 1877 did he become a more generally acceptable symbol of reconciliation. Also, Lincoln was appealing to late-nineteenth-century Americans in ways that the great Washington was not. Lincoln was no aristocrat: he was born and raised in humble circumstances, and he was the rail-splitter, who had labored hard with his hands, studied books, and succeeded. He was more accessible, more human, than the great, silent, distant gentleman Washington. In 1909, the centennial year of Lincoln's birth, three more states commemorated his birthday, and his image appeared on the one-cent coin. By 1959, more than 30 states officially recognized Lincoln's birthday as a holiday. But February 12 never became a national holiday in its own right.

Together, Washington and Lincoln became a composite hero, their birthdays (conveniently and somewhat mystically both in February) becoming holidays in most of the states. But in the twentieth century, overexposure from historians, debunkers of history, merchants hawking all sorts of goods, and both fascist and antifascist groups invoking their names for modern agendas, saturated the public with their images, eroding and trivializing their significance. Washington especially suffered in the aftermath of the bicentennial of his birth; historian Karal Ann Marling wrote that by late 1930s Washington "had been too popular for too long . . . from sheer overexposure, Washington had become a bore."

In more recent decades, the decline of Washington and Lincoln as icons reflects a diversification of concerns in an increasingly multicultural society. In the 1960s, writes Matthew Dennis, Americans "generally shared a sense of ambivalence, or estrangement, toward familiar icons." But it was Congress that may have dealt our "star" presidents the mortal blow, when in 1968, as part of the Monday Holidays Act, it moved the official observance of Washington's Birthday for all federal workers to the third Monday in February (thereby guaranteeing that the official celebration would never again fall on his actual birthday, the 22nd of the month). Although Congress designated the day as Washington's Birthday, some states dropped their separate observances of Lincoln's Birthday, combining it with Washington's and calling it Presidents' Day. The Monday Holidays Act thus diluted the images of Washington and Lincoln, but the situation was made worse by public confusion over the change. Many Americans still believe that the federal holiday is called Presidents' Day, and also that Presidents' Day is meant to honor *all* past presidents, whereas most states intend that the presidents to be honored are the traditional ones, Washington and Lincoln. Few citizens can become enthusiastic about celebrating Millard Fillmore, or Rutherford B. Hayes. But perhaps the slow eclipse of Washington and Lincoln in popular memory should not surprise; Barry Schwartz, who has studied the progress of Washington's reputation in America, concludes that "to expect that a nation should turn out, year after year, in heartfelt veneration for a man who died many generations ago is to make unreasonable demands on its capacity for emotional attachment."

"We live in a post-heroic age," argues Matthew Dennis, and "Presidents' Day is as unheroic as it gets." Modern Americans seem ambivalent about heroes, anyway. Firefighters and police in general became the new popular heroes after the terrorist attacks of September 2001, but "heroes" are announced nearly every night on the evening news: soldiers returning from Iraq (whatever their actual service); people who rescue pets from storm drains; and perhaps most fleeting of all, sports figures. On the other hand, modern Americans seem to want their heroes to be perfect, and "heroes" of the moment fade when any number of human frailties are subsequently exposed in the glare of modern media. George Washington and Abraham Lincoln were certainly not perfect, and so even they cannot measure up to our exacting standards. If heroism has become democratized, it has also become well nigh impossible to sustain. Presidents' Day, a lackluster and watered-down replacement for the birthday observances of the "Father of his Country" and the "Savior of his Country," now often little more than an excuse for a sale, seems to reflect Americans' growing detachment from the founding generations of their nation.

MARDI GRAS
AND CARNIVAL

Of the more than 10 thousand festive occasions taking place annually in the United States, slightly more than one percent call themselves Mardi Gras, Carnival, or similar terms. Yet the terms and the festival to which they refer are no less familiar to most Americans today than the great national holidays of Thanksgiving, Christmas, Halloween, and the Fourth of July. This familiarity has grown over the past two generations because of the mass media's affection for Mardi Gras's most renowned paradigm in the United States, the festival at New Orleans, which changes its date each year, depending on the date of Ash Wednesday. The renown of Carnival has also grown because of a shift in middle-class America's ideas of leisure time. For today's more affluent and more sedentary (but still work-driven) Americans, a glittering spectacle, where the main thing that one has to do is relax and look, has special appeal. Easily accessible "otherness," sunshine, and media-familiar glitter have become the prime elements of leisure-time desire. *Mardi gras* (French for "Fat Tuesday," the day before Lent begins in ashes and penitence) had quite different characteristics in the European mother countries of most Americans only a few generations ago. Carnivalesque excess in food, drink, and sexual play was the alternative to the slow tempo of winter work, before sunlight and warmth returned, and before the resumption of long hours and often feverish tempos in agricultural work, ship-going commerce, and artisanal manufacturing. Mardi Gras/Fastnacht/Carnestolendas/Shrove Tuesday/Carnavale took its meaning from the rhythms of locally experienced, religiously sanctioned everyday life. After the Industrial Revolution in the increasingly secular United States of the nineteenth

MARDI GRAS AND CARNIVAL

- ☐ Mardi Gras and Carnival have traditionally been periods of sexual license, and for excessive eating and drinking.

- ☐ Mardi Gras is French for "Fat Tuesday." Fat Tuesday is the day before Ash Wednesday, which marks the beginning of Lent and occurs between early February and early March every year.

- ☐ Organized Mardi Gras celebrations were first recorded in New Orleans in the 1830s. Large numbers of out-of-towners began to travel to New Orleans for Mardi Gras in the 1880s.

- ☐ While the vast majority of Mardi Gras and Carnival celebrations occur along the Gulf Coast, many cities throughout the Unites States celebrate the holiday too, including New York City, Hartford, Chicago, Seattle, and Memphis.

A Mardi Gras parade in New Orleans, 1907. Courtesy of the Library of Congress.

and twentieth centuries, Carnival lost its meaning as a prelude to the new-year rekindling of faith and replenishing of physical energies.

The dominant image of Mardi Gras in today's mass media has suppressed recognition of half a dozen other types of Carnival celebration in this country. New Orleans's festival, and that of its sister versions in Mobile, Alabama, and in other Gulf Coast Carnivals from Florida to Texas represent the best-known forms. Carnival festivity in Tampa, Florida, Brooklyn, New York, and rural Louisiana differ from the New Orleans–Mobile type primarily because of the power of local ethnic groups to orient celebration toward their native traditions. But if one looks closely at the deep history of the New Orleans and Mobile festivals, one sees that they, like these present-day variants, also developed by means of mixture. American Carnivals, unlike most of their European forebears, began and have continued to flourish by acknowledging, fusing, and sometimes juxtaposing social, cultural, and even biological differences, at least in its publicly shared forms.

For historical reasons as well as for reasons of changing national patterns of leisure-time consumption, the area commonly identified with American

Carnival is the Gulf Coast and its hinterlands. Most of the hundred or so pre-Lenten celebrations there are less than three generations old. Among them, the two oldest foundations in New Orleans and Mobile stand out as the models for nearly all others except those in south central ("Cajun") Louisiana.

City boosters in Mobile and New Orleans claim that their first inhabitants began celebrating Fat Tuesday as soon as they stepped off their French ships at the beginning of the eighteenth century. But the earliest reliable testimony for collectively organized carnivalesque performances, as opposed to individual masking in the streets and private masquerade revelry, dates only from the 1830s and 1840s. The "Bedouins" and the "Mardi Gras Rangers" roamed New Orleans streets at the beginning of the 1840s, but they shortly disbanded. In 1831 at Mobile, however, a carnivalesque society was founded that endured for 60 years and gave birth in 1857 to Comus, New Orleans' oldest and most prestigious Carnival organization. The bizarre name of the Mobilian foundation evokes the society's social (Anglo-American, with a small minority of French families) and cultural (French plus Western-American) eclecticism. After the Civil War this Mobilian group paraded on Fat Tuesday, but earlier they ambled about the streets on New Year's Eve with an emblematic rake draped with cowbells, calling themselves the Cowbellion de Rakin Society. "Cowbellion de Rakin" plays ironically upon the city's political and economic beginnings. Mobile is a port city surrounded by rich farm land, founded in 1699 by French noblemen; "Cowbellion de Rakin" undermines the name's Frenchified pretentiousness with homespun frontier impudence: rebellion and cowbells, rakin(g)/raising a ruckus.

The Cowbellions perhaps shifted their parades after the Civil War to Fat Tuesday due to rivalry with New Orleans, whose pre-Lenten celebrations were rapidly outstripping Mobile's festive play in renown. The spirit of half-whimsical elitism inspiring these first festive organizations in both cities, however, has proved to be a stimulus so congenial to the carnivalesque imagination that it has remained a guide to all subsequent permutations. These Carnival societies, whether old or new, create glittering dreams of themselves, which fascinate the rest of the nation with their defiant distance from the grinding capitalist-industrialist assumptions guiding life elsewhere. The prevalence among whites of reactionary ideologies for a half century after the Civil War ensured popular support for the escapist extravaganzas of Carnival. In 1866 an ex-Confederate soldier named Joe Cain paraded with several other veterans in Mobile's Carnival as an undefeated Indian warrior, "Chief Slackabamorinico," who, Cain said, had just emerged from nearby Wrang Swamp; the following year the group appeared again in increased numbers, announcing themselves less ambiguously as the Lost Cause Minstrels. The "Joe Cain parade," although it eventually died out, reappeared in the mid-twentieth century in less racist guise as "the people's parade," welcoming anyone in costume to join in, provided that they registered as part of a group with city authorities. The parade still exists today.

Krewe of Comus Ball during Mardi Gras in New Orleans, 1997. © Philip Gould / Corbis.

The reputation of New Orleans as the "City that Care Forgot" emerged in the period between the end of Reconstruction in 1878 and the end of World War I, half composed and half imposed by economic depression and political reaction. That reputation soon proved darkly attractive to people elsewhere in the country. Trainloads of visitors to Carnival began arriving in the 1880s. An entire chapter in the scholarly *Standard History of New Orleans* published in 1900 was understandably devoted to the Carnival: in that year Carnival tourists were estimated at 100,000.

Until the 1920s Mobile's downtown parades were, like those in New Orleans, restricted to whites. Mobile never developed something like New Orleans's "superkrewes," dating from 1969, which anyone regardless of sex, race, or residence might join. Whatever eagerness middle and lower classes have displayed for participation in Mobile's "mystic societies" has never outlasted the reluctance of more moneyed elites to relax their grip on what they consider proper merry-making. In New Orleans the edges available for developing Carnival games have always been more ample and various. Divisions of every kind, ethnic, religious, political, and above all racial, fracture the city. But Carnival is the day on which fractiousness should be cast aside by all good citizens—for the sake of the tourists at least. Divisions yes, but quarrels no! Little by little the core idea of the New Orleans–Mobile model, big public parades maintained

A poster announcing the Mardi Gras Carnival in Mobile, Alabama, 1900. Courtesy of the Library of Congress.

by Carnival societies of like-minded persons of similar social rank, came to be expanded beyond the wealthy few to any group organizing a "krewe" (this is the New Orleans name; in Mobile the proper name for a Carnival group is "mystic society"). The public activity is complemented by a private banquet and dance for krewe members and their invited friends.

Most Carnival societies in the two cities start preparation for Mardi Gras within a month or two after the end of Lent at Easter. They choose a theme for next year's parade floats, an exercise that blends the esoteric with the commonplace in fantasmatic spectacles. The most popular of all themes has been children's stories and fairy tales; the second mythology (not only Greco-Roman but Near Eastern and Far Eastern), the third history (European and American, especially military), and the fourth geography (the Rocky Mountains, Egyptian pyramids, etc.). The societies hand over articulation of the theme to committees of society members, each with responsibility for a particular float. Carnival societies have 3 to 13 or even more floats today, so elaborate adjustments are needed to coordinate the floats. The desire to preserve preceding years' structures for reasons of tradition and economics assists in this, but also tends to undercut originality.

Action in the Carnival streets has two aspects in this Mardi Gras model. The parading side moves Mardi Gras toward spectacle. This however does not induce mere awed passivity in those who watch. Float-riders and spectators engage in what might be called "the throwing game," a much-transformed descendant of what were in preindustrial conditions "queting exchanges" (quests for food). Beads and doubloons dominate the throws in New Orleans; sugary confections called moonpies are thrown from floats in Mobile. Confetti throwing, even in showers of paper rather than of plaster bits as of yore, has almost disappeared.

Each Carnival society, each form of throwing, each mode of costuming and float-making in the two cities has its special history. Because society members invest much time and money in their play, these special histories endure. But all these Carnival elements also evolve, and this is especially easy to see in the second kind of public behavior, that which maximizes participatory interchange because it is conducted on foot and often one-to-one rather than in carefully planned big-street parades. On Fat Tuesday, those without any masking or costuming element in their appearance in New Orleans's French Quarter are a bizarre minority. Exuberant individualism in costuming rules the day, challenging the passerby at every step to equal the masker in repartee. In the run-down black back streets east and north of the Quarter, troops of African Americans garbed in an inimitable combination of nineteenth-century Plains-Indian and African feathered, sequined splendor walk and chant. They are accompanied by uncostumed dancers and musicians, devotees of each such so-called "gang" or "tribe;" these devotees are called the gang's "second line." The interchange here is mostly group to group rather than individual to individual. For many decades after 1909 the famous Zulu tribe of African Americans also paraded in that ghettoized area, with the same group-oriented exchanges—comic patter, wildly thrown fish and gilt coconuts, and constant interruption of the parade-path to enter taverns and houses for alcoholic cheer. But the civil rights movements of the 1960s changed this, and the Zulus have now joined the first kind of street action, parading down the main streets of the city with elaborate floats. They retain some of their tradition of satiric imitation of the white societies' elite pretensions in decking out their "kings" in Elizabethan grandeur. That is, while today's Zulus have admitted some whites as members, their king still parades in grass-skirted splendor, and they still hand out gilt coconuts labeled as "African gold."

There are also today some black members of "Rex," the once all-white and now the most prestigious Carnival society in New Orleans. But the division between black and white modes of playing Carnival in New Orleans remains visible and even geographical with a few exceptions like the Zulus' main-street activity and the sometimes racially mixed mini-groups who mask in French Quarter streets. In Mobile the color line remains even more strictly observed. Two Carnival kings, one white, one black, parade on different days. In sum, participation in the first form of Carnival—its elite and spectacular parading form—has evolved from being the preserve of an upper middle class toward being available to anyone with the money—and it costs several thousand dollars today to join even a modest krewe or mystic society, marching at a disadvantageous time on a day earlier than Fat Tuesday.

The two sides of the New Orleans-Mobile model of Carnival thus still perpetuate duplicitous qualities. The model is receptive to most moneyed minorities, especially those with local business and marital connections; it is also interested in the power of even poor crowds (applause is important), but less so if the crowds have dark faces. These qualities, already attractive beyond the home cities as early as the 1880s, have been avidly imitated along the Gulf Coast since World War II. The recipe of parades in public and banquets and balls in private, stably carried on by cohorts of friends in Carnival societies (with slowly growing assistance from public authorities), has spread in this region for more reasons than factors of leisure time and affluence. Here there is not only sunshine but its proper ambience; warm, sandy beaches begin to beckon in February and March. There is also, among the locally civic-minded, the impulse to do what your neighbors a few miles away are doing. Moreover, when Americans after 1945 began careening toward new technologically driven, worldwide-connected lifestyles, the elements of tradition that could be preserved amid the juggernaut of modernity acquired a nostalgic value. The quality of the many Gulf Coast Carnivals developed in the wake of Mobile and New Orleans is well captured in this vignette from *Coasting Through Mardi Gras, A Guide to Carnival Along the Gulf Coast*:

> On the night before Mardi Gras Day [here at Fairhope, a town not far from Mobile, this day is Monday, not Tuesday, so people can go to Mobile the next day] another enthusiastic bunch of ladies takes to the streets with nine floats and nine lady marshals. These gals began parading in 1993 and their first theme was appropriately named "Maiden Voyage." Frolicking on their emblem float each year is their "mascot," a beautiful court jester dressed in purple and gold and named *Frolic*, of course. Along with candy, doubloons, and Frisbees, this fun-loving group also throws garters complete with their logo. Catch one.

The eastern end of the Gulf Coast in the present-day state of Florida was for more than two and a half centuries a Spanish possession. Pensacola and Tampa, two large port cities on the west side of the Florida peninsula, both possess Carnivals a century or more old. Although both were Spanish settlements, their Carnivals were first modeled after Mobile (Pensacola organized "mystic societies" from 1900) and New Orleans (the Tampanians called their first soci-

The Jesters' float makes its way along Canal Street during the Rex parade on Mardi Gras in New Orleans, Tuesday February 8, 2005. © AP / Wide World Photos.

ety in 1904 a "krewe"). But neither city has hesitated to adapt its festivity to more local parameters. Tampa's adaptation was especially inventive. Some miles south of Tampa Bay is another bay; one of the seaways into it is called Gasparilla Pass because it was the hideout area of the pirate Jose Gaspar or Gasparilla, who terrorized passing merchant ships between 1783 and 1822. This nearby pirate's reputation fired the imagination of a Carnival society founded in 1904 in Tampa, which called itself Ye Mystic Krewe of Gasparilla. On Mardi Gras the krewe, having arrived by sea, flocks ashore and pretends to take the mayor of Tampa captive for the day; members march through the town waving swords and menacing spectators. This fine invention remains an elite, essentially mainstreet and spectacle-oriented aspect of a Carnival whose context has profoundly changed since it was inaugurated in 1904. The city began to grow rapidly from the 1850s onward and soon included on its edges a Hispanic suburb, Ybor City, which became a center of cigar-making in the 1880s and eventually spawned a more Latin American version of Carnival. To judge from the Internet's advertisement of "Gasparilla Carnival" in 2001, however, one would scarcely suspect that anything goes on in Tampa at Carnival-time except romanticized playfulness with the region's most notorious former resident:

> Gasparilla is the one time of year regular folks can go down to the richest street in Tampa, Bayshore Boulevard—where million-dollar mansions stand—and party. . . . The parade route is a

party in itself. You'll see nurses and doctors and people who have 9 to 5 jobs pushing grocery carts full of ice and beer, or Radio Flyer red wagons of Captain Morgan's rum. . . . Members of Ye Mystic Krewe—the all-male, nearly all-white social club . . . board the replica of a real 18th century pirate ship, the Jose Gasparilla . . . The pirates lead the flotilla and are the big draw of the parade partly because they started it and pay for much of the cost. . . . You'll see lots of kids reaching for beads thrown from the floats—and adults doing the same.

One in every five Tampa residents claimed "Hispanic and Latino" ethnicity in 2004 (total population: 303,447). By the 1980s the "Fiesta Day" accompanying Gasparilla Carnival advertised Cuban and Italian foods and games, strolling musicians, and puppeteers and mimers of many kinds, so that the two aspects noted in New Orleans and Mobile—organized processions and on-foot fooling—have acquired contrastive tonalities, similar to the parades of Mardi Gras Indians or Zulus as compared to the main-street parades of "krewes" in New Orleans. The pleasant Gulf Coast climate has played its part, perhaps, in blending different ethnic traditions and different social allegiances into an imagination of what could have happened once upon a time. Tampa's Gasparilla Invasion occurs on the second Saturday in February; it is not now and perhaps never was dated with respect to the beginning of Lent.

Unlike the case in Tampa, "exotic" ethnicity has been the actual rather than legendary spur to the creation of Carnival in New York, Chicago, Detroit, Hartford, San Francisco, Washington, D.C., and allegedly another 17 locales in the United States with large West Indian populations. Celebrations take place whose main tenor is to reproduce the singularly famed Trinidad pre-Lenten celebration. As in the case of Tampa, none of these festivals takes place on the days leading up to Roman Catholic Lent. None of them developed in the circumstances of protest that gave Trinidad's Carnival its special general character and its particular kind of carnivalesque quality. There is nevertheless little doubt that the main features of Carnival-as-spectacle, as practiced today in Trinidad's capital Port of Spain, have been successfully transplanted to many American cities. The largest of them takes place in Brooklyn, New York. Carnival was celebrated by West Indians already in the 1920s in Harlem; the occasion moved in the 1960s to Brooklyn and today accommodates over ten thousand paraders and more than two million spectators on Labor Day Monday in September. The mayor of New York and a high-ranking police official have, understandably enough on the occasion of such a mammoth festival, led the parade during the last four years.

Brooklyn's Carnival parades are not centered around floats. The only motorized vehicles are sound-trucks, which blare live or recorded "soca" ("soul" plus "calypso") music to which parades of people shuffle, march, and dance along the street. The rhythm of the music and the "jump-up," two-step style of dancing is well adapted to dancing alone, in pairs, or in gigantic groups of a thousand or more costumed revelers. The revelers in the parade are divided into 60-person groups wearing identical costumes, who follow 4 to 10 lead maskers. These lead maskers carry headdresses that are extraordinarily high and wide—15 to 20 feet—with arm attachments that depict insects, dragons, devils, and other phantasms. The making of such heavy and complex yet individually propelled costumes is evidently no less an engineering than an artistic feat.

Organization of the costumed bands is entrepreneurial rather than based on social class, residence, or family ties. For several months before Labor Day, 25 to 30 store fronts in Brooklyn, located especially along Nostrand and Church Avenues, an area full of food and clothing shops catering to West Indian tastes, are turned into "mas' camps," mask- and costume-making enterprises. Anyone can go into one of these enterprises and decide to purchase a Carnival costume from among the half-dozen or more models sketched in color on two- by three-foot-long white paper by the mas camp artist. Costumes today cost from 50 to 150 dollars.

On the days before Monday's parade, as costume selection culminates, there is an accumulating hubbub in these streets, pulling people out of their apartments to shop and look and listen, to eat and chat and "chip" (a two-step dance shuffle) to the music emanating from apartment windows as well as from record stores. Steelbands also have their "yards," where during the last few days the players, mostly young men and women in their teens and twenties, gather nightly to practice. Each of these yards, accommodating 50 or 60 players with their specially tooled oil-barrel-shaped instruments, takes up more room than a "mas camp" store, so they are more widely scattered over Brooklyn. This on-the-street excitement during the week before Labor Day—or West Indian Carnival Day as local people insist on calling it—is as much a part of the Carnival as the parade itself. There is little masking by non-paraders during this week or during the parade. Nor is there any bead- or moonpie-throwing. The action of spectators takes a different form. People from 15 West Indian nations take part in this Carnival. Their homelands are all English- and French-speaking; Spanish-speaking West Indians have separate festivities and scarcely participate in this Carnival. More than half the people in the huge crowds buy small, 7-by-11-inch flags, which they wave furiously when a contingent of their island nation parades by. Still another dimension of West Indian Carnival is a more helter-skelter parade of individuals and small friendship groups which is called "J'ouvert" and takes place in darkness between three and eight o'clock Monday morning.

The basic structure of individualized revelry pulling together in (and against) the enterprises of privately organized societies is what has maintained and developed this 80-year-old ethnic (rather than seasonal or religious) version of Carnival in America's largest metropolis. The other 20-odd West Indian Carnivals in the United States all follow that Trinidad-inspired organization and styling, and all with less success, somewhat in the same way that most Gulf Coast Carnivals vary little from their models in New Orleans and Mobile.

In 1763 the French who had emigrated from their homeland since the early seventeenth century were forcibly expelled from their farmsteads in eastern

Canada. By the 1820s, after many vicissitudes, large numbers of these "Cajuns" from Canadian Acadia settled down in small rural communities in south-central Louisiana. Sometime between 1850 and the later nineteenth century their agriculturally based customs, their nuclear-family-based collective solidarity, and their stubborn resistance to the Anglo-American lifestyle surrounding their area, not to mention their pleasure-loving Gallic spirit, gave rise to a special form of Carnival celebration called "the Fat Tuesday run" (*courir de mardi gras*). The form was adopted and changed in a few particulars (especially musical) by French-speaking African Americans living in the same geographical area, who called themselves "black Creoles."

With the exception of the celebrations in New Orleans and Mobile, this *courir* form is the only mode of American Carnival that has attracted impressive scholarly attention. Thirty slightly varying instances of it are known today, which involve Carnival players ranging from a few dozen to a few hundred, and which engage the attention of a hundred onlookers in some cases to a few thousand in others. Such numbers cannot compare with those turning out for a single big parade during New Orleans's Mardi Gras. But small is beautiful in this case as in many others, both esthetically and anthropologically.

Mardi Gras celebration in New Orleans, late nineteenth century. © Brown Brothers.

The *courir* is a swing through Cajun countryside from one farmhouse to the next. In only a few cases today the *courir* is still a horseback "run." In most cases revelers move from one place to the next in a tractor-drawn truck. Maskers are called *sauvages* (wild people, savages), or *paillasses* (buffoons, clowns), *soldats* (soldiers), or simply *Mardi Gras* (i.e., people of Fat Tuesday), and their face coverings variously reflect these names. The main action of the countryside tour is to beg for food, and especially for live chickens, which are chased by the revelers until caught and killed. The chickens and other donated ingredients and money are used to make a community gumbo on Fat Tuesday evening, an event followed by a masked ball. Everyone who cares to come is invited to share in the food and dancing. This engaging sequence is made more piquant by the antics of the Mardi Gras as they beg throughout the long day not only from the farmhouse hosts but from anyone at all within their ribald reach. Even the barefaced, cape-wearing supervisor of the begging game, the *capitaine*, who gives flag signals to begin and end a visit, may be pulled into the action and playfully mishandled—above all by women. Until the 1970s the *courir* was exclusively male; today women play in increasing numbers.

The tenacious coherence with which this Carnival celebration has been played for at least four generations, with its special music (sung in French as the revelers arrive at each homestead) and special costuming, has been as important as the recent fame of the Cajun lifestyle in the national media since the 1970s. Zydeco music, country-style dancing, and Cajun cooking have become such attractive emblems that curiosity-seekers are becoming a nuisance in these once strictly local festivals. Organizers of the flag-waving, frantic "jump-up" revelers on West Indian Day in Brooklyn ardently but vainly hope for more non-Caribbean spectators. But those who play Mardi Gras in Basile, Grand Marais, or Tee Mamou worry instead about the dwindling local support of new business elites and the growing numbers of spectacle-seeking outsiders.

Ethnos and ethos here combined to create a festive form whose single components, like those in New Orleans and Mobile's big-parade forms, can all be traced to European antecedents. But the cohesiveness of the festive form also derives from astute incorporation of factors of local ecology and economy, as well as from responsiveness to local popular culture.

At the end of this chapter I have listed 128 public festivals calling themselves Carnivals or a similar term. Certainly many more remain to be located, but probably not more than twice this number. Three-fourths of those listed are located along the Gulf Coast and in its hinterlands, which is more than twice the number that I have found in all the rest of the nation. Slightly less than 25 percent of these known, well-advertised Carnivals come from the small central-Louisiana area called Cajun Country. They are a sociological and demographic exception, for nearly all the other Carnivals are found in large urban areas. Big-city Carnivals all over the United States, like those in New Orleans and Mobile, waver between honoring broad ideals of happy-go-lucky behavior during this festival and yielding to deep-seated feelings of resentment and hatred. Riots against homosexuals, violence against women, animosity between blacks and whites disrupt Carnival's jovial atmosphere time and again. Are such breakdowns the consequence of Carnival's openness, its untrammeled, overarching, overweening reach toward expressive freedom?

Carnival is a total cultural phenomenon. It draws upon and nourishes all the human capacities for representation—verbal, visual, gestural, musical, gustatory—in a limitless gamut of display and performance genres that play across and arbitrarily amalgamate satiric, hortatory, celebratory, and ritualistic distinctions. It stimulates something even deeper and wider than the amplitude of our esthetic-expressive talents. Despite the periodic attempts of state and church and business people to regulate or even co-opt this occasion, Carnival continually escapes their clutches, just as it smoothes over or rolls over the fools and fanatics who scar its freedom. How has that been possible? Surely above all by the way its forms recast the everyday limits of perception and conception by treating those limits as nothing more (but also nothing less) than comic possibilities. No particular Carnival at any particular time ever realizes such jovially conceived openness in ways satisfying to every one of its actors or spectators, and out of that too may emerge an irrationally destructive urge. But this totalizing experience of laughing acceptance, collectively explored, nonetheless remains the occasion's horizon of intent. That is perhaps the real reason that this statistically negligible mode of play called Carnival has such a prominent place in the American imagination of festivity.

AMERICAN CARNIVALS: AN INDEX

The following list is arranged first in two sections: Gulf Coast Carnivals and non–Gulf Coast Carnivals. Within these sections the places of activity are listed alphabetically by locality, followed by the date of the first known or estimated publicly organized activity. Internet advertisers, local tourist agencies, and chambers of commerce do not care to acknowledge the foundation date of their festivities unless it is to their financial advantage. The many dates with question marks are my deductions. Unless a date is definitively a first initiative by a named group, I assume that the date that I have found (usually the date of the publication in which the Carnival is described simply as a current practice) refers to an already established custom; the estimated date of origin is then placed five to seven years before that documented date.

The Carnivals with dates between the 1860s and 1910s were often abandoned and then resumed a generation or more later, but such intermittency is not signaled here. Cajun Carnivals are indicated with an asterisk (*). They are all given a questionable foundation date in the 1850s unless a definite foundation date has been found.

Half of the Carnivals listed in the first section (65) are located in Louisiana. Louisiana is the only state endorsing Mardi Gras as a state holiday, surely a reason circularly entwined with factors like the climate, the location of Louisianan Acadia, and the inspiration of New Orleans in the explanation of such a preponderance.

Gulf Coast Carnivals

		Gulfport, MS	1960s?
		Gulf Shores, AL	1979
Alexandria, LA	1993	Hammond, LA	1990s?
Atlanta, GA	1873–80	Hollywood, FL	1936
*Basile, LA	1850?	Houma, LA	1947
Baton Rouge, LA	1990s?	Houston, TX	1899
Bay St. Louis, AL	1896	Indian Point, MS	1990s?
Berwick, LA	1980s?	*Iota, LA	1850s?
Biloxi, MS	1908	*Iowa, LA	1850s?
Boca Raton, FL	1960?–70?	Kaplan, LA	1980s?
Bogalusa, LA	1990s?	*Kinder, LA	1850s?
Bolivar, TX	1990s?	*Lacassine, LA	1850s?
Brownsville, TX	1960s?	Lacombe, LA	1980s?
Carencro, LA	1960s?	*Lafayette, LA	1850s?
Catahoula, LA	1980s?	*Lake Arthur, LA	1990s?
*Chackbay, LA	1850s	Lake Charles, LA	1882
Chataignier, LA	1850s?	Lake Wales, LA	1984
Chauvin, LA	1990s?	Larose, LA	1990s?
*Choupique, LA	1850s?	*L'Anse Maigre, LA	1850s?
*Church Point, LA	1850s?	*L'Anse de 'prien noir, LA	1850s?
Covington, LA	1952?	*LeJeune Cove, LA	1850s?
*Crowley, LA	2001	Livonia, LA	1990s?
Dauphin Island, AL	1990	Lockport, LA	1990s?
DeRidder, AL	1980s?	Long Beach, MS	1990s?
Diamondhead, MS	1980s?	Madisonville, LA	1980s?
Donaldson, LA	1901	*Mamou, LA	1850s?
*Dulac, LA	1850s?	Mandeville, LA	1980s?
*Egan, LA	1850s?	Maringouin, LA	1980s?
*Eunice, LA	1850s?	Mermentau, LA	1900?
*Evangeline, LA	1850s?	Mobile, AL	1830s
Fairhope, AL	1985	Monroe, LA	1985
Franklin, LA	1990s?	Morgan City, LA	1980s?
*Gaines, LA	1850s?	Moss Point, MS	1990s
Galveston, TX	1867	Natchez, MS	1875
Gautier, MS	1990s?	New Iberia, LA	1890s
*Gheens-Vacherie, LA	1850s?	New Orleans, LA	1841
*Grand Marais, LA	1850s?	Norwood, LA	1980s?
Gretna, LA	1980s?	*Oberlin, LA	1850s?

Ocean Springs, MS	1990s?		Columbia, TN	1990s?
Orange Beach, MS	1990s?		Dallas, TX	2002
*Ossun, LA	1850s?		Detroit, MI	1990s?
Pascagoula, MS	1935?		Fayetteville, AR	1990s?
Pass Christian, MS	1925?		Fort Lauderdale, FL	1990s?
Pensacola, FL	1900		Hartford, CT	1990s
Port Allen, LA	1980s?		Helvetia, WV	1869
Port Arthur, TX	1990s?		Hollywood, FL	1936
Prichard, AL	1978		Jackson, MS	1970s?
*Rayne, LA	1850s?		Liberal, KS	1950
*Scott, LA	1850s?		Los Angeles, CA	1960s?
Shreveport, LA	1900?		Manitou Springs, CO	1996
Slidell, LA	1950s?		Memphis, TN	1872
*Soileau, LA	1850s?		Miami, FL	1950s?
Sunset, LA	1980s?		Montgomery, AL	1962
Tampa, FL	1904		Nashville, TN	1990s?
*Tee Mamou, LA	1850s?		New York, NY	1947
Thibodaux, LA	1990s?		(Harlem, Brooklyn)	
*Ville Platte, LA	1850s?		Norman, OK	1994
Waveland, MS	1990s?		Oakland, CA	1990s
White Castle, LA	1948		Ogden, UT	1890
Youngsville, LA	1980s?		Saint Louis, MO	1960s?

Non-Gulf Coast Carnivals

			San Francisco, CA	1986
			San Jose, CA	1990s
Austin, TX	1990s		San Luis Obispo, CA	1979
Baltimore, MD	1881		Seattle, WA	1960s
Benicia, CA	1994		Tuscaloosa, AL	1960s?
Birmingham, AL	1896		Washington, DC	1980s?
Chicago, IL	1990?			
Cincinnati, OH	1883			

FURTHER READING

Ancelet, Barry. "*Capitaine, voyage ton flag:*" *The Traditional Cajun Country Mardi Gras.* Lafayette: Center For Louisiana Studies, 1989.

Dean, Bennett Wayne. *Mardi Gras, Mobile's Illogical Whoopdedo.* Mobile, Ala.: Adams Press, 1971.

Kasinitz, Philip. "New York Equalize You?" Change and Continuity in Brooklyn's Labor Day Carnival." In *Carnival: Culture in Action—The Trinidad Experience*, ed. M. C. Riggio. New York: Routledge, 2004.

Kinser, Samuel. *Carnival American Style: Mardi Gras at New Orleans and Mobile.* Chicago: University of Chicago Press, 1990.

Mauldin, Barbara, ed. *Carnaval!* Seattle: University of Washington Press, 2004.

Samuel Kinser

ST. PATRICK'S DAY

The Irish were not alone as an ethnic or immigrant group in celebrating feast and saints days in colonial and early republican America. The variety and frequency of various types of commemoration within that developing society was impressive. While St. Patrick's Day was not an invention of America, Irish Americans have done more than anyone else in the world to mark March 17 as special. The celebrations back in Ireland were, for many years, low-key affairs focusing on religious services, family gatherings, and dinners. In colonial America, St. Patrick's Day began in similar fashion but evolved slowly into an ostentatious public display of Irishness in America, with parades in numerous towns and cities and the adoption of customs and rituals peculiar to St. Patrick's Day itself—some transplanted from Ireland, others of local inspiration.

In America today, the commemoration of St. Patrick's Day is associated most strongly with the Irish Catholic diaspora and the Ancient Order of Hibernians, long-time stalwarts of parades in honor of the Patron Saint of Ireland. However, the origins of Patrician observance in America lie with transplanted Ulster Protestants. This point is really no surprise: Protestants had dominated Irish migration to British North America in the early eighteenth century, and those arriving in Massachusetts were already familiar with formal and private observance of St. Patrick's Day by the Anglo-Irish elite. In this tradition St. Patrick's Day celebrations at Dublin Castle were stylish affairs organized by the British government, honoring both the patron saint of Ireland and the importance of Anglo-Irish solidarity. However, St. Patrick's Day among the American Irish

ST. PATRICK'S DAY

☐ St. Patrick's Day celebrations in colonial America were brought over and initiated by Ulster Protestants, following those in Northern Ireland that focused on Anglo-Irish solidarity.

☐ The first St. Patrick's Day celebration in America took place on March 17, 1737, in Boston.

☐ The first unified parade down Fifth Avenue in New York City was in 1851. Prior to that St. Patrick's Day was celebrated locally, in neighborhoods.

☐ The first St. Patrick's Day greeting cards were created in 1898. Through the twentieth century, the cards became more humorous than serious, and in 1910 the AOH (Ancient Order of Hibernians) declared that the cards were offensive and requested that St. Patrick's Day cards be destroyed.

☐ By the 1870s over 120 American and 9 Canadian cities held St Patrick's Day parades.

☐ St. Patrick's Day celebrations in America often reflected political divides and tensions in Ireland over southern Home-Rule and northern Union with England, especially during the turbulent years following the Easter Rising in 1916.

☐ In 1952, Pan American Airlines advertised their first direct commercial flight from Ireland to the United States by flying 100,000 fresh shamrocks from Shannon, Ireland to New York City, to be used for free distribution along Fifth Avenue.

☐ The 1992 parade in New York almost floundered when the city refused to issue a parade permit after the event's sponsor, the AOH (Ancient Order of Hibernians) refused to allow the Irish Lesbian and Gay Organization (ILGO) to march in the parade.

☐ As of the late 1990s, the four most popular and well-attended St. Patrick's Day parades were held in New York City, Boston, Savannah, and Kansas City.

☐ Corned beef and cabbage, a popular meal served on St. Patrick's Day, is an American, not an Irish dish.

eventually took on very different modes of expression and divergent ways of interpretation.

ST. PATRICK'S DAY IN THE AMERICAN COLONIES

John D. Crimmins, who in 1902 published a chronology of St. Patrick's Day celebrations in America, contends that the first recorded St. Patrick's Day celebration in the colonies took place in the early eighteenth century:

> The Irish gentlemen and merchants who met convivially in Boston on March 17, 1737, to honour St Patrick, and founded a benevolent society with quaint officials bearing silver keys described themselves as Irish or of Irish extraction and of Protestant faith.

On that day the Charitable Irish Society of Boston (CISB) was formed to provide relief for "those of the Irish nation who might be reduced by sickness, age or other infirmities and accidents or distress." This vision of charity to Irish compatriots portrays an inclusive picture, but the structure of the society was narrowly prescribed and elitist. Its rules stated that the managers of the charity fund and officers of the society would have to be "Protestants and inhabitants of Boston." The "respectable" social cachet of the CISB was circumscribed in a by-law stating that all members had to be clean and decently dressed, "not in cap or apron." Inexplicably, for the next 57 years the society did not formally observe St. Patrick's Day, meeting instead in April every year. Not until 1794 was March 17 restored as the group's major date of assembly. Therefore, the inaugural celebrant of St. Patrick's Day in America did very little to foster appreciation of March 17 as significant.

In the same era, though, several other charitable and fellowship societies were created by Irish Protestants, and it soon became customary for them to organize a dinner and religious service to commemorate St. Patrick's Day. In 1775, for instance, the officers of the Sons of St. Patrick, some 70 in all, marched in unison to the Unitarian King's Chapel to hear a dedicated sermon, after which they assembled for dinner at "Mr Ingersolls in King Street." The officers in question comprised Irish members of the 47th regiment of the Most Ancient and Benevolent Order of the Friendly Brothers of St. Patrick. It appears, therefore, that an Irish contingent of the British army may have unwittingly staged the first St. Patrick's Day parade through the streets of Boston. Exactly one year later, however, Boston-based Crown soldiers were marching hastily in retreat. For on St. Patrick's Day 1776, General Sullivan, an Irish-born soldier serving the Continental forces, led George Washington into Boston, thereafter assuming military control of the city after British forces evacuated. Since then March 17 has been remembered as "Evacuation Day" in Boston. Yet the significance of St. Patrick's Day in Boston remained. Irish Americans who chose to celebrate the "liberation" of Boston on March 17 could also boast Irish leadership of that process. Hence they took part in a dual celebration—local independence from British rule, and, by remembrance of St. Patrick, their connection with the Irish homeland.

Early commemorations of St. Patrick's Day in New York were similar to those of Boston. The first recorded Patrician festivities took place on March 17, 1762, in the house of John Marshall, an Irish Protestant. Such localized St. Patrick's Day observances soon became customary in New York, with "Irish residents of the city" meeting on March 17 each year "in loving remembrance of the parent land." Two main forms of Patrician observance seem to have emerged in colonial New York. The first type of custom was private and formal. Irish charitable societies, which were invariably formed by "well to do" Protestants, staged official St. Patrick's Day dinners with the aim of raising funds to support Irish nationals who had fallen on hard times in the new world. These events invariably included speeches by prominent local Irishmen, who tended to see both Ireland and the American colonies as parts of the British Empire; hence there were not only tributes to St. Patrick but expressions of loyalty to the English monarch. The second type of St. Patrick's Day custom was predominantly Catholic, public, and unpretentious. It featured family gatherings, church services, and lowbrow Irish customs like drowning the shamrock. This social group tended to be mobile, transient, and illiterate, leaving little record of its St. Patrick's Day observances.

The St. Patrick's Day parade, such a major part of March 17 celebrations today, had indecisive and unsystematic beginnings in America. The earliest Patrician spectacle in New York appears to have come in the form of a military procession in 1766. John. T. Ridge, who seemed particularly attuned to the aesthetics of such occasions, wrote:

> the day of St Patrick, tutelar Saint of Ireland, was ushered in at dawn, with Fifes and Drums, which produced a very agreeable harmony before the doors of many Gentlemen of the nation and others.

But this comment reveals nothing about why and how Irishmen were marching on St. Patrick's Day in a military cavalcade. For Irish-Catholic immigrants in colonial America, enlistment in the British army was a rare career opportunity. Catholic soldiers were, however, not usually found beyond the rank and file of the military. This was a stark contrast to Irish-born Protestants, several of whom served as officers in the British Army. So despite a common national background, differences of rank and status were apparent in the Irish soldiers' observance of St. Patrick's Day. For example, on March 17, 1779, a march of the "Volunteers," which consisted of rank and file Catholics in the British army, was led by its Irish-Protestant leader Colonel Lord Rawdon, who presented the troops to Britain's esteemed ally, the Hessian General Knyphausen. The march naturally enough drew honor to the patron saint of Ireland, but it had a broader purpose here in encouraging Irish American recruits to join the British army. New York's *Weekly Mercury* reported that "the Volunteers of Ireland, preceded by their band of music" marched out to the Bowery, where a St. Patrick's Day dinner was held for 500 people. Elsewhere in America, the British Army provided similar encouragement for Irish troops to commemorate their patron saint, albeit in a context of a common loyalty to Britain. There were military parades on St. Patrick's Day at Fort William on Lake George in 1757, and at Fort Pitt (now Pittsburgh) in 1763. Subsequently, during the 1770s, there were similar processions in South Carolina, Maryland, Kentucky, Baltimore, and Charleston.

The American War of Independence (1775–1783) involved Irish soldiers in both Loyalist and American camps. Hence St. Patrick's Day in revolutionary America was observed separately by groups of Irishmen committed to killing each other. The heroics of Irish soldiers in the victorious Continental army suggested that the Irish people in America—despite many of them having supported Crown forces—had earned themselves a place in the new republic. This heightened sense of profile and purpose was reflected, in part, by the key role of several Irish immigrants in the political culture of the new nation. Irish Americans soon featured prominently in Fourth of July parades, symbolizing by this process their sense of citizenship in a wider polity. St. Patrick's Day, too, gained impetus as Irish people took to the streets in parade on March 17. As part of an independent American Republic they were effectively announcing pride in an Irish heritage while also committing themselves to a new land.

ST. PATRICK'S DAY IN THE NINETEENTH CENTURY

By the early nineteenth century the United States was attracting significant numbers of emigrants from Ireland, particularly now from its southern, Catholic-dominated regions. This flow reflected greater religious freedoms for Catholics in America. In Massachusetts, for example, the state constitution of 1780 allowed Catholics liberty of public worship and rights of citizenship, such as voting and eligibility to hold public office. In the British colony of Ireland, by contrast, Catholics faced restrictions on religious practice, suffrage, and political representation. No wonder Irish Catholic emigration to America rose between 1780–1825. Eventually, Irish Catholics assumed greater influence, even control, over Irish charitable societies that had a staunchly Protestant history. But their commitment to social causes remained. The ecumenical Friendly Sons of St Patrick, for example, made 2,850 charitable donations to individuals in New York between 1805 and 1829. An increasing presence of Catholics in organizations like these eventually had implications for the manner in which St. Patrick's Day was remembered in America. For, as will become apparent, Catholics generally commemorated March 17 in a more public and gregarious manner than did Protestants.

The most prominent Irish Catholic charitable organization in the United States was the Hibernian Universal Benevolent Society. With this group's support the annual St. Patrick's Day parade in New York grew in importance, becoming an ever more potent display of Irish Catholic presence. Ridge writes that on March 17, 1831, members of the society carried "the richest and most splendid banners we have ever witnessed, with other appropriate insignia of the Emerald Isle and mottoes of most of the revolutionary characters." In other words, St. Patrick's Day parades in New York now ostentatiously celebrated the Irish Catholic presence in America; Irish Protestants, though dominant in the eighteenth century, were now on the margins. To the chagrin of Ulster Loyalists, March 17 had become an opportunity to parade Irish republican symbols through the streets of New York, such as with banners depicting revolutionary martyrs Wolfe Tone and Robert Emmett.

By the early 1840s, many working-class Irish Americans had established respectable roles in mainstream society, most notably through jobs in the police force, fire department, and railways. The Irish American elite had also made its presence felt in municipal government and small business. All this created a gradual self-confidence among Irish Americans that was reflected, in part, by the rising significance of St. Patrick's Day. The Irish were, by this time, numerically significant in the United States, but the famine accelerated the Irish presence way beyond expectations. For resident Irish Americans, the mass arrival of impoverished immigrants from Ireland during the late 1840s and 1850s eroded their localized sense of progress in the host community. The Anglo-American majority now stereotyped the Irish, more than ever, as economically backward and socially dysfunctional. Despite this fall from grace, there was a determination by many Irish Americans to declare their "rightful place" in a so-called free society. Henceforth, the commemoration of St. Patrick's Day became a once-a-year vehicle for the Irish to symbolically claim their "stake" in the United States, and to declare their allegiance to a homeland vividly remembered.

The growing number of Irish people in America affected both the scale and nature of St. Patrick's Day observances. The sheer volume of immigrants, although not welcomed by all sections of the host society, gave the Irish constituency within America a numerical boost. The Irish became a significant population group in major cities such as New York, Boston, and Chicago, and were becoming prominent elsewhere, such as in Savannah and New Orleans. In this respect the St. Patrick's Day parade became an annual barometer of how potentially powerful (or at least numerous) Irish Americans were in such places. The parades also allowed Irish Americans to project a set of beliefs and aspirations to both their cohorts and other Americans generally. Hence a key aim of Patrician processions, particularly in the wake of the controversial 1848 rebellion in Ireland, was not simply to celebrate Ireland and the place of the Irish in America, but to affirm a dual sense of loyalty to homeland and adopted society. Patriotism of this kind intended to win the confidence of Anglo-Protestant Americans who found the growing local Irish presence both threatening and unnerving. These themes were apparent during the 1852 St. Patrick's Day parade in New York:

> This delight in display, a reminder of the recruiting drives of 1848 with their fife and drum bands, pikes and tricolours, was soon to be formalized in annual procession, on the one day of the year when Irish-Americans took control of public ceremonial space. The pattern was established in 1852: at the first massed St. Patrick's Day procession in New York, pride of place went to the military companies, followed by benevolent, temperance, burial and other forms of Irish associational culture, with the women in carriages bringing up the rear.

That said, the sheer weight of Irish numbers in major American cities, reflected in their mass assembly on St. Patrick's Day, was also a show of latent force. The parade aimed to impress upon politicians seeking reelection that the Irish were now a powerful interest group that could not be ignored. Irish American civic leaders quickly realized that if their urban ethnic population could be brought together politically, socially, and culturally, they might form a significant voting bloc within the body politic. Influential members of the Irish American community, such as newspaper editors, entrepreneurs, and politicians, envisaged a shared Irish American perspective on key issues of the day. In that regard, "the annual St. Patrick's Day parade became a visible symbol of the bonds of Irish communal solidarity;" it was the one day of the year when "the Irish took over the streets of New York and announced to its non-Irish residents that they were a force to be contended with." The symbolic cohesion of the parade was evident by the disparate range of organizations that took part. From the late 1840s, marchers included the Operative Masons, the Quarrymen's United Protective Society, the Laborer's United Benevolent Society, and 14 other labor organizations. This social mix, while dominated by the working classes, provided clear evidence of the broad appeal of "Irishness" in America.

The St. Patrick's Day parade in New York city, which had been driven by the enthusiasm of the Laborer's United Benevolent Association, came under the organizational control of an umbrella group from 1851. The newly formed Convention of Irish Societies was professional in outlook, meeting every Friday throughout the year to plan and stage the parade; the organization of the March 17 street procession was, indeed, the sole function of this body. Centralization of the parade management meant that localized, neighborhood marches were now less likely, with interested parties invited to parade in unison down Fifth Avenue. A single march of impressive scale and color was likely to capture more public attention than a series of smaller neighborhood parades on St. Patrick's Day. The profile of the Fifth Avenue parade was also heightened by the appointment of a "grand marshal" to head the march. As the spectacle and hype of the parade grew, so greater publicity followed in the daily press; St. Patrick's Day was emerging as a social "event" in New York City. This transformation was reflected, as much as anything, by the active involvement of non-Irish politicians on St. Patrick's Day; they paid attention to the parade so as to ingratiate themselves with their Irish constituency. In order to win Irish

American votes, they "attended diligently to immigrant sensitivities; green flags and much bombast flew from the steps of Tammany Hall on St. Patrick's Day." By 1853, the annual parade included enough marchers to bring traffic in New York City to a standstill; this sign of growing ethnic presence and power could not have been lost on those of an anti-Irish and anti-Catholic persuasion. Yet in the same year, the city's mayor and council elected to review the parade from a specially constructed stand. This established a precedent for subsequent years, elevating further the significance of Irish Americans and their annual parade in New York City.

The year 1853 was also significant in that the Ancient Order of Hibernians (AOH) took its place in the parade for the first time. This group was supported by a large local membership, and its leadership strove for prominence in the Irish American community. Indeed, by the end of the 1850s the AOH dominated the organization of the New York parade and has controlled it ever since. The modern organization of the AOH again raised the profile of St. Patrick's Day: the group tapped into its growing national network of affiliated Irish clubs, prompting a marked upturn in the number of marchers on St. Patrick's Day. By 1860, the New York parade included over 10,000 marchers, a number bolstered by the AOH's invitation to Irish groups outside the city to join in the procession. Another successful initiative was the welcome of various expatriate Irish County societies in the festivities; the first of these, the County Monaghan Social Club, marched in 1860. A major impetus for the rise of the AOH, and the gathering together of the Irish societies in one parade, was reaction to the anti-Irish campaigns of the nativist movement. The amalgamated Irish parade became "an oppositional event meant to demonstrate not only the strength and unity of Irish Catholics, but also the determination of Irish Catholics to be accepted as American."

The increased organization of the New York parade during the 1850s, and its move from a localized and ad hoc event to central control by a committee, certainly raised the profile of the event annually. It was now, for better or worse, more of a stage-managed performance. The parade followed an understood format, making it familiar and accessible to those who watched. Because it was so recognizable it was also potentially powerful. The crowds expected the parade to impress and entertain them; in meeting these expectations the performers were also able to convey messages about their self-declared significance in a host society, and their proud connection with an Irish homeland. The New York parade, which included marchers from across the nation, became an annual performance and spectacle of the Irish presence in America. It offered the "irresistible drama that only massed marchers could provide," and it "employed that drama to underscore the celebration's major themes," such as the strength of labor, the success of the Irish in America, and the force of Irish nationalism.

St. Patrick's Day parades were now appearing across America, involving a diverse cross-section of Irish American society. In Jacksonville, Florida,

St. Patrick's Day celebrations in the 1850 and 1860s were organized and staged by various Irish railroad and roadwork gangs. These groups were rarely in the same place because of their labor commitments, but the Jacksonville Irish still managed to assemble on St. Patrick's Day. The March 17 parade, held under the joint auspices of the Hibernian Temperance and Benevolent Society and the Catholic Men's Association, was the high point of the year for the local Irish. With its messages of charity and abstinence, the procession did much to boost the image of Irish Catholics among the Protestant teetotal community. By 1860, St. Patrick's Day celebrations were reported in 14 states and 3 Canadian provinces, including Parkersburg, Virginia, Covington, Kentucky, New Albany, Indiana, Adrian, Michigan, and Ontario. The steady growth of the Irish across America, and their concentration in specific cities and ghettos, meant that they were easily organized into groups, clubs, and associations—a process that was furthered by a growing number of Irish American newspapers. These Irish societies, especially those that managed St. Patrick's Day celebrations, "allowed immigrants to express their nationality freely," a chance they took full advantage of with "monster parades" on March 17.

But what did the increase in Patrician observance signal and represent in this period? First, it appears that St. Patrick's Day was used by Irish Americans as a way of focusing attention on the position of the Irish back home, and for Irish nationalists the ongoing political battle against the British presence in Ireland. These perspectives invariably functioned along religious lines, with Protestants more likely to support the Union with Britain and Catholics an independent Irish nation. Second, St. Patrick's Day turned the spotlight on the position of the diaspora within their host society. In having these twin functions, St. Patrick's Day became a key time for Irish American public expression: this was no more important than in New York, which developed, during the second half of the nineteenth century, as "the international headquarters of Irish nationalist agitation." All radical groups, such as the Fenians, Clan na Gael and the Land League, found political support and campaign funds in New York, and the enthusiasm in the city for such causes, and for the Irish generally, made St. Patrick's Day all the more important.

America's *Irish World* newspaper regularly described St. Patrick's Day parades across the country as virtuous moral undertakings and was careful to always locate the celebration of the Irish saint within the broader context of respect for liberties offered by the American nation. In 1874 the newspaper reported the president of the United States and his cabinet reviewing the St. Patrick's Day parade in Washington. The picture of this event was draped with the American flag as well as an Irish flag featuring harp and sunbursts. The related text argued that the importance of President Grant's observance of the parade was its "complete and sufficient refutation of the calumny which says that it is 'a parade of foreigners.'" Reports from elsewhere in the country reflected the same obsessions; the orderliness of the marchers, their embrace by national or state officials, the involvement of members of the military, and links between the Irish role in the success of the American nation and the future self-government of Ireland. The parades were now widely reported in the press: they spread from San Francisco in the west to New York in the east, Savannah in the south, and Wisconsin to the north, and included over 120 processions in the United States and 9 in Canada.

ST. PATRICK'S DAY IN THE FIRST HALF OF THE TWENTIETH CENTURY

During the late nineteenth and early twentieth centuries, there was an expectation among Irish Americans that Britain would grant Home Rule to Ireland, as had happened already in the Dominions of Canada, Australia, and New Zealand. This was particularly so, it was felt, as so many Irishmen—Protestant and Catholic—fought for Britain in World War I. The Easter Rising in Dublin was, in part, an expression of frustration that Britain had not lived up to its promise of Irish self-government. Just as importantly, British government reprisals against the Dublin militants and their supporters—including executions and incarcerations—worked strongly against the reformist cause and effectively radicalized political opinion both in Ireland and the United States.

Tension about Anglo-Irish relations was reflected and indeed expressed on St. Patrick's Day in America. This was apparent even before the Easter Rising: in New York the 1916 parade was an abject failure because of local infighting about the political situation in Ireland. At this point the key argument centered on whether or not Home Ruler John Redmond warranted the support of Irish America, or whether Irish Americans should align themselves behind groups seeking radical change. The organizer of the 1916 parade was P. J. McNulty, treacherously described by the *Gaelic American* as "a pro-Britisher who supports Redmond in his treason to Ireland and a political schemer." The procession attracted only 1,700 marchers, and a comparably small presence of spectators. The traditional stalwarts of the parade, including the bulk of the AOH, the Sixty-Ninth regiment, and Cardinal Farley all refused to take part as a result of McNulty's open support for Redmond. The *Gaelic American* concluded that the low turnout was a direct result of the divisiveness of McNulty's stance, and that the message from New York to London was that there was no approval for "John Redmond's sale of Ireland." nor were they "in favour of England in the war." This is but one example of the significance of St. Patrick's Day as an annual barometer for the political thinking of influential Irish Americans.

By the end of World War I the Irish Parliamentary Party was in retreat and Sinn Féin had begun its meteoric political rise. In 1918, therefore, the New York St. Patrick's Day parade organizers had to juggle competing issues. First, they had to come to terms with recent political changes in Ireland and the immediate legacy of the 1916 Rising. Second, they had to balance Irish Republican rejection of Eire's involvement in World War I with the active local participation, since 1917, of the America they swore allegiance to, in that very conflict. The position of the Irish in the New World often took precedence on St. Patrick's Day, and this was no exception. The parade offered patriotic sentiments to Americans serving in the war and emphasized pride that Irish Americans were among them. Moreover, the American Irish Republican organization, Clan na Gael, rejoined the parade in 1918, thereby ending its St. Patrick's Day boycott against Redmond and Home Rule, which had begun in 1909. The 1918 New York parade was also notable for its inclusion of the militant republican women's group, Cumann na mBan, while the nationalist group Friends of Irish Freedom also marched for the first time.

The involvement of these three bodies in the parade marked a new radicalism within St. Patrick's Day celebrations, which increasingly allied Irish America with the cause of Irish Republicanism. That link was embodied in 1920 by the appearance in America of the leader of Sinn Féin, Eamon de Valera, on the St. Patrick's Day parade review stand in New York. The liturgy of the new Ireland being fought for in the Irish War of Independence was made clear. For the first time in the history of New York's St. Patrick's Day parade, the orange, green, and white Irish tricolor of the new Irish Free State replaced the all green flags that had traditionally been used to represent Ireland. In the march itself, nostalgic symbolism about the Emerald Isle was overshadowed by the livery of the new Irish Free State. By the mid-1920s, however, political messages on St. Patrick's Day in America were less triumphal. The Irish Civil War had eroded political certainties; commentators from abroad, in particular, were left wondering what the "Irish cause" now meant.

Although politics played a key role in the commemoration of St. Patrick's Day in America, the nature and intensity of ideological differences waxed and waned. A more constant, though far more benign part of St. Patrick's day in the United States, has been custom and nostalgia. In March 1930, the American magazine *Good Housekeeping* reminded its readers that "the celebration of St. Patrick's Day has become a universal custom." Henceforth recipes for suitable food on March 17, as well as arts and crafts to embellish the day, were printed in numerous women's magazines, such as *Ladies' Home Journal, Delineator,* and *Women's Home Companion.* Since the early twentieth century these magazines, with a largely middle-class readership, had been encouraging women to try out different St. Patrick's Day menus, and to decorate their table with an Irish theme. This annual advice was most pronounced in the 1950s, not only through mass circulation of women's magazines but the inclusion in many newspapers of a "woman's page."

The exchange of cards for all sorts of anniversaries was a traditional part of American popular culture by the late nineteenth century. It appears that the first St. Patrick's Day postcards emerged on the American market in 1898 and were dominated in the early years by those produced by the International Art

Company and Raphael Tuck and Sons. At first, the greeting cards were adorned with images of shamrock and St. Patrick, or else idealized depictions of the Irish rural landscape. During the twentieth century, however, there was a significant increase in the volume of humorous St. Patrick's Day cards depicting leprechauns, pots of gold, blarney stones, and the like, that had the effect—perhaps unwittingly—of trivializing the Irish anniversary. As early as 1910, the AOH had requested that the U.S. Post Office destroy all St. Patrick's Day postcards it considered were offensive to the Irish. In a similar fashion the *Boston Pilot* pleaded with its readers not to buy such "offensive" cards, which it argued ignored the holy and sacred nature of St. Patrick's Day. The paper especially condemned cards that "even when read with an Irish humour [are] insulting to normal Irish sensibilities. Nearly naked women, slobbering drunk men, cavorting pigs—all with suggestive phrases added—do nothing to promote either decent merriment or happy sentiments." The *Boston Daily Globe,* meanwhile, argued that the "true purpose" of March 17 was to venerate and celebrate the teachings of St. Patrick. The day should not be honored, the paper argued, by "the gyrations in South Boston … the green ties, verdant [and] phoney commercialised shamrock."

One of the problems for the image of St. Patrick's Day celebrations in North America was that the "stage Irish" stereotype, which included stories and images of wanton drunkenness on St. Patrick's Day, were readily projected by newspapers, observers, and commercial enterprises, and reinforced by many marchers and spectators themselves. As a widely celebrated annual event, St. Patrick's Day offered an easy newspaper story—which could readily be positive or negative. At the start of spring along came the Irish preparations for March 17, and all the old clichés could be given their yearly airing. The weather was a constant source of lame headlines. If it was good, and the sun shone, this reflected the "proverbial luck of the Irish." If, as was more often the case, the rain or snow fell, then "a leprechaun of a weather man played a nasty trick." The St. Patrick's Day meteorological lottery, rather than being a product of the season, was described mystically by the *Daily News* as a result of "evil ones who sought to put the curse on the parade of the Irish." St. Patrick's Day accessories, including green ties and hats, were also cause for comment. The *New York World Telegram and Sun* reported that "Young girls wore lapel buttons bearing this invitation in green letters: "Kiss Me, I'm Irish." A number of girls said the message did not go unanswered." Overall, then, various adornments and enticing behavior suggested, implicitly at least, that the flirtatious greeting cards the *Boston Pilot* objected to nonetheless had some basis in reality.

ST. PATRICK'S DAY IN THE SECOND HALF OF THE TWENTIETH CENTURY

The immediate post–World War II era evinced rapid change in the United States. The collapse of the British Empire and the advent of the Cold War brought new dynamics to international relations. The world appeared to be a smaller place. Radio communication was being supplemented by television with its visual images from across the globe, while the introduction of mass air travel across continents made for simpler travel associated with emigration and tourism. In urban America the 1950s also featured development of new suburbs, the continued championing of the automobile, and the realization, for many people, of discretionary spending power. In this context advertising and commercialism in America boomed—and, as part of this trend, festivals and celebrations became the target of marketing experts. The celebration of St. Patrick's Day now received their attention.

Because of changes in technology, the shamrock was now readily available for international distribution from Ireland. Regular commercial air services across the Atlantic meant that this tiny yet precious symbol of Irishness could be transported to places where it was not easily grown in late spring, such as bitterly cold New York and Montreal. In March 1952, to advertise the first direct commercial flight from Shannon airport to New York, Pan American Airlines flew 100,000 fresh shamrocks across the Atlantic for free distribution to Fifth Avenue marchers. This most Irish of plants could thus be worn proudly, or provided as a gift to loved ones. Either way, Pan American got their point across: Ireland and America were now connected like never before as a tourist and trade destination. And St. Patrick's Day was a key moment for both of these to take place. The marketing of real shamrocks was, of course, only part of the commercialization of St. Patrick's Day. More frequently, the image or symbol of the shamrock was employed artistically—adorning souvenirs, advertisements, decorations, greeting cards, and clothing. This pattern was not, however, restricted to America. St. Patrick's day was also marketed in Canada and Australia, and Irish people across the globe became accustomed to receiving small boxes full of shamrock, or else a St. Patrick's Day greetings card.

By the 1950s, the United States boasted the most extensive telecommunication network of any nation. In terms of the celebration of St. Patrick's Day, this meant that Patrician festivities across the country were closely monitored by the media. At a typical St. Patrick's Day parade, local newspaper reporters and radio commentators relayed their impressions of the event, while in some of the major cities television coverage also brought moving pictures and sounds of the festivities to a very large audience. The commercial opportunities of such blanket coverage were not lost on American business, so sponsorship duly became part and parcel of the St. Patrick's Day parade. This also helped bring Irish performers to the United States on St. Patrick's Day. In 1959, for instance, the St. Laurence O'Toole Pipe Band was flown from Dublin to New York to take part in the festivities; their flight and other costs were met by sponsor Rheingold Beer. They were the first band from Ireland to appear in a New York St. Patrick's Day parade.

In addition to commercial and media opportunities associated with St. Patrick's Day, there were chances for politicians to elevate themselves before live audiences. The trend of politicians either seeking or responding to the Irish vote was never more important than in the case of Mayor Richard J. Daly of Chicago. Throughout his career, Daly courted the Irish of Chicago and ran many aspects of his administration in a way that benefited them. It was as a result of Daly's initiative that the St. Patrick's Day parade in Chicago was reintroduced as a major city event. The tradition of staging an official city St. Patrick's Day parade, which began in 1843, had ceased in Chicago by 1869. The mayor's inaugural parade took place in 1956, attracting 10,000 marchers and 250,000 spectators, support that grew steadily thereafter. In addition to the downtown parade, there was a south-side event that began in 1953. Started by Father Thomas J. McMahon and Jack Allen, the south-side event grew steadily in the postwar years. In 1955, television star Ed Sullivan led the parade, and by 1958, 250,000 spectators lined the procession route. Although competing with the downtown parade, especially during the Daly years, the south-side event has, with a few breaks, survived, and is now larger than the parade held in the city center.

For many Americans, television broadcasts provided a window into St. Patrick's Day parades around the nation. Festivities from New York and Boston were beamed into living rooms, and there were even programs covering events in Ireland. Regional television broadcasters now also made an effort to capture local celebrations. The growth of such television programming, most noticeable in the United States with its large number of broadcasters, brought a demand for addresses from the Irish Taoiseach on St. Patrick's Day, as well as a call for programs about the state of contemporary Ireland. In 1963, Milwaukee station WISN TV Channel 12 broadcast a 30-minute film entitled "Ireland Yesterday and Today" as part of its St. Patrick's Day program. To accompany this, WISN also wanted to show a five-minute address from the Taoiseach. The Irish Consul General in Chicago replied to the broadcaster that the Taoiseach, Sean Lemass, had accepted the request because of the large local Irish population and the favorable impact that such coverage of Ireland might have for tourist revenue. Lemass's St. Patrick's Day address of 1963, a general overview of Irish agriculture and industry, was duly filmed, then flown to WISN courtesy of Aer Lingus.

In the post–World War II era, many Irish Americans were the third, fourth, and fifth generations of those who had emigrated in the post-famine era. As the years passed, many of the younger sections of the family lost the day-to-day connection with their Irish roots. While they were happy to "celebrate St. Patrick's Day once a year, to enjoy a bit of Irish music and to spend an evening with their friends at a local Irish pub," their links with a common ethnic and family background were diminishing, as were their ties with traditional Irish neighborhoods. One observer wryly concluded: "As their fortunes brightened they gladly left the districts where their families had lived for generations and moved to new split levels and ranch houses in the suburbs." Despite this lack of connectedness to Irish roots, the number of St. Patrick's Day events across America during the 1960s grew to heights that would have been unimaginable at the beginning of the century. To the far west in California, the first Los Angeles St. Patrick's Day parade had taken place in 1870, and the state had witnessed a steady growth of large- and small-scale celebrations ever since. Press coverage of March 17 in the *San Francisco Chronicle, Oakland Tribune, San Francisco Examiner,* and *Los Angeles Examiner* indicates that St. Patrick's Day had become a major social event in the postwar years. As the *San Francisco News* explained in a 1951 article:

> [E]ven if you don't happen to be Irish, it's hard to ignore St. Patrick's Day. For the Irish are rightfully proud of being Irish, and not diffident about displaying their pride to the world. And St. Patrick's Day of course gives an Irishman a special reason to boast of his ancestry, for it honors a saint who had ability and courage in considerable quality … Even if there was no St. Patrick's Day to celebrate it would not discourage the average Irishman. He would still be an Irishman and, as all the world knows, that's cause enough for celebration.

Despite occasional criticisms about the commercial and political opportunism on St. Patrick's Day, its celebration was still revered and processions in honor of March 17 grew in size and scope. New York still claimed the most imposing annual parade, which, by 1966, involved 123,000 marchers and an estimated 1.25 million spectators. The AOH was aware of negative images that could be attached to St. Patrick's Day, and that the appearance and conduct of the marchers helped to shape the public's perception of the Irish. To counter pejorative images and patronizing clichés about the New York parade, the AOH made considerable efforts to promote what it understood to be the authentic meaning of St. Patrick's Day. Through its newspaper, the *National Hibernian Digest,* the Order reminded its members that:

> [T]he St. Patrick's Day parade in New York is a semi-religious parade, and also very Irish in character and tradition. Every marcher is a person dedicated to the honor and glory of St Patrick on March 17th. It is this state of mind that has made and keeps this parade an outstandingly worthy and glorious one, in a City that has many great parades throughout the year.

To ensure that a desirable image of Irish Americans was presented on March 17, the St. Patrick's Day Parade and Celebration Committee issued "Rules and Regulations for the Government of the Parade." Participation in the New York and other Patrician parades held under the auspices of the AOH was restricted to affiliated organizations approved by the committee. In keeping with the Irish nationalist ethos of the AOH, only patriotic Irish and American marching airs could be played by parade bands. English tunes, such as "God Save the King" and "It's a Long Way to Tipperary," were deemed unsuitable, and thus prohibited. Organizers also declared that no mottoes, advertisements, or signs "that might tend to bring the parade or the Order into disrepute, or anything controversial, will be allowed." The only objects that could be carried were the official banners of each organization marching in the parade, and the American and Irish flags. Rules were even established about the appearance of marchers.

While the parade committee accepted that it could not prescribe people's dress, it would not allow "any burlesque or dress that will look immoral or ridiculous." Equally, the committee countered a common belief among marchers that "sticking something on their hats like green quills, or decorations that are distasteful, if they are green in colour, are perfectly in order." This was "an erroneous impression." stressed the parade organizers. All this, it was hoped, would help to counter press comments about cheap, tacky, and tasteless forms of dress and accessory on St. Patrick's Day.

POLITICS OF PARTICIPATION: THE 1990s

Over the last couple of decades there has been intense debate about which groups are welcome to march in St. Patrick's Day parades. The Fifth Avenue cavalcade and many others across America were organized under the aegis of the Ancient Order of Hibernians, a staunchly Catholic body with a conservative moral outlook. AOH-run St. Patrick's Day parades were therefore supposed to be bastions of traditional family values, even though some revelers certainly let their hair down, dressed up theatrically, and overindulged in drink. Occasional disorderly conduct and insobriety could be addressed by parade organizers with the assistance, where necessary, of local authorities. This effrontery was, however, not a key issue for the AOH in the early 1990s. Rather, the 1991 New York parade saw the attempted involvement of the Irish Lesbian and Gay Organization (ILGO), a nonconformist group that had emerged "from seemingly nowhere chanting 'we're here, we're queer, we're Irish.'" The subsequent ILGO campaign to be allowed to march in the parade was "a validation of their larger efforts to gain the full measure of respect and [civil] rights they believe they deserve." But the St. Patrick's Day parade was no easy political vehicle upon which to ride. Devoutly Catholic sectors of the Irish American community bitterly opposed the ILGO's claim of a right to march. The ILGO had hoped to take part as a group in the New York parade of 1991, but its application was turned down by the (AOH) official organizing committee. From the outset, however, the ILGO was widely supported by the mainstream media, which dismissed as bigotry the opposition of the AOH and other organizations to ILGO participation in the parade. In an effort to reach some kind of compromise, an "ordinary" Irish group that had been accepted into the parade, Division 7 from Manhattan, invited the ILGO to march with them. That the ILGO had been subsumed into the main body of the parade would have been frustrating enough to the parade committee, but the decision of New York's Mayor Dinkins to march with Division 7 and the ILGO contingent, rather than in the mayor's customary position at the head of the parade, raised the stakes further. While Dinkins's decision was applauded by many liberals, the traditionally conservative Irish American supporters of the parade, which included the Catholic dominated AOH, were very displeased with the mayor's decision.

As Dinkins marched, he was booed by many in the crowd, and even shelled with beer cans. Meanwhile New York's Catholic Cardinal O'Connor, although opposed to homosexuality, refused to take a public position on the mayor's action during the parade. Yet the Catholic Church's stance on gay and lesbian involvement in the parade went on to assume utmost importance in the battle between the organizing committee and the ILGO.

In 1992, the parade committee, led by the conservative Francis Beirne, took the position that no group would be granted admittance to the parade "that has a position contrary to the teachings of the Catholic faith." As a result of the committee's decision, the ideals of the ILGO were considered contrary to the qualification rules—and the AOH claimed that they ran what was, in effect, a private parade so were entitled to include and exclude according to Catholic teachings. The ILGO was once more banned from taking a place in the parade, but this time also excluded from joining the march under the auspices of someone else's banner. These decisions placed the parade committee outside of the spirit of New York's human rights legislation. As a result, City Hall removed the permit to organize the parade from the division of the AOH that had been organizing the event for over a century. The issue went to court and a federal judge ruled that the AOH was within its constitutional rights to deny the ILGO permission to march in the parade. The judge dismissed the New York City Human Rights Organization, which had supported the ILGO, as comparable to "the thought police of [Orwell's] 1984." The 1992 parade went ahead with the ILGO excluded. As the controversy in New York grew, gay and lesbian groups campaigned to be included in St. Patrick's Day parades and other public celebrations across America. Many cities had no objections to gay and lesbian participation; indeed places such as Savannah used their open policies as a method of promoting their parades. So the AOH, while a very influential umbrella organization for the running of St. Patrick's Day parades and festivities in America, is no longer all-powerful with respect to March 17 and its commemoration.

CONCLUSION

From the 1960s the number of St. Patrick's Day parades staged across America grew year by year. Even towns and cities without a noticeable Irish population and no historic links to Ireland began staging an annual celebration. In the late 1990s the Irish American magazine, *World of Hibernia,* listed the major St. Patrick's Day festivities around the United States. It reported that the largest was the parade through Manhattan, which attracted 150,000 marchers and a crowd of 1.5 million. Second came Boston with 10,000 marchers in 1999, and a crowd of a million. The most important parade of the southern states, Savannah, was third. St. Patrick's Day in the state of Georgia has been celebrated since 1824; today it is a bank and school holiday, and the four-hour parade in Savannah typically attracts a crowd of some 400,000. The fourth largest parade, in Kansas City, Missouri, was founded in 1973; it now attracts a crowd of some 250,000 and around 1,200 marchers. Similarly, the Cleveland parade involves 10,000 marchers and an annual crowd of approximately 250,000. Chicago's south side gathers 12,000 marchers and 230,000 spectators, while the seventh-largest parade is across the city in downtown Chicago, featuring 2,000 marchers and 200,000 watching from the sidelines. The final two parades in the list of St. Patrick's Day big draws are those in Philadelphia and Pearl River, New York. These attracted 12,000 and 10,000 marchers, and crowds of 150,000 and 90,000 respectively in the late 1990s.

The continued significance of St. Patrick's Day parades in America lies in the psyche of the American, rather than Irish, nation. In that respect, St. Patrick's Day celebrations are as much about American patriotism as any affinity towards Ireland. Indeed, many of the marchers have never even been to the "homeland." As historian Wallace Evan Davies has put it:

> Americans have long been a nation of joiners ... Americans have also long been ardently and aggressively patriotic ... being thus both gregarious and nationalistic, Americans have naturally turned to forming numerous patriotic societies.

That said, Irish Americans have remained acutely aware of the links between their chosen home and the land of their forebears. St. Patrick's Day parades are in some way symbolic markers of the success of Irish enterprise, and a celebration of the liberty they won in America. The parades also serve an important purpose in interpreting events back in Ireland. As Jack Holland argued in *The American Connection: U.S. Guns, Money, and Influence in Northern Ireland* (1987), St. Patrick's Day celebrations are assertions of "a powerful conviction that Ireland's destiny would be determined as much by what happened in America." This dual vision of Irish America, one part of which looks to America, the other to Ireland, continues today.

As early as the 1960s St. Patrick's Day was celebrated within an Irish American community that had largely assimilated into the so-called "melting pot," climbed the social ladder, and suburbanized. The annual Patrician celebrations were little changed, but the previous dynamic where Irish Americans strove to be recognized as equals by a wider society was no longer relevant. Irish Americans were clearly part and parcel of American society. Such assimilation also meant that celebrating St. Patrick's Day was an unquestioned part of the annual fabric of American life. Reginald Byron, author of *Irish America* (1999), recalled:

> On St. Patrick's Day, I wore something green to school like everyone else. It was merely something that we did without ever asking why, like exchanging cards on St Valentine's day.

In the early twenty-first century it is possible to understand the American experience of St. Patrick's Day not as representing a largely distinctive Irish American ethnic experience, as had been necessary in the past, but instead as a celebration of an assimilated American Irish population. As Byron observes,

St. Patrick's Day is now "a quintessentially American institution that owes relatively little to Ireland, and is Irish in only superficial ways." While the politics of Ireland (and later Northern Ireland) shaped St. Patrick's Day celebrations in America, its principal focus was internal (American), rather than external (Irish). The St. Patrick's Day celebrations of the late twentieth century should be understood not as displays of *ethnic* Irishness, but rather as large-scale and warm-hearted embraces of Irish *citizenship* in America. Byron concludes that to assert or to "be Irish on St. Patrick's Day is to claim membership of the fully assimilated mainstream of middle Americans who have left the cultural baggage of their immigrant origins behind them." Such themes of successful assimilation and Americanization nonetheless papered over real changes. By the 1960s and 1970s, the Irish population in America was dwindling and growing older. The attendance at Irish clubs and cultural events fell year by year, with many such operations closing their doors for good. Yet the St. Patrick's Day parade remained the most visible symbol of the American Irish. Indeed, the New York parade chairman argued 25 years ago that "without the parade many people wouldn't think there were any Irish in New York." Despite such misgivings, St. Patrick's Day continues to capture the public spotlight on March 17 each year in America. Henceforth Irish American traditions and values will either be confirmed or (re)invented on this day annually, almost as if they were floated on a parade.

FURTHER READING

Byron, Reginald. *Irish America.* Oxford: Oxford University Press, 1999.

Crimmins, J. D. *St. Patrick's Day: Its Early Celebrations in New York and Other American Places, 1737–1845.* New York: The author, 1902.

Davies, Wallace Evan. *Patriotism on Parade: The Story of the Veterans and Hereditary Organizations in America, 1783–1900.* Cambridge, Mass.: Harvard University Press, 1955.

Holland, Jack. *The American Connection: U.S. Guns, Money, and Influence in Northern Ireland.* New York: Viking, 1987.

O'Hanlon, Ray. *The New Irish Americans.* Boulder, Colo.: Roberts Rinehart Publishers, 1998.

Ridge, John T. *The St. Patrick's Day Parade in New York.* New York: St Patrick's Day Committee, 1988.

Mike Cronin and Daryl Adair

PASSOVER IN AMERICA

- [ ] Passover, no matter where celebrated, commemorates the Jews' biblical passage from slavery to freedom.

- [ ] The first Passover celebration in North America most likely occurred in 1654 in the Dutch colony of New Amsterdam (now New York City).

- [ ] The dates when Passover are celebrated are determined by the lunar calendar and fall in March or April, beginning on the first full moon after the spring equinox during the Jewish calendar month *Nisan.*

- [ ] Celebrations last for seven or eight days.

- [ ] *Keeping kosher* is observing strict Passover dietary restrictions that prohibit eating or owning leavened foods and require removing any traces of bread from the household and cleaning or substituting any object, including plates, cutlery, appliances, and furniture, that may have come into contact with bread or bread-like products.

- [ ] *Matzah*—unleavened bread—can be mixed with water and kneaded for no more than 18 minutes before being baked to remain *kosher.* Rabbis observe matzah manufacturing to ensure compliance with Hebraic law.

- [ ] The *Haggadot,* the liturgical part of the *Seder,* is based on the flight of the Jews from captivity. In America the haggadot has been used by companies to sell their goods—Maxwell House coffee offered a copy in its cans during the 1930s—and its content has been adapted to address social concerns such as the Holocaust, racial prejudice, and even animal rights.

- [ ] The Seder itself often reflects contemporary social issues such as women's equality.

PASSOVER IN AMERICA

Passover (called *Pesach* in Hebrew) is a spring holiday that Jews around the world observe in order to remember and celebrate the liberation of the Israelites from Egyptian bondage, as recounted in the book of Exodus in the Old Testament (or *Torah*). The name *Pesach* comes from the Hebrew root literally meaning to pass over, exempt, or spare, and refers to the fact that God passed over the houses of the Jews when slaying the firstborn of Egypt. *Pesach* is also the name of the sacrificial offering (a lamb) that was made in the Temple in Jerusalem during this festival. Before its destruction in 70 C.E., the Temple was the central place of worship for Jews, where sacrifices were offered through priests; after its destruction, animal sacrifice and priestly worship were replaced with the symbolic rituals and prayer that have characterized Judaism ever since.

Passover is not only a central historical holiday for Jews that commemorates the biblical passage from slavery to freedom, but also a festival of nature that denotes the beginning of spring and has parallels in other agrarian cultures. Passover is sometimes referred to as *Chag he-Aviv* (the Spring Festival), *Chag ha-Matzot* (the Festival of Matzahs), or *Z'man Cherutenu* (the Time of Our Freedom). Theologically, Passover marks the start of the covenant between God and the Jews as an entire people; ideologically, the holiday celebrates redemption and creation, rebirth and revival. The first Passover in what would eventually become America most probably occurred in 1654, the year that 23 Jews fled from the Portuguese who had conquered the Dutch colony in Recife, Brazil. These Jews settled in the Dutch colony of New Amsterdam (now New York City), marking the beginning of an organized Jewish community in America. More American

Jews celebrate Passover than any other Jewish festival—even Yom Kippur, the Day of Atonement, considered the holiest day of the Jewish year.

Passover occurs in the spring, but since Judaism relies on a lunar calendar, in America the holiday can fall any time during the months of March or April. In the Jewish calendar, Passover begins on the fifteenth day of the month of Nisan and continues for seven days, though many Diaspora Jews (those outside the land of Israel, including those in America) observe eight days. This practice of adding an extra day to festivals goes back to the Second Temple Period, when the Jewish calendar was set by eyewitness testimony, rather than calculations. An eyewitness at the high court in Jerusalem would proclaim the new month based on his sighting of the new moon, and then the Jews of the Diaspora were notified of the start of the month by a signal-fire system. This system was eventually deemed faulty by the rabbis, who devised the second festival day for the Diaspora—*Yom Tov Sheni Shel Galuyot*—to replace the signal system and serve as a buffer to make sure those outside Israel were celebrating the holiday on the correct day. All Orthodox and many Conservative Jews in America continue to observe eight days of Passover, while most American Reform Jews observe only seven days of the holiday, as do Israeli Jews.

PASSOVER DIETARY LAWS

Dietary regulations for Passover are very strict and stem from the prohibition against eating any leaven (called *hametz*) for the full seven (or eight) days in remembrance of the Israelites' hurried departure from Egypt, which left no time for their bread to rise. In place of bread (which includes cookies, cake, pasta, beer, and anything containing wheat, barley, rye, oats, or spelt that came into contact with liquid), Jews eat unleavened bread, called *matzah*. The instruction to eat matzah comes from the book of Exodus (12:20): "You shall eat nothing leavened; in all your habitations shall you eat unleavened bread." According to historian Hasia Diner, matzah is the only Jewish food that was not absorbed from surrounding cultures and remains unique to Jews.

Ashkenazi Jews (of Central and Eastern European descent) extend the dietary prohibitions on leaven during Passover to incorporate *kitniyot*—legumes and grain-like foods, including rice, peas, lentils, beans, corn, soy products, and peanuts—while Sephardic Jews (of Spanish, African, Asian, or Middle Eastern origin) continue to eat these foods during Passover. The Ashkenazi prohibition against eating *kitniyot* is a post-biblical addition that dates back to the Middle Ages; rabbis felt that these additional banned foods were similar in appearance to wheat and were often stored in the same bags, so they banned them to avoid confusion. The majority of the American Jewish population is Ashkenazi, and as a result of the extended Ashkenazi Passover dietary restrictions, many popular American food products are manufactured in special kosher-for-Passover versions each spring. For example, both Coca-Cola and Pepsi make special Passover runs of their beverages in which they substitute sugar for the corn syrup they ordinarily use to sweeten their beverages. These products are marked discreetly with the letters OUP (Orthodox Union Passover) or KP (kosher for Passover). In neighborhoods across America with large Jewish populations—especially those in the Northeast—it is not uncommon for bagel stores and pizza places to close during the Passover holiday.

In addition to not eating leaven, Jews must not own any leaven during Passover (as stated in Exodus 13:6–7 and 12:17–20). As a result of this prohibition, Jews are required to remove all traces of bread from their houses in a massive spring cleaning effort, which culminates the night before Passover in a final search for leaven: family members scour their house with a candle and feather for crumbs, which are then burned. This search is known in Hebrew as *bedikat hametz,* and some Jews also see it as a symbolic way of removing the puffiness—the arrogance and pride—from their souls. Many Jews will give food that is not kosher for Passover away to non-Jewish acquaintances or neighbors; some Jewish communities host food drives for poor people in the days before Passover so that they can donate their leavened products to soup kitchens or homeless shelters. In Orthodox communities, Rabbis will often arrange for families to contractually sell their *hametz* to a non-Jew for a nominal fee, who will then let the family purchase it back after the holiday is over.

Passover dietary laws also call for using a set of dishes that are either re-koshered for the occasion, or set aside strictly for once-a-year Passover use. The houses of extremely wealthy observant Jews sometimes include a separate "Passover kitchen" that is only in use for the holiday. It is important to emphasize that the process of cleaning the entire home of all *hametz* to prepare for Passover is an enormous task. It can take several weeks of full-time scrubbing, which often includes going over kitchen appliances with Q-tips and toothpicks, boiling utensils, shampooing upholstery, and covering all surfaces that come into contact with food with foil or shelf-liner. While Passover is traditionally a holiday based in the home, beginning in the 1930s, observant American Jews who wanted to avoid the hard work of koshering their entire houses for Passover instead vacationed at kosher-for-Passover hotels in New York, New Jersey, and Michigan. After World War II, family resorts in New York's Catskill Mountains and in and around Miami, Florida became fashionable places to celebrate Passover away from home. Kosher for Passover cruises have also gained in popularity in the last 20 years, though the Cunard Line began offering them as early as 1935.

Historian Andrew Heinze argues that by the turn of the twentieth century in the United States, Passover became the foremost occasion among Jews for buying new things; progress eclipsed purity as the dominant theme of American Passover. He points to a *New York Tribune* report from the Passover of 1902, which chronicles all the abandoned furniture and bedding that Lower

East Side Jewish residents dumped into city streets in an effort to both purify and upgrade their households. Passover, according to Heinze, provided an annual occasion for Jews to buy new products, which sanctioned the American belief in progress and a rising standard of living, while simultaneously reinforcing Jewish identity by couching consumerism within the celebration of a traditional festival.

MATZAH

Passover is a key component of Jewish existence in the United States, and the most recognizable contemporary symbol of the holiday for most American Jews are the green, white, and orange boxes of Manischewitz matzah that turn up on supermarket shelves each spring. Traditionally, in America and elsewhere, matzah was round, irregularly shaped, hand-mixed, kneaded, and baked under rabbinic supervision in local synagogue basements or bakeries, and sold wrapped in newspaper until 1850, when the matzah kneading and baking machine came to America, and matzah went from being handmade to machine-produced. The 1850s were also the decade in which American newspapers began to depict Passover celebrations, usually by showing the process of matzah-baking via illustrations to explain how Jews celebrate Passover, as matzah was considered the most unique and identifiable marker of the holiday for their non-Jewish readers. In 1888, Manischewitz, the oldest and largest matzah company in America, began machine-baking and distributing uniformly shaped, seven-by-seven inch squares of matzah in cardboard boxes from their bakery in Cincinnati, Ohio. Historian Jonathan Sarna has charted how matzah companies embraced this new technology and used it to sell more matzah. A 1919 Manischewitz newspaper ad boasted that, "no human hand touches these matzas in their manufacture," while competitors Horowitz Brothers and Margareten declared, "we have raised the kneading and baking of Matzoh from a haphazard, careless, hit-or-miss process to a science."

Timing is of critical importance in matzah-making—according to Jewish law, the entire process (from the start of the mixing to the finished matzah) must not take longer than 18 minutes, because if the dough is idle for longer than 18 minutes, it is considered leavened. As a result, despite the mechanization of matzah-making, rabbis continue to monitor every phase of production in factories to make sure that the 18-minute rule is observed and the machinery is continuously cleaned so no bits of dough are left behind to contaminate subsequent batches. At Streit's, the second-largest matzah bakery in the United States, which opened its factory in 1925 on the Lower East Side of Manhattan and is currently the only remaining family-owned matzah producer in America, the 18-minute matzah-making process is usually completed with three or four minutes to spare.

Today's mass-produced American matzah bears little resemblance to the cakes of unleavened wheat flour and water eaten in the desert during the Exodus from Egypt. Manischewitz offers 11 different varieties of matzah, including Apple Cinnamon, Egg & Onion, Savory Garlic, and Everything Matzo. For those who want more culinary variety over Passover, Streit's manufactures stuffing, cereal, potato chips, pasta, cookies, 11 kinds of cake mix, and even a blueberry pancake mix—all certified kosher-for-Passover. In the last decade, with the rise of consumer interest in nonprocessed, organic foods, *shmura* matzah has been making a comeback. Literally meaning "guarded matzah," *shmura* is a reference to the requirement that a rabbi watch every stage of matzah production, from the harvesting of the wheat, through its threshing and milling, to its mixing and baking, in order to ensure that no water comes in contact with the grain before the proper time. This practice is based on Exodus 12:17: "And you shall guard the matzot." *Shmura* matzah is hand-made in small batches, often of whole-grain flour, and is hand-formed into round wafers that many Jews consider more authentic, or at least closer to the biblical version of unleavened bread. However, *shmura* matzah is generally only available in areas with large Jewish populations, where it is sold to the local community.

THE HAGGADAH

Jews usher in the holiday of Passover in the home with a highly ritualized festival meal and liturgical service known as a *Seder* (the Aramaic word for "order"), held on the first night of Passover with family and friends. (Jews who celebrate the second festival day will usually conduct Seders on both the first and second nights of Passover.) The principal religious purpose of the Seder is the recounting of the Exodus story, and the book that provides the liturgy for the Seder and functions as its manual is known as the *Haggadah* (plural, *Haggadot*)—literally "the telling." There are many editions of the Haggadah from around the world, each with the same core Hebrew text, composed from a pastiche of Jewish sources: biblical passages, prayers, instructions for the conduct of the Seder, rabbinic commentary originally found in the Mishnah and the Talmud, and liturgical poems and songs (many of which were added in the Middle Ages). The reading of the Haggadah is based on a verse from Exodus 13:8: "You shall tell your son on that day: it is because of what the Lord did for me when I came forth out of Egypt."

The arrangement of the Seder table, psalms, benedictions, and other parts of the Haggadah that Jews recite today can be traced back to the Mishnah (the core text of rabbinic literature), which was edited around 200 C.E. Commentaries were added, and a large portion of the current version was completed by the end of the Talmudic period (500–600 C.E.) The original version of the Haggadah was a section within the Jewish prayer book, but the earliest version of a stand-alone Haggadah can be traced back to the thirteenth century Spain; the earliest printed version appeared in 1486, though the invention of printing did not mark the end of handwritten Haggadot. Since the fifteenth century, more than 3,500 printed editions of the Haggadah have been published. Due to the second commandment, which warns against creating graven images, traditional Jewish books are not illustrated with human forms, with the one exception of the Haggadah. Because the book is meant as an educational tool— particularly one that should be appealing to children—it became acceptable to illustrate Haggadot. As a result, there are many famous illuminated and illustrated versions; *The Sarajevo Haggadah,* which dates back to the mid-fourteenth century, and *The Prague Haggadah* of 1526 are two of the most well-known. In the sixteenth century, versions of Haggadot with translations of the Hebrew text into local vernacular began to appear.

The Haggadah is the Jewish book with the largest number of copies in print in America. Many Jews brought Haggadot with them from their home countries when they immigrated to America, but the first Haggadah printed in the United States, officially titled *Service for the Two First Nights of the Passover in Hebrew and English, According to the Custom of the German and Spanish Jews,* was published in New York by S. H. Jackson in 1837. The first rendition of a distinctly American Haggadah was the 1879 Liberman-Chicago edition. While other illustrated nineteenth-century American Haggadot used European drawings, this Haggadah actually contained contemporary drawings that reflected American Jewish life in nineteenth-century Chicago, as well as local holiday customs. In 1908 the Reform movement's Central Conference of American Rabbis (CCAR) issued the *Union Haggadah,* which included content and translation changes. The CCAR added English poems and hymns to the book and also transliterated important Hebrew blessings into English. Perhaps the most popular American Haggadah, however, has been the Maxwell House version. First published in the 1930s as a promotion for Maxwell House coffee, copies came free with a coffee purchase, which made it easy to provide each Seder-goer with their own copy of the Haggadah. The first corporate-sponsored Haggadah, it was ultimately reprinted many times; more than 20 million copies have been distributed, and it is still used today in many American homes. Since the early 1900s, the Haggadah has been used as a marketing device in America, with copies printed and sponsored by butcher shops, wine companies, banks, and other corporate concerns that provide goods and services to the Jewish community.

Haggadot must include certain elements: they must tell the Exodus story in the first person and the present tense so that each person speaks of being freed by God; they must mention each symbolic food present at the Seder and explain its significance; and they must offer children a chance to ask specific questions meant to join them to the community and cue the telling of the Passover story. But along with the essentials, American Haggadot reflect the customs and concerns of various groups and time periods in the United States.

The 1940s through the 1960s saw the growth of overtly political content in various American Haggadot, which dealt with issues such as prejudice, the new state of Israel, and the Holocaust by adding commentary or including readings about these subjects both around and instead of the traditional texts. Various versions of Holocaust Haggadot juxtaposed images of concentration camps and survivors' testimony with traditional text, linking the memory of the destruction of European Jewry with the Israelites' enslavement and emancipation from Egypt. With the establishment of the State of Israel in 1947, new Haggadot were published in America that reflected modern Zionist sentiments—especially those of the *kibbutzim* (collective communities in Israel), whose Haggadot mirrored their socialist, nationalist, and agricultural concerns. Israel's 1967 victory in the Six Day War also spawned a fresh selection of Haggadot, which emphasized that the Jewish people could finally fulfill the Seder's concluding line of "Next year in Jerusalem." In the United States, the 1960s were a time of political radicalism and upheaval, which was reflected in many homegrown Haggadot, some of which only existed in typescript or photocopied editions. Labor-activist Haggadot added union-organizing songs to the Seder, antiwar editions included peace anthems and prayers, and versions concerned with racial justice had civil rights ballads accompanying more familiar tunes. In the 1970s, Haggadot often contained prayers for Soviet Jews trapped behind the Iron Curtain, and in the 1980s there were versions emphasizing freedom in South Africa.

Recent decades have seen egalitarian, environmental, feminist, social justice, meditative, atheist, and interactive children's Haggadot published by various groups. Noteworthy alternative Haggadot include Rabbi Arthur Waskow's groundbreaking prototype—a 1969 Freedom Seder, motivated by the death of Martin Luther King Jr., titled "A Radical Haggadah for Passover" (published in *Ramparts* magazine). *Haggadah for the Liberated Lamb* (Micha Publications, 1985) links the liberation of all God's creatures with the Passover story to create a vegetarian Haggadah celebrating compassion, while *The Santa Cruz Haggadah* (Hineni Consciousness Press, 1991) stresses self-liberation as a new-age-inspired Haggadah of evolving consciousness. *The Shalom Seders* (New Jewish Agenda, 1984) offers three different Haggadot within one book—the Waskow Freedom Seder mentioned above, a Seder of the Children of Abraham to build bridges between Muslims and Jews, and a Haggadah of Liberation, which focuses on women's equality and tales of resistance. *The Journey Continues* (Ma'yan, 2002) is one of the most recent and comprehensive women's Haggadot, while *The Women's Seder Sourcebook* (Jewish Lights Publishing, 2003) functions as a companion text for participants who wish to add feminist readings or interpretations to their Seders. In the last decade, Haggadot from the Reform and Reconstructionist movements, like *The Open Door* (Central Conference of American Rabbis, 2002) and *A Night of Questions* (Reconstructionist Press, 2000), have revised traditional Seder texts with gender-inclusive language, marginalia, extra commentary, and historical notes.

Contemporary American versions of the Haggadah contain varying degrees of Hebrew and generally have extensive English translations (often creatively interpreted) of the traditional Hebrew text. With the advent of cheap photocopying and computer-printing technology in the late 1980s through today, individuals and families have started to make their own unique Haggadot culled from various source materials. The Internet also has a number of downloadable versions of the Haggadah, both from official Jewish movement Web sites, and individuals who have constructed their own versions and displayed them for public use. Some Internet Passover projects worth noting include the 2003 anticopyright, self-published *Love and Justice in Times of War Haggadah*, which bills itself as a politically progressive, multicultural, antiracist, gender-radical, queer-friendly Haggadah zine. Also innovative—especially in its use of technology—is *The Open Source Haggadah Project*, started and maintained by writer Douglas Rushkoff in order to reinvigorate inquiry into Jewish texts and make them readily accessible to all Jews. This Web site allows anyone to add text and interpretations to an online database of Haggadah sections; a user can then compile a unique Haggadah with segments and commentary from multiple sources. In the same vein, Rabbi Mark Hurvitz engages in a constantly changing, ongoing hypertext Passover project, called *A Growing Haggadah.*

Why is the Haggadah arguably the most well-known and well-loved form of Jewish liturgy? What is at the heart of the active relationship between this text and its modern community, and why do so many Jews feel empowered to add to it or alter it? As liturgy, the Haggadah is pedagogical, as are the actual rituals that occur during the Seder, because it is geared toward instructing children. Due to the learning-friendly environment that the liturgy itself creates, even adults generally feel comfortable asking questions about material in the Haggadah, or the rituals of the Seder itself. The Seder also takes place in the home, is lay-led, and encourages active involvement by all who are present—generally every attendee participates in the reading of the Haggadah. The story of the Exodus is narrative (as opposed to the more lyric liturgy of the daily prayer book), and the symbols that the Seder revolves around are tangible to all participants via the Seder plate and other foods (like matzah) that are distributed over the course of the meal. Because the Seder is home-based, many Haggadot are home-grown; individual families, groups of friends, or communities with specific personal, spiritual, and political agendas feel empowered to compile their own versions using various amounts of the traditional liturgy, combined with other Jewish and non-Jewish sources.

THE SEDER

Participation in a Seder is central to the celebration of Passover. The Seder is predominantly a home-based ritual, and it originates both from the description of the meal that the Israelites prepared before the Exodus from Egypt (in Exodus 12:3–11), and from the prescription repeated four times in the bible that commands fathers to tell the story of the exodus to their children (Exodus 12:26–27; 13:8; 13:14; Deuteronomy 6:20–21). Besides Haggadot for each participant, and whatever food will be served at the Passover meal, the items needed for a Seder include a Seder plate, matzah, and wine. The Seder plate contains all the symbols of the Seder and is placed in the middle of the table for all attendees to see. Some items on it are passed out to participants and eaten, while others function as nonedible symbols that are merely pointed to during the Seder. While any dish may be used as a Seder plate, many Jews own elaborately decorated silver, glass, metal, or ceramic plates with places marked for each item in Hebrew or English.

In the last 40 years, ritual Jewish items like Seder and matzah plates, menorahs, Kiddush cups, and candlesticks have become bearers of personal expression and taste, rather than more general objects of Judaic art. There are many artists and craftspeople that specialize in producing unique Jewish objects tailored to various aesthetic styles. Some of the more recognizable designs in contemporary artistic American Judaica include Gary Rosenthal's industrial-eclectic glass and welded metal pieces, Tamara Baskin's colorful fused glass, and Sharon Muchnick's ceramic ritual objects decorated with floral motifs.

Historian and material culture scholar Jenna Weissman Joselit points to the idea that while Passover has been about family unity, it has also been an aesthetic opportunity. In her studies of *The Jewish Home Beautiful* (a Jewish domestic ladies' periodical) from the 1880s through the 1950s, she found that more pages were devoted to Passover than to any other Jewish holiday. In addition, the Seder table itself embodied each family's history and sense of collective memory due to the pastiche of items assembled over time and distance that were on display for Passover eve: mismatched glasses and goblets, china, flatware, and ritual objects from various relatives throughout the generations, which came together to create a material record of family experiences and solidarity.

The foods on the Seder plate include: *karpas,* a green vegetable (usually parsley), which symbolizes spring, and is eaten dipped in salt-water; *haroset,* a puree of chopped nuts, apples, wine, and spices, which symbolizes the mortar that the slaves used for bricks in Egypt; *maror,* or bitter herbs (typically horseradish) which are a symbol of the bitterness of slavery; *beitzah,* a roasted egg, which is not eaten, and which symbolizes the festival sacrifice that Jews used to bring as an offering to the temple in Jerusalem before its destruction; and *zeroa,* a roasted shank bone, which is the symbol of the Passover sacrifice. Vegetarians in the Jewish community have tried to find an appropriate replacement for the shank bone on the Seder plate; the most popular option is a beet, because its blood-red color serves as a reminder of the Passover sacrifice. An extra glass of wine is also placed on the table for the prophet Elijah, usually in an ornate goblet, as according to Jewish legend, Elijah visits every home on Passover and drinks from his cup.

The order of a traditional Seder is as follows:

1. Participants sanctify the holiday by reciting a blessing over, and drinking, the first cup of wine.

2. They then wash their hands, without reciting the traditional hand-washing blessing. The omission of the blessing is meant to make children curious and lead up to the question that the youngest child asks later: "Why is this night different from all other nights?"

3. Participants eat a green vegetable—usually parsley—dipped in salt water. The vegetable symbolizes the renewal of the earth each spring, while the salt water evokes the bitter tears shed by the slaves in Egypt.

4. Three matzahs are set aside on a special plate during the Seder. At this point in the proceedings, the Seder leader breaks the middle of the three in half. The larger piece is wrapped in a napkin and set aside as the *afikomen*—the matzah eaten at the end of the meal; the smaller piece is replaced between the other two matzahs. It is common practice for an adult at the Seder to hide the *afikomen* during the meal; the children are sent to find it and are usually rewarded for returning it to the table so that the Seder can continue, as the Seder cannot end until the *afikomen* is eaten. (Alternately, the children at a Seder might attempt the steal the *afikomen* from the table while the Seder leader isn't paying attention; the leader will then bargain with the children for the return of the *afikomen*.) This custom is clearly intended to keep the children awake and attentive until after dinner.

5. The *maggid*—the telling of the Passover narrative, which includes the story of the exodus from Egypt—is the heart of the Haggadah. The narrative is preceded with an invitation for all who are hungry to join participants at the Seder, and continues on to express hope for redemption. The youngest child then recites "The Four Questions," which ask participants about various unusual customs that occur during the Seder and leads into the telling, which begins, "We were slaves to Pharaoh . . . " It is common for participants to take turns reading parts of the Haggadah's narrative, which is specifically told in the first person plural "we" so that participants feel as if the story is their own: "In each generation, every individual should feel personally redeemed." The central symbols of the Passover table are pointed to and explained, praise psalms are recited, drops of wine are spilled for each of the 10 plagues, and the second cup of wine is blessed and consumed.

6. Participants ritually wash their hands again, this time reciting the hand-washing blessing.

7. Two blessings—the regular blessing for bread and a special blessing for matzah—are recited, and pieces of matzah are passed around the table and eaten.

8. Participants eat the bitter herb (usually horseradish) either alone, or with the sweet *haroset* mixture.

9. Out of respect for the sage Hillel, who believed that matzah and the Passover sacrifice (in this case, symbolized by the *maror*) were eaten together in temple times, participants eat a sandwich of matzah and bitter herbs, called a "Hillel sandwich."

10. Participants eat the Passover meal, which often begins with hard-boiled eggs dipped in salt water to simultaneously symbolize both joy and fertility, and the tears of the slaves in bondage. There are no specific foods or rituals required during the actual meal, and most families use this as social time.

11. Children are sent to find the *afikomen,* which is then broken up and distributed around the table, so each Seder participant can eat a piece for dessert. In temple times, the Passover sacrifice was eaten at the end of a meal, when everyone's hunger was sated. In honor of this custom, the *afikomen* is the very last food eaten at Seder.

12. Participants recite grace after the meal, and at the conclusion, they drink the third cup of wine. It is at this point in the Seder that the door is opened to let in the prophet Elijah, who is said to be the herald of the Messiah and a symbol of future redemption. While the door is being opened, participants recite a passage known as the *shefoch chamatcha* ("Pour out your wrath"). Added in the Middle Ages as a response to anti-Semitic persecution, this section of the Haggadah calls for harsh punishment of those who oppressed the Jews and destroyed the temple. This appeal to God for vengeance makes many American Jews uncomfortable. As a result, some Haggadot simply leave out this passage, or replace it with psalms of praise, prayers for peace, or readings that emphasize the dangers of retributive justice.

13. The Hallel (Psalms 113–118) and other hymns of thanksgiving are recited over the fourth cup of wine.

14. The Seder concludes with traditional songs added in medieval times—like "*Ehad mi Yodea*" ("Who Knows One") and "*Had Gadya*" ("One Kid")—and with a prayer for future hope that ends with the line, "Next year in Jerusalem."

In addition to the rituals above, there are many Seder customs that participants may choose to practice. In the ancient world, reclining while eating was a sign of freedom. Because of this tradition, Seder participants are supposed to recline on their left sides (using armchairs or pillows) when partaking of the four cups of wine, the matzah, the Hillel sandwich, and the *afikomen*. (The reclining action, in practice, usually involves participants leaning to the left, rather than fully reclining, due to space constraints at crowded tables.) However, participants are not supposed to recline while eating symbols of slavery, like *maror*. In more traditional households, the leader of the Seder might wear a *kittel*—a white robe reminiscent of the priestly garments worn during the temple service, that also functions simultaneously as both festive dress and burial shroud and is often worn during times of transition (like at one's wedding, and on Yom Kippur). In many Sephardic families it is customary to be more literal about the reenactment of the Exodus from Egypt. One Sephardic custom has Seder participants taking a turn playing an Egyptian taskmaster, lightly beating another person with celery, chives, scallions, or leeks. North African, Yemenite, Turkish, and Greek Sephardim all practice variations on a custom that involves having the Seder leader circling the table with a walking stick and the *afikomen* in a sack over his shoulder, while he tells everyone at the Passover Seder table about the miracles he witnessed as he came forth in the Exodus from Egypt.

Since the women's liberation movement of the 1960s and 1970s in the United States, women's involvement in recreating Jewish rituals to include themselves in more active ways has breathed new life into ritual objects, prayer language, and worship services for both women and men. The first feminist Seder in the United States took place in New York City in 1976, using *The Women's Haggadah*, which was written by Esther Broner and Naomi Nimrod. In the 30 years since, this Passover ritual has been one of the mainstays of the Jewish women's movement; Jewish women's groups across the country hold them both in addition to, and instead of, traditional Seders. Some of the most visible changes to Passover traditions have come from feminist additions to the Seder table. During a visit to Oberlin College in the early 1980s, Jewish scholar Susannah Heschel encountered a student Haggadah that included a crust of bread on the Seder plate as a sign of solidarity with Jewish lesbians. This inspired her to add an orange to her family's Seder plate. During the Seder, she asked each family member to bless and eat a segment of the fruit as a gesture of solidarity with those who were marginalized within the Jewish community (including Jewish lesbians, gay men, widows, and orphans). The orange, for Heschel, symbolized the fruitfulness for all Jews when those who were marginalized were included within the Jewish community. The story of what the orange stands for, however, managed to change as it circulated and has been eclipsed by a false, but more widespread version: a male rabbi tells Heschel that a woman belongs on the *bimah* (or pulpit) like an orange belongs on the Seder plate. Proponents of this version of the story see the orange on the Seder plate as a symbol of feminist defiance, and as a way to support female rabbis. Regardless of the story behind it, many families now include an orange on their Seder plate as a nod to women's equality in Judaism.

While many traditionalists would not consider taking part in innovations such as this, for many liberal Jews new rituals bring a contemporary focus to holidays and hold enormous meaning. In addition to the orange that graces some Seder plates, a number of people have added a novel ritual object called a Miriam's Cup—another modern feminist symbol—to their Seder tables. A Miriam's Cup is placed beside the Cup of Elijah and is filled with water to represent Miriam's Well, which was a source of water for the Israelites in the desert. This cup draws awareness to the often overlooked importance of Miriam and the other women of the Exodus story and sends the signal to Seder participants that a household is generally inclusive and egalitarian.

INTERFAITH SEDERS

America is a predominantly Christian country, and Passover is one of the few holidays that manage to cross the Jewish-Christian divide. The topic of whether or not Jesus's Last Supper was a Passover Seder is a hotly contested one among biblical scholars, but regardless of which side they take in the debate, most scholars do agree that the Last Supper took place on or near Passover and contained some elements of a Jewish ritual meal. With the growing popularity of evangelical Christianity in America, there has also been increasing interest among Christians in Passover. Christian bookstores carry literature on celebrating the biblical feasts at home, and some churches even recreate Christian versions of the Passover Seder, which reinterpret the significance of the holiday and its symbols to fit Christian theology. These Seders might speak of the paschal lamb as a prophecy of Jesus, or say that the three symbolic pieces of Seder matzah represent the Trinity. Other Christians choose to let Jewish people define their own holidays, rather than reinterpreting or appropriating them, and instead join Jewish families or attend local synagogues as Seder guests.

While Passover is a family holiday, a central invocation in the Haggadah intones, "Let all who are hungry come and eat." As a result, it is customary, and some Jews would argue obligatory, to invite people from the community (and especially those in need) to one's Seder. In recent years the Jewish community has conducted special interfaith Seders to explain the holiday to non-Jews, and to build bridges between Jewish and non-Jewish communities. Some interfaith Seders specifically reach out to other established religions, inviting Baha'i, Buddhist, Catholic, Jewish, Muslim, Protestant, and Unitarian-Universalist congregations to join with them. Other interfaith Seders target people in need by inviting residents from local soup kitchens or homeless shelters to partake in festivities. In recent years, Black-Jewish Liberation Seders (also called Freedom Seders) have grown in popularity—especially on college campuses—where students trace the parallels between the Jewish Exodus and the African-American struggle for freedom from slavery, highlighting liberation journeys through racism and anti-Semitism in America. These Seders often include readings from Martin Luther King Jr.'s writings, and the singing of spirituals like "We Shall Overcome," in addition to the traditional holiday texts and songs.

VARIATIONS IN PASSOVER PRACTICES

As with any religious rituals, Passover practices and observances vary widely among Jews in America depending on their denominational affiliation, ethnic background, and personal preferences. Some may attend a Seder with family or friends the first night of the holiday but choose not to keep kosher for the remaining days of Passover; others may attend Seders and keep kosher for Passover by avoiding leaven without going through the process of purifying their houses or changing their dishes; still others may follow Jewish law to the letter. The three major branches of Judaism in America (Orthodox, Conservative, and Reform) and the two major ethnic groups (Ashkenazi Jews of central and eastern European backgrounds, and Sephardic Jews originally from Spain and Portugal), all also have different official policies on Passover observances. The Reform movement leaves it up to each individual to decide how to observe the dietary rules of Passover. The Orthodox and Conservative movements both stand by the strictest prohibitions on any foods made from barley, oats, rye, spelt, and wheat. Ashkenazi Jews are also supposed to refrain from eating corn, legumes, millet, or rice, while Sephardic Jews continue to eat these foods during Passover. The majority of the American Jewish population is Ashkenazi—however, many American Jews choose to keep a Sephardic version of Passover. Additionally, many Jews use the holiday as a time to eat in an intentionally "healthier" way, by sticking to vegetables, meat, and other nonprocessed foods, in addition to avoiding leaven.

According to the 2000 National Jewish Population Survey (NJPS), 70 percent of Jews in America either hold or attend a Passover Seder each year. For Jews who remain unaffiliated with any specific branch of Judaism, many of whom consider themselves "secular Jews" or "cultural Jews," Passover remains a beloved and regularly observed holiday due to its universal manifesto of liberty and freedom for all, and the Haggadah's ethical message of compassion toward the stranger, the poor, and the disadvantaged. These Jews enjoy the sense of community and ritual that the Passover Seder offers, as well as the chance to reconnect with family and celebrate their Jewish heritage over the course of the holiday. The major themes of Passover—redemption and creation, rebirth and revival, exile and liberation—are attractive because they feel contemporary, and personally or politically relevant. As a result, many Jews who aren't normally observant of Jewish dietary laws, or other Jewish laws, choose to keep kosher for Passover in some way, shape, or form.

Many observant or Orthodox Jews consider the practice of keeping kosher only for Passover inconsistent, contradictory, illogical, or absurd; some dismiss those who keep kosher for Passover as too lazy to make the commitment to keeping kosher year-round. But there are various heartfelt convictions and motivations behind why generally nonobservant Jews choose to keep kosher for Passover. The practice provides solidarity with or connection to other Jews, as well as to Jewish history and one's Jewish heritage, and presents them with the opportunity to engage in Jewish tradition. Keeping Passover dietary restrictions also helps Jews maintain a connection to their families—either emotionally, or physically, through holding Seders with them at the start of the holiday. Other Jews focus on the symbolism of the holiday, and the themes it advocates, or take a more corporeal approach, and view Passover as a chance to cleanse their system of certain foods and improve their health. Some enjoy the challenge of avoiding particular foods for the week, or appreciate the relationship of food to marking time in a specific way. In a more spiritual vein, many Jews connect the holiday's themes to their own personal psychological issues, or their faith, or view Passover as a time to bring more consciousness and awareness to their eating practices. Other Jews keep kosher for Passover because they think it is important for non-Jews to see Jews respecting their religion in a public way, while some people keep kosher for Passover due to habit, or to honor the notion of sacrifice that the holiday entails. Regardless of the personal motivations behind American Jews' observances, or their wide varieties of ritual practice, Passover manages to simultaneously retain its myriad of unique American innovations, while continuing to tie American Jews to the worldwide Jewish community.

FURTHER READING

Geffen, David. *American Heritage Haggadah: The Passover Experience.* New York: Gefen Publishing House, 1992.

Glatzer, Nahum N. *The Schocken Passover Haggadah.* New York: Schocken Books, 1996.

Heinze, Andrew. *Adapting to Abundance: Jewish Immigrants, Mass Consumption, and the Search for American Identity.* New York: Columbia University Press, 1992.

Joselit, Jenna Weissman. *The Wonders of America.* New York: Hill and Wang, 2002.

Strassfeld, Michael. *The Jewish Holidays: A Guide and Commentary.* Philadelphia: Harper and Row, 1985.

Erika Meitner

EASTER

- [ ] Easter celebrates the resurrection of Jesus of Nazareth and is the most important Christian annual feast.

- [ ] The English word Easter is derived from ancient Norse terms for springtime, which in turn were derived from the Norse term for East, the direction of the sunrise.

- [ ] In the fourth century Church Fathers set the day of celebration of Easter on the Sunday following the first full moon after the spring equinox.

- [ ] Pre-Christian springtime rituals such as lighting bonfires and greeting the dawn on Easter morning, and fertility symbols like eggs and hares continue in contemporary popular Easter practices.

- [ ] G.F. Handel's *Messiah,* with its libretto of biblical texts meditating upon the birth, life, passion, and exaltation of Christ, was originally performed as a Lenten benefit concert for the Foundling Hospital in Dublin, Ireland.

- [ ] Puritan settlers in New England discouraged Easter celebrations (much as they did those of Christmas), considering them tainted by papism.

- [ ] The large, elegant white Easter lily is native to Japan and became a popular decorative Easter symbol in the 1880s.

- [ ] What began in 1870s New York City as a walk of fashionable Easter worshipers up and down Fifth Avenue to view the floral decorations in the various churches at the conclusion of morning services became, in just 20 years, a cultural institution known as the Easter Parade.

- [ ] Easter is often celebrated on different days in America. Eastern European immigrant Byzantine Catholics observe the Roman (Gregorian) calendar, while the Orthodox in America follow the older Julian calendar, which in any given year can cause a discrepancy in Easter's date of up to several weeks.

EASTER

Easter is Christianity's most important annual feast, a solemn and joyous celebration of the religion's foundational belief, namely, that the God of biblical faith raised from the dead Jesus of Nazareth, a first century C.E. Galilean Jew whom the Roman occupational government had executed by crucifixion. Jesus's execution occurred during the annual Jewish Passover festival in Jerusalem. The Jewish roots of the Christian religion largely figure in the name, date, and duration of Easter as the high point and longest season in the liturgical cycle, or calendar of worship, of the Christian year. While the key to Easter's religious content and meaning lies in the origins of Christianity as it emerged as a distinct religion in the late Greco-Roman world, its eventual development as a springtime festival in Europe and, subsequently, America brought about a rich tradition of customs that both endure and continue to evolve today.

A survey of names for the feast in various European languages is indicative of the holiday's blending of Christian and other sociocultural traditions. The English and German titles, Easter and Ostern, respectively, have their roots in ancient Norse terminology for springtime (Eastur, Eostur, Ostar), which included a feast celebrating the new life or birth manifested by the growing (warmer, longer) sun. East or Ost refers to the direction from which the sun rises. As Christianity spread in Northern Europe, its springtime feast of Christ's rising from the dead easily coincided with the imagery of the indigenous festival of new life. Among the languages of the more southern European peoples the titles for the Christian feast—Pascua (Spanish and Portuguese), Pasqua (Italian), Pâques (French)—derive from the common Latin and Greek word *pascha*, which, in turn, comes from *pesach*, the proper Hebrew name for the Jewish feast of Passover. This Jewish root word points to the historical development of Easter.

ORIGINS OF THE FEAST AND SEASON

As a proper annual feast, Easter only emerged gradually during the second century of Christianity. The first several generations of Christians marked time not according to an annual but a weekly calendar. Sunday was the feast day, while Wednesday and Friday were fast days. From its origins, the Christian Church proclaimed that God raised Jesus the Christ (or Messiah) from the dead on the first day of the week. The early Christian communities quickly entitled the day on which they assembled to commemorate Christ's death and resurrection the Lord's Day, designating Sunday as their ritual celebration not only of what happened to Jesus in the past but also of his continued presence experienced in their sacred meal of bread and wine they called the Eucharist (Greek for thanksgiving). A further designation of Sunday as the Eighth Day bespoke a hopeful, future-oriented dimension. Building on the Jewish biblical creation story (in the Book of Genesis), early Christian leaders proclaimed Sunday as not only the first day of creation but also, based on what God had done in Jesus the Christ, the first day of the new creation. Whereas Judaism celebrated the seventh day of the week as the Sabbath, a holy day of rest imitating God's relaxation after a week's worth of creating the cosmos, believers in Jesus saw in Sunday an eighth day of creation, amounting to the dawn of a new age of righteousness and salvation for the whole world. In the New Testament (the Christian biblical books), a letter attributed to Saint Peter speaks of the promise of "a new heaven and a new earth" begun in Christ (2 Pet. 3:13), while in the Book of Revelation (or Apocalypse), written at the end of the first century C.E., the Christian prophet John describes being taken up in ecstatic visions on the Lord's Day (Rev. 1:10), culminating in his arrival at "a new heaven and a new earth" (Rev. 21:1).

Sunday was (and remains) the primordial Christian feast, a day for celebrating faith in the crucified Jesus as the beloved Son God raised from the dead, hope in the promised fulfillment of the new creation begun in Christ, and love shared through the Eucharistic ritual whereby believers recognize Christ's presence among them "in the breaking of the bread" (see Luke 24:35). The second century C.E., nonetheless, saw across the Roman Empire the gradual development of Christians celebrating an annual memorial of Christ's death and resurrection, coinciding with the Passover, the annual Jewish festival season during which Jesus had been executed. The timing and meaning of the Christian pascha, however, varied among the local churches. Passover occurs on the first full moon after the spring equinox, the fourteenth day of the month of Nisan. Churches in the regions of Rome, Palestine, and North Africa developed Easter with an emphasis on Christ's resurrection. Thus, they set its annual date on the

Sunday after the fourteenth of Nisan. Churches in Asia Minor, on the other hand, placed theological emphasis for Easter on Jesus's death by crucifixion as the ultimate meaning and fulfillment of the annual Jewish sacrificing of lambs on Pesach. These churches, which became known as Quartodecimans (or "Four-teeners"), celebrated their pascha on the date of the annual Jewish Passover, 14 Nisan, whatever day of the week that might be.

By the end of the second century the bishop of Rome insisted that all Christian churches should celebrate Easter on the Sunday, but his fellow bishops rebuked him when he went so far as to threaten the Quartodecimans with excommunication. In 325 C.E. the Council of Nicea, an assembly of all Christian bishops convoked by the Emperor Constantine, called for a single system of dating and celebrating Easter. Still, universal acceptance for the annual timing of that Sunday was only realized in the sixth century, and even then with difficulty, since both Jewish and Christian leaders found it difficult to calculate the exact paschal date in relation to the spring equinox and subsequent full moon. Official Roman ritual books eventually included rather complex tables for determining Easter's date in any given year.

The fourth century was the period in which not only the annual dating of Easter Sunday became more unified but also the celebration of the paschal mystery split into a series of feast days, each commemorating one event in the scenario of Jesus' final days and execution. Jerusalem was the center for this ritual elaboration of Easter, which rapidly spread throughout Christianity. Bishop Cyril developed distinct religious services extending back from Easter Sunday into the preceding eight days. The Friday and Saturday, which were already solemn fast days in preparation for the Sunday festival, took on the role of marking the events of Jesus's crucifixion (Good Friday) and watchfulness for his resurrection as he lay in the tomb (Holy Saturday and its night Vigil of Easter). Thursday evening commemorated Christ establishing the Eucharistic meal on the eve of his execution, while the Sunday before Easter became Palm Sunday, a festival for carrying palm branches and chanting hosannas (praises) in imitation of the biblical reports of a crowd doing this for Jesus when he entered Jerusalem for the final time. Even the day before that took on significance, as it was named Lazarus Saturday, memorializing Jesus's raising his friend and disciple Lazarus of Bethany from the dead, an event which the Gospel of John attributes to the Judean leadership's resolve to do away with him. The entire period running from Palm Sunday to Easter became known as Holy Week.

Although the elaboration of official rituals and popular customs for Holy Week is what would persist and grow throughout the Church right through the Middle Ages, another crucial development in the Christian worship (or liturgy) and religious formation (or catechesis) had significant impact on the theology and ritual of Easter as both a pivotal day and an entire season in the Church year: the practice of initiating new Christians within the annual Easter cycle. By the latter fourth century churches all the way around the Mediterranean—from Milan to Constantinople to Antioch to Alexandria—had developed lengthy (often years long) programs for the religious formation of converts to the faith, culminating in a multistaged liturgy running from Holy Saturday night into the early morning hours of Easter Sunday. The local Christian community kept the Vigil (night watch) in their basilica or church building by lighting candles and then listening to a long series of biblical readings from Hebrew creation stories through New Testament texts, interspersed with the chanting of psalms and prayers. Meanwhile, the bishop and his assistants (presbyters, deacons and deaconesses) were baptizing the worthy candidates in an elaborate water rite held in a separate, symbolically charged place called the baptistery. Having been immersed (attended by ministers of the same sex) in water that symbolized both dying to sin (drowning) and passing naked through birth (amniotic fluid), the neophytes were raised from the pool, clothed in white robes, and (most often) sealed with the Holy Spirit by the bishop's prayerful application of holy oils to the head. The entire entourage then processed into the vigil-keeping church, with the gleaming initiates symbolizing the continued presence and life of the resurrected Christ in the persons of these new members of his body. Alleluia hymns joyously accompanied the proclamation of biblical accounts of the first Easter, followed by preaching and prayerful petitions. The bishop then confirmed for the assembly that the baptisms had validly occurred, doing or repeating the sealing with oils, and then inviting the neophytes into the sanctuary as honored participants around the altar of the Eucharist, which they were now qualified to share for the first time.

If the Easter Vigil's emergence as the most important and elaborate ritual of the Church year was due to the identification of the feast with the initiation of new Christians, the entire ritual-formation process for the neophytes likewise played a key role in the development of the 50-day Easter Season that followed, as well as the 40-day season of Lent that preceded it. Once established as an annual feast, Easter quickly became a 50-day festival culminating in Pentecost, another Jewish feast (50 days after Passover). Christians adapted Pentecost, a Jewish harvest festival that had evolved into a celebration of their divine covenant, with a new meaning, namely, the descent of the Holy Spirit the risen Christ had promised to share with his disciples. Fourth-century bishops exhorted their faithful to celebrate the entire period as an octave of Sundays or "a week of weeks," with Saint Basil of Caesarea teaching that Pentecost reminds believers of the resurrection awaiting them in the promised new creation. Not surprisingly, then, many churches in this period also baptized new members on this last Sunday of Easter, with Pentecost acquiring its own vigil. Meanwhile, earlier in the season, those baptized at the Easter Vigil wore their white robes and were the subject of special instruction at daily Eucharistic liturgies throughout the first week of Easter. At the conclusion of the octave, that is, on the Second Sunday of Easter, the bishop instructed them to set aside those garments and take a regular place among the rest of the assembled worshiping community.

Easter's governing role in the development of the annual Christian calendar gradually reached in the other direction as well. By the fourth century the two-day fasting period in preparation for Easter expanded first to three weeks and then, finally, to a 40-day period called Lent. In biblical tradition the number 40 symbolized people's purification and journeying to redemption (Noah's ark riding out the destructive flood for 40 days; the Israelites' 40-year trek to the Promised Land). Three of the gospels recount how Jesus, as the fulfillment of Israel's redemption, underwent 40 days of prayer and fasting in the desert before beginning his public mission. The Church applied this timing and imagery to those about to be baptized, making Lent the final period of intense purification and preparation for their sacramental initiation at the Easter Vigil. During this period another liturgical process developed in conjunction with Lent, in response to the problem of purifying and renewing Christians who had failed their baptismal promises. At the start of Lent the local bishop excluded from Sunday Eucharist those who had seriously, publicly sinned. He and all the faithful committed themselves in solidarity with this Order of Penitents, joining them in prayer, fasting, and almsgiving throughout the Lenten season. On Holy Thursday the bishop received the penitents back to communion.

In most churches around the Empire the six-week Lenten season began with its First Sunday, exactly 40 days before the Easter Triduum's commencement on the evening of Holy Thursday. A problem developed, however, with regard to fasting. Being fundamentally the Day of the Lord (celebrating Christ's resurrection), Sunday could not be a fast day, even in Lent. Thus, the total number of fast days, including Good Friday and Holy Saturday, only amounted to 36. By the seventh century most Western churches had made up the difference of the four extra days by moving the start of Lent back to the Wednesday prior to the First Sunday of the season. The traditional singing of an antiphon calling for the donning of sackcloth and ashes as signs of penitence gave rise to the imposition of ashes on the heads of the faithful on that day. The Roman church, always conservative and spare in ritual matters, only mandated the practice of Ash Wednesday in the eleventh century. By that time, the elaborate, extended process of initiating adults into the Church had all but universally vanished. Having become the imperial religion of both East and West, Christianity became synonymous with membership in society, and baptism was performed in infancy, not long after birth. The rigors of the Order of Penitents did not much survive the end of the first Christian millennium. Individual confession of sins to a priest, at any time of year, became the practice for sinners, with Lent becoming the annual, communal reminder to all believers of their need for humble repentance.

DEVELOPMENT OF EUROPEAN EASTER CUSTOMS AND PRACTICES

With neither initiates nor official penitents any longer at the ritual center of Lent and Easter, these seasons, especially Holy Week, took on the character of pious devotional acts, religious dramas, and a panoply of folk customs across Europe. By the Middle Ages the Christian liturgical domain had divided into two clearly distinct divisions of labor—clergy and lay people. The former performed in church edifices official rites that were beyond the scope of most of the faithful due to the accretion of complex ministerial roles and increasingly obscure gestures and symbols, all done in Latin, a language incomprehensible to most of the laity and often little better understood by many of the clergy. The liturgy of Holy Week and Easter largely became a matter of spectacle, that is, of visual enactments bound to biblical imagery associated with specific days on the calendar. While people attended the clerically performed rites in great numbers, they also developed their own popular practices that paralleled, interacted with, or even significantly differed from the clerical ritual activities. Here we shall survey just some of the vast array of European rituals and customs that later influenced Easter traditions practiced in America.

Processions were the form of ritual activity that provided lay people a corporate role in the liturgical drama of Holy Week. The people not only followed the clergy in processions within the church rites but also took to the streets in popular processions marked by music and displays of sacred images. Everywhere the Mass for Palm Sunday included a procession. By the early medieval period this entailed clergy and laity moving from an outlying chapel to the main church at the town or city's center, carrying blessed palms and seasonal flowers. Another feature was a wooden statue of Christ on a donkey mounted on wheels and pulled through the center of the procession. In Slavic and Bavarian countries farm families carried the blessed palms with songs and prayers through their barns and fields, sticking slips of the branches in each locale for protection from bad weather and disease. Holy Thursday's evening Eucharist concluded with a procession transporting the remaining consecrated bread (the Blessed Sacrament) from the main altar to a chapel or side altar, where it lay in repose amidst candles and flowers. In the Latin countries people dressed in black would visit seven such repository shrines in the vicinity, praying the rosary as they processed from one to the next. The Good Friday liturgy featured the priest carrying a cross through the church, stopping three times to call the faithful to worship, before placing it on a pillow in front of the altar, where all processed forward to venerate it with a kiss. In Latin countries, especially Spain, people developed street processions in which they wore hooded cowls, carried candles, and depicted the events of the Passion with statues of the suffering Christ and his mother Mary. After Easter Sunday Mass in medieval Central Europe the people would walk through the fields singing hymns. To this day in Echternach, Luxembourg, the bishop leads the entire population in a step-danced procession through the winding streets on Pentecost Monday (which remains a civic holiday in Europe).

European Easter practices did not, however, originate only from the rituals, biblical stories, and images of Christianity. The pre-Christian roots of the springtime celebration were deep and enduring, as well. In Ireland Saint Patrick christened Druidic springtime bonfires by establishing the tradition of lighting a fire in the churchyard at the start of the Easter Vigil to symbolize Christ, the Light of the World. Irish missionaries in the sixth and seventh centuries brought this new meaning to the widely popular springtime bonfires in the Germanic countries. Throughout medieval Europe people came to celebrate the dawn of Easter on hilltops or open plains, professing to the see the sun taking leaps of joy and angels shimmering in its rays, as well as finding healing powers in flowing waters. In Northern countries water figured in youthful games on Easter Monday and Tuesday, with the opposite sexes splashing each other—the vestiges of ancient fertility rites—while costumed children performed songs from home to home with finales of sprinkling, for which they were rewarded with eggs and sweet goodies. The Easter egg was based on Indo-European folklore, a symbol of spring fertility and the miracle of birth. Christian eyes saw the egg as the tomb from which Christ broke forth, giving new life to the world. Decorated according to various regional styles, eggs were also more simply dyed in vegetable-based colorings and then used in games whose objectives were to see whose egg, colliding with others by either rolling or knocking, could endure without cracking. The bunny, a most fertile animal, was another pre-Christian symbol of spring's new life with the mythic power of producing colored eggs for children in many lands. By the early nineteenth century sugar or pastry bunnies were

Elaborately decorated Easter eggs. © Corbis

gracing Easter tables, along with a wide board of traditional breads, cheeses, garnishes, and such meats as lamb (Christ, the Lamb of God), sausage, and ham (pigs being a European symbol of good luck).

Events in the 1500s brought about divisions in the Church that resulted in the variety of Christian sects that would arrive on American shores in subsequent centuries. Indeed, the schism between the Western Roman Church and the Orthodox Churches of the East was already hundreds of years old. While East and West had always practiced distinctive liturgies and other forms of piety, a further difference developed in 1582. Pope Gregory XIII decreed that a new calendar replace the ancient Julian calendar, which was increasingly inaccurate due to its inability to accommodate the earth's taking 365 and one-quarter days to circle the sun. The Orthodox Churches did not adopt the Gregorian calendar. To this day, while the Orthodox and all other Christians continue to celebrate Easter on the first Sunday after the first full moon of the spring equinox, they differ in determining when exactly that date comes about. In any given year the discrepancy can amount up to several weeks (with the Orthodox always being later), while occasionally the two calendars' dates for Easter coincide.

The sixteenth century witnessed the fracturing of Western Christianity into a number of religious bodies separated from the Roman Church. One of the hallmarks of the Protestant Reformers was their principle of placing authority in biblical texts alone and rejecting much of the governmental, liturgical, and doctrinal structures of Roman Catholicism. The church calendar was a primary object for revision, as it had become freighted with saint's days and other holy days that the reformers said detracted from faith in Christ's once-for-all saving deeds. Martin Luther and John Calvin both retained the annual "feasts of the Lord" (Christmas, Good Friday, Easter, Ascension, and Pentecost). Many reformed churches on both the Continent and British Isles, however, came to reject the Church Year entirely, arguing that even the feasts of the Lord had no biblical warrant, Sunday alone comprised the weekly Lord's Day, and the traditional holy days had become occasions for sinful merrymaking and superstitious evils. From its break with Roman Catholicism, the Church of England maintained a strong church calendar and rituals. Separatists from the Anglican Church at the turn of the seventeenth century, on the other hand, following the Anabaptists and Calvinists, rejected Anglicanism as sternly as Roman Catholicism. In the first half of that century these Puritans would establish the Massachusetts Bay Colony, where leaders kept vigilance against all things papist, including such holidays as Christmas and Easter.

Perhaps the most notable contribution the Protestant traditions—especially Lutheranism, Anglicanism, and its eighteenth-century offshoot, Methodism—have made to the observance of Easter has been in the realm of music. Theologically and musically gifted composers in these churches developed rich repertoires of not only hymnody but also religious oratorios and other sacred music to be performed during the Lenten and Easter Seasons. In Germany the only type of musical performance allowed during Lent was sacred pieces based on biblical texts; opera and secular cantatas were forbidden. These conditions gave rise to sacred oratorios, among which arguably the greatest are J. S. Bach's two *Passion*s (according to Saint John and Saint Matthew), although he also composed splendid oratorios for the other feasts of the Lord. G. F. Handel's *Messiah*, with its libretto of biblical texts meditating upon the birth, life, passion, and exaltation of Christ, was originally performed as a Lenten benefit concert for the Foundling Hospital in Dublin, Ireland, where seasonal restrictions on secular entertainment also applied. While Handel's masterpiece drew on the Anglican anthem tradition, Bach's oratorios came out of a German heritage of musical Passion dramas, whose own history reaches back to medieval miracle plays. The first of those plays, in fact, developed as part of the Easter Morning Mass, a clerical dramatization of the eleventh century chant, "Victimae Paschali Laudes," describing the events surrounding Christ's resurrection. Local traditions of miracle plays and biblical dramas for various liturgical seasons spread throughout Europe, with the most famous today being the Passion Play performed every 10 years at Oberammergau, Germany—a tradition begun during the plague and Thirty Years War of the seventeenth century. Finally, note must be made of the prolific and widely used hymn compositions, including much for Passiontide and Easter, by the Methodist Charles Wesley, who with his brother John had a missionary stint in the American colony of Georgia in the eighteenth century.

EASTER AS AN AMERICAN HOLIDAY

The second half of the nineteenth century witnessed Easter's emergence as an American holiday. Whereas up to that time observances of the Easter season were isolated in Roman Catholic, Anglican, and Lutheran churches and neighborhoods, beginning in the 1860s culturally mainstream Protestant churches (e.g., Congregational, Methodist, Baptist, Presbyterian) adopted the annual holy day. Easter also appealed to the burgeoning middle-class Victorian fascination with ritual traditions, especially as these could be incorporated into home-focused celebrations. The Easter festival's interactive engagement of the religious, social, economic, and cultural dimensions of American life over the ensuing decades made it a holiday blending the sacred and secular, Christianity and commerce, biblical messages and popular tastes, as robustly as these had converged in medieval feasts.

The celebration of Easter in American churches, as well as wider society, proved a new moment in the feast's long tradition of combining Christian beliefs with exultation in the newness of the spring season. Increasingly elaborate floral displays became the distinctive feature of the American church interior at Easter. In the 1880s a florist named W. K. Harris introduced to the Easter season a large, elegant white lily native to Japan and cultivated in Bermuda. Achieving immediate popularity, the "Easter lily" became the key feature in church sanctuaries, often with dozens of pots arranged in pyramids, cross-patterns, or alongside banners with such inscriptions as "Christ Is Risen!" and "Alleluia!" In the more liturgically oriented Churches, the splendid sight and smell of Easter lilies and other flowers, set against the brilliant white draping and vestments traditional for any feast of the Lord, dispelled the gloom of the somber fasting season of Lent. Large churches in the major cities began to outdo each other in their Easter decorations, importing exotic flowers from great distances and constructing veritable glades around their altars.

Nor were the church buildings the only bearers of Easter finery. The congregants were, as well. Just as Irish tradition, among others in Europe, had long

An Easter lily. Courtesy of Getty Images / PhotoDisc.

associated Christmas with food and drink but Easter with new clothes, American Christians of all denominations in the latter nineteenth century made the donning of fresh attire part of their Easter practice. The debuting of new fashions at Easter morning services bespoke not only Christian faith but also faith in the American dream of prosperity and affluence, to the point that some Protestant ministers began to vocally critique the association of Easter with expensive new finery. Merchants, on the other hand, embraced the newfound religious popularity of Easter not merely for trade purposes but often in synchrony with the churches, creating seasonal displays in their windows (complete with crosses and biblical slogans) that mirrored the elaborately decorated sanctuaries. By the early twentieth century Easter had become a genuine season in the annual American shopping cycle.

The results went on parade. What began in 1870s New York City as a walk of fashionable Easter worshipers up and down Fifth Avenue to view the floral decorations in the various churches at the conclusion of morning services became, in just 20 years, a cultural institution known as the Easter Parade. Thousands

Hundreds gather at the Rockefeller Center for an Easter Parade. Courtesy of Getty Images / PhotoDisc.

came to see and be seen for the afternoon, with people even traveling from Long Island and New Jersey to view the pageant of privilege and fashion. As New York's Easter Parade grew in the twentieth century to the point of attracting hundreds of thousands, the event was unable to retain its elitist character and unique location. In the 1920s such tourist destinations as Atlantic City and Coney Island mixed the fashion-show aspect with other carnival attractions, laying the groundwork for Easter's becoming another American vacation. Still, that the widespread American association of Easter with energetic shopping as a celebration of springtime display—and with New York as the symbolic center of

The cover from the sheet music for Irving Berlin's "Easter Parade," 1948. © Culver Pictures.

the tradition—stood the test of time is evident in the 1948 musical *Easter Parade* based on the hit tune of the same name by Irving Berlin.

The film industry's role in the American observance of Easter, however, would prove mostly to focus not on popular and commercial culture but, rather, on the biblical domain. Movie theater hits of the 1950s and 1960s, including *The Robe* (starring Richard Burton), Cecil B. DeMille's *The Ten Commandments* (starring Charlton Heston and Yul Brenner), and George Stevens's *The Greatest Story Ever Told,* became regular Easter offerings on the three major television networks from the late 1960s onward. In 1977 NBC premiered Franco Zeffirelli's *Jesus of Nazareth,* making it a mini-series for Holy Week. Still, the annual television cycle around Easter was not exclusively of such serious religious fare. Part of CBS's early springtime ritual during the same period included an annual Sunday evening showing of *The Wizard of Oz* (film release, 1939), a fanciful, miraculous tale of deliverance from deadly evil that exalted the goodness of family, home, virtue, and friends in a way that mythically resonated with American viewers of all ages. The advent and proliferation of cable channels since the 1980s, along with increasingly sophisticated technology for personal movie viewing, have diminished the ritualized patterns (daily, weekly, and annual) that characterized the first decades of American television. Recently, however, a commercially successful biblical film well attuned to current popular tastes for both sentimental religious piety and graphic screen violence entered the Easter cycle. Mel Gibson's *The Passion of the Christ* premiered in the United States for Lent of 2004 and in the following year was already showing on television during Holy Week.

VARIETIES OF EASTER TRADITIONS
IN AMERICA TODAY

The religious practice of Easter in twentieth century America is, nevertheless, primarily a story of traditions of church and home steeped in the ethnic heritages of successive waves of immigrants, along with American-grown rituals and customs. A survey of some of these can serve as a description of practices that continue, albeit with inevitable ongoing modification, in this new century.

During the earliest decades of the twentieth century large numbers of immigrants from the Slavic lands of Central Europe settled in the New England, Middle Atlantic, and Great Lakes states. These peoples mostly belonged to churches in union with Rome that nonetheless practiced liturgical rites and religious customs proper to Eastern Europe. Often called Byzantine or Greek or even Uniate Catholics, the names of their churches also reflect regions from which they came. For example, the Ruthenian Catholic Church has its roots in the Carpathian Mountains (territories now in Slovakia and southern Poland), while the Ukrainian Catholics come from the country that once again independently bears that name. Others arrived in America as Russian Orthodox Christians, whose church attained a practical autonomy from the Patriarchate in Moscow in the 1920s, because of the severe restrictions in external communications the Soviet government imposed on the Russian Church. This was the origin of what became the Orthodox Church in America, which attracted not only Russian, Romanian, Bulgarian, and Albanian Orthodox immigrants but also received Byzantine Catholics who became disaffected by the treatment they received from the American Roman Catholic hierarchy. Since the fall of the Soviet Empire, the Orthodox Church in America, as well as local Greek Orthodox churches, have been receiving new waves of the immigrant faithful from the former Soviet Bloc. All of this brief history is to explain why there is at once much overlap in Easter folklore, customs, food, piety, and liturgy (ritual) among these various nationally based churches and yet a difference in when they celebrate Lent and Easter. The Byzantine Catholics observe the Roman (Gregorian) calendar, while the Orthodox in America follow the older Julian calendar, which in any given year can cause a discrepancy in Easter's date of up to several weeks.

The Orthodox Church at this point in history stands out as the Christian denomination practicing the most elaborate liturgical rites and calendar, for which Easter is the dazzling apex. The annual Easter cycle begins with the 40 days of Great Lent, a season of prayer, fasting, and almsgiving (charity to those in need) that is intended not to be morose but, rather, charged with faith in Christ's resurrection-victory over death, in which it already participates. This indicates the mystical quality of Orthodox worship, a perception of symbol and ritual as drawing believers into a timeless divine reality that nonetheless touches all moments in life's present, ongoing story. The Lenten fast is highly demanding, and while strictly expected of clergy and monks, functions as an ideal for each of the faithful to pursue to the best of one's abilities and fortitude. Meat, eggs, dairy products, and fish are all prohibited from the Lenten diet, although many Orthodox keep this comprehensive fast only in the first and final weeks of the season.

While Lent entails special weekly church services, the liturgical activity reaches its crescendo in Passion Week (Holy Week), especially from Holy Thursday evening through the wee hours of Easter Sunday morning. On Good Friday afternoon the middle of each church has a tomb enshrined with flowers into which a cloth painted with an icon (sacred image) of the dead Jesus (the "winding sheet" or *plaschanitsa* in Slavonic) is laid. A subsequent ritual of Holy Saturday includes processing outdoors around the church with the priest carrying the winding sheet over his head to signify Christ's victory over death and redemption of the universe. An exterior procession also figures prominently in the vigil of Easter, which begins at midnight with the clergy and people, candles in hand, circling the church. Returning to the front doors they hear the announcement of Christ's resurrection, enter the church to find in the center a splendid icon depicting the event, and proceed with a joyous service replete with much chanting of psalms and hymns, incensing of all the (many) icons in the church, proclamation of the Gospel, and finally the Divine Liturgy of the Eucharist.

Slavic American Christians—Orthodox and Catholic—share a rich tradition of foods and domestic customs for Easter. On Holy Saturday evening the faithful bring to the church for blessing baskets covered with a symbolic white cloth and laden with the special foods for the Sunday feast: butter, salt, ham, sausage, hardboiled eggs, horseradish with beets, pascha (a bread of flour, eggs, milk, sugar, yeast, and yellow raisins), a ball of sweet cheese emblazoned with cloves in a cruciform pattern, a bottle of wine, and a candle, which is lit for the blessing ceremony but will also grace the table back home. At the beginning of dinner on Easter Sunday the father of the household ceremoniously gives a portion of one of the blessed eggs to each person at the table, proclaiming, "Christ is Risen," to which each replies, "Indeed, he has risen!" Indeed, this dialogue is the expected form of salutation for the entire day. Among the home's decorations are *pysanki,* eggs covered with intricate designs applied by hot wax that seals the patterns on the shells before submersion in brilliant, deep vegetable dyes. Greek Orthodox Christians, on the other hand, simply color their boiled eggs crimson to signify the blood of Christ. Their tables include lamb, as well as an array of special cookies and pastries.

Distinctive to the American Protestant celebration of Easter, across denominational and racial lines, is the sunrise service. Gathering in the dark a half hour before dawn causes this ritual practice to have a similar affective impact on its worshipers as the Saturday night Easter vigils in Catholic and Orthodox churches. Sunrise services variably take place in churches, on hilltops and mountainsides, along lakes and other bodies of water, and even in cemeteries. When celebrated in the cemetery, a tradition among southern black Christians, for example, the Easter sunrise service includes the events of Christ's passion and death as well as his resurrection, since these churches do not observe the rites of Holy Week. In many southern towns and cities the sunrise service is an ecumenical (or interchurch) affair in addition to the regularly scheduled worship held later by each congregation. People bring along flashlights, blankets, and lawn chairs to such services. Local political or community leaders often take leading roles in the worship, while the choirs from the various churches try to outdo one another. The order of service includes hymns (nearly always "Christ the Lord Is Risen Today"), scripture readings, psalms, and prayers, all of which is often followed by a much anticipated pancake breakfast.

The community pancake breakfast is but one indication of the family-oriented quality of Protestant Easter Sunday (indeed, southern Christians consider the main holidays to be Christmas, Easter, and Mother's Day). After the late morning regular church services, families go to grandmothers' or other matriarchal homes for generously prepared dinners, often featuring lamb or pork. An Easter egg hunt usually takes place for the children out in the yard. The child who finds the most eggs wins a prize or, in another variation, the eggs have other treats attached to them. Easter baskets full of candy and featuring a chocolate bunny might also be hidden for each child in the home, with parents telling the

A little girl picks up an egg during an Easter egg hunt. Courtesy of Getty Images / PhotoDisc.

little ones that the Easter bunny brought the treats during the night. This is, in fact, a typical custom throughout America. The children's sermon at church often includes the story of how the bunny was in the garden where Jesus was entombed and became the first to witness his resurrection.

Protestant churches do not have special rites for Easter but, rather, on that Sunday morning the worship is of a higher or more intense quality. The first evidence for this is the attire of the congregants, including new outfits and shoes and often featuring hats. The scripture readings may include a conflating of the passion and resurrection stories from all four gospels into one continuous, lengthy narrative. Music, a key feature in Protestant worship, includes such favorite hymns as "Lord of the Dance," "Lo! In the Grave He Lay," "He Lives," "Come to Jesus Just Now," and "I Come to the Garden Alone." A children's choir often performs, while the adult choir offers special anthems. Flowers adorn the pulpit and communion table. In southern black churches mums are the special bloom for Easter. African American worship, which features passionate preaching and a call-and-response pattern, rocks with even greater participation through shouts and song, including spirituals and hymns that bear emotions and convey the church's spirituality. A notable ritual difference for this day in Baptist churches, nonetheless, is the omission of the usual Sunday evening service, unless they gather for a reading of Luke's account of Jesus's walk with two disconsolate disciples on the day of his resurrection, for which the climax is their recognizing him in the breaking of the bread at the evening meal.

American Protestant worship, however, is not devoid of commemorations on various days of Holy Week. Palm Sunday is observed in even the most liturgically minimalist of denominations, if only by the reading of one of the gospel accounts of Jesus's fateful entrance into Jerusalem. Many churches across the country observe Good Friday with a service of the Seven Last Words either during the afternoon (three o'clock is the traditionally held hour of Jesus's death) or the evening. The ceremony is a collection of the gospel accounts of what Jesus said as he hung on the cross, which totals seven different statements. These are read successively, accompanied by preaching, hymns, and prayers. Interestingly, the historical origins of this service lie in Lima, Peru, where a Jesuit priest in the eighteenth century created the Three Hours Devotion (Tre Ore). The practice quickly spread through Latin America and back to Spain, Portugal, and Italy, whence it was later exported to the United States. In recent decades Protestant churches engaged in the liturgical and ecumenical movements have begun celebrating, to varying degrees, services on Ash Wednesday, Holy Thursday, Good Friday, and even Easter Vigils on Saturday evening. Leaders in these movements are taken with the ancient historical roots of the rites for the various days, an interest that has converged with an increased desire for ritual among some Baptists and other churches that focus more exclusively on biblical proclamation. In contrast, there are others who have taken a stand against these recent explorations in liturgy, arguing that Protestant worship is characterized by Sunday services alone.

The rapidly growing Hispanic/Latino population in the United States is bridging the Protestant-Catholic divide. Immigrants from Mexico, and Central and South America bring a tradition of Roman Catholicism characterized by close communal bonds, ritual hospitality, home-based piety, and affectionate interpersonal relationships. This enculturation of Christianity has collided with the more clerically dominated and privatized Catholicism widely typical of American parishes. One outcome has been an increasing attraction of Hispanic/Latino believers to Pentecostal and other locally founded Protestant churches, where they enjoy personal support, participatory worship full of biblical proclamation and accessible song, and preaching that engages the joys and struggles of their lives. This adoption of Protestant worship, however, has not come at the price of their culturally based Christian practices, including the full range of domestic and communal Easter customs that are their Latin heritage—what religious scholars call "popular religion." Not surprisingly, on the other hand, Hispanics/Latinos in the United States have stayed with the Roman Catholic Church in parishes where their experience of God as interpersonal companionship with Jesus (and his mother Mary) is given full range of communal and liturgical expression. This is most powerfully evident in Hispanic/Latino Catholic celebrations of Holy Week and Easter.

Good Friday is the ritual center of the Hispanic/Latino observance of Easter. Believers' deep personal identification with Jesus comes to powerful expression beginning on Holy Thursday night, especially as the liturgy shifts from the Mass of the Lord's Supper to the reposing of the Blessed Sacrament for ongoing nocturnal adoration and prayer. The people experience this moment as being with Jesus for his agony in the Garden of Gethsemane in the hours leading to his arrest. The ritual of Good Friday often entails a live enactment of the Stations of the Cross, a series of 14 scenes (based on details from the four gospels and other folkloric traditions) depicting Jesus' condemnation, torture, bearing of his cross to the execution site of Calvary, and death. Whether done with costumed actors playing the parts of Jesus, the Roman officials and soldiers, Mary, and the other women and men disciples or, alternatively, using statues or other artistic depictions of the scenes, this procession-based ritual is not play-acting but, rather, a performed communal meditation on God's love that draws many to tears. Later on Good Friday the liturgy includes people's processing forward to kiss the feet of a large crucifix and, in some parishes, a further service of meditation, shared prayer, and song before a statue of Mary holding the body of her dead son. These rituals, along with other processions on Palm Sunday morning and Holy Saturday night, are for the Hispanic/Latino faithful present-tense experiences integrating their life-stories with the master narrative of their communal religious heritage.

While Hispanic/Latino Catholicism continues to preserve medieval-rooted customs of popular processions, biblical dramas, and personal devotions, it is part of a wider American Roman Catholic Church 40 years into a liturgical reform mandated by the world's bishops at the Second Vatican Council (1962–65). Although often misconceived merely as a process of modernizing the faith, this fundamental overhaul in Catholic worship is actually based on more than a century of research into the earliest centuries of Christian liturgy in an effort to reform its practice today. The goal is a renewal of active participation in the liturgy by the lay people along with the clergy, enabled by the use of local language (rather than Latin), ritual simplification (through the elimination of centuries of excess symbolic accumulation), restoration of the fundamental role of biblical readings and preaching in all the rites, and a primary theological return to understanding all liturgy as believers sharing in the mystery of Christ's death and resurrection (the paschal mystery). A fundamental impact this reform has had on the Church calendar has been the renewal of the Easter Vigil as the most important liturgy of the year.

Even if American Catholics still assist at Christmas Eve and Easter morning Masses in numbers that far outpace attendance at the Easter Vigil, the Vigil is nonetheless the ritual-theological key to the reform and renewal of the entire Lenten and Easter Seasons. This is due to the recovery of Christian initiation— baptism, along with confirmation and the Eucharist—as the sacramental heart and soul of the Vigil. Drawing heavily upon fourth-century C.E. liturgical sources, the Rite of Christian Initiation of Adults (RCIA) is a months-long (or even years-long) process of guiding converts into the Catholic faith through stages of inquiry and formation marked by pastorally attuned rituals. Lent has thus become, once again, a season of purification and enlightenment for those to be baptized at Easter, with these neophytes functioning as sacramental (visible, bodily) reminders to all of their own baptisms. The prayer, fasting, and almsgiving of Lent thus recovers its communal dimension as solidarity with those soon to be baptized, as well as with those who are repenting of their failure to keep their baptismal commitments. The third, fourth, and fifth Sundays of Lent include rituals of self-scrutiny for the neophytes in light of special gospel readings. Holy Saturday includes a session at which they recite the creed and Lord's Prayer they were given to learn at the beginning of Lent, while they and their sponsors and other ministers keep a fast for the approaching climactic Easter Vigil that night.

The Vigil, which once again moves through the four stages developed in the fourth century (see above), is at once solemn and joyous, formal and informal. The recovery of baptism as the total soaking of neophytes by either submersion or pouring in a baptismal pool (which can be either a permanent or temporary fixture in the church) changes the entire feel of the Easter celebration from one of keeping new hats and clothes pressed and proper to neophytes having to change from sopping garments into white robes, only to have their heads rubbed with consecrated olive oil. Thus do they move into the sanctuary for the celebration of the Eucharist, even as the presiding priest moves through the church sprinkling the entire congregation, who vocally renew their baptismal profession. The cumulative ritual effect is a night of bonding with one another in the crucified and risen Christ.

Easter Sunday morning Masses in American Catholic parishes, on the other hand, continue to be scripted more according to the cultural conventions of less frequent (often semiannual) church goers, sporting new springtime attire and bonding with family members (rather than with a wider faith community). American Catholics celebrate dinners, hunt for Easter eggs, enjoy chocolate and other candy, and take strolls as much as their Protestant and Episcopalian counterparts across the country. The severity of Lenten fasting customs followed by many Catholics prior to the Second Vatican Council have given way to just two fast days, Ash Wednesday and Good Friday, along with abstaining from meat on all Fridays of the season. Even these regulations are loosely interpreted, if not widely ignored. Ash Wednesday and Palm Sunday remain popular occasions for Roman Catholics to turn out for services, while the Stations of the Cross are a weekly Friday practice that has largely fallen off. Communal penance services held sometime during the latter weeks of Lent have become a popular means for parishioners to assemble for the Sacrament of Reconciliation, replacing earlier lines of Catholics outside confessional booths, where they spoke their sins to a priest through screened walls. The communal and family dimensions of the faith are evident in the 50-day Easter season, as well, with first communions being held for children who had been baptized as infants, sacramental confirmation being conferred on teens, and each Sunday Mass opening with sprinkling rites to celebrate the baptismal calling of all.

AMERICAN EASTER IN THE NEW MILLENNIUM

As the United States continues to receive new immigrants from Africa, Asia, and the Pacific Rim, Christians from those countries are bringing further variations to the common religious themes for Easter. Their religious heritages bear both the influence of the particular European missionaries who came to their countries and the subsequent histories of the enculturation of Christianity in each locale, generating distinct customs of food, decoration, music, and dance. The French brought Catholicism to Vietnam, for example, while the Presbyterian and Methodist churches took hold in Korea. Filipino Catholicism exudes many characteristics of Portuguese piety, while great numbers in the southern countries of Africa belong to the worldwide Anglican Communion. Recently revised hymnals in many American Christian denominations contain selections from these various cultures. Such beautiful folk songs from Ghana as "Jesu, Jesu" and "Christ the Lord Has Risen" are making their way into the Holy Thursday and Easter Sunday repertoires of American churches, to cite but one example.

Easter, of course, continues to function as a holiday in wider American society, as well, exerting various degrees of influence in the economic, cultural, and political spheres and even sparking occasional controversy. Concert halls host performances of not only the Bach *Passion*s but also the *Requiem*s of Duruflé, Fauré, and other great composers, while in such cities as Atlanta highly sophisticated live productions of the Passion Play attract large crowds to theaters. As department chain stores run promotions for new clothing at Easter, advertisements for exquisite gold and diamond-studded crosses grace the pages of magazines and front sections of newspapers. The New York Stock Exchange closes for Good Friday. On the Saturday of Easter Weekend the president and first lady host children for an Easter egg rolling party on the South Lawn of the White House. Resorts such as Walt Disney World offer special events to attract Easter

Children and adults on the White House lawn during the annual White House Easter egg roll, 1923. Courtesy of the Library of Congress.

vacationers, and increasing numbers of better-off Americans take cruises during the holiday, often with chaplains on board.

Mediating such significant religious and social power, Easter not surprisingly prompts practices that become contested at times. Recently a national candy company mass-produced chocolate crosses, targeting the market of Hispanic Christians, for whom such confections are familiar in both Latin America and Europe. Some Anglo-Christian clergy, however, protested in the press that the product was offensive. Tensions exist within churches, as well. Over the past decade the Roman Catholic ritual practice of washing feet during the Holy Thursday Mass (in imitation of Jesus doing so for his disciples at the Last Supper) has become controversial in some American dioceses. Many bishops insist that only the ordained celebrant at the liturgy should wash feet and, furthermore, that the recipients should be exclusively male. The symbolism is an identification of the priest with Jesus and the disciples with men alone, a strong statement about leadership and participation in the Roman Catholic Church not lost on those, especially women, seeking further church reform.

Over the years such weeklies as *Time, Newsweek,* and the *New York Times Magazine* have annually featured cover stories on Christianity at Easter time.

These often concern the current biblical, historical, and theological state of the question about some aspect of Jesus: his life, mission, death, or resurrection. The stories and sidebars seek to raise interest among the readership by exposing them to scholarly and religious debates about the origins of Christianity. Such questions, of course, are just as much about the present and future course of the Christian religion in America—significant indication that Easter will continue as a vibrant holiday on the American calendar.

FURTHER READING

Costen, Melva. *African American Christian Worship*. Nashville, Tenn.: Abingdon Press 1993.

Goizueta, Roberto. *Caminemos con Jesús: Toward a Hispanic/Latino Theology of Accompaniment*. Maryknoll, N.Y.: Orbis Books, 1995.

Nardone, Richard. *The Story of the Christian Year*. New York: Paulist Press, 1991.

Schmidt, Leigh Eric. "The Easter Parade: Piety, Fashion, and Display." *Religion and American Culture* 4 (Summer 1994): 135–64.

Weiser, Francis X. *Handbook of Christian Feasts and Customs: The Year of the Lord in Liturgy and Folklore*. New York: Harcourt, Brace and World, 1952.

Bruce T. Morrill

VE DAY AND VJ DAY

Victory in Europe Day and Victory over Japan Day are two "holidays" that either failed to take root in the United States or fell victim to the Cold War and the threat of nuclear war. For Europeans the victory over the Axis nations was tremendously significant, but VE Day never had a firm footing in the United States. While VE Day has been largely forgotten in America, it is still celebrated in Europe, especially Russia, which suffered so terribly. On the other hand, in the United States VJ Day as "Victory Day" persisted, but in a diminishing fashion until only Rhode Island marks it as a state holiday called "Victory Day." During the Cold War old enemies became allies, and it seemed inappropriate to continue to celebrate the defeat of either Germany or Japan. More than that, the remembrance of VJ Day increasingly became entangled in atomic and nuclear-bomb politics, and the United States was put on the defensive for having been the only nation to have used the bomb, regardless of its justification. Furthermore, as the issue of racial oppression became an international concern, the unfinished business of cleansing the United States of its own racial failures gained greater significance. The continuation of the "Double V" campaign of African Americans after the war meant that, for them, the war was not over. VE Day and VJ Day did not have the same meaning to African Americans who pledged to fight the Double V campaign.

THE PROBLEM OF DATING THE END OF THE WAR

European nations erupted with relief and joy at the surrender of the Nazis in May 1945, after nearly six years of devastation and carnage, but the United

VE DAY AND VJ DAY

- VE and VJ Days commemorate the end of fighting in Europe (Victory in Europe) and with Japan (Victory over Japan). More broadly they commemorate American participation and triumph in World War II (1941–45).

- Victory in Europe Day is, or more to the point was, celebrated on May 9.

- Victory over Japan Day is marked on either August 14, the day Japan announced surrender, or September 2, the day Japan formally signed surrender papers.

- President Harry S. Truman in 1946 declared August 14 "Victory Day," but Victory Day is legally observed only in Rhode Island.

- The Cold War and quick rehabilitation of Germany and Japan as U.S. allies undercut the triumphalism of VE and VJ Days.

- The atomic bombing of Japan by the United States to end the war injected moral ambivalence into the days as well, an issue that was used by Cold War foes and domestic critics of U.S. involvement in the Vietnam War.

- Continued segregation and racism in the United States during and after World War II brought lingering criticism from the African American community, bringing further moral ambivalence to World War II victory celebrations.

States allowed itself only a temporary celebration. The sense of victory was tempered by the fact that Japan remained to be defeated. The war against Japan was principally an American undertaking, and a bloody invasion of the Japanese homeland loomed for the fall of 1945. What the toll might be was hammered home in the savage battles of Iwo Jima and Okinawa. The Battle of Iwo Jima (February 19 to March 26, 1945) had been won at a cost of 6,821 Americans killed, 19,217 wounded, and 2,648 removed because of "combat fatigue." Of the Japanese garrison of over 21,000 only 1,082 were taken prisoner.

At the very moment that Germany surrendered, the battle of Okinawa was raging. This battle (April 1 to June 29, 1945) took more lives than the atomic bombs dropped later on Hiroshima and Nagasaki. The ground invasion began on April 1, 1945, but kamikaze planes starting attacking the assembled American fleet as early as March 18. By the time the battle was over, more than 12,000 U.S. service personnel had been killed and 36,000 wounded. In addition, U.S. forces suffered another 26,000 "battle fatigue" casualties. More than 20 percent of all American naval deaths in the entire war were inflicted by the Japanese kamikaze attacks, which sank 36 ships and damaged 368 others. Japanese losses were staggering: at least 131,000 military personnel were killed along with an estimated 142,000 civilians—one third of Okinawa's civilian population. The carnage made the American military and public believe that a terrible price was yet to be paid in the Pacific, even if the European conflict was over. Many of the troops in Europe knew that they were headed for the Pacific theater. Consequently, VE Day never meant as much to Americans as it did to Europeans.

What day should be celebrated as VE Day? While the Western nations mark May 8, Russia and former Soviet states celebrate May 9. German General Alfred Jodl signed surrender papers in the wee hours of May 7 in Reims, France, for the Americans, British, and French. The fighting was to cease on May 8. General Dwight Eisenhower insisted that the surrender had to include the Soviet Union, and the Allies intended to announce the surrender at a formal ceremony on May 9. However, Western journalists began to leak the news of the surrender, so the United States and Britain declared the victory on May 8. The Soviet Union would not recognize the end of the war until the formal signing on May 9. Moreover, some fighting occurred on May 9 between German and Soviet troops in Czechoslovakia. Consequently, even to the present time VE Day is celebrated on different days in Western and Eastern Europe.

There is also some confusion about what day is VJ Day. Is it August 14, or is it September 2? August 14 certainly is most remembered because the Japanese announced their surrender that day, but the official surrender ceremony took place on September 2, 1945 on the deck of the battleship USS *Missouri*. These different dates led to some early disagreement. In an effort to establish a single day to encompass the entire war, in 1946 President Harry S. Truman designated August 14 as "Victory Day." Truman's proclamation noted that August 14, 1945 had "terminated a conflict world-wide in scope and freed the people of

The Japanese sign a surrender, bringing the end to World War II. © Brown Brothers.

the world from the threat of enslavement of body and spirit." As such, Victory Day could commemorate the defeat of both Japan and Germany, but it never became a national holiday. A bill introduced in the House of Representatives in March 1947 to make August 14 a national holiday went nowhere. On March 9, 1948 Rhode Island became the first state to make "Victory Day" a legal state holiday; however, Governor Thomas Dewey of New York proclaimed September 2 as VJ Day. Dewey did the same thing the next year, but various towns even in New York celebrated either in August or September. In 1949 Arkansas became the second state to make August 14 a state holiday called "World War

II Memorial Day." Sidney McMath, a World War II veteran, was the governor, and considerable anti-Japanese feeling lingered in Arkansas, which had been the site of two large relocation camps for Japanese Americans during the war. Some other states considered making Victory Day a state holiday, but by 1949 and 1950 the world situation had made the celebration of the end of World War II seem problematic.

POSTWAR OBSTACLES

The almost immediate onset of the Cold War and the lack of peace in so much of the world caused the *New York Times* in 1949 to editorialize, "We knew, then, that the war was over. Today, four years later, we are not so sure." It cited the problems in Korea, China, India and Pakistan, and Indonesia. Furthermore, to an astonishing degree, the bitterness toward the Japanese melted in response to the rapid "Americanization" of Japan during the occupation. Within the first year the national news media were filled with glowing reports of the reforms in, and progress of, Japan. Because hundreds of American GIs wanted to marry Japanese women during the occupation, in 1947 Congress passed the Soldier Brides Act, which waived the racial exclusion of such brides. Under the 1924 National Origins Act, Asians were completely excluded from immigration and naturalization, but this 1947 act opened the door somewhat, signaling improvement in Japanese-American relations. When, in February 1950, 14 members of the Japanese Diet visited Boston, they were warmly welcomed in the state senate and were present when the Massachusetts Senate rejected a bill to make August 14 a legal holiday. They were also heartily applauded in the Massachusetts House of Representatives. In 1955 Arkansas revised its state holiday list and dropped August 14, leaving only Rhode Island with Victory Day as a legal holiday despite repeated efforts to rename or abolish it.

As the world became increasingly concerned about nuclear weapons, the fact that the United States had used the atomic bomb to end the war with Japan placed a special moral burden on the nation. Indeed, the threat of nuclear war shifted the attention from VJ Day to the day that the atomic bomb fell on Hiroshima, August 6. Increasingly, remembering the day the bomb fell overshadowed the end of the war itself. After the Soviet Union signed a treaty with Japan officially ending the war in 1956, Communist bloc nations joined the commemoration of the bombing of Hiroshima in order to embarrass the United States and to score diplomatic points in the Cold War. Over time, Japan emerged as a victim of the war, not the aggressor.

THE CONTESTED MEMORY OF WORLD WAR II

In the 1960s, opponents of the Vietnam War marked the atomic bomb day as a day of protest. When President Lyndon Johnson's daughter Luci was

The famous kiss in Times Square as New York City celebrates the end of World War II, August 14, 1945. © AP / Wide World Photos.

married on August 6, 1966, antiwar groups denounced him, saying that he had scheduled the wedding in order to divert attention from Hiroshima day and the Vietnam War. The Congress of Racial Equality called it "the worst possible taste" to schedule the wedding that day, and antiwar protestors picketed the church where Luci was married. By 1969 the significance of August 6 had totally overpowered August 14 as services were held at the Cathedral of St. John the Divine in New York City to remember the dead at Hiroshima, but nothing was done to commemorate Victory Day. The following year, on the 25th

The crew of the Enola Gay pose in front of the World War II airplane. © AP / Wide World Photos.

anniversary of the dropping of the bomb, great antiwar and peace rallies were held across the nation, and memorial services were held in New York at the Roman Catholic Church of St. Paul the Apostle. On August 15, a tiny item on page 10 of the *New York Times* reported that VJ Day was observed in Fall River, Massachusetts, the day before.

Of course, local commemorations always occurred here and there across the nation, including one Colorado town that marked VJ Day for over 25 years with a parade. Since the end of World War II a host of commemorations of wartime events have been held and various memorials and monuments have been erected, such as the Iwo Jima monument. Various World War II ships float in harbors as monuments and museums, including the USS *Massachusetts* at Fall River, Massachusetts, the USS *Enterprise* at Patriots Point Naval Museum at Mount Pleasant, South Carolina, and the USS *Missouri* at Pearl Harbor, Hawaii. The attack at Pearl Harbor (December 7) is always observed, and D-Day (June 6) celebrations occurred often, especially on special anniversary years, such as the 25th, 40th, 50th, or 60th. But no day has been set aside

The utter destruction of Hiroshima after the atomic bomb, 1945. Courtesy of the Library of Congress.

to mark the victory in the war, and construction of the National World War II Memorial was not begun until 2001.

In 1995, for the 50th anniversary of VJ Day, the United States planned to issue a commemorative stamp that depicted the Enola Gay and a mushroom cloud rising over Hiroshima, but it was withdrawn out of sensitivity to Japanese opinion. The Smithsonian's exhibit of the B-29 Enola Gay itself turned into a nasty battle over conflicting interpretations with the result that the plane was shown without much explanation and the museum's director was forced to resign. Veterans' groups were outraged that the interpretation that was first proposed focused on the suffering of the Japanese without emphasizing the horrors of Japanese expansionism and atrocities. A Smithsonian official summed up the clash of interpretations: "The veterans want the exhibit to stop when the doors to the bomb bay opened. And that's where the Japanese want it to begin."

The clarity of the war was clouded by historical revisionism that developed especially in the 1960s. Since 1945, the defenders of the decision to annihilate Hiroshima and Nagasaki claimed that the bombs were dropped to save

American lives that would to be lost in the planned invasion of the home islands. Revisionists came to argue that the atomic bomb was not needed to end the war but was dropped to impress the Soviet Union in the postwar world. Others argued that using the atomic bomb was an act of racism, that it would not have been dropped on Germany. Another argument was that the bomb was dropped to justify the expenditure of the billions to create it. All of these revisionist themes undermined support for Victory Day and made the nation more sensitive to Japanese protests about the day. Every commemoration raised the atomic-bomb issue, shifting the argument from why there was a war to whether the bomb should have dropped. Each observance highlighted the fact that United States was the only country to use an atomic weapon in war, which created a sense of guilt about a war that seemed morally right in all other respects.

AFRICAN AMERICAN MEMORIES OF SERVICE

A contributing cause of the decline and fall of VJ Day was the fact that many in the African American community viewed World War II differently from much of the rest of the country. They remembered that World War I had ended with no progress toward recognition of their rights. That war had been followed by race riots in the "red summer" of 1919 and many individual lynchings. They were determined that this would not be repeated after World War II.

As the United States began gearing up for war in 1941, African American leaders pressed for equal treatment. The March on Washington Movement pressured President Franklin Roosevelt into issuing Executive Order #8802 on June 25, prohibiting discrimination in defense industries and government agencies and creating the wartime Fair Employment Practices Commission. On February 7, 1942, the *Pittsburgh Courier* began its "Double V for Victory" campaign, which soon spread through the black newspapers. The *Courier* called for "victory over our enemies at home and victory over our enemies on the battlefields abroad." In November 1942 the poet Alaine Locke wrote that the nation's treatment of black Americans was "now a touchstone the world over of our democratic integrity." The March on Washington Movement used the symbolism of the Double V in its continuing efforts to achieve equal rights.

The Double V ideal energized African Americans to keep up the pressure at home as the war went on abroad. Many whites resisted such changes, and racial tensions exploded in Detroit on June 20, 1943, leaving 34 dead. Then, when the war ended, African Americans faced a wave of repression and killings. At least 60 black southerners were violently killed from the end of the summer of 1945 to the end of 1946. Victory over the enemies abroad had been achieved; victory over the enemies at home was yet to be won. Victory in war did not have the same exhilarating sense to Americans who faced discrimination, segregation, and inequality in the United States.

The issue of racial discrimination became a weapon in the Cold War, and the United States was put on the defensive all through the 1950s and 1960s because of its manifest racial problems. Even the dropping of the atomic bomb on a nonwhite people was used against the United States. It was touted as additional proof of the racism of the nation. As the bombing of Hiroshima overshadowed the end of the war, the issue of race was emphasized by some opponents.

VICTORY DAY IN RHODE ISLAND

The tenacity of Rhode Island in celebrating August 14 deserves special attention for its interplay of state, local, national, and even international politics in the formation of commemorative days. In the first place, the influence of veterans, especially naval veterans, is unusually high. During World War II, Rhode Island had Navy and Seabee facilities for hundreds of thousands of men, many of whom served in the Pacific theater. A considerable number of these later retired in the state. Rhode Island residents suffered a proportionally larger number of war deaths than nearly any other state. The veteran influence pushed to make a legal holiday of Victory Day, and veterans' organizations have adamantly opposed any attempt to demote the day, even to change the name. In addition, Rhode Island is a strong labor union state, and once the holiday became part of labor contracts, it became extremely difficult to get rid of a paid holiday. (In Arkansas unions were far weaker and less influential, and state employees dropped their opposition to eliminating the holiday when they were promised an alternative paid holiday.)

Celebrated as "Victory Day" on August 14 since 1948, the observance of the day in Rhode Island was switched to the second Monday of August, beginning in 1987, but every effort to drop the holiday or to rename it has been resoundingly defeated. Indeed, defenders of the day reinforced it by passing legislation that forbids it being called by any other name than "Victory Day" by any government agency or department and requiring that employees who must work on the day be paid time-and-a-half or be given an alternative paid holiday.

Opponents of Victory Day argued that it was racist, unfairly stigmatized the Japanese, kindled anti-Asian feeling, and impeded investment by Japanese concerns in the state. Although the official name has always been "Victory Day," it was commonly called "VJ Day" by the public and in newspaper advertisements for "VJ Day" sales. The Greater Providence Chamber of Commerce argued that, because Rhode Island was out of step with its neighboring states (and the federal government), production and sales were lost in Rhode Island on what was a regular business day everywhere else. State Representative Elizabeth Morancy, one of four Catholic Sisters of Mercy in the nation who left her religious order rather than drop out of politics, introduced a bill in 1985 to rename the day to "World Peace Day." Her bill passed the House Committee on Labor but was rejected 63–20 by the full House. During the hearings on the bill, Morancy was denounced as a "traitor" and as a "Communist" by opponents. The following year her bill failed even to get out of committee. In 1989 Representative Linda Kushner, representing a liberal East Side district in Providence, submitted a bill to rename the day as "Remembrance Day." Heated and bitter hearings were held, and the bill died in committee. Opponents of these changes even proposed that the name should revert to "Victory over Japan Day." Seeing that it was hopeless to try to change the name to something that left out the veterans, in 1992 State Senator Rhoda E. Perry from the East Side and Representative Paul W. Crowley of Newport offered a bill to change the name to "Rhode Island Veterans Day." Governor Bruce Sundlun publicly supported their proposal. The bill made it to the House floor, but the House voted overwhelmingly (82–9) to recommit the bill to committee, killing it for 1992. The attitude of opponents to the name change might be summed up by the comment of Representative David W. Dumas from East Greenwich who said, "If our friends in Japan are upset, all I can say is: 'Deal with it.' We won that war."

The effort to change the name to "Rhode Island Veterans Day" continued each legislative session until 1995, and another bill by Representative Sandra Barone and Senator Charles Walton, the only African American elected as a Rhode Island state senator, to rename the day "Peace and Remembrance Day" was likewise utterly rejected. Both bills were unanimously defeated by the legislative committees after impassioned and harrowing testimony by aging World War II veterans. Afterward, Representative Barone said that renaming Victory Day was a dead issue as far as she was concerned. And so it was: no bill to change the name has been introduced since 1995.

In fact, the official name of Victory Day was cemented more firmly by a measure adopted in 1999 that prohibited Victory Day from being called anything else. This step was taken largely because the name and meaning of Victory Day had begun to be obscured when Governor Edward DiPrete initiated the practice of calling the second Monday in August "Governor's Bay Day," when state beach parking fees were lifted for the day. DiPrete proclaimed this in 1989 to attract tourists to Rhode Island's beaches after the oil tanker *World Prodigy* went aground in the spring, spilling millions of gallons into Narragansett Bay. The operative feature of DiPrete's move was free admission to the state parks and beaches because the governor had the power to waive fees only on holidays. Victory Day 1989 was the first available holiday after the *World Prodigy* oil spill. Veterans were angered at this, saying that Bay Day took attention from Victory Day, and eventually, Governor Lincoln Almond changed Bay Day to July 31 in 1999. The defenders of Victory Day introduced legislation in 1997 to prohibit "any state or local government or agency of government from referring to 'Victory Day' by any other name." Not enacted in 1997, this became law in 1999 when it passed the House 78–4.

Finally, the intensified attention in the rapidly diminishing generation of World War II veterans (as symbolized in recent popular film and literature) shifted public focus on the war to the sacrifice of the military personnel and quieted opponents of the war commemoration. After the attack of September 11, 2001 and the start of the Afghan and Iraq wars, it became political suicide to oppose celebrating World War II veterans.

A STILLBORN HOLIDAY

With the exception of Martin Luther King Jr. Day, most American holidays generally have had to serve a long apprenticeship before gaining national recognition. Even the meaning of an obvious holiday like the Fourth of July has been contested and developed slowly. Part of the fate of Victory Day lay in the fact that it had no time to get rooted before being overtaken by other wars and concerns. Armistice Day had nearly two decades of observance before World War II began, but its meaning was almost lost in the new global conflagration. The veterans managed to rescue it in some fashion in the 1960s and 1970s, but its new name, Veterans Day, has detached it from its origin. Victory Day never had sufficient time to develop before the Cold War, Korean War, and Vietnam War made it seem pointless. It is noteworthy that 59 years after the war ended the World War II Memorial in Washington, D.C. was dedicated on Memorial Day, 2004, not August 14. (On the other hand, Rhode Island dedicated its new World War II memorial on August 14, 2004, VJ Day.) Victory Day / VJ Day has been nearly eclipsed. It was buried in world affairs, in other wars, in the fear of nuclear war, and in the international concern about racism. Most of all victory over Japan did not usher in a season of peace to the United States; instead, the means employed to end the war came to overshadow Victory Day.

J. Stanley Lemons

EARTH DAY

Although not an official national holiday, Earth Day is an annual event in which Americans acknowledge both the threat to the world's natural environment and the need for perpetual protection. The first Earth Day on April 22, 1970 constituted one of the largest demonstrations in American history and symbolized the potency of a new environmental movement concerned not just with wise-use conservation but overall environmental quality. The new environmentalists recognized that the unrestrained urbanization and industrialization characteristic of the nation's post–World War II economic boom mandated more than merely the judicious utilization of natural resources. Expanding upon the tradition of Progressive-era preservationists, they sought protection for the intrinsic condition of the world's air, water, and land. They viewed the world as an ecosystem with humans only a part, a part that nevertheless threatened the whole. In the more than three decades since the first Earth Day, America has responded with significant legislation, institutionalizing environmental protection as a central responsibility of our federal and state governments. While these restrictions have improved the environment, they have also engendered public complacency, many Americans no longer sensing an imminent threat. New environmental laws have also spawned a backlash from industry chafing under restrictions it perceives as onerous, ideological conservatives, and others who believe environmental protection and economic growth mutually exclusive. In recent years, therefore, Earth Day celebrations have been much more subdued. In the end, the story of Earth Day reflects the maturation of the environmental movement and the ebb and flow of American environmentalism.

EARTH DAY

- [ ] Earth Day is not, and has never been, recognized by the United States federal government as an official holiday.

- [ ] Post–World War II economic growth and the spread of suburbia intensified popular appreciation of nature and environmental conservation while quickening the pace of environmental degradation, leading to a groundswell in environmental activism in the 1960s and 1970s.

- [ ] The first Earth Day celebration/demonstration in America occurred on April 22, 1970, as environmental activists sought protection for the intrinsic condition of the world's air, water and land.

- [ ] In 1971, United Nations Secretary-General U Thant declared March 21 the official U.N. Earth Day.

- [ ] Earth Day celebrations had become a truly global phenomenon by 2000, when 5,000 environmental groups in 184 countries marked the event.

EARTH DAY 1970

The first Earth Day drew an estimated 20 million participants and involved over 10,000 schools and 2,000 colleges and universities. It was an odd gathering of businesspeople, housewives, college students, children, workers, and radical antiestablishment militants. Indeed, the amazing turnout represented every strata of American society. In New York, over 100,000 people participated in festivities in Union Square. In Washington, thousands gathered on the Mall. In cities from Philadelphia to Los Angeles, a citizenry often divided over issues such as the Vietnam War, racial desegregation, and the economy united in an event part celebration and part earnest protest. The sheer size of the turnout ensured significant media coverage, but the demonstrators themselves occasionally devised tactics to seize headlines. At the University of Minnesota, members of the "Students for Environmental Defense" conducted a mock funeral service for the internal combustion engine, lowering an engine into a coffin buried in downtown Minneapolis. A New Jersey housewife spent weeks sewing red banners with black skulls and crossbones, which she then placed on dredging equipment she believed sullied nearby beaches. Self-styled Yippies at Indiana University were more aggressive, plugging municipal sewage pipes with concrete, while their more orderly colleagues tossed birth control pills at the crowds. Protesters intended such actions to garner attention—and their efforts proved successful. All three major television networks devoted considerable coverage to the event, while the public broadcasting stations devoted all of their daytime programs to the protection of environmental quality. Only a handful of incidents nationally resulted in arrests—an amazing fact given the magnitude of the turnout. When protesters blocked access to part of Boston's Logan airport, police arrested 13. A young Florida man faced jail for violating a local sanitary code. His crime was protesting the thermal pollution of Biscayne Bay by showing up at a utility company's offices with a cart of decaying fish and a dead octopus.

Politicians, of course, noticed. Both houses of Congress adjourned for the day, allowing their members to participate in the various activities, invariably extolling their own interest in the matter. Politicians of every stripe, from liberal South Dakota senator George McGovern to conservative Arizona senator Barry Goldwater, found themselves in agreement—if only for a day. Federal officials were not the only ones rallying to the environmental bandwagon; state and local officials added their collective voice to the chorus of environmentalism. Massachusetts' legislature unanimously amended the state constitution to declare a pollution-free environment a constitutional right. The Albuquerque, New Mexico City Commission slashed public transportation fares to one cent for the day as an incentive to use mass transit and as a symbol of its support. Many of the promises and speeches proved banalities, but the importance of environmentalism as a political issue was hard to deny. Although with perhaps

More than 1,200 students assembled a five-story globe on the National Mall in Washington to mark the 35th anniversary of Earth Day, 2005. © Joyce Naltchayan / AFP / Getty Images.

a bit of hyperbole, *American Heritage Magazine* summed up the day succinctly. Earth Day, it claimed, was "one of the most remarkable happenings in the history of democracy."

SEEDS OF THE ENVIRONMENTAL MOVEMENT

The magnitude of the first Earth Day—the apparent breadth of public concern—surprised many observers, for the problems on which the demonstration focused had multiplied rather suddenly, paralleling the nation's rapid postwar economic growth. In the decade and a half after the conclusion of hostilities, the United States emerged as the "affluent society," in the words of Harvard economist John Kenneth Galbraith. By 1960, the nation's population had increased by 35 million, with the population growth rate approaching that of India. The census that year reported a population of 180 million, almost a 20 percent increase over the previous decade. The gross national product was $500 million, more than double the $200 million GNP in 1945. The median family income approached $5,700, an increase of almost 50 percent adjusted for inflation.

This growth had a tremendous impact on the way Americans regarded their environment. Rising standards of living allowed more recreational time as well as greater discretionary income. Americans had more time for qualitative experiences along with material necessities and thus had the means for a greater appreciation of environmental amenities. A host of new appliances appeared on the market—automatic washing machines and dryers, dishwashers, waste disposal units, power lawn mowers, and many others—all significantly reducing the time necessary for normal domestic chores. At the same time the average work week declined from 44 to almost 40 hours. The result was a boom in the recreation business. The making and servicing of pleasure boats, camping equipment, sporting goods, and hunting and fishing gear became multimillion-dollar businesses. Americans purchased almost four million pleasure boats in the 1950s alone. In short, they now had the opportunity to enjoy the outdoors as never before.

The growth of the automobile industry made a retreat to more natural surroundings much easier. From 1945 to 1960 the number of cars increased by 133 percent. Middle-class America now meant two cars, each successive model longer and wider, with more gadgets and bigger fins. The government did its share to facilitate easy access to nature, passing the massive Highway Act of 1956, which provided for 33 billion dollars to construct over 41,000 miles of new interstate roads. Vacations in the country were no longer the exclusive domain of the super-wealthy. Although few Americans yet saw the recreation business itself as a threat, most Americans now realized that the environment offered more than simply the extraction of natural resources.

America's phenomenal growth following World War II did more than stir a new-found appreciation of nature. It also noticeably began to affect overall environmental quality, to erode the very intrinsic value of nature Americans were just learning to appreciate. The expansion of the population and economy contributed to massive urbanization. The growth of suburbs characterized this urbanization and brought more than simply a comfortable lifestyle; it also brought unforeseen environmental consequences.

Suburbs were not new to America. Satellite communities had grown around American urban centers since the days of horse cars and trolleys. The new migration after World War II, however, dwarfed these earlier movements. Mass-produced and prefabricated, and best represented by the Levittown Community on Long Island, suburbs offered affordable homes away from the problems of inner cities. After 15 years of depression and war, America had a severe housing shortage. Together with the spread of the automobile, the new suburbs offered a solution. During the 1950s, suburbs grew six times faster than established cities, with a total of 18 million new suburbanites. By 1960, one-quarter of Americans lived in such suburban homes. Americans now spoke of a "megalopolis" to describe the miles of sprawling single-family homes that surrounded established urban centers.

The new suburbanite, however, faced a cruel paradox in his or her existence. Economic growth had made suburban life possible, but it also threatened the amenities he or she had sought in the first place. Landowners, real estate developers, financial institutions, and utility companies all fostered more intensive use of land. Local governments joined in with the hope of securing more tax revenue from higher land values. Two-lane roads became four-lane roads, utility poles replaced trees, and shopping centers replaced open fields. By 1960, over 2,000 shopping centers had sprung up in previously undeveloped land. Billboards, part of the growth of the advertising industry during the same period, soon blighted what natural beauty remained. Suburbia had become in many ways just like the urban areas from which it grew.

The nation's growth contributed to the deterioration of environmental quality in other ways. In many areas construction of waste treatment centers did not keep pace with the greater population density. This meant that many communities simply dumped raw sewage into nearby rivers and lakes, magnifying the problem of water pollution. The dumping of such sewage led to eutrophication, the overfertilization of water plants. The resulting algal growth blocked the sun from deeper plants, whose subsequent death and decay eliminated the remaining oxygen in the water. This ensured the death of any aquatic wildlife, including fish. In time, the water was devoid of all life, its ecosystem destroyed.

More people and more suburbs meant more waste, more trash. Municipal waste—residential, commercial, and institutional refuse—constituted millions of tons a year, the elimination of which composed a municipal expense that only education and roads surpassed. During the 1950s, Americans, with their appetite for automobiles, junked almost as many cars per year as they manufactured. Most communities disposed of their waste in city dumps, incinerators, or landfills. Open dumps contributed to disease, contaminating the surrounding air and the water tables, while municipal incinerators often lacked even the most rudimentary control equipment. Although they were the best alternative, sanitary landfills were the most expensive, and rarely did municipalities allocate adequate funds.

The greatest threat to the quality of the nation's air, however, was not municipal waste, but the growth of the automobile so crucial to the development of the suburban life. The internal combustion engine produced unhealthy levels of hydrocarbons, carbon monoxide, and nitrogen oxide vehicular-exhaust emissions. In certain urban areas on hot days the result was a grey, choking haze, air pollution that decreased visibility and irritated eyes. Residents in the rapidly growing community of Los Angeles soon coined a term for this nasty vapor—smog, an amalgam of smoke and fog—a term Americans throughout the country soon recognized and adopted.

The automobile was not the only culprit. The electric-power industry, together with other heavy industry, also contributed. America needed her heavy industry to construct suburbia, and it in turn needed its electricity; both saw

Dead fish on this beach are an alarming sign of global pollution.
Courtesy of Getty Images / PhotoDisc.

a significant increase in the 1950s. Most of these industries burned fossil fuels and in doing so contributed to the problem. The burning of oil, gas, and coal released particulate matter and sulfur oxide into the air. This produced an acrid yellow gas, especially from those plants burning high-sulfur coal. Many large industrial cities had reeked with this foul stench since the dawn of the Industrial Revolution, but in the postwar years the problem only compounded, much to the chagrin of the nearby populace.

This manifold threat to the nation's environmental quality—the complex problems facing America's air, water, and land in the postwar world—ensured a

Los Angeles has often been thought of as the city with the worst smog problem in the United States. Courtesy of Getty Images / PhotoDisc.

popular protest for adequate reform. It was not until the 1960s, however, that the problems worsened to the point that any significant national movement emerged, a movement that ultimately culminated in the first Earth Day in 1970. In 1962, a former researcher for U.S. Fish and Wildlife Service, Rachel Carson, published *Silent Spring*, a text that bemoaned the environmental impact of indiscriminate insecticide use but had ramifications far beyond the agricultural community. Carson shocked many Americans with her warning that the impetuous pace of human development threatened the natural world. Quickly a best seller, *Silent Spring* arguably opened the eyes of the American public to the problems that accompanied the prosperity of the postwar world. Carson's book found a receptive audience in the 1960s, an era rapidly evolving as one of the most rebellious, tumultuous decades in American history. Growing numbers of Americans, most notably many among the nation's youth, countered traditional assumptions by rallying against the evils they perceived in American life. The repression of African Americans and women, the apparent pointlessness of the war in Vietnam, the greed of large corporations, and the drudgery of the average middle-class existence—all increasingly galvanized the young into a potent cultural force that welcomed the basic tenets of the new environmentalism. For many, America needed fundamental change, with protection for environmental quality only one of many examples.

Biologist/author Rachel Carson examines a specimen in a jar by the ocean.
© Alfred Eisenstaedt / Time Life Pictures / Getty Images.

The growth of environmental organizations, both in terms of the number of organizations and the membership within each, reflected the nation's shifting attitudes. Prior to 1960 an average of only 3 new conservation groups per year appeared on the American scene. Throughout the remainder of the 1960s, the average was 18. The number of environmental journals and periodicals skyrocketed. Older conservation organizations, such as the National Audubon Society, the National Wildlife Federation, the Sierra Club, and the Izaak Walton League were slow to adapt to the new environmental awareness, and, when still advocating the wise-use doctrine or pressing for resource development, often found themselves at odds with the new environmentalism. Frequently focusing on specific, narrow interests such as national parks, their efforts failed to appreciate the diversity of the threat to environmental quality and thus capture a broader audience. Although relations were at times strained, most of the traditional organizations began to adapt their message and found that their membership rose. The Wilderness Society, for example, doubled its membership over the decade, while the Sierra Club and the National Audubon Society more than doubled theirs. "We cannot suitably quarrel with youth who seek a new direction," concluded the Wilderness Society.

POLITICS AND ACTIVISM

The potential of this grassroots environmentalism was evident from the start, its successes slowly building as the movement grew. By the 1960s, President Lyndon Johnson's Great Society witnessed the first significant legislation to address the problem of pollution. New laws to create air and water quality standards were revolutionary for their day, if not stringent enough to meet the growing problem. Laws to protect unspoiled wilderness from development, to create a permanent fund for the purchase of park land, to limit solid waste, and to create a wildlife-refuge system were critical steps in the evolution of federal environmental policy. Most notably, Johnson's Interior Department secretary, Stewart Udall, emerged a forceful champion of the natural world, in many respects challenging the dominant utilitarian biases of his predecessors. Perhaps even more apparent to the public was Johnson's wife, Lady Bird. Although many first ladies had adopted a pet cause, Lady Bird's was unique—the preservation of the country's natural beauty. Chairing a presidential commission and hosting a White House conference on the subject, Lady Bird helped pass legislation to limit roadside blight. Her real significance, however, lay in the example she set. The American people should, she insisted, care about their environment.

All of this was, however, only a foundation. The problems appeared to worsen still, simultaneously leading two individuals into activism who otherwise had little in common. Early in 1969, in the counterculture capital of San Francisco, John McConnell, a former writer and journalist with an interest in space, proposed to Peter Tamaras, head of the city's Board of Supervisors, that the city issue a proclamation that declared March 21 "Earth Day." This was the day of the Vernal Equinox, McConnell explained, the annual time when the sun crosses the equator, resulting in a 12-hour day and 12-hour night throughout the world. To McConnell, the day symbolized global equilibrium and thus constituted a great chance to publicize the need for harmony and balance between nature and humanity. San Francisco was the perfect location, he argued; its name came from St. Francis, the patron saint of ecology. Just as San Francisco accepted the proclamation, McConnell presented the idea of an Earth Day to a

November 1969, United Nations Conference on "Man and His Environment." There delegates warmly embraced the concept, ultimately agreeing to sponsor Earth Day celebrations.

By this time, however, another individual—one with more power and thus more ability to garner publicity—had begun his own efforts to organize a day of environmental awareness. In his Washington office, Wisconsin Democratic Senator Gaylord Nelson was a continent away and, arguably, in a different world. He shared McConnell's concerns, however, if not his mystical considerations. Nelson had sought for a way to rally more public support since the early 1960s when he convinced President John F. Kennedy to launch a five-day, 11-state "conservation tour." This September 1963 tour, however, did not garner the attention for which Nelson had hoped, leaving him searching for another vehicle. By the end of the decade, antiwar demonstrators routinely organized "teach-ins," public gatherings popular at many large universities. In such events, students boycotted classes to attend meetings, where activists led panel discussions, symposia, and lectures. A grassroots "environmental teach-in," Nelson assumed, might gain the necessary publicity. Nelson's goals were twofold. First, he recognized that the Johnson-era legislation was insufficient and that Congress would have to act soon. "I wanted to shake up the political establishment and force this issue further onto the national agenda," he confidently declared. While he did not openly acknowledge it, he also wanted to dissociate environmentalism from the New Left. He knew that it was critical to involve America's youth—to tap into their activism and idealism—but worried that too close an alliance with one group or one party might hamper progress. Environmental degradation, he believed, transcended political, cultural, social, economic, and geographic boundaries. At a conference in September 1969, Nelson unveiled his plans and invited everyone to participate.

The response was tremendous. After wire reports carried his announcement, telegraphs, telephone calls, and letters poured in from around the country. Two of Nelson's staff, John Heritage and Linda Billings, initially handled the arrangements from his Senate office. To ensure that the organization had sufficient bipartisan support, Nelson enlisted the aid of California Republican congressman Paul McCloskey as formal co-chair. After an article by reporter Gladwin Hill appeared in the November 30, 1969 edition of the *New York Times*, momentum gained but the necessary planning outstripped Nelson's resources. In January 1970, John Gardner, founder of the group Common Cause, provided temporary space for a Washington, D.C. headquarters. Nelson arranged for college students to volunteer in the office and selected Stanford University graduate and Harvard law student Denis Hayes as national coordinator. The date they selected for the first "national environmental teach-in," increasingly called Earth Day in spite of McConnell's efforts, was April 22, 1970.

Although only 25 years old, Hayes was an excellent choice. Ambitious and intelligent, Hayes recruited fellow activists from his alma mater. With Nelson's

Dennis Hayes, head of Environment Teach-In, Inc., the Washington organization coordinating activities for Earth Day is shown at the group's Washington, D.C. office, 1970. © AP / Wide World Photos.

help, a new independent organization grew—Environmental Teach-In, Incorporated. Some of Hayes's youthful staff occasionally let their politics show, hampering Nelson and McCloskey's efforts to broaden their base. One volunteer trashed the Nixon administration's environmental promises as a "billow of smog" while another refused to meet with John D. Ehrlichman, Assistant to the President for Domestic Affairs and one of Nixon's closest advisors. Such an impertinent snub to an incumbent presidential administration did not seem to bother them. "We didn't think we had anything to chat about," a spokesman for the organizers sarcastically explained. For the most part, however, Hayes hid his liberal inclinations and adopted the centrist approach of his mentor Nelson. Eschewing the confrontational politics of the New Left, he sought to unite rather than polarize. "We didn't want to alienate the middle class," Hayes recalled. "We didn't want to lose the 'Silent Majority' just because of style issues." Hayes also wisely adopted a decentralized approach, encouraging local groups to take the initiative and offering only loose coordination and advice. He sought to make the day an educational opportunity as much as a protest, corresponding with schools from the elementary to the university level. In only one example, an Illinois sixth-grade class braved cold temperatures to plant a tree on its playground in anticipation of the day. This positive, centrist approach alienated some of the more radical elements in the emerging environmental movement, those who equated activism with militancy and found the tempered Earth Day rhetoric too tame.

Overshadowed by Nelson and Hayes, McConnell proceeded with his own plans in San Francisco. He coordinated with the Sierra Club, centered in the city, and the Junior Chamber of Commerce. Like Hayes, he corresponded with grade schools and arranged special educational programs. When the Vernal Equinox arrived on March 21, 1970, his efforts paid dividends even if most participants already looked to the national environmental teach-in as the key event. San Franciscans raised an "Earth Flag" in Golden Gate Park. The park provided seedlings, which McConnell and his allies distributed to the Red Cross and schools in the Bay area. In later years, McConnell was somewhat resentful that his efforts had fallen into the historical shadows even if the larger cause of environmental protection had gained the requisite publicity. "Earth Day is not April 22," he told all who would listen. In fact, McConnell had won his own legacy. Going on to lead Earth Society, McConnell convinced United Nations Secretary-General U Thant in 1971 to declare March 21 the official U.N. Earth Day. Every year at U.N. headquarters participants ring a "Peace Bell" to symbolize the world's collective efforts. Two minutes of silence and reflection traditionally follow. In the first year, the celebration included a "Global Village," including booths and displays, the "Street of Mysteries," the "Avenue of Spring," and the "Street of Crafts." In the second year, the new U.N. Secretary General Kurt Waldheim did the honors as a special 12-hour environmental television broadcast emanated from New York.

In the White House President Richard Nixon barely noticed the United Nations celebrations, offering words of support when questioned but giving it little thought. The efforts of Nelson and Hayes—the larger Earth Day—were another matter. As April 22, 1970 approached, a debate raged. Ever the astute politician, Nixon had recognized the potential power of the new environmentalism sweeping the country even before Hayes and the others began molding their "teach-in" into the truly momentous event it became. In addition, his political opposition stood poised to take advantage of the situation if the administration somehow appeared indifferent. Predictably, Maine Democratic senator Edmund Muskie, a probable 1972 opponent, prepared an offensive, planning to venture to Harvard and the University of Pennsylvania for speeches demanding additional environmental protection. Muskie had not joined Nelson in promoting Earth Day, top aide Leon Billings recalled, but he recognized it "as an opportunity to provide political strength to his lonely crusade." Other presidential-caliber Democrats planned to make the most of the occasion as well. Minnesota senator Hubert Humphrey scheduled a major speech at an Indiana high school, while Washington senator Henry Jackson planned the same at the University of Washington. Senator McGovern scheduled his address for Purdue University, while Massachusetts senator Edward Kennedy chose Yale University. The Democrats knew the power of this political bloc, Nixon assumed, and to ignore it completely might prove foolish.

On the other hand, however, many advisors warned Nixon that environmentalists were "social activists on the left side of the political spectrum," harboring a natural antagonism difficult to bridge. Still remaining were serious questions about whether Nixon could reach America's youth in any event. So many other factors—the war, the administration's position on civil rights—played into the equation. Any efforts might simply prove futile, a waste of time. Worse was the possibility of alienating traditional conservative allies. Many industries anticipated facing the full wrath of environmentalists' anger on this, their designated day. Dow Chemical, which had suffered protests against its manufacture of napalm and chemical pesticides, figured the best defense was a good offensive, sending its public relations team into overdrive to present the most environmentally friendly face possible. Other companies more readily participated, reflecting a market-savvy realization of their own consumers' concerns if not a genuine concern for environmental quality. Much of American industry simply feared that such a wide popular demand for environmental protection might result in additional burdensome regulations, regulations that had the potential to slash employment and hamper the economy. They did not want to appear to counter publicly such a popular movement as the new environmentalism, but neither did they plan to support a president who actively and ardently pushed the environmental agenda. Nixon realized that various industry representatives and a number of conservatives had already voiced in private, if not in public, their displeasure over the administration's environmental accomplishments to date. To appear at the forefront on Earth Day might risk pushing them into direct opposition.

The first White House staffer to recommend a strong administration response in favor of Earth Day was aide Christopher DeMuth, who recommended to Ehrlichman and Deputy Assistant to the President for Domestic Affairs John Whitaker, his immediate supervisor, that Nixon deliver a "substantial presidential address." Ehrlichman had just appointed Whitaker as the White House's top environmental advisor, and Whitaker, in turn, had realized the intelligence of DeMuth. A recent graduate of Harvard and the same age as Hayes and the other Earth Day organizers, DeMuth argued that a forceful presidential response before the day itself would ensure the "supremacy of the moderate students," not the radical fringe. DeMuth promised to keep in close contact with various congressional leaders and with his contemporaries in the Earth Day national headquarters in Washington.

Whitaker quickly agreed with DeMuth. A former advance man and scheduler with the Nixon campaign, Whitaker held a doctorate in geology and a long-standing interest in environmental protection. Ehrlichman, however, was another question. A year older than Whitaker, he also had a background in the environment; he had served for 15 years as a land-use attorney. He too recognized the importance of cleaning up the environment and the political potency of the new environmentalism, but as a closer aide to Nixon and with responsibilities beyond simply natural resources, Ehrlichman had reservations about such a strong endorsement as the one Whitaker and DeMuth proposed.

Ehrlichman worried that preparations for Earth Day were not sufficiently bipartisan. Nelson's promises and the participation of McCloskey did not convince Ehrlichman, who warned Nixon that the entire affair had the potential to turn "anti-Administration." Nelson had come uncomfortably close, in Ehrlichman's eyes, to encouraging the same radical elements the administration feared. In a speaking tour the previous year, for example, Nelson had remarked that youthful activism promised to take leadership away from "indifferent, venal men who are concerned with progress and profit for the sake of progress and profit alone, and who consider the environment the problem of birdwatchers and butterfly chasers." Rather than directly endorsing Earth Day, Ehrlichman concluded, Nixon should organize federal workers' participation, but personally remain aloof.

Nixon made no immediate decision, allowing the debate within the administration to spread. Secretary of Interior Walter Hickel, together with his chief advisor, Undersecretary Russell Train, argued that Nixon declare Earth Day a national holiday and issue an executive order directing government employees to aid their local efforts. "This action would be beneficial not only to our fight for the environment," Hickel wrote, "but also to our continued efforts to involve young people in national concerns." Hickel noted that the Interior Department had already begun to court the young environmental vote on its own, forming a student advisory body termed the Student Council on Pollution and the Environment. In addition, the Interior Department had arranged a series of nine regional seminars on the environment in cities from Boston to San Francisco—and in not one had the participants turned anti-administration. With still no decision from Nixon, Whitaker wrote Train to ensure that, at the very least, the department adequately publicized the seminars, including mailing environmental organizations press releases of its efforts. If nothing else, this would help inoculate the White House from possible criticism.

Nixon recognized that preparations were necessary in any event, and thus he could not delay his decision. Weighing the options, Nixon decided on a middle course, a low-risk plan along the lines of what Ehrlichman recommended. The White House would ensure the active participation of its key staff, who would speak throughout the country lauding the president's concern for environmental quality. Nixon, however, would remain quiet, neither issuing an executive order nor even making an official statement beforehand. If it appeared that events were proceeding smoothly—that is, with little violence or criticism of the White House—then Nixon might issue a quick statement to the press, hopefully in time for the evening news. A certain amount of criticism was inevitable, Nixon assumed. He had promised a major environmental address in the future and had his staff actively preparing a program of legislative initiatives. It was an agenda, Nixon hoped, that would establish his environmental credentials regardless of his response to Earth Day, a complete program sufficient in its own right to win the environmental vote. If he tried to steal some of the spotlight on Earth Day, an event for which he had contributed nothing, some would criticize him for grandstanding.

Whitaker and DeMuth had their marching orders. They sent a memorandum to the Departments of Interior, Agriculture, Labor, Transportation, and Health, Education and Welfare requesting each to develop a plan of action for the coming day. DeMuth would in turn coordinate publicity. The administration, Whitaker wrote DeMuth, should "hit Carson, Cavett and the think-type programs," referring to popular late-night television talk shows. It should include "young fellas" in its agenda, not simply higher administration figures. DeMuth notified Patrick Buchanan, a young aide and speech writer, that if any administration figure were asked about Earth Day, he should respond positively, noting that Nixon planned future environmental initiatives. To ensure that no administration figure encountered a hostile reception for which he was unprepared, Whitaker instructed DeMuth to "categorize our potential speakers as 'establishment' or 'teach-in' types."

When Earth Day finally arrived, hundreds of administration staffers fanned out as planned, their scripts in hand. His own speech scheduled for Harvard, Train recalled the staff "very engaged around the country." William Reilly, who later headed the Environmental Protection Agency under President George Bush, gave a speech on solid waste, prompting a man in the back to ask, "Mr. Reilly, where were you when it was garbage?" It was, Reilly recalled, "my baptism under fire." Any such fire, thankfully, was not real; the White House's fear of violence proved unfounded. With neither the major riot so many feared nor a significant Vietnam story, the media had more time to assess and critique the event, and the focus quickly turned to the administration. Ignoring the administration's efforts, the headline declared neglect by the White House—the very criticism Nixon had hoped to avoid. His actions—or, more correctly, lack of action—ensured condemnation. In the end, despite the best efforts of Whitaker and DeMuth, only two cabinet members gave speeches on the environment,

Secretary of Transportation John Volpe and Hickel. Hickel's topic did little to appease critics: support for the Alaskan oil pipeline, a major federal project that environmentalists argued would destroy the pristine beauty of America's last wilderness. Aware of the possibility of a fuel shortage, Nixon approved of the speech. Hickel, the ex-governor of Alaska, wanted to use the opportunity to argue that construction posed no hazard. With campus unrest prevalent and his speech scheduled for the University of Alaska, Hickel was, according to Whitaker, "understandably nervous." Nixon made no statement or proclamation, although White House proclamations appeared that week for National Boating Week and National Archery Week. The speeches of the many participating subcabinet officials, of Whitaker, Train, Reilly, and of other prominent individuals friendly to the White House reaped little coverage.

EARTH DAY AS POLITICAL AMMUNITION

"There was little doubt," Whitaker later wrote, "that the Nixon administration took its licks on Earth Day." CBS's much-admired newsman Walter Cronkite characterized the crowds as "predominantly anti-Nixon." Newsman Daniel Schorr added that while the event offered a rare chance for reconciliation between the nation's youth and its presidential administration, "they went their polarized ways." White House correspondent Dan Rather was more pointed, describing Nixon's reaction as "benign neglect." In many instances, the speakers themselves added jabs at the White House. Addressing a crowd in New York City's Bryant Park, noted author Kurt Vonnegut Jr., remarked, "If we don't get our President's attention, this planet may soon die . . . I'm sorry he's a lawyer; I wish to God that he was a biologist." Protesters in Washington threw oil on the front steps of the Department of Interior, a mess maintenance crews rapidly bathed away before television cameras arrived. Most politicians, in the vein that Nelson intended, avoided direct criticism of Nixon, but for many of the younger protesters, tying environmental protection in with criticism of Nixon's war policies was hard to resist. Even organizer Hayes quietly concluded, "We cannot save the environment as long as the war goes on."

The week of Earth Day, White House staffers participated in a symbolic clean-up of the polluted Potomac River, with the media properly alerted. The administration, the staged event seemed to declare, did, after all, care. The White House had scheduled the event prior to Earth Day and had in fact touted it for some time to all who would listen. After the criticism of the day, however, the clean-up appeared a lame attempt to shield the administration from further rebuke, far from any genuine expression of concern.

In the end, the first Earth Day and the criticism the administration endured reinforced in Nixon the importance of environmentalism politically. It helped launch a political competition as Republicans and Democrats each sought the banner of environmental champion. The years that followed Earth Day were the most productive for the natural world in all of congressional history. Within three years of Earth Day, Americans gained both the Environmental Protection Agency and the monumental National Environmental Policy Act. New amendments to air and water pollution legislation dramatically strengthened restrictions and increased funding. New limits on pesticides, most notably DDT, and new legislation to protect the nation's coastal zones and marine mammals added to an amazing slate of legislative accomplishment. Congress passed bills encouraging recycling and protecting not only endangered species but their habitats. Washington intervened to stop egregious reclamation projects, the Cross Florida Barge Canal only one example, and halted construction of a Miami airport that threatened the Everglades.

It was the height of American environmentalism, which subsequent Earth Days reflected. The following year, 1971, Nelson introduced a congressional resolution declaring the third week in April as "Earth Week." Nixon initially refused, which dumbfounded Whitaker. "It costs us nothing," Whitaker complained. "I think we are painting ourselves into a corner for nothing." Whitaker continued to lobby and reminded Nixon of the success of the first Earth Day and the political criticism he faced. In the end, Nixon agreed and issued the proclamation. It was a good decision. While the celebrations were not as big as the previous year, they covered a week and thus garnered almost as much publicity. In New York City, Mayor John Lindsay closed Madison Avenue in midtown Manhattan for a pedestrian mall. Thousands pushed strollers and ate lunch as speakers extolled the virtues of environmentalism. Many of the original sponsors of the first Earth Day had formed Environmental Action to continue their activism. They were clearly not alone. In 1972, Earth Week events continued around the country. In Pittsburgh, 1,200 delegates to a national Young Men's Christian Association convention selected an environmental project to improve their respective home communities. Their efforts ultimately involved almost 750,000 people. In Kansas City, Mayor Richard Walsh arranged for National Guard trucks to aid in regular trash collection and disposal. In addition to the planting of trees, seminars, and speeches that had characterized the previous two years, participants tested soils, organized a number of clean-up campaigns, and even took part in film festivals and bicycle tours. As popular artist Marvin Gaye sang "Mercy, Mercy Me, the Ecology," the United Nations Conference on the Environment in Stockholm, Sweden declared a "World Environment Day." This designated date was June 5, completely separate from the both the respective March and April Earth Days. In many respects, it appeared, Earth Day and environmentalism had become dominant traits in the American psyche.

EARTH DAY AND THE WANING OF THE ENVIRONMENTAL MOVEMENT

The American psyche has never been constant, however; the times continued to change. Several months after Earth Week, 1973, Syria and Egypt launched the Yom Kippur War with an attack on Israel. Nixon quickly reinforced the Jewish state, which, in turn, prompted the Arab countries of OPEC to launch a complete oil embargo against the United States. For months Americans had feared an energy crisis. Now, however, it was a reality. Gasoline prices skyrocketed and shortages were commonplace. Increasingly, Americans called for a relaxation of environmental law, convinced that restrictions exacerbated the economy.

Indeed, environmental advocates soon faced steep obstacles. The heyday of environmentalism had begun to fade, the movement's ability to captivate the public slowly waning with new economic and international developments. The era of abundance, which the nation had enjoyed since the conclusion of World War II, was petering out. In its place grew a new reality, labeled "the energy crisis," that dominated public concern throughout the remainder of the decade and the administrations of Gerald Ford and Jimmy Carter. Increasingly, fewer Americans assumed eternal plenty, and an ever-expanding economy that allowed for the perpetual removal of natural resources from potential production. Environmentalism spoke for the spiritual and nonutilitarian values of these resources, contrary to the historic patterns of economic endeavor. In times of prosperity, the nation could easily cherish these values as signs of a compassionate and rational culture that understood its technological limitations. However, in times of economic strain—begun with the energy crisis—they became to many a luxury the nation unfortunately could no longer afford. The goals of environmentalism increasingly appeared class-based and insensitive to more basic concerns of economic survival, a difficult obstacle for environmentalists to overcome.

Not surprisingly, Earth Day celebrations reflected America's shifting attitudes. As early as 1972, the *New York Times* added a solemn note, wondering if Earth Day would suffer "the danger inherent in all anniversaries . . . that pious observance may replace inspiration." In 1974 the crowds were the smallest ever with most speakers rather subdued. In Wisconsin, several hundred citizens agreed to reduce electricity and gas consumption as an indication of the importance they placed on the environment. In doing so, however, they arguably reinforced the assumption that energy production and environmental protection were mutually exclusive. Massachusetts governor Frances Sargent offered his official state car as a test case for new emission control technology, required on all cars in Boston the following year. Much to his dismay, his car flunked the test. Environmentalist David Brower tried to put the best possible perspective on Earth Day's obvious depreciation. "Earth Day started out as an orgasm," he stated, "and then they couldn't quite repeat that kind of success."

While the energy crisis obviously played a role in Earth Day's sudden loss in stature, other factors contributed. In many respects, the very legislative success that the first Earth Day helped spawn removed the sense of crisis so pivotal to motivating the public. In another sense, the diminished nature of

Earth Day simply proved the struggle to protect the environment in a new phase. With the initial wave of Earth Day–era legislation now on the books, the conflict shifted to a new arena, one dependent upon bureaucrats and lawyers as much as grassroots volunteers. It revolved around legal implementation, the intricacies of interpretation, and the complex minutiae of science. With debate increasingly narrow and technical, rarely in the national headlines, there existed a "tendency to go to sleep on implementation," according to environmentalist Brent Blackwelder. In addition, the movement had always enjoyed convenient enemies—greedy corporations or ignorant governments. Increasingly, all recognized, solutions revolved around the individual sacrifices of the everyday citizen. On Earth Day, author Barry Commoner charged that many common conveniences, the same enjoyed by the average housewife, were "ecological idiocy." The car, air conditioning, a large family—all staples of suburban life and all a threat. Clearly, sustaining enthusiasm was no simple task.

In the broader context, the liberalism of the Great Society era had begun to spark the inevitable backlash, a backlash the economic malaise helped fuel. A new, rejuvenated conservatism grew, which flourished in the years that followed. Among many Republicans, pragmatism gave way to a more ideologically driven distrust of government. Moving from the traditional New England base of Republicanism, this new conservatism centered in the south and west, the areas of least environmentalism. Combining social conservatism with a strong faith in the free market, it did not overtly oppose environmental protection but did challenge the legitimacy of the federal regulations upon which such protections depended.

EARTH DAY'S STAYING POWER

The threats to American environmentalism were manifold but, in the end, did not succeed in halting Earth Day. With the passage of years came notable anniversaries: the tenth in 1980, the twentieth in 1990, the twenty-fifth in 1995, and, most recently, the thirtieth in 2000, each an indication that environmentalism persisted. Denis Hayes returned for the tenth anniversary to lead Earth Day 1980. The organization's goal, he declared, was to "build nationwide political support for a counterattack." Once again, a street fair was the focus of the New York festivities, this time on the Avenue of the Americas. As if to remind the public that environmental threats remained, a fire at a nearby Elizabeth, New Jersey chemical waste site sent potentially toxic clouds of smoke into Manhattan. Hayes did a remarkable job and when environmental leaders began to organize the 1990 celebrations, they once again turned to his experienced hands. Perhaps reflecting the earlier efforts of McConnell if not growing globalization, Hayes and his allies mobilized almost 200 million people in 141 countries. In France, participants formed a 500-mile human chain while in Italy 5,000 people lay down in the streets to protest car fumes. Hikers climbed up Mount Everest in a "trash-picking trek" and in Japan protesters held an "ecofair" in a landfill. Recycling was a major focus for most nations, even if the day won more publicity abroad than in the United States. President George H. W. Bush, fishing in Key West, Florida, used a telephone hookup to address an Earth Day crowd in George, Washington. Cynical pundits noted that the American turnout paled to 20 years before, one writing that "even the music was recycled." Nevertheless, the day was a success by all objective accounts and arguably helped build momentum for the 1992 United Nations Earth Summit in Rio de Janeiro.

By 1995 it was obvious that far from wilting under the threats to environmentalism, Earth Day appeared almost rejuvenated. Nelson had won the Presidential Medal of Freedom for his role in organizing the inaugural event and returned to lead Earth Day XXV. Together with Project Earthlink, an organization of 13 government agencies, and Earth Day USA, another volunteer group, Nelson hoped to match the day a quarter of a century before. According to the *New York Times,* "Everybody wants a piece of the action, including the [President Bill] Clinton administration, the environmental movement and even big business." The latter was particularly telling. The new Earth Day enjoyed a budget of millions and tremendous support from corporate America, a somewhat ironic twist for many observers. According to one, "Corporations realized that they could co-opt Earth Day by sponsoring or hosting events, transforming the earnest day of observance into an indulgent observance of themselves." According to *Time Magazine,* Earth Day was a "commercial mugging." The first Earth Day of the new millennium was no different. By the time April 22, 2000 arrived, 5,000 environmental groups around the world were on board, reaching a record 184 countries. In only one event, a talking drum chain traveled from village to village in Gabon, Africa. In America, thousands gathered, if not with the enthusiasm of their parents' generation. The irony even more apparent, one of the biggest sponsors was the Ford Motor Company, hardly an unfamiliar litigant in the environmental community.

The fate of Earth Day reflects the role of environmentalism in modern society. Today an overwhelming majority of Americans claim to support environmental protection. The public may lack the enthusiasm of the first generation of environmentalists, its commitment may be less firm, but neither does it perceive itself in opposition. Even industry today professes to be environment-friendly, although at closer inspection partisan politics often demonstrate deeper fissures. In one sense this makes environmentalism a less potent force, Earth Day a superficial shell of its former self. In another sense, however, it indicates that environmentalism—and Earth Day—are here to stay.

FURTHER READING

Flippen, J. Brooks. *Nixon and the Environment.* Albuquerque: University of New Mexico Press, 2000.

Oelschlaeger, Max, ed. *After Earth Day: Continuing the Conservation Effort.* Denton: University of North Texas Press, 1992.

Rothman, Hal K. *The Greening of a Nation? Environmentalism in the United States Since 1945.* Fort Worth, Tex.: Harcourt Brace, 1998.

Stefoff, Rebecca. *The American Environmental Movement.* New York: Facts on File, 1995.

J. Brooks Flippen

ARBOR DAY

Arbor Day is a holiday dedicated to the planting and appreciation of trees, and it is a common part of the American school experience and a familiar feature of the annual calendar. It is no accident that this is the case, since the Arbor Day holiday has a dedicated staff that works throughout the year to promote its observance. Created in 1872, it is a day devoted to contemplation of the future rather than the past, and it comes with a specific task: encouraging the public to plant trees. As such, it joins Earth Day as the American holidays most oriented to nature. In its first century, the holiday had two explicit and equal goals: to improve the environment, and to foster good citizenship through the encouragement of active stewardship of the land. The start of the holiday's second century was marked by the creation of the National Arbor Day Foundation, which took custody of the observance of and education about tree planting in the United States. By that time, Arbor Day observance had spread to many other countries, reflecting the character of the holiday, which is civic rather than national.

The National Arbor Day Foundation seeks to encourage as many people as possible to improve the world by planting trees, and to commemorate the holiday's founder, J. Sterling Morton (1832–1903). Morton and others argued that people who planted trees, and were surrounded by them, were better, more moral people. Today the Foundation goes so far as to suggest that anyone who plants a tree is a hero. Thus the commemoration of the holiday celebrates those who celebrate the holiday, in a loop of good feeling and self-satisfaction. The actual impact of the holiday on the environment is somewhat more abstract. While it is certain that millions of trees—indeed tens of millions of trees—have

ARBOR DAY

- [ ] Arbor Day was first observed in 1872 and now is celebrated each year on the last Friday in April, although some states have designated other dates.

- [ ] Founded by J. Sterling Morton, Arbor Day is devoted to contemplation of the future rather than the past and comes with a specific task: encouraging the public to plant trees.

- [ ] Arbor Day aims to improve the environment and foster good citizenship by encouraging active stewardship of the land.

- [ ] The roots of the holiday lie in the deforestation of America's East coast, and westward migration into the relatively treeless plains region.

- [ ] Morton's adopted home Nebraska was the first state to institute Arbor Day, in 1874.

- [ ] By 1892 the holiday had officially been adopted and was being observed by schools in 40 U.S. states and territories.

- [ ] In 1971 John Rosenow created the National Arbor Day Foundation to build Arbor Day's legacy.

- [ ] The foundation started the successful "Tree City U.S.A." program, which is designed to promote healthy urban forests. To achieve "Tree City" status municipalities must hold an annual city-sponsored Arbor Day observance.

been planted due to the inspiration of Arbor Day, the environmental problems that the trees are intended to address continue to grow. The history of Arbor Day falls into four periods: the American precursors of "official" tree planting, the life and times of Morton, the rapid growth of the holiday following its inception, and the modern incarnation with the National Arbor Day Foundation.

TREES IN THE EARLY UNITED STATES

The dominant narrative of the early European experience in North America is one of encounter with a vast forest, and the challenges entailed in clearing and settling the land. Indeed, forests were viewed as a barrier to agriculture, and those who cut trees were doing the work of the nation, and of God. Virtue was in the towns and clearings, vice and danger was in the forests. As opposed to the dark and massive forest, wood was valued for fuel and large trees were prized as ship masts, and other commercial uses of trees were encouraged as well. In 1624, for instance, the Colonial Assembly of Virginia directed property owners to plant mulberry trees in support of a budding (and ultimately unsuccessful) silk industry. In that decade the first commercial tree nurseries were created, and towns began naming streets after common trees. In the eighteenth century, English elms, American chestnuts, and a variety of other trees were planted for beautification of streets and parks in Boston, Georgetown, New Haven, and other cities.

Before long, however, residents of some areas experienced a shortage of wood that had two primary causes. East of the Mississippi it was due to excessive destruction of the forests and a growing demand for domestic and industrial fuel; what was cut down was not replaced, and the lack caused hardship particularly during the winters. West of the Mississippi the shortage was due to the conditions of the prairie, where trees were largely confined to riverbanks and small, widely scattered groves. For Americans in the east the shortage of wood came as a rude surprise, given the prevailing sentiment, increasingly less accurate, that the continent was covered with forest. For those pushing west, the transition from eastern forests to the prairies posed new challenges, as a fundamental resource was suddenly absent from the landscape. The transition from an over-abundance of forest to a sense of shortage was gradual and only articulated by a small number of astute observers, despite the massive change that was taking place. It gave rise, however, to an increased interest in tree planting and deliberate environmental manipulation.

J. STERLING MORTON AND THE BIRTH OF ARBOR DAY

J. (Julius) Sterling Morton was born in New York in 1832, educated in Michigan, and made his way soon thereafter to the Nebraska territory, arriving in 1854. He came during a period of heightening awareness of the need for and benefits of environmental stewardship. Andrew Jackson Downing, the influential horticultural writer and editor, felt that tree planting was a patriotic duty. Three factors contributed to the desire to increase timber supply: the growing population and destruction of forests east of the Mississippi, the increase in settlement in the barely forested Great Plains, and, some years later, the consumption and destruction of forests caused by the Civil War. Downing suggested that "Pleasure and profit are certain, sooner or later, to awaken a large portion of our countrymen to the advantages of improving their own private grounds." These were sentiments that resonated powerfully with Morton, who began his professional career as a newspaper publisher and local politician. In these roles, Morton served as a strong promoter of the Nebraska territory, and he was eager to draw new settlers to the area. Trees were a way to both beautify the land and foster sound agricultural practices, and these, Morton was convinced, led to population growth, which in turn generated power and profit.

As a politician Morton had a checkered career, and he was defeated in a run for the governorship of Nebraska when it first became a state. He continued his public work, however, by serving on the State Board of Agriculture, and it was there that he first proposed a day dedicated to planting trees, a proposition that he advocated in his journalistic work as well. Morton argued that "The cultivation of trees is the cultivation of the good, the beautiful, and the ennobling in man, and for one, I wish to see this culture become universal in the State." The State Board obliged Morton's desire, and issued a proclamation declaring:

> That Wednesday, the 10th day of April, 1872, be, and the same is hereby, especially set apart and consecrated for tree planting in the State of Nebraska, and the State Board of Agriculture hereby name it Arbor Day; and to urge upon the people of the State the vital importance of tree planting, hereby offer a special premium of one hundred dollars to the agricultural society of that county in Nebraska which shall, upon that day, plant properly the largest number of trees; and a farm library of twenty-five dollars worth of books to that person who, on that day, shall plant properly, in Nebraska, the greatest number of trees.

On the first Arbor Day it is reported that over one million trees were planted in Nebraska, and the effort was declared a rousing success. Two years later, the governor of Nebraska made Arbor Day an official state holiday, and its observance in the capital in 1875 drew upon 1,000 children from different schools to march in a parade and plant trees on behalf of their classes. With these early observances, Arbor Day made a name for itself, and began its rapid spread. Morton's star was linked to Arbor Day, which was shifted by the Nebraska legislature to coincide with his birthday, April 22. More tangibly, President Grover Cleveland later appointed Morton Secretary of Agriculture for the United States, a post he held from 1893–1897, providing him with a platform to further his advocacy of tree planting for environmental change.

THE GROWTH OF ARBOR DAY

As noted, the mid-nineteenth century was a time of rising environmental concern, and a period of grand thinking in terms of environmental steward-ship. One area of experimentation was the Great Plains, and Morton's Arbor Day was part of a series of proposals to take charge of the environment and craft it to address human needs. Some of the ambitious settlers in the plains states recalled that east of the Mississippi there were both forests and rainfall, and they suffered from the lack of each in their new homes. A connection was made between the two, and the hypothesis that forests generated rainfall gained currency. An obvious reflection of this supposed link was the Timber Cultures Act, which was passed by Congress in 1873, just as Arbor Day was emerging. The act was proposed by Phineas Hitchcock, a journalist like Morton, and the U.S. Senator from Nebraska at the time. It offered free land to settlers, up to 160 acres, in return for planting one-quarter of it with trees. The intent was to bring rain to the plains by altering the landscape. Although millions of trees were planted under the sponsorship of the act, the climate did not respond, and it was repealed in 1891. Despite that failure, many states fostered tree-plant-ing programs, and there was widespread support for large-scale tree planting through the end of the century. It is in this atmosphere that Arbor Day spread beyond Nebraska and became a holiday observed throughout the nation.

Other states were quick to emulate Nebraska and adopt Arbor Day as a holi-day, but the holiday got an even greater boost in 1882, when a national for-estry convention meeting in Cincinnati called upon school children around the country to plant Arbor Day groves. The groves were to be commemorative of famous figures in American history, and this was seen as an apt educational tool. The following year, a forestry committee proposed that Arbor Day be commemorated in all schools in the United States and be a part of the regular curriculum. By 1892 the holiday had officially been adopted and was being observed by schools in 40 U.S. states and territories. This rapid proliferation gave rise to a cottage industry that produced materials to assist in conducting Arbor Day ceremonies and to help teachers with lesson plans. The anthologies and programs that were generated contained poems, songs, speeches by nota-bles, and craft activities, along with basic information about trees. The tone of the material was lofty and ambitious and celebrated not only the trees, but also the people who were wise and caring enough to plant them. Typical of the sentiments of the time were the comments of J. T. Rothrock, a leading forester and Pennsylvania State Commissioner for Forestry, who said on Arbor Day in 1895 that tree planting would:

> Exemplify the noble justice of leaving the world in as good condition for the prosperity of your children as you found it for yourselves. All this you may do by simply planting a tree, which will grow while you sleep and draw its strength and its long life and large usefulness

from the sunshine and the storm, costing nothing, harming no one, blessing everyone, and pleasing God.

J. M. Carlisle, Superintendent of Schools in Texas, felt that through Arbor Day observances, "the sentiment in favor of both physical and moral cleanliness is greatly strengthened, while patriotic feelings are aroused and the people are drawn together by the contemplation of so many great themes in which all have a common interest." A compendium of Arbor Day material from 1909 carried the words of the famous to America's school children, including a letter from Teddy Roosevelt and the tree-related writing of Washington Irving, William Cullen Bryant, Walt Whitman, George Perkins Marsh, Gifford Pinchot, John Muir, and, to lend an international flavor, William Shakespeare.

Yet, while the early spread of Arbor Day and its entrance into the school curriculum are impressive, the holiday was not transformative of the American people, or of the American landscape, in the way that its founder and promoters hoped and asserted it would be. As time passed, Arbor Day was largely relegated to a once-a-year school activity, a small civic observance, a booster club project, existing as a brief mention in the news each spring, but failing to sustain its early momentum. And, due to different climate conditions across the United States, the holiday was observed on a variety of dates, subject to suitable local planting conditions (federal designation in 1970 of Arbor Day as the last Friday in April notwithstanding). Thus Arbor Day did not fix a single day for everyone and had, other than children, a small and poorly defined constituency. Even the national organization, American Forests, founded in 1875, struggled to maintain a membership and purpose in the next 100 years. But, with the coming of Arbor Day's centenary, a new force sought to revitalize its observance.

THE RISE OF THE NATIONAL ARBOR DAY FOUNDATION

Just as Arbor Day is the result of the vision of one man, J. Sterling Morton, so, too, is the National Arbor Day Foundation the creation of its founder John Rosenow. Like Morton before him, Rosenow blended public relations skills with a love of trees and concern for the landscape. So too, Rosenow sought to inspire the masses through the Arbor Day holiday and believed that it can be a transformative force. In 1971 Rosenow left his job at the Nebraska Bureau of Tourism and began organizing events to celebrate the 100th anniversary of Arbor Day and its founding father, one of Nebraska's most famous citizens. From the humble beginnings of a 21-year-old idealist, the National Arbor Day Foundation has grown to an organization that has had millions of members (membership currently hovers around one million, but there is regular turnover), each of whom has received bundles of tree saplings ready for planting. More than that, the foundation has taken on a range of conservation and educational projects focused on tree planting, going well beyond a one-day annual observance. It has also become the "clearinghouse" of Arbor Day celebrations, providing material to schools, to members, on a Web site, and through public service announcements on radio, television, in movies, and newspapers. Indeed, it has worked hard, and with some success, to make the holiday and its associated values inseparable from the foundation itself.

One of the most successful programs sponsored by the Foundation is "Tree City U.S.A.," designed to promote healthy urban forests. In order to achieve "Tree City" status, municipalities are required to fulfill a number of conditions, among them holding an annual city-sponsored Arbor Day observance. The number of Americans living in designated "Tree Cities" is approaching 90 million; thus there is a large potential audience for the official observances. The foundation also reaffirmed the patriotic aspect of Arbor Day with an "election" in 2001 of a national tree, a beauty contest won by an undesignated species of oak, with the results endorsed by a 2004 Congressional act making the oak a legal national symbol. At the time, Nebraska's Senator Ben Nelson commented that "The oak tree will now be as much a symbol of America as Thanksgiving Day, Old Glory, the Star Spangled Banner, and the bald eagle. It is a fine choice to represent our nation's strength, as it grows from just an acorn into a powerful entity whose many branches continue to strengthen and reach skyward with every passing year."

For those who might not be inspired by acts of Congress, the foundation has other ways of promoting Arbor Day, including direct mass-mailing, announcements printed on grocery bags in Wal-Mart and other stores, billboards, celebrity events, and prominent space in government publications and agency Web sites. Through the National Arbor Day Foundation, the holiday has a staff of professional promoters, a permanent place in school curricula, and a cadre of government boosters unlike any other celebratory day. It is apolitical, upbeat, low-key, pro-America, and profitable, a perfect springtime holiday package.

Yet, even as Arbor Day is presented as a forward-looking holiday, its annual observance provides an opportunity to take stock of the world that tree planting is supposed to transform. Arbor Day was born in 1872 during a period of growing environmental concern and was promoted as a way to solve the challenges of that time. Today the holiday addresses serious environmental problems that, despite 100 years of tree planting, continue to grow rather than diminish. Trees are presented as an ideal tool for abating the damage that people cause to nature, and the holiday celebrates the power that they and their planters have to create a more perfect world.

Of course trees and tree planters cannot create a perfect world, although there may be something to the claim that the holiday fosters a civic attitude and a positive outlook. And if the symbolism and rhetoric of Arbor Day exists on a plane that is increasingly distant from the day-to-day reality of life in America, it is thus like many other holidays that have suffered from commercialization or dilution of their original spirit and intent. At the same time, like other American holidays, Arbor Day continues to be a cause for celebration, a source of inspiration and excitement for children, and an opportunity for politicians and community leaders to engage nature, even if only briefly. And if American culture is less sentimental about Arbor Day than it once was, no longer writing poems and odes to the beauty of trees to be declaimed in an unselfconscious manner, it is also true that trees continue to hold a special place in American (and other) societies. Because of this, Arbor Day can be a forward-looking holiday, one that marks many individuals through their specific act of planting something that may well outlast them. Indeed, the fact that Arbor Day has not solved our environmental problems seems to ensure its continued relevance in generations to come.

FURTHER READING

Cohen, Shaul. *Planting Nature: Trees and the Manipulation of Environmental Stewardship in America.* Berkeley: University of California Press, 2004.

Lipkis, Andy, and Kate Lipkis. *The Simple Act of Planting a Tree: Healing Your Neighborhood, Your City, and Your World.* Los Angeles: Tarcher Publishing, 1990.

Samuels, Gail. *Enduring Roots: Encounters With Trees, History, and the American Landscape.* New Brunswick, N.J.: Rutgers University Press, 1999.

Skinner, Charles R. *Arbor Day Manual: An Aid in Preparing Programs for Arbor Day Exercises.* Freeport, N.Y.: Books for Libraries, 1890, repr. 1977.

Williams, Michael. *Americans and Their Forests: A Historical Geography.* Cambridge: Cambridge University Press, 1992.

Shaul Cohen

MAY DAY IN
URBAN AMERICA

Celebrated for centuries as a rite of spring, May Day took on new meaning in the late nineteenth century. The labor movement in America initially set aside May 1 in 1886 to make a nationwide demand for the eight-hour workday. From that moment on, May Day became known as something other than just the herald of spring: it became an annual event for labor's push for the shorter workday. In time new agendas were added to this secular holiday; most notably, anarchists, socialists, and communists claimed May Day as their own. For them it was to be more than a day to usher in the eight-hour demand; it was to be the harbinger of the new international socialist order to come after the anticipated demise of capitalism. May Day also became a vehicle through which these radical Americans publicly defined and expressed their political identities. Consequently, May Day celebrations were diverse and varied over time as the social and political profiles and concerns of their participants changed. In their May 1 demonstrations, radicals found ways to display their adherence both to a particular strand of anarchism, socialism, or communism and to a specific conception of American citizenship. Each May 1 they thereby publicly defined radical American identities.

The history of the annual May Day holiday illuminates the self-images of radicals who were not union or party leaders. They were less likely than prominent public figures to have left a written record of how they understood their place in society. Instead, the public arena of urban American political culture was where they defined the meaning of their left-wing political affiliations and aspirations. Those who did leave a written record recalled May Day as one

MAY DAY

- [ ] American labor organizations first took to the streets on May 1, 1886 to demand the eight-hour workday.

- [ ] May Day is an informal holiday, unrecognized by the United States federal government.

- [ ] May Day soon become a touchstone event in late nineteenth- and early twentieth-century American political radicalism, providing a public platform to socialists, communists, anarchists, and other left-leaning, anticapitalist labor and political organizations.

- [ ] The radicalism associated with May Day spurred the federal government to officially recognize September's Labor Day, which was supported by more moderate labor organizations.

- [ ] Immigrants and urban dwellers were May Day's largest supporters and participants.

- [ ] May Day celebrations diminished or were forced out of the public eye by a conservative backlash against left-wing political and labor organizations during the post-World War I "Red Scare."

- [ ] During the Red Scare groups critical of left-wing or progressive politics failed to win widespread acceptance for competing holidays celebrated on May 1 such as "American Day," "Ceremony for the Massing of the Colors," and "Loyalty Day."

- [ ] May Day celebrations revived along with working-class mobilization during the Great Depression but were called off during World War II.

- [ ] Competing Loyalty Day parades overshadowed May Day celebrations during the Cold War, gaining the support of large veterans' groups and prominent politicians and others coming together under the umbrella of anticommunism.

of the more important moments for expressing personal solidarity with the political left in America. In their autobiographies, the communists Peggy Dennis, Howard Fast, and Robert Schrank, for example, each vividly recalled lively May Day celebrations. As children, they publicly proclaimed their difference from other classmates and declared their solidarity with other radical families by staying out of school and marching in the local May Day parade instead. As adults, they joined the Communist Party and continued to turn out on May 1 to reinforce their unity as radicals and publicize their political message. Although Dennis, Fast, and Schrank eventually came to question the validity of their radical politics, their memories of the significance of May Day in shaping those beliefs are clearly, even fondly, presented in their autobiographies.

As one communist, Karl Millens, recalled to Vivian Gornick in her study of American radicals, May Day was the most important public event for those on the left. He remembered how, "for weeks before. . .every wall, every storefront, every lamp post in the neighborhood was plastered with 'All Out May One.'" According to Millens, "*that* was our election day, our Fourth of July, our Hanukkah, and our Christmas." Although it never became a national holiday in America, May Day was once central to the formation and expression of individual and collective radical identities. Because the largest concentrations of laborers and labor organizations were in America's cities, May Day was almost exclusively an urban phenomenon. New York City and Chicago housed two of the largest populations of anarchists, socialists, and communists in the nation from the late nineteenth through the mid-twentieth centuries, but May Day was just as important among the radical political communities in other American cities, such as Boston, Philadelphia, Newark, and Seattle.

RADICAL ASSOCIATIONS

May Day originated in a loose coalition of trade unionists, anarchists, and socialists who turned out for the first nationwide protest for the eight-hour day on May 1, 1886. The occasion soon became an annual event. Almost immediately this new holiday was used for different purposes by different groups. The American Federation of Labor (AFL) and most of its affiliated unions continued to use May 1 as the focus for their drive for a shorter work day in the 1890s but restricted their efforts in this struggle to one trade per year. Not only did this limited approach provide a more achievable goal for the Federation's efforts, but it also provided a way for the organization to distance itself from the more radical economic changes that were being advanced by anarchists and socialists. In addition, by the end of the 1890s politically moderate trade unionists increasingly gave their support to the September Labor Day holiday instead of large May Day demonstrations. Especially after Labor Day became a nationally recognized holiday in 1894, workers had an occasion to celebrate the accomplishments of the organized labor movement in the United States, without associating their goals with the overthrow of capitalism. Labor Day gave the nation's workers an opportunity to present themselves as patriotic Americans to help win their bread-and-butter workplace demands.

In the years following the first politicized May Day in 1886, anarchists and socialists took a very different path from that followed by the AFL, embracing instead the radical implications of May Day. They defined this new holiday, which they created in their annual parades and mass meetings in the 1890s, as the harbinger of the international socialist order that they hoped to realize. Significantly for its subsequent history, the birth of May Day in America in 1886 was quickly connected in the popular imagination with the infamous Haymarket bombing affair, which took place only three days later in Chicago. For May Day's radical adherents, this association symbolized the repression of radical thought in America and the heroism of resistance, and even martyrdom, in the face of it.

For the holiday's opponents, May Day and the Haymarket incident represented the growing threat in America posed by radical European immigrants and their socialist and anarchist doctrines. Most native-born Americans, whether working-class, middle-class, or elite, soon looked upon May Day as "un-American." The event's changing social profile reinforced this perception. The vision of May Day's revolutionary potential, voiced first among Chicago's

An engraving from an 1886 issue of *Harper's Weekly* of a bomb going off among the police during the Haymarket Riot in Chicago. Courtesy of the Library of Congress.

German American anarchists, was shared among those in the growing Italian American anarchist communities there and in New York. Although they were a minority within the massive wave of Italian immigrants that began arriving in America in the late 1890s, these anarchists and their refugee leaders contributed to the character and content of May Day celebrations. They added songs, poems, and plays in their native tongue to the annual event, like Pietro Gori's one-act play, *Primo Maggio.* First performed by an anarchist group in Paterson, New Jersey in 1896 with Gori in the cast, it became a favorite centerpiece of many Italian American May Day gatherings. Along with radical immigrants from other ethnic backgrounds, Italian American anarchists sustained these celebrations at the turn of the century, since by then most politically moderate native-born and immigrant laborers had begun to abandon May Day demonstrations altogether.

Yet some of these radicals also constructed more complex sociopolitical identities that expressed their understanding of themselves as both radicals *and* Americans. By carrying the Stars and Stripes alongside the red flag in their May Day parades, for example, these socialists voiced their belief that the nation's banner symbolized more than just the "law-and-order" patriotism it had come to represent by the end of the nineteenth century. Instead, they gave the American flag a new meaning by presenting it as a symbol of the *promise* of democracy and freedom inherent in the American political system, a promise that they believed would be fulfilled only through the creation of a socialist commonwealth.

MAY DAY IN PROGRESSIVE AMERICA

By the 1900s and 1910s, the Socialist Labor Party (SLP) and the more recently established Socialist Party observed May Day separately. Each group used this holiday to refine its collective radical political identity and vied with the other over custodianship of the annual event. The SLP, more ideologically orthodox than the Socialist Party, refused to take up the cause of social or economic reforms in its May 1 demonstrations, focusing only on the ultimate goal of socialist revolution. As a result, the SLP's message did not resonate with most of the urban working class. Instead, the party's following came primarily from within the cities' small radical ethnic communities. These groups gathered together in their local meeting halls on May Day to express, in the distinctive accents of their particular ethnic heritage, their shared beliefs and values as socialists.

The Socialist Party, on the other hand, embraced a wide array of working-class political and economic concerns, such as the call for sweatshop reforms, better wages, and the end of child labor, and was therefore able to forge broader coalitions than the SLP. The Socialist Party organized large-scale parades with up to 60,000 participants in these years, including many trade unions that unofficially affiliated themselves with the party in its fight for workplace changes.

Many of these unionists joined the marches to demonstrate as proud workers who were ready to fight for higher wages from their employers. For example, striking Jewish bakers marched in New York in 1911, and shirtwaist factory girls, who had just won a pay increase, joined the line in celebration in 1916. Workers such as these, turning out to voice their concerns each May Day, may not necessarily have shared in the revolutionary visions of the Socialist Party. Yet the party used the annual parades as a way to spread its political agenda and try to build up its working-class ranks. In their May Day demonstrations, Socialist Party members, like the SLP members, also vigorously defended their right to carry the American flag alongside the red flag as socialist Americans.

THE RED SCARE AND THE 1920s

Despite the best efforts of Socialist Party leaders to assert their party's legitimacy and their recognition of America's democratic heritage, their May Day parades and mass meetings became targets of both political persecution and vigilante violence during the first Red Scare. Unable to distribute its party literature on May 1 or to secure permits for its processions and outdoor gatherings, the Socialist Party took its May Day commemorations indoors and sponsored smaller meetings for most of the 1920s. The same held true for the nascent Workers (Communist) Party. While the Socialist Party continued to defend its vision of a radical political fulfillment of America's democratic heritage (understood as the completion of the "unfinished" revolution of 1776), the young Communist Party instead embraced the 1917 Bolshevik Revolution as a step toward the establishment of an international communist order. The communists used the annual May Day holiday not only to demonstrate the solidarity of its members with the workers of the world, but also to stage cooperative ventures with community reform groups in local working-class neighborhoods. Such work continued at the grass-roots level through the onset of the Great Depression, as the communists, such as those in the Communist Party, came above ground to work toward their vision of working-class revolution.

While some progressive labor organizations joined the May Day demonstrations of the Socialist Party and the Communist Party in these years, the AFL continued to distance itself from the holiday. By the 1920s, the Federation had rejected several resolutions asking for its official recognition of May Day, and cast the holiday as an un-American celebration, which it believed was observed by only radicals and foreigners. Prioritizing their need to foster agreements with sympathetic employers at a time when many businesses pushed for the open shop, Samuel Gompers and the AFL leadership believed that any association with the radical May 1 observances posed a political liability for them. Instead, they encouraged their member unions to embrace the September Labor Day parades, which they saw as an ideal opportunity for the expression of labor's solidarity, strength, and respectability. In the Labor Day parades that were held in the 1910s and 1920s, the AFL and its member unions presented themselves as a predominantly white, male, skilled labor force that wanted to secure their position in the industrializing economy through collective bargaining. The AFL's definition of the patriotic laborer-citizen in its Labor Day parades was therefore a socially and politically exclusive one.

The same was true for the definitions of Americanism that patriotic societies expressed in the public observances that they organized in the 1920s in reaction to May Day. These included the short-lived "American Day," which was sponsored by the American Defense Society from 1919 to 1924; the Ceremony of the Massing of the Colors, which was organized by the Society for the Massing of the Colors from 1924 through the 1940s; the Loyalty Day parades, which were supported by the Rotary Club and Boy Scouts from 1920 to 1925; and National Child Health Day school and community events, which were advocated by a coalition of progressive reformers and the AFL beginning in the late 1920s. Intended to displace May Day demonstrations from the streets of New York and Chicago, each of these events advanced a socially and politically narrow understanding of what it meant to be an American. In their aesthetics and design, these gatherings were militant and masculine demonstrations of loyalty to the state, in which organizers sought to instill narrowly defined patriotic values into the nation's youth.

Despite the efforts of the many organizations that coordinated these events to displace May Day demonstrations, socialists and communists continued to

School children dance around maypoles in Central Park, New York City. Courtesy of the Library of Congress.

observe the holiday during the 1920s. Children of socialists and communists, who were considered the future of these movements, also joined in the annual observance. For many of these second-generation ethnic Americans, participation in May Day was a central event in their political awakening that led them to join the Socialist Party or Communist Party, and to carry on the tradition of the holiday for the next two decades.

REVIVAL IN THE GREAT DEPRESSION

With the onset of the Great Depression at the end of 1929, both the Socialist Party and the Communist Party witnessed a resurgence in membership, due in part to the influx of this younger generation. Numbers also increased as the Socialist Party continued its work within sympathetic unions for an end to wage cuts and more relief pay, and as the Communist Party worked for mass mobilization against hunger and unemployment. As both parties brought their respective May Day celebrations back onto the streets in the late 1920s and early 1930s, they found themselves in competition over access to those streets and the allegiance of the urban working class. Although the threat of fascism in Germany and the desire to strengthen its own ranks inspired the Communist Party to call for a united front of all progressive and labor forces on May Day after 1933, efforts at cooperation between the two parties failed due to ideological and tactical divisions. It was not until the "right-wing" of the Socialist Party broke from the party in protest against attempts at such united action that the militant socialists were able to coordinate a joint May Day event with the communists in 1936 and 1937. But even then, internal divisions remained strong enough for the Socialist Party and its affiliated unions to pull out of this temporary alliance and once again hold independent Socialist Party events.

At the same time, the Communist Party, having shifted from its revolutionary "third period" class analysis of the early 1930s, worked to build a united Popular Front May Day with unions and any local Socialist Party branches that remained open to cooperation. In supporting the Popular Front the Communist Party made manifest its recognition that it needed to engage more with the wider political and social environment in America, particularly the nation's democratic heritage and ethnic pluralism. This recognition was based on policy pronouncements from the party leadership, who declared that "Communism [was] Twentieth-Century Americanism," and from grass-roots experience since before the Great Depression of organizing at the level of city neighborhoods. The party and its affiliated fraternal organization, the International Workers Organization (IWO), organized large-scale May Day parades and mass meetings in the late 1930s, in which they symbolically presented this new understanding of radical Americanism. One of the visible expressions of this identity was the overwhelming presence of American flags interspersed with the red flag. Many of the flag bearers held the standards in their right hand and lifted their left fists in salute, further integrating symbols from two political traditions. In so doing they made visible their support for a militant American democracy that would be based on strong worker solidarity.

In addition, the Communist Party expressed renewed recognition of the distinct ethnic traditions within America. In order to organize successfully within the nation's diverse urban communities, the Communist Party found it beneficial not only to establish local party branches, but to work within existing community organizations, which were often based on race or ethnicity. Celebration of this democratic ethnic pluralism, considered part and parcel of the American experience, became another defining characteristic of the communist-led Popular Front May Day demonstrations after 1938. In 1939, for example, several sections paraded under a banner that proclaimed, "Immigrants All—Americans All" in what they called a "March of All Nations." Younger members in the IWO's Junior Section paraded in costumes that represented the garb native to their particular ancestral homeland. In part these demonstrations were sincere expressions of ethnic pride by rank-and-file party members and affiliates. Yet the official decision to highlight such pluralism as part of the Popular Front May Day was most likely also an instrumental one, used to widen the appeal, and the ranks, of the Communist Party U.S.A.

The Communist Party and IWO contingents were joined during May Day celebrations by numerous labor unions. Many were locals that had broken with their internationals and with the Socialist Party to form a united Popular Front with the Communists, in order to campaign against fascism and war and for civil rights, jobs, and peace. These workers, who came from traditional craft unions, like the Painters Union in New York, as well as from the newer industrial and professional unions like the Steel Workers Organizing Committee or the Artists Union, turned out en masse on May Day to create what became a celebration of the "common man:" the "everybody who's nobody and the nobody who's everybody."

Through these communist-led Popular Front May Day parades the holiday reached a climax, in terms of both the degree of its cultural resonance within American society and the number of participants. In New York alone, nearly a quarter of a million marchers turned out by the end of the decade. Its left-progressive message of social inclusion and economic equality was attractive to Americans suffering from the effects of the prolonged depression and was rhetorically broad enough, in its celebration of the common man, to house a wide coalition of communists, left-leaning socialists, union members, and social reformers.

COLD WAR BACKLASH AND DECLINE

Once the United States entered World War II, the grand Popular Front May Day parades in New York City and Chicago were suspended. By 1944, *The Daily Worker* reported that party members would not honor May Day with mass demonstrations or strikes but instead go to work for the war effort. The temporary abandonment of May Day celebrations resulted, in part, from the Communist Party's decision to support the allied fight against fascism after the Nazis attacked the Soviets in June 1941. Beginning in May 1942, the Communist Party subordinated its May Day demonstrations to the imperatives of the war, scaling back the event so that their members' money and time would be focused on mobilizing the country for battle. The Socialist Party held smaller indoor meetings and dinners instead of lavish parades.

With the end of World War II, great outdoor May Day celebrations were temporarily revived. In New York in 1946 the Communist Party hosted a large parade, featuring a contingent of recently returned war veterans and some 150,000 participants. The revival of the May Day parade, and of the radical left's presence in public culture, however, was short-lived. By the late 1940s, the Communist Party retreated into a revolutionary orthodoxy that made united front activity difficult. At the same time, the currents of the Cold War were already running swiftly through American politics. May Day and the radical left, which had become its custodian, suffered under both the political pressures of the second Red Scare and the challenges of rival demonstrations by patriotic organizations.

The Veterans of Foreign Wars (VFW) directly challenged the Communist Party–dominated May Day parades by organizing Loyalty Day demonstrations on May 1 in the late 1940s and early 1950s. Although the conservative veterans' group had coordinated smaller Loyalty Day parades in the early 1930s, it was not until after the war that these demonstrations won official government support and widespread press attention. In 1948, for example, New York Mayor William O'Dwyer, who was an honorary chairman for the day's events, stood at the parade's reviewing stand. U.S. Attorney General Thomas Clark joined him. At the time Clark was leading the legal prosecution against 11 national Communist Party leaders who, under the Smith Act, had been charged with conspiracy to advocate revolution by violence. In subsequent years, the VFW was joined by other veterans' organizations (including the American Legion and the Catholic and Jewish War Veterans), youth organizations such as the Boy Scouts, and contingents from local Catholic schools. The *New York Times* reported the events favorably, highlighting the large number of patriotic marchers that turned out. It compared the growing size of the Loyalty Day parade to the flagging May Day demonstrations, interpreting the difference as proof of New Yorkers' steadfast rejection of communism. One year, for example, it boasted that Loyalty Day had produced 750,000 spectators compared with May Day's 50,000. As a result, the city's VFW commander proudly asserted that his troops had "walked them [Communists] off the streets."

The VFW's efforts in the public sphere had a wider resonance in the late 1940s than they did during the early 1930s because the Cold War fostered a new conception of the American nation. Loyalty Day resonated with the idea of America as the leader of the "free world." Central elements of this idea were individual freedom and unfettered capitalism, both of which were understood to need vigorous defending at home and abroad against the threat of the collectivist ideologies of socialism and communism. Loyalty Day parades were one of many overt demonstrations in support of this new idea of America, along with the well-known anticommunist crusades of Attorney General Clark, Senator Joseph McCarthy, and the House Un-American Activities Committee. By staging these parades to eradicate the radicals' holiday, the VFW joined in the Cold War anticommunist fervor. Communists and communist sympathizers were supplanted from the streets and squares of American cities so that they could no longer voice their party line or work the crowds for recruits.

The vigilantly anticommunist Roman Catholic Church also sought to redefine the meaning of May Day during the 1950s by offering an alternative focus. Defense of religious freedom, or freedom of conscience, was offered in place of the radicals' attention to economic rights. Although the Catholic Church had long opposed communism because of its rejection of private property and acceptance of revolutionary violence, the Church's hostility took on a new focus during the Cold War when it experienced repression under the communist regimes in eastern Europe. When Pope Pius XII instituted the special "Mass for St. Joseph the Worker" on May 1, 1955, which was to be observed annually on May 1, he promoted veneration of the saint as part of a broader anticommunist crusade. As he stated at its inauguration, the special mass was to become the "'Christian Baptism of May Day." Church leaders like Francis Cardinal Spellman eagerly adopted the mass and made it a part of their popular crusade against communism.

By the mid-1950s these conservative demonstrations came to dominate the city's streets each spring, as the disproportionate numbers between the Loyalty Day and May Day crowds in New York indicated. The Socialist Party and SLP celebrations were all but gone from the public eye, as the two parties essentially faded from the political landscape. The Communist Party also witnessed a decline in membership, as the inner core of the party shifted once again to a position of rigid orthodoxy that precluded it from forming coalitions. In addition, the prosecution of communist leaders under the Smith Act and the popular anticommunism sweeping the nation eventually rendered the party impotent.

Because of the intensity of anticommunist sentiment, radicals also found themselves isolated from the labor unions that they and their parents had helped to build. By the late 1940s, any association with communists or communism was a major liability even for the Congress of Industrial Organizations (CIO), which had long had strong radical ties. With passage of the Taft-Hartley Act in 1947, the right to strike was limited and the closed shop outlawed. In this new, constrained position, most unions did not want to tempt further legal limitations by becoming targets for anticommunist persecution. Leaders of organized labor were pushed by Taft-Hartley and the Cold War anticommunist agenda to favor labor peace and control their rank and file in the interests of maintaining their bargaining power. Purging their ranks of communists became an essential part of this new equation, which the labor unions began to do in 1946, even within the CIO unions that the Communist Party had helped to build in the 1930s. Without any significant support from the unions, Communist May Day demonstrations dwindled.

As the majority of the AFL-affiliated unions had been doing for nearly half a century, organized labor in America now turned its full attention to the September Labor Day holiday instead, when it could celebrate itself as a distinctly American labor movement on a holiday unique to the United States. Consequently, most American laborers distanced themselves from solidarity with workers around the world, who continued to observe May Day. On the September holiday, which essentially had become a celebration of leisure by mid-century, American workers felt pride in their nation's exceptional postwar economic boom and culture of consumption in which, it was believed, real class divisions did not exist.

The few radicals who held out during the 1950s and organized small May Day meetings in Union Square were totally marginalized within the nation's Cold War political culture. By 1956, there were very few Communist Party members and supporters left, and their numbers dwindled even further after Soviet Premier Khruschev's revelations of Stalin's reign of terror. Disillusionment led many party faithful to leave the ranks and to abandon the holiday that had been a central part of their collective self-definition for decades. Not only did the anticommunist crusade alienate the party from the unions at the same moment organized labor sought a less confrontational posture in the new postwar boom economy, but the internal collapse of the communist movement in America after 1956 doomed it, and May Day, to oblivion in the United States.

By the late 1950s, then, the holiday that had represented the aspirations of those who embraced radical politics was now all but abandoned. May Day had become so strongly identified with the Soviet Union and global communism that it had been rendered useless as a vehicle for democratic protest in the United States. Even after the second Red Scare in the late 1940s and early 1950s waned, May Day could not be revived to its former glory. The holiday lost its mass audience, as the class divisions that were laid bare during the Great Depression faded in a postwar wave of consumption. The old radical and working-class holiday, born in the streets of Chicago and New York in the movement for the eight-hour day, and expanded into an annual protest for the end of capitalism and the rise of socialism, rang hollow in a land of uneasy peace and unusual plenty.

As a result, the presence of May Day in the history of American political culture became a purposefully forgotten component of postwar Americans' "purposeful remembering," as they constructed a new public memory for their

Protesters walk through the financial district of Chicago in their opposition to economic and political exploitation, 2000. © AP / Wide World Photos.

nation in the latter half of the twentieth century. While protest and dissent have remained possible within American political culture, their economic focus has been limited. They have not included a questioning of the nation's capitalist economy, nor have those who voiced them been able to capture and redefine the core symbols of the nation. The implications of this for the political left in the latter half of the twentieth century have been profound.

Yet the legacy of May Day was not entirely lost after the 1950s. A day of labor protest that originated in America had found its way around the globe, first along the currents of the international labor and socialist movements and later through the channels of the international Communist Party. Even in America, where the great socialist and communist urban parades are no longer held, vestiges of the holiday could be found in the sporadic efforts of radical student-based movements of the 1960s and 1970s to revive the holiday around contemporary issues. Today many anti-globalization protestors have claimed May Day as their own, making their protests against world-wide capitalist development and defining their collective identity as an international movement struggling to find more humane, environmentally responsible, and socially inclusive forms of economic and political relations. Although the Old Left socialists and communists who first associated May Day with radical politics are no more, the holiday remains a useful medium for the expression of insurgent political identities elsewhere in the world. It remains one of America's most unusual and controversial cultural exports, and its history illuminates the changing nature of American political culture from the late nineteenth to the mid-twentieth centuries.

FURTHER READING

Foner, Philip S. *May Day: A Short History of the International Workers' Holiday, 1886–1986.* New York: International Publishers, 1986.

Haverty-Stacke, Donna Truglio. "Constructing Radical America: A Cultural and Social History of May Day in New York City and Chicago, 1867–1945." Ph.D. diss., Cornell University, 2003.

Kazin, Michael, and Steven J. Ross. "America's Labor Day: The Dilemma of a Worker's Celebration." *Journal of American History* 78, no. 4 (1992): 1294–323.

Panaccione, Andrea. *The Memory of May Day: An Iconographic History of the Origins and Implanting of a Workers' Holiday.* Venice, Italy: Marsilio Editori, 1989.

Donna T. Haverty-Stacke

CINCO DE MAYO AND 16TH OF SEPTEMBER

Two of the most important Mexican holidays, both widely celebrated by Mexican Americans and other Americans, are often misunderstood in the United States. Cinco de Mayo, the fifth of May, is the more commercialized of the two, and is often confused with Mexico's Independence Day, which is celebrated on September 16. These two Mexican national holidays are referred to as the *fiestas patrias*. Cinco de Mayo (May 5) commemorates General Ignacio Zaragosa's victory on May 5, 1862, over the French army at Puebla, Mexico, the victory at *La Battalla de Puebla*. *Diez y Seis de Septiembre* (September 16), commemorates the events on that date in 1810, when Father Miguel Hidalgo rallied Mexicans to overthrow the Spanish colonial government in a speech called "El Grito de Dolores," the cry of Dolores, the town where Father Hidalgo lived. While both holidays have political and military origins, they have grown and changed over time and are both closely tied to Mexican nationalism and identity. Many writers and commentators only refer to *Fiestas Patrias* as September 16, Mexican Independence Day. In any respect, the celebrations in the United States are often more a statement of cultural roots than a patriotic or political statement. The common thread, though, is a celebration of Mexican ethnicity, and a history and culture born out of European conquest, African slavery, and indigenous cultures.

HISTORY

The history of Cinco de Mayo is one of the major David and Goliath stories in North America. A poorly trained and organized Mexican Army defeated a

CINCO DE MAYO AND
16TH OF SEPTEMBER

- Both are popular celebrations of Mexican independence brought to the United States by immigrants, where they serve as an affirmation of Mexican identity.

- *Cinco de Mayo* (May 5) commemorates General Ignacio Zaragosa's victory on May 5, 1862, over the French army at Puebla, Mexico.

- *Diez y Seis de Septiembre* (September 16) commemorates when, in 1810, Father Miguel Hidalgo rallied Mexicans to overthrow the Spanish colonial government in a speech called "El Grito de Dolores," the cry of Dolores.

- *Cinco de Mayo* is celebrated more widely in the United States than it is in Mexico.

- 16th of September is considered Mexico's Fourth of July.

- In 1988 the U.S. Congress designated September 15 to October 15 National Hispanic Heritage Month.

- Both holidays are celebrated throughout the United States, but the largest celebrations are in areas with the most immigrants from Mexico and their descendants, like California, Texas, the American Southwest, and large cities like Chicago.

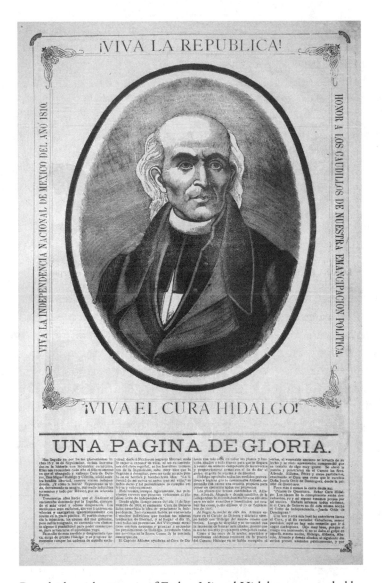

Broadside with portrait of Father Miguel Hidalgo surrounded by text celebrating Mexican Independence. Courtesy of the Library of Congress.

highly trained and well-organized French Army. During the 1850s, the decade after the Mexican-American War and the Treaty of Guadalupe Hidalgo, a financially unstable Mexico experienced a severe economic crisis. In 1855 Benito Juarez became the Minister of Justice and issued a series of reforms that limited the power of the Catholic Church. In 1857 the progressives led by Juarez adopted a new constitution for Mexico in hopes of dealing with the unstable political and financial situation; conservatives vigorously opposed it. These events lead to civil war that brought the country to the brink of bankruptcy. In response to the financial disaster Juarez suspended foreign debt payments for a two-year period. European banks rejected the moratorium on repayment, and Spanish, British, and French forces seized the gulf coast city of Veracruz. The Mexican government agreed to resume payments, and the Spanish and British forces withdrew. Much of the debt was owed to France, and Napoleon III of France used the conflict as an excuse to expand French influence in Mexico and establish a French Catholic monarchy in Mexico City. Napoleon III was led to believe by Mexican conservatives that the French would be seen as liberators, and that Mexicans would welcome the stability of a European-styled government.

A French Army of 6,000 men was sent to Veracruz and marched overland toward Mexico City. The French decided to attack the city of Puebla on May 5, 1862. The Mexican forces under the leadership of General Ignacio Zaragosa, who was born in Texas, numbered about 5,000 troops and were not as well armed as the French forces. Captain Porfirio Zamora, the commander of a cavalry troop that fought under Zaragosa, was born and raised in south Texas; thus a second American connection. The Mexican troops were mostly indigenous peasants and were poorly trained and equipped; for example, they included many state militiamen who lacked uniforms and were sometimes armed only with machetes. At the time, the French army was considered one of the best in the world and did not expect much resistance. In addition, the United States was embroiled in its Civil War and thus was thought unlikely to interfere in French plans to control Mexico. Three times the French army attacked the fortified positions surrounding Puebla and was repulsed all three times. After the third assault General Zaragosa ordered his cavalry to attack the retreating French army; only the intervention of a thunderstorm ended the fighting, and the defeated French withdrew. Leading the attack on General Zaragosa's right flank was young Brigadier General Porfirio Diaz, a future leader of Mexico. Fewer than 100 Mexican soldiers were killed, while the French losses numbered between 460 and 1,000. Despite its tremendous advantages, an army of one of the most powerful nations in the world was defeated by the smaller, less experienced, and outgunned Mexican army.

While news of the victory inspired many in Mexico, Napoleon III answered with more troops, and Puebla fell to the French in May 1863. They soon entered Mexico City, and the Juarez government was forced to flee. The majority of Mexicans continued to support Juarez and used guerilla tactics to harass the French and Mexican Imperial forces. In March 1867, nearly four years later, the French left, tired of their experiment in Mexico. Forces loyal to Juarez soon defeated the Mexican Imperial army, and Archduke Maximillian of Austria, who had accepted the crown of Mexico from Napoleon III, was captured and executed. President Juarez returned to power and triumphantly entered Mexico City to take over control of the government.

THE SIGNIFICANCE OF "EL CINCO DE MAYO"

Although the Battle of Puebla, *La Batalla de Puebla,* was rendered insignificant by later French victories, it infused the Mexican people with pride and patriotism it had rarely enjoyed, especially after the defeat by the United States in the Mexican-American War. Thus, after many tragedies and setbacks, at the Battle at Puebla the Mexican people were able to rally against the French invasion and be justly proud of being Mexican. *Yo soy Mexicano,* I am Mexican, became a positive statement, a symbol of Mexican unity, and a source of pride. For Mexicans, Cinco de Mayo has come to represent national sovereignty and the right of self-determination. There is also an ethnic dimension; the ability of an indigenous people to defend themselves from military and cultural takeover and preserve their traditions. The later defeat of the French also symbolized an end to foreign intervention, the last time a large-scale European army would invade the Americas. Hence, it is a day of joyous affirmation of political and cultural identity.

From an American standpoint, Jose Antonio Burciaga and other scholars believe that if the French had won the first battle of Puebla, France would have provided additional aid to the South in the American Civil War. At that time,

Performers reenact the "Batalla de Puebla" in San Diego during Cinco de Mayo celebrations, 2003. © Jorge Uzon/AFP/Getty Images.

Confederate General Robert E. Lee was enjoying some success, and the French could have aided the South in freeing southern ports of the Union blockade. Union troops defeated the Confederate Army just 14 months after the Battle of Puebla, essentially ending the Civil War. One reason for the Union Army's success was that the French defeat at Puebla cut off the flow of arms that had been shipped to the confederacy from the part of Mexico controlled by the French. Thus, the U.S. Civil War was shortened, and assistance was given that helped end American slavery. In response, the United States came to the aid of the Juarez government with weapons and ammunition and thus helped to ultimately defeat the French in 1867. American soldiers were even encouraged to join the Mexican army to fight the French. In the victory parade in Mexico City, the American Legion of Honor marched along with Mexican soldiers. It may be somewhat of a historical stretch to pin the survival of the United States on the success of a small Mexican army at Puebla on May 5, 1862, although it is at least a possibility that history might have been changed by this one event. Thus, Cinco de Mayo has a historical significance for millions of people who are not of Mexican ancestry. In addition, many historians maintain that because of the failure of the French to defeat Mexico's sovereignty, Mexican nationalism and self-esteem began to grow substantially for the first time in Mexico's short but turbulent history.

On a final note, there are jokes about the origins of Cinco de Mayo. For example, the Chicano cartoonist and commentator Lalo Alcaraz has a humorous history of Cinco de Mayo on the pocho.com Web site that satirizes the commercialization of this holiday. For example, he discusses the huge profits made on Cinco de Mayo by major corporations, including the beverage industry. One rather labored joke goes like this: Hellmann's mayonnaise at one time was manufactured in England. A ship was carrying 12,000 jars of the condiment for delivery in Vera Cruz, Mexico. This was to be the largest single shipment of mayonnaise ever to Mexico. However, the ship was lost at sea, and the cargo was forever lost. Hellman's mayonnaise had become very popular with the people of Mexico, and they had been eagerly awaiting the arrival of the large shipment. When they heard the news of the sinking, many people were very upset. Their anguish was so great that they convinced the Mexican government to declare a national day of mourning. It occurs each year on May 5, and is known as . . . Sinko de Mayo.

CELEBRATIONS—MEXICO AND THE UNITED STATES

Cinco de Mayo is a national holiday in Mexico and was first celebrated under French rule. The name of the city, Puebla, was even changed to Puebla de Zaragosa. However, It is not celebrated in Mexico to the same extent that it is by Mexican Americans in the United States, mainly because in Mexico the 16th of September (Independence Day) is considered the more important holiday. In Mexico it is more of a regional holiday and is celebrated most vigorously in the state of Puebla, especially in its capital city of the same name. Although there are celebrations nationwide, they are all on a lesser scale than in Puebla. In the United States, Cinco de Mayo celebrations range from the three-day extravaganza on Olvera Street and in other parts of downtown Los Angeles, to small events sponsored by schools, community organizations, and commercial businesses. It is celebrated throughout the United States, wherever there are communities of people of Mexican ancestry, including the Southwest, southern California, and parts of the Northwest, Midwest, Northeast, and the South. Particularly well known is the celebration in Los Angeles, on the streets near City Hall. Common festivities include parades, mariachi and other kinds of Mexican music, dancing, meals featuring Mexican food, sports events, beauty contests, and more. Piñatas are also common at Cinco de Mayo events. Thus, it is a time to celebrate being of Mexican ancestry, and to share with community folks and others Mexican and Mexican American culture. Many of the large events in the United States have parades, car shows, music, and food as part of the festivities. Today it has become much more commercialized in both the United States and Mexico, and the holiday is promoted by businesses with products such as food and beverages. Many restaurants and bars also exploit Cinco de Mayo and provide a venue for celebrators. This is one indication of both the growing economic strength of the population of persons of Mexican ancestry in the United States, and the increased popularity of Cinco de Mayo beyond this ethnic group. Unfortunately a number of advertisements have perpetuated traditional stereotypes of Mexicans.

As in Mexico, commercial interests in the United States have increasingly promoted Cinco de Mayo in order to sell food, beverages, and a variety of other products. Many restaurants and nightclubs are more than happy to provide a place for people to celebrate Cinco de Mayo. Some even view it as a Mexican Saint Patrick's Day, basically a day/evening to drink beer and other alcoholic beverages. However, there are also many public and private noncommercial Cinco de Mayo celebrations throughout the United States, some very small and some quite large. Many community activists accuse the major beer companies of "hijacking" Cinco de Mayo, similar to what has happened to Saint Patrick's Day, and turning it into an excuse to sell beer and tequila. Marketing the holiday to both Mexican Americans and other Americans, millions of dollars are spent each year to promote Cinco de Mayo as a drinking holiday, oftentimes by Mexican breweries, blurring its significance. A number of cities have sponsored alcohol-free Cinco de Mayo celebrations in an effort to restore the original meaning of the holiday. For example, in San Diego more than 10,000 people have gathered at Chicano Park for an alcohol-free Cinco de Mayo event.

In the United States, Cinco de Mayo is seen as a day to celebrate Mexican American heritage more than a day to commemorate a battle victory. Besides being an excuse to party for some people, events and celebrations on this day educate the American people about Mexican American culture and history. It is a day for people of Mexican ancestry to maintain and reaffirm their roots; a day to celebrate their ethnic and cultural traditions. Mexican Americans celebrate the holiday as an appreciation of its cultural significance—victory in the face of great odds and the patriotism it generated—more than its historical significance. It is and can be used as a learning experience to close the cultural gap between Mexican Americans and other ethnic groups. Other reasons why Cinco de Mayo is widely celebrated in the United States include the fact that General Zaragosa, the leader of *La Battala de Puebla,* was born in Texas while it was still part of Mexico; thus for many he is the first Chicano hero. To attract voters, politicians give speeches and attend events on Cinco de Mayo and September 16. In the United States, non-Mexican American candidates often attempt to show their knowledge of people of Mexican ancestry and their commitment to community concerns by participating in Cinco de Mayo events. For example, presidential candidate John Kerry spoke in East Los Angeles on May 5, 2005 on issues important to the Mexican American community, and George W. Bush responded that as a former governor of the State of Texas he had long been committed to helping Mexican Americans. It was not by accident that John Kerry's national co-chair for his election campaign was Antonio Villaraigosa, a Los Angeles city councilman elected mayor of Los Angeles in 2005.

A SAMPLING OF AMERICAN CINCO DE MAYO EVENTS

California

The largest event is held in Los Angeles. The Los Angeles event begins with a huge downtown fiesta on Broadway, and continues the next weekend with food, dancing, and music. Over 600,000 people typically crowd into a 36-square block area of downtown Los Angles to participate in the world's largest Cinco de Mayo celebration. The streets are colored in red, white, and green, the colors of the Mexican flag, while well known and local orchestras and bands play patriotic songs and other Mexican and Mexican American tunes. Many people, young and old, come dressed in traditional Mexican clothing, and young girls can be seen in red and green ruffled dresses with wide skirts. A stage is set up at City Hall with a picture of General Zaragosa, flanked by American and Mexican flags. Both American politicians and Mexican dignitaries speak about their peoples' shared history and the heritage of Cinco de Mayo. There are also sports events, dances, and picnics in other parts of Los Angeles as part of the celebration.

San Diego has a three-day event centered around Old Town that attracts more than 200,000 people. Similar to many other celebrations, there is mariachi and other types of Mexican and American music including jazz and hip-hop, dancing, food, and handicrafts. There is also a showcase of hands-on exhibits designed to promote the arts, culture, and industries of the local area. An interesting part of the San Diego event is a live reenactment of the Battle of Puebla. San Jose,

California also has a major parade and festival that has been somewhat curtailed in recent years. Unfortunately, the celebration in San Jose is best known today for a large riot in 1997, which led to many arrests and property damage. While many people blamed the police for overreacting to drunk and unruly young adults in the crowd, the easy availability of alcohol played a role. Alcohol was also involved in 2005 when police clashed with a crowd of about 500 at a Cinco de Mayo celebration in Richmond, California. There are many other events throughout California, including a fairly large one in Santa Barbara, and many cities and towns also have special celebrations on Cinco de Mayo. University student organizations at many campuses sponsor Cinco de Mayo events in order to educate other students and the larger community about the historical events surrounding Cinco de Mayo, and its cultural importance.

Texas

One of the more interesting Cinco de Mayo events is held at Goliad, Texas, a town of only 2,000 residents with strong ties to the battle of Puebla because General Zaragosa was born there. He was also baptized there and later moved to Matamoros, Mexico with his family after Mexico's defeat in the Texas Revolution. Goliad has a small museum honoring General Zaragosa, and a huge statue of him, a gift from the state of Puebla in 1980. An important part of Cinco de Mayo in Goliad is the educational programs by the Zaragosa society, a local volunteer group that sponsors classroom visits and distributes educational materials to the schools. Goliad has celebrated Cinco de Mayo for many years, although the event has grown in popularity in recent years and has been named the official venue for the celebration by the Texas Senate in 1999. Even the name Goliad is steeped in Mexican history; it is an anagram of Miguel Hidalgo y Costilla, the father of Mexican independence. Goliad's event includes a Catholic mass at the Zaragosa Amphitheater, a parade, a beauty pageant, and of course lots of food, music, and arts and crafts. They also have historical figures dressed in period clothing who interact with the participants.

San Antonio has a large celebration over three days, as do Austin and other Texas cities. At the Dallas celebration a wreath-laying ceremony is normally held at the statue of General Zaragosa in Jaycee Zaragosa Park. There is also a significant three-day celebration in San Marcos, Texas, which has celebrated Cinco de Mayo with a state menudo cook-off since 1974. San Marcos also hosts concerts, a parade, folklorico dancing, and a beauty pageant. Alpine schedules an annual Cabrito Cookoff on a weekend for their Cinco de Mayo celebration.

Arizona, Colorado, and Nevada

A unique Cinco de Mayo celebration is held in Chandler, Arizona where people gather for mariachi music, dance, games, and food. The highlight of the festival, though, is races and a pageant featuring Chihuahuas. Proud owners parade their dogs through the park, race them, and compete to see whose dogs will be crowned King and Queen of Chihuahuas. Another interesting way to celebrate Cinco de Mayo is at Rawhide Wild-West-Town, in Scottsdale, Arizona. Besides music, food, fireworks, and bull riding, they also have a running of the bulls, which requires participants to sign a release of liability and assumption of risk agreement.

Denver, Colorado's two-day festival is held at Civic Center Park in front of the state capitol and draws more than 400,000 people. There are many choices of Mexican food, and people listen to nortena, banda, and other types of Mexican/Mexican American music.

Reno, Nevada has a three-day festival, partially sponsored by local casinos. It rivals in size the celebration in Los Angles and attracts well over 100,000 people. It includes charros and a dancing horse show, a foot race, live music, and dance on a number of stages. Las Vegas, Nevada also hosts a major event at Freedom Park with many food and handicraft vendors. Along with California, Texas and a number of other states, Nevada has one of the most rapidly rising populations of people of Mexican ancestry.

Outside the Southwest

There are literally hundreds of celebrations in other parts of the United States. Chicago, the city with the second-largest number of people of Mexican ancestry in the United States, has a huge event that attracts nearly 200,000 people to Douglas Park. Many other towns and cities in the Midwest and Northwest, such as Portland, have celebrations and festivals, an indication that people of Mexican ancestry can be found nearly everywhere in the United States. St. Paul, Minnesota also holds a two-day event and a parade. It is held in the city's District del Sol and has many food vendors and various dance troupes, plus a street dance. Orlando, Florida has a celebration with a street fair, strolling mariachis and other Mexican music, dancing, and a tortilla-eating contest. An unusual example of a small celebration is held at North Carolina's Morrison Correctional Institution. Participants, which include inmates, staff, and guests, are provided with many types of Mexican food, such as tacos, bunuelos, pico de gallo, and horchata, and they listen to Latino music. There is also folk dancing, and singing, including the Mexican national anthem. It is a time for inmates and staff to celebrate and recognize the contributions of Mexican culture in the United States.

In sum, Cinco de Mayo events in the United States come in all sizes and can be found nearly everywhere. This holiday is an opportunity to celebrate Mexican history and culture and to educate all Americans about the contributions of both Mexicans and Mexican Americans to the American mosaic. Many of these events have corporate and local business sponsorship, including

Hispanic chambers of commerce. Schools and community organizations also often take an active role in planning the events.

16TH OF SEPTEMBER (DIEZ Y SEIS DE SEPTIEMBRE): HISTORY OF MEXICAN INDEPENDENCE DAY

On the September 16, citizens of Mexico and people of Mexican ancestry in the United States and other countries celebrate Mexico's independence from Spanish rule. This holiday has its origins in events that occurred three centuries prior to Mexico's independence when the Spanish captured Cuauhtemoc, the last Aztec emperor, in 1521. This event marked the beginning of 300 years of Spanish rule. Colonial society was highly stratified, with Spaniards born in Spain at the top, followed by Criollos or creoles (born in Mexico of Spanish parents), Mestizos and Mulattos (mixed bloods), and the indigenous peoples and Africans. The Criollos were treated as second-class subjects and would become the group that sparked the independence movement.

In 1808 Napoleon invaded Spain and selected his brother Jose (or Joseph) Bonaparte, as king of the Spanish Empire (1808–1810). This distraction gave Mexicans the opportunity to begin an independence movement from Spanish control. The French Revolution and its concepts of democracy, liberty, and equality derived from the French philosophers Rousseau, Montesquieu, and Voltaire, and the American Revolution, inspired many educated Mexicans to start a revolt against Spain. In the early hours of September 16, 1810, a 57-year-old Catholic priest, Padre Miguel Hidalgo y Costilla, rang the bell of his small church near Guanajuato and gave the cry—el Grito de Dolores (the cry of Dolores) to his congregation. It was a call to Mexicans of all races and backgrounds to fight for liberty, and the beginning of the Mexican War of Independence that would last 10 years. The plan had been to start the revolt on October 2, but Hidalgo's friend Ignacio Allende had informed him that the Gachupines (a derisive term for Spanish born in Spain, also known as Peninsulares) had discovered the plot by Criollos to establish an independent Mexico and had sent soldiers to arrest him. Hidalgo was an unlikely revolutionary leader; an educated Catholic priest, the former dean of the College of San Nicolas at Valladolid in Michoacan (now Morelia), and the son of a Hacienda overseer. Although Mexican-born of Spanish ancestry, he believed in empowering the Mestizo and indigenous masses, and the end of Spanish tyranny. In this respect the revolt was similar to independence movements in many other Latin American countries, led by men such as Jose Gervasio Artigas, Jose de San Martin, Bernardo O'Higgins, Jose Antonio Paez, and Simon Bolivar. What Hidalgo actually told the people at Dolores is unknown. It is widely believed that he said "Viva la Virgen de Guadalupe! Death to bad government! Death to the Gachupines!" Some believe he also said

"Viva Mexico," but this is unlikely since the term "Mexico" at that time referred to Mexico City and not the country, which was called New Spain. The Virgin of Guadalupe would come to symbolize the Mexican liberation movement.

In the days following this speech in Dolores, a large army of mostly Mestizo and Indian peasants captured the cities of San Miguel, Celya, and Guanajuato, and almost entered Mexico City, only to be ordered to retreat by Hidalgo. He was apparently a compassionate man, and he was worried that his unruly army would devastate the city as they had done in previous instances. This gave the Spanish colonial army time to regroup, and Hidalgo's poorly armed peasant army was soon on the run. Hidalgo was later captured and executed by the Inquisition for both heresy and treason in July of 1811. However, he had started a revolt that would ultimately succeed a decade later. Thus, Hidalgo is known as the Father of Mexican Independence because his "Grito" started the revolution and helped gain Mexico's independence from Spain. After Father Hidalgo's death, Jose Maria Morelos, a priest from a small town, rallied the revolutionary forces until his capture and execution in 1815. As the decade came to a close Vicente Guerrero became leader of the revolutionary forces and continued the struggle until the Spanish forces were finally defeated. In recognition of their contributions, three states in Mexico are named Hidalgo, Morelos, and Guerrero, and many hospitals, schools, colleges, parks, and government buildings bear their names.

THE SIGNIFICANCE OF THE 16TH OF SEPTEMBER

September 16 is similar to July 4 in the United States. It is regarded as much more important and is celebrated more widely and vigorously in Mexico than is Cinco de Mayo. It is a time to show one's pride in being Mexican. There are rodeos, charro performances, dancing, and much more. There is much food and noisemaking, flags wave from nearly every building, lighted decorations appear everywhere, and the people decorate statues of Father Hidalgo with flowers representing the Mexican flag: red, white, and green. Green symbolizes independence, white symbolizes the Catholic faith, and red symbolizes the union of Spanish, creoles, Indians, and other people in Mexico. People of all ages join in for Mexico's biggest fiesta. While it arguably does not have as much significance for the United States as does Cinco de Mayo, celebrating independence from Spain is shared by all of the former colonial countries of Latin America

But even in the United States, September is recognized as the most important time of year to celebrate independence and pride in one's Hispanic heritage. The week of September 15–22 was proclaimed Hispanic Heritage Week by the U.S. Congress in 1968, and in 1988 Congress designated September 15 to October 15 National Hispanic Heritage Month. In 1967, President Lyndon Johnson in a proclamation recognized September 16 as Hispanic Heritage Day, and each year since then the president issues a proclamation requesting that everyone recognize and celebrate the history, culture, and contributions of Latinos in the United States. The tragic events of September 11, 2001 in New York City and Washington, D.C. led President Vicente Fox to cancel the annual celebration on September 16 at diplomatic and consular offices in the United States. Thus, in victory and in tragedy, there are close ties between Mexico and the United States, and at least a certain degree of solidarity and common purpose. Hence, Mexican Independence Day is now part of a wider recognition of the history, culture, and traditions of Latinos in the United States. This is one way of recognizing the shared history of colonialization, and subsequent independence from

Vicente Fox and his wife, Marta Sahagun de Fox, celebrate Cinco de Mayo in Mexico City, 2003. © AP / Wide World Photos.

a European nation. As a final note, the 16th of September, like Cinco de Mayo, is often used to promote the Chicano heritage in the United States rather than a strictly Mexican heritage and culture.

The 16th of September is not as commercialized in the United States as Cinco de Mayo, although many events are corporate- and local business-sponsored, and the food and beverage industry, and other companies, use it to sell their products.

CELEBRATIONS: MEXICO AND THE UNITED STATES

Today Mexican Independence Day is a much bigger celebration than Cinco de Mayo. The people of Mexico celebrate with a fiesta unlike any other. The celebration actually begins the night before in the plazas and zócolas (town meeting places) in nearly every city, town, and village in Mexico. The most spectacular celebration is in Mexico City. When the clock strikes 11 o'clock in Mexico City the crowd becomes quiet, and the president of Mexico steps out onto the palace balcony and rings the historic bell that Father Hidalgo rang to call the people in 1810. Then the president gives the Grito de Dolores, and shouts "Viva Mexico" and "Viva independencia," and the crowd echoes back. The president also waves the Mexican flag, and the people sing the Mexican national anthem. Recently, there have been videos available of the president of Mexico giving the reenactment of "El Grito." This is repeated all over Mexico at the same time, and the governors of the various states, mayors, and government officials in other countries all reenact "El Grito" in hundreds of locations. Toward the end of the ceremony the crowd joins and loudly yell the names of the heroes of the independence movement, and at the conclusion there is a fireworks display, and the people throw confetti, blow whistles and horns, and generally make lots of noise.

This tradition dates to a well-known celebration of the *grito de independencia* on the night of September 10, 1910. It was the 100th anniversary of Father Hidalgo's initial *grito,* and government dignitaries had gathered to view the most important fiesta on the Mexican civil calendar. At 11:00 P.M. President Porfirio Diaz stood on the main balcony of the national palace, rang the same bell that Father Hidalgo had rung in Dolores, and shouted, "Long live the heroes of the nation!" President Diaz had chosen the night before the actual event (dawn on the 16th) because September 15 was Saint Porfirio's feast day (a Greek saint of the fourth century, and the birthday of President Porfirio Diaz.) It is still celebrated on the 15th today, and "El Grito" is reenacted at precisely 11:00 P.M. in plazas or zocalos all over Mexico. Streets, houses, buildings, cars, and trucks are decorated throughout the country. Merchants and street vendors sell flags, balloons, sombreros, and *rehiletes* (shuttlecocks), and nearly everything is painted in the colors of the Mexican flag. There are also many

Members of the dance group Danza Teocalt perform in Los Angeles, May 2003. © AP / Wide World Photos.

kinds of food, including *Antojitos,* that is, finger food and candies, and various fruit punches made from guayabas, sugarcane, raisins, and apples are sold on the street and in temporary stands. Traditional foods, such as mole poblano and posole are very popular on this holiday. Many men dress as charros, and women in China Poblanas, or indegenous dresses. Others dress in the colors of the Mexican flag: green, white, and red. Mariachi and other types of popular music are played on the street and many other locations. Flags seem to be everywhere, lighted decorations are common at most events, and noisemakers, whistles, and other instruments are widely available. The people are ready to make as much noise as possible, and there is fireworks, music, and a fiesta that lasts long into the night. The actual day of September 16 is celebrated similarly to July 4 in the United States. There are civic ceremonies, rodeos, parades, and bullfights, among many other events.

A popular Mexican Independence Day celebration for visitors from the United States is at San Miguel de Allende, near where Father Hidalgo made his famous speech. It is the birthplace of another hero of the initial struggle for independence from Spain, Ignacio Allende, who gave his last name to San Miguel. As in Mexico city, there is the reenactment of "El Grito" and fireworks on the evening of the 15th. On the 16th, there is a large parade, with many people dressed in red, white, and green, and a reenactment of a battle between the Spanish army and the insurgents. In addition, there are food, arts and crafts, and many public and private fiestas throughout the city.

A SAMPLING OF MEXICAN INDEPENDENCE DAY CELEBRATIONS IN THE UNITED STATES

Texas

The first celebration on September 16, the first *Fiestas Patrias* in Texas, was held in the early 1820s. Festivities included music, dances, food, elaborate costumes, and homage to the heroes of the revolution. Celebrations in Texas continued into the post–Civil War years and spread to many towns along the border, and to other Texas towns. By 1900 San Antonio held an elaborate three-day fiesta from September 15–17, which was coordinated by a committee called the *Junta Patriotica* (Patriotic Board), and local organizations. There was a large parade, including participation by local groups called *sociedades mutualistas* (mutual aid societies). There were singing of patriotic songs, games, food, and fireworks. Today, it is a traditional celebration rooted in historic events and devoted to preserving the multiethnic nature of Texas. Today the San Antonio celebration occurs over three days, and Market Square in downtown is the center of the festivities. There is also a multiday festival in Lubbock at the Memorial Civic Center.

San Angelo also has a long tradition of celebrating September 16. By 1910 there was a large parade, and a two-day celebration at the Lake Concho Pavilion. In later years the celebration moved into the community and included baseball games, concerts, and other activities. The first event in Houston was during the 1920s, when the Mexican population became large enough to have a Mexican consulate. The celebration expanded into a number of activities, including a parade, and by 2004 had evolved into a series of events throughout September, including beauty pageants. In Austin there are more than two dozen concerts held during a six-day festivity. Local chapters of the League of United Latin American Citizens (LULAC) and the G.I. forum, major community organizations in Texas, often assist in coordinating events. In Port Arthur, on the second weekend of September, the celebration is called the Mexican Fiesta, and there is folkloric and other entertainment along with food and music.

California

In Los Angeles the festivities begin on the evening of September 15 with "El Grito de Dolores" on the steps of City Hall. The evening begins with music, and at 11 o'clock the Mexican consul reenacts Hidalgo's call for independence. The mayor of Los Angeles and other local politicians, plus community leaders, join him. This event is also televised. There is also a major festival in San Diego, in Old Town and a number of other locations, with music, folk dancing, food, and so on. Close by in Tijuana there is also a huge fiesta sponsored by the Instituto de Cultura de Baja California.

Outside the Southwest

Mexican Independence Day is celebrated in hundreds of towns and cities throughout the United States, everywhere people of Mexican ancestry reside. For example, The Mexican Cultural Center in Philadelphia commemorates this holiday with a corporate-sponsored festival at the Great Plaza at Penn's Landing. In Philadelphia it has become a reunion of all Latino communities, including Puerto Ricans, Cubans, Colombians, Venezuelans, and so on, plus, of course, Chicanos and Mexican immigrants. At this fiesta there is Latino music including mariachis, folk dancing, food, and arts and crafts.

FURTHER READING

Chartrand, Rene, and Richard Hook (Illustrator). *The Mexican Adventure 1861–67.* London: Osprey Press, 1994.

Garcia, James. *Cinco de Mayo: A Mexican Holiday about Unity and Pride.* Chanhassen, Minn.: The Child's World, 2003.

Gnojewski, Carol. *Cinco de Mayo: Celebrating Hispanic Pride.* Berkeley Heights, N.J.: Enslow Publishers, 2002.

Harris, Zoe, and Suzanne Williams, *Piñatas and Smiling Skeletons: Celebrating Mexican Festivals.* Berkeley, Calif.: Pacific View Press, 1998.

Palacios, Argentina. *Viva Mexico! A Story of Benito Juarez and Cinco de Mayo.* Orlando, Fla.: Steck-Vaughn, 1992.

Louis M. Holscher

MOTHER'S DAY

- Mother's Day is observed on the second Sunday in May; it is not a federally recognized holiday.

- Its roots lie in the centuries-old English tradition of visiting one's mother with a bouquet of wildflowers on "Mothering Sunday."

- Anna Jarvis organized America's first modern Mother's Day celebration in Philadelphia in 1908.

- Jarvis asked people to wear a carnation to honor their mother on the holiday.

- Mother's Day observations have been used to promote many contentious progressive and conservative aims over the years, among them women's suffrage, pacifism, child welfare, domesticity, prevention of "racial decline," women's health, the Equal Rights Amendment, moral purity in men, and antipoverty efforts.

- In 1914 President Woodrow Wilson issued the first Presidential Mother's Day Proclamation, praising American mothers for their services to the nation.

- Angered by the deepening commercialization of the holiday she had helped popularize, Anna Jarvis later campaigned against those who sought to exploit Mother's Day for profit.

- Gift-giving has become such a pervasive part of Mother's Day festivities that in 2005 the National Retail Federation projected that sales would exceed $11 billion.

- Mother's Day celebrations have international appeal, as countries the world over currently celebrate the holiday.

MOTHER'S DAY

The holiday known as Mother's Day is celebrated each year in the United States and many other countries on the second Sunday in May. It is a day of sentimental remembrance that, in the words of the day's founder, Anna Jarvis, is meant to honor the "best mother who ever lived." More long-distance phone calls are placed on Mother's Day than on any other day of the year. Restaurateurs report that the second Sunday in May is their busiest day. The Hallmark greeting card company reported in 2005 that Mother's Day is the third-largest card-sending occasion. Florists are exceptionally busy in early May making and delivering special Mother's Day arrangements, and they mark the day as an especially profitable one, and, retailers hail the day as the second-highest gift-giving holiday in the year, exceeded only by Christmas. As a public demonstration of filial devotion, the holiday was unknown in the United States before 1908 when Anna Jarvis organized the first modern Mother's Day celebration in Philadelphia. Yet, in less than a century, Mother's Day became one of the most popular of American holidays, and one that is celebrated in more than 40 nations.

EARLY IMPULSES

In England the custom of visiting mothers with bouquets of wildflowers apparently extends back hundreds of years. Called "Mothering Sunday," this British counterpart of the American holiday continues to be celebrated on the fourth Sunday of Lent (in March or April). During the nineteenth century, on Mothering

Sunday, apprentices and domestic servants were given time off from their duties in their masters' households to return home for the weekend to their families of origin. The concept of a day honoring mothers also has been traced back to the mythology of ancient Greece and to rituals in Asia. The roots of the modern custom, however, are generally assumed to be found in the Victorian era of the late nineteenth century, because it is the genteel Victorian concept of the devoted, self-sacrificing mother that reigns in the literature and rituals of the modern celebration.

In the United States, Julia Ward Howe, abolitionist, suffragist, and author of "The Battle Hymn of the Republic," is sometimes credited as the founder of Mother's Day. The Mother's Day celebration she proposed in 1872 was intended as a day of female protest against the horrors of war perpetrated by men, not a day to honor individual mothers. Howe urged mothers to "arise" and leave their homes for a "great and earnest day of counsel." Together, she proclaimed, women would seek the means "whereby the great human family can live in peace." Writing just after the tragedy of the Civil War, Howe believed that because of their common bond of motherhood, women held the key to disarmament, peace, national unity, and international harmony.

Howe was not alone in thinking that women held the key to restoring ties shattered by the Civil War. Soon after hostilities ended, Mrs. Anna Reeves Jarvis, wife of a Grafton, West Virginia merchant, organized the mothers of the town for a "Mother's Friendship Day" meant to be a day of reconciliation. Mrs. Jarvis, like Julia Ward Howe, thought that mothers, because of their innate abhorrence of conflict (a common belief in the nineteenth century) were especially suited to rebuild the community that had been torn apart by war.

ANNA JARVIS'S CRUSADE

Anna Jarvis, who is usually credited with the creation of Mother's Day, was born in 1864, the daughter of Anna Reeves Jarvis. Living in Grafton, West Virginia, Anna as the oldest daughter had been especially close to her mother, although like many young women at the turn of the century, Anna also wanted to establish her independence. At age 27, Anna asked to live with an uncle in Chattanooga, Tennessee, but Mrs. Jarvis vetoed the move. The following year, however, Anna joined her brother, Claude, the wealthy owner of a thriving taxi business in Philadelphia. What was to have been a temporary visit became permanent when Anna was employed as a writer in the advertising department of the Fidelity Mutual Life Association and immersed herself in upper-class Philadelphia society. Letters between mother and daughter sustained the strong family ties, until in 1902, on the death of her husband, Mrs. Jarvis moved to Philadelphia to live with her daughter.

When Mrs. Jarvis died in 1905, Anna found the loss unbearable. Her mourning was prolonged and intense, a fact that the historian James P. Johnson has attributed to a deep depression complicated by a sense of guilt. Coworkers,

Anna Jarvis, the founder of Mother's Day. © Bettmann / Corbis.

noticing Anna's grief, urged her to turn her emotional turmoil into a blessing by taking up the work of her "devoted, loving and noble Christian mother." In response, Anna put her organizing skills and social connections to work. In 1907, she persuaded the congregation of the Andrews Methodist Episcopal Church in Grafton to hold a special service to mark the second anniversary of her mother's death; in honor of her mother, she distributed Mrs. Jarvis's favorite flower, the carnation, to the parishioners. In Philadelphia, she convinced several ministers to use the Sunday services for special sermons on motherhood.

From this time until her death in 1948, Anna Jarvis devoted herself to honoring the memory of her mother by obsessively promoting a public holiday on which all children paid homage to motherhood. Her first step was to organize a Mother's Day committee with prominent Philadelphians as members. In addition to her brother Claude, Jarvis's committee included Henry J. Heinz, whose wealth came from the manufacture of food products, the owner of Wanamaker's department store, and the editor of the Philadelphia *Inquirer*. It was a group that provided social legitimacy, financial support, and a forum for her message. On the third anniversary of her mother's death, in 1908, Jarvis inaugurated her drive for the universal celebration of Mother's Day at a special ceremony in the massive auditorium of Wanamaker's department store. Her committee was incorporated in 1912 as the Mother's Day International Association as Jarvis left her position at Fidelity Mutual and made the promotion of Mother's Day a full-time vocation.

Each year she wrote letters to public officials seeking their support for her holiday. In response, the governor of West Virginia, William Glasscock, issued the first Mother's Day proclamation in 1910, in which he asked all West Virginians to "attend church on that day and wear white carnations." Jarvis also wanted the federal government to acknowledge her holiday, but her first effort met with derision on the floor of the Senate. In 1908, Senator Elmer Burkett from Nebraska introduced a resolution in the United States Senate that would have recognized May 10 as Mother's Day and encouraged Senate members to wear a white flower to honor the occasion. On behalf of his resolution, Burkett argued that as more and more young people moved from their families to live independent lives in the city (where they might be corrupted by the evil ways of urban life), Mother's Day would "get the boys together and make them think of home and mother and the surroundings there." Senators engaged in a 40-minute debate over the resolution with one urging the Senate to substitute the fifth commandment in place of Burkett's language and another suggesting that the resolution belittled motherhood. The *New York Times* reported that the resolution was "gravely" referred to the judiciary committee where it was permitted to "sleep peacefully."

Jarvis was more successful in 1914 when Congress passed a joint resolution directing the president to ask Americans to display the flag on the second Sunday in May as a "public expression of our love and reverence for the mothers of our country." President Woodrow Wilson then issued the first Presidential Mother's Day Proclamation, praising American mothers for their services to the nation. Presidents since this time have followed Wilson's lead; in 2001 President George W. Bush encouraged "all Americans to honor the importance of mothers and to celebrate how their love and devotion are crucial to the well-being of children, families, and our society."

THE POLITICAL AND SOCIAL USES OF MOTHER'S DAY

Throughout her life, Anna Jarvis was an indefatigable campaigner for Mother's Day, but it took more than the grief and the energy of one woman to turn

Mother's Day into a national celebration and annual ritual. The nation's Sunday schools were among the most active supporters of Jarvis's efforts; their endeavors to celebrate Mother's Day certainly contributed to the popular acceptance of the holiday. In 1910, Jarvis approached George W. Bailey, chair of the executive committee of the World's Sunday School Association, with her idea, and Bailey persuaded a national Sunday school convention to endorse the celebration of Mother's Day. In the early twentieth century, Sunday schools observed as many as 200 special commemorative days, festivities that helped to draw children into the church. Children's Day was one of the most popular among the anniversary days, patriotic days, and days to encourage charitable and reform activities. Given these traditions, observance of Mother's Day quickly became a regular ritual in Protestant Sunday schools. By 1912, religious publishing houses were offering special programs, invitation cards, and celluloid carnations to help the Sunday schools celebrate Mother's Day.

In the churches proper, Mother's Day also became a regular feature of the religious calendar. Sermons designed for the adult church service praised the sacrifices of mothers and urged adults to honor their mothers. In 1912 during a General Conference of the Methodist Episcopal Church in Minneapolis, a delegate from Grafton called on his denomination and others to observe the second Sunday in May as Mother's Day. The resolution passed at the meeting, however, merely acknowledged what had already occurred. By 1911, Mother's Day celebrations were reportedly held in every state. Although Protestant churches were the first to incorporate Mother's Day into church festivities, before long, celebrations could be found in many different congregations, a unifying ritual and symbol of a common identity in an era rent by severe social and political upheavals.

Religion was only one of the many forces dividing Americans during the early twentieth century. Immigrants brought new customs to the United States, labor unrest fostered a fear of class warfare, and cities pulled young people away from their rural roots and conservative social values. Mother's Day provided Americans with an opportunity to celebrate a shared ritual. Protestants, Catholics, and Jews, in immigrant churches and those of native-born Americans, among the poor and the well-to-do, and both city dwellers and those from the countryside held Mother's Day festivities. Mother's Day was a reminder that though they may have shared little else in common, everyone had a mother. As a west coast magazine expressed it at the time, Mother's Day "is to commemorate no anniversary related to creed, to class, or to country; it is to observe generally the common debt of all mankind, our obligation to our mothers."

When used to pay reverence to the institution of motherhood rather than to individual mothers, Mother's Day proved to be a more contentious holiday. As was so much in American society in the early twentieth century, gender roles, too, were undergoing rapid and far-reaching changes. Some ministers saw Mother's Day as an opportunity to remind women of their maternal duties and to valorize an ideal of motherhood and domesticity that was challenged by the activities of suffragists, working girls, and college-educated social activists. Then too, as the birth rate among native-born white women declined, alarmists worried that modern women were shunning motherhood and contributing to "race suicide." As one Protestant minister told his congregation during one of the first Mother's Day celebrations, true Christian mothers "organized no crusades in the interest of so-called 'women's rights,'" and "never postured upon the platform as social and political revolutionists, but in a larger and higher sense they contributed to the real need of the times, inspiring honesty, loyalty, and patriotism in the hearts of their children and so strengthening and guaranteeing the foundation of our National greatness." During the services on Mother's Day, churches began to bestow special honors on the oldest mother present, or the one with the most children. The churches were among the first American institutions to use Mother's Day to promote a specific social arrangement; in this instance, Mother's Day became a vehicle for reminding women that domesticity was their destiny.

If the antisuffragists used Mother's Day to honor the woman who shunned a political or economic role outside the home, early twentieth-century feminists also laid claim to both maternal imagery and to Mother's Day. When suffragists claimed that women needed the vote because they brought values to political decision making that men neglected, they argued that it was maternal sentiment that was lacking in a government without female participation. It would have come as no surprise, then, when suffragists attempted to turn the holiday into a political event. In 1914, for example, the Women's Political Union, a radical suffragist organization, offered a $5.00 prize for the "best baby belonging to a suffragist mother." The group intended to prove that votes for women meant better babies, not neglected children as the antis charged. Anna Jarvis, too, was a suffragist, and she sometimes represented her holiday as a way to include women in what was otherwise a very masculine calendar. "Washington's Birthday is for the 'Father of our Country'; Memorial Day for our 'Heroic Fathers'; 4th of July for 'Patriot Fathers'; Labor Day for 'Laboring Fathers'; Thanksgiving Day for 'Pilgrim Father[s]'; and even New Year's Day is for 'Old Father Time.'" Surely, Mother deserved one day during the year. And, if the symbolism of Mother's Day did not encompass every woman (indeed, Anna Jarvis was herself unmarried and childless), nonetheless, the spirit of the day endorsed the maternalism that was such a powerful tool in the hands of the suffragists.

The success of Mother's Day in the early twentieth century and later, therefore, hinged in part on how, in addition to evoking private familial sentiment, the symbolism could be manipulated to espouse popular public or social agendas. Almost immediately, the holiday became identified with measures to improve maternal and child health—a pressing problem for social activists when Anna Jarvis first initiated Mother's Day ceremonies. The National Congress of Mothers (precursor of the Parent-Teacher Association) initially seemed lukewarm to the idea of Mother's Day; however, by 1910, this group of reform-minded women was so enthusiastic about the day's possibilities to publicize the group's work that Anna Jarvis accused them of selfishly ignoring the real meaning of the day. Women who belonged to the National Congress of Mothers shared a belief that motherhood should be put on a scientific basis. They dismissed the notion that a mother instinctively knew what was best for her children, and they promoted reliance on the advice of medical and psychological experts.

Maternal and child health reform was a component of this "scientific motherhood," and the National Congress of Mothers was not alone in using Mother's Day to generate support for both private and government efforts to provide birth control, prenatal services, and healthy baby clinics. On Mother's Day in 1931, the Maternity Center Association of New York planned to "direct the attention of the American people to the deplorable maternal death rate" in the United States, reportedly the highest in the "civilized world." And, the editor of the women's magazine *Good Housekeeping* suggested in that same year that Mother's Day would be a good time to "pour scorn" on the head of the Oklahoma senator who had filibustered a federal maternity bill. During the 1930s, Eleanor Roosevelt worked to establish the Golden Rule Foundation, an organization that used Mother's Day to advocate for maternal health activities, and in 1936 working-class women in Chicago rallied on Mother's Day to lend their support to the issue. So common was the association of Mother's Day and maternal and child welfare that by 1948 George W. Hecht, publisher of *Parent's Magazine* and chairman of the National Committee on the Observance of Mother's Day, Inc., a group not endorsed by Anna Jarvis, thought that Mother's Day was becoming an "increasingly important factor in the development of healthier, happier families." As *Good Housekeeping* editorialized, "Loving one's own mother should make one thoughtful of all mothers."

Throughout the twentieth century, annual Mother's Day celebrations continued to provide opportunities for women's issues. During the 1970s, the National Organization of Women, a powerful feminist group, held rallies on Mother's Day to support the Equal Rights Amendment and sponsored "Give-Equality-for-Mother's-Day" banquets. On Mother's Day during the 1980s, groups protesting the sale of infant formula to mothers in the Third World (because its use has been associated with increases in infant mortality rates) advertised their boycott of the offending multinational corporations. Even more recently, races have been held throughout the world on Mother's Day to promote breast cancer awareness and raise money to support medical research.

Individual politicians have sought personal political benefit from Mother's Day celebrations, and they have used the day's symbolism to further political objectives. In 1923 Alfred E. Smith, the governor of New York, planned a huge Mother's Day celebration in New York City. To enhance his popularity with voters in the 1920s, the mayor of Boston, John "Honey Fitz" Fitzgerald,

Coretta Scott King (center, dark glasses), shown walking hand in hand with Mrs. Harry Belafonte, leads a Mother's Day march for welfare rights. © Bettmann / Corbis.

sponsored a Mother's Day municipal picnic that reportedly hosted between 15 and 20 thousand mothers and children. In 1933, in the midst of the Great Depression, newly elected President Franklin D. Roosevelt issued a Mother's Day proclamation that called attention to the "unprecedentedly large number of mothers and dependent children" who, because of the economic catastrophe lacked "many of the necessities of life." For Roosevelt, of course, this was an unabashedly political statement, a way of publicizing his New Deal agenda for combating the Depression. Years later, in 1968, Coretta Scott King, wife of slain civil rights leader Martin Luther King Jr., led a Mother's Day march in support of poor mothers and their children. Taking "Mother Power" as her slogan, she called on "all women of the nation" ("black women, white women, brown women and red women") to take up what she called a "campaign of conscience." The Mother's Day march was an activity of the Poor People's Campaign organized by the Southern Christian Leadership Conference in 1967 to promote antipoverty legislation.

The political uses of Mother's Day have also included support for peace and for specific wars. Motherhood was, and continues to be a symbol of pacifism, and at times Mother's Day festivities have been appropriated for demonstrations on behalf of peace and disarmament. This practice is a legacy that recalls the nineteenth-century community-building work of Anna Jarvis, senior, in Grafton, and also the efforts of Julia Ward Howe to establish a "Mother's Peace Day." As Americans watched the war clouds gathering in Europe and the Pacific during the 1930s, a "Mother's Peace Day" parade was held on Mother's Day in 1938. During the 1980s, Helen Caldicott, pediatrician, antinuclear activist, and founder of the Women's Party for Survival, led demonstrations on Mother's Day against the proliferation of nuclear arms and nuclear energy. More often, however, Mother's Day has been seen as a means to boost morale and promote patriotism during periods of war. This was particularly true of World War I, when the military's use of Mother's Day helped to secularize a celebration that was still strongly identified with the church calendar.

HARNESSING THE POWER OF SENTIMENT FOR WAR

With Mother's Day presented in the churches, in the press, and in government proclamations as a time when all Americans regardless of race, creed, or religion could come together to honor a shared symbol of loyalty and self-sacrifice, the holiday proved to be a powerful vehicle for promoting the national war effort in 1917. The sentiments associated with Mother's Day allowed some Americans to address two troubling issues. First, the day's celebrations reassured soldiers that the war was a battle to protect a personal relationship as well as an abstract concept (Wilson's "war to end all wars"); and, second, the holiday rituals affirmed the patriotism of American women (a loyalty that seemed in doubt in light of the prewar activities of suffragists and women pacifists).

The Mother's Day stories popularized in church journals provided the framework for turning the holiday into a soldiers' celebration. Initially these stories made the holiday an occasion for grown sons to honor the mothers they left behind as the men made their way in the world. The men in the stories, as they became preoccupied with business, neglected their mothers. More importantly, these men risked losing the values inculcated in childhood by a pious mother. The essence of work and family in the early twentieth century were thought to be fundamentally antithetical. In this context, Mother's Day became a ritual reminder of the ethics of love, honor, and sacrifice that contrasted with the savagery and self-interest valued in business enterprise. The tale of a successful businessman who locked his office door while he read a letter from Mother and withdrew into the world she represented was typical of Mother's Day stories for adults in church magazines.

The vision of mother and home was an amulet meant to protect sons who had gone off to the city to make their fortune. Frequently the evils of the city tempted the son and only the memory of his mother could strengthen his resolve and enable him to lead a life worthy of his mother's trust. If in the story a son did succumb to city temptations (alcohol was an explicit temptation, sex was only hinted at), the memory of mother was often all that was needed to bring about repentance. Even hardened criminals could be reformed by reminding them of the expectations of a pious Christian mother. These stories can be read as expressions of uneasiness about the secular bent of American (and in particular masculine) society and an ambivalence about the individualistic ethic that ruled the industrial capitalist workplace of the early twentieth century. Ritualistic acknowledgment on Mother's Day of the values embedded in community and family helped alleviate these cultural anxieties. These representations from the church magazine stories were easily adapted to meet the needs of a nation at war.

Mother's Day tales had a special poignancy during the war; joining the army was no metaphorical sailing away from home to face the dangers of the world. To be the "feller your mother thinks you are" was to be brave in the trenches, loyal to home and country, and above all pure of mind, body, and soul. Because the boys were off on their own and unsupervised at training camps or in foreign countries, leaders worried that the draftees would be easy targets for purveyors of alcohol and sex. The army wanted and needed men who remembered the values that were embodied in mother love, so it was not surprising that the military ordered special Mother's Day services in army camps (along with more aggressive antiprostitution and antivenereal disease campaigns). Anna Jarvis attended and approved of the Camp Chillicothe, Ohio observances. Soldiers stood at attention for one minute in honor of their mothers and then recited the Lord's Prayer.

Another activity Anna Jarvis would have approved was the special Mother's Day mail proposed in 1918 by *Stars and Stripes,* the newspaper of the American Expeditionary Force. All military men were asked to take time on Mother's Day to write a letter home. The Secretary of War supported the idea, and on the second Sunday in May, the YMCA distributed stationery to all men in uniform. "Pack the page with love and good cheer," the *Stars and Stripes* advised. "Fill it to the brim with reassurance, for you know how mothers worry." Soldiers were told to mark the envelope "Mother's Letter" for special handling, and it was reported that censors worked extra shifts to speed the delivery process. A congressman who helped sponsor the letter-writing campaign said of these letters, "It is a tribute at once to the name of 'Mother,' to the traditions of the service of the Army and the Navy of the United States, and is at the same time indicative of the wonderful esteem in which woman is held in our Republic." The special mail inaugurated during World War I may have become a perennial custom in the military; in 1938, *Time* magazine reported that the Secretary of War urged every U.S. soldier to write home in honor of Mother's Day.

During World War I, women at home as well as men in uniform became the subjects of Mother's Day rhetoric. From both pulpits and Congress in 1917 and 1918, mothers were praised for their willing sacrifice of sons to the war effort. Mother's Day was "special" these years because, according to the church journal, the *Presbyterian,* women felt "most deeply the pangs of war." Congress passed another Mother's Day resolution in 1918, directing the attention of the whole nation "to the patriotic sacrifice made by the mothers of our land in freely offering their sons to bear arms and, if need be, die in defense of liberty and justice." Mrs. Bixby, a mother who had lost five sons during the Civil War, was held up as the exemplary Mother's Day heroine; her sacrifice was a model for all mothers during the "war to end all wars."

Mother's Day rhetoric emphasized a mother's willingness to part with her sons in part because the loyalty of women to the war effort was in doubt. Americans definitely were not united over entry into the European war, and antiwar protesters clashed often with "100% Americans" over the decision to send troops overseas. Women, especially suffragists, however, seemed to be a particularly troublesome lot to the supporters of conflict. Before the war, feminist arguments for suffrage had held out the promise of perpetual peace as a bonus result of votes for women. Women were represented as innately pacifist, less warlike than the aggressive male, and determined to protect their young from harm. Suffragists argued that if government were directly responsible to mothers as well as to men, legislators would be less likely to take the nation into war. While the National American Woman Suffrage Association, the largest of the suffrage organizations, lent its support to military efforts, there were other suffragists and female activists whose opposition to the war was vocal and uncompromising. The wartime Mother's Day rhetoric set standards by which the patriotism of American mothers could be judged, and the sentiment honored on Mother's Day helped to reassure Americans that women would willingly support this war even though they had no voice in the decision.

During World War II, Mother's Day celebrations once again became a time to unite patriotic ritual and a gushing sentimental image of motherhood. Mothers of decorated war heroes led Mother's Day parades; speakers praised the sacrifices of mothers (like a Mrs. Emma Van Coutren, named Mother of the Year in 1944 because 11 of her 12 children were in the armed services); and one lieutenant colonel suggested that their names belonged in the nation's hall of fame, along with the names of servicemen. Indicative of the patriotic sentimentalism that surrounded wartime Mother's Day was a feature article in *Life* magazine from May 25, 1942 that documented Mother's Day events at military bases. A group of servicemen at Langley Field in Virginia made a heart-shaped formation around Mrs. Blanche Carr, who was holding the hand of her son. At Camp Forrest, Tennessee, a military jeep drove Mrs. Covington to a ceremony in her honor, where she was crowned "Dear Mom." And cadets at an army training school in Enid, Oklahoma used parachute packs to spell out "Hi Mom," a greeting captured by aerial photography. Where else but in America, Philip Wylie, author of *Generation of Vipers,* bemoaned in 1942, would an entire military division be used during wartime to spell out the word "mom" on a drill field. Wylie was one of the most vituperative critics of what he called "megaloid momworship," but he was not alone in critiquing American motherhood. His condemnation of "momism" drew on the works of eminent psychiatrists who feared that sentimental motherhood had emasculated American men. Nonetheless, for the duration of the war, the Mother's Day mom was not the modern woman who balanced work and childrearing, although this, too, was an image—captured in the figure of Rosie the Riveter—that served the war effort during the 1940s. Rather, she was a self-sacrificing woman whose sons worshipped her and dutifully served in the military as her protector.

"Gold Star Mothers," the mothers of soldiers who had died in combat, were honored figures during World War II. The practice of displaying a gold star to commemorate a son's death was begun in 1917 by a group of women in Indiana. Organizing themselves as "American War Mothers," they urged families to display a blue star for each son in the military. If a son died in battle a gold star was to be sewn over the blue one, and in May 1918, President Wilson called these grieving women "Gold Star Mothers." In 1925, the War Mothers held a convention in Philadelphia and a very determined Anna Jarvis disrupted their meeting. In a loud voice, she harangued the group for selling Mother's Day white carnations at a profit, and she stopped only when arrested by police for disturbing the peace. The War Mothers further infuriated Jarvis in 1929 when they awarded their Victory Medal to Frank E. Hering, a man who claimed to be Father of Mother's Day. Hering based his claim on a celebration of motherhood he had organized in 1904 on behalf of a chapter of the Fraternal Order of Eagles.

MOTHER'S DAY AND COMMERCIALISM

Although she quickly lost control over the rituals and customs associated with Mother's Day, throughout her life Anna Jarvis tried to retain for herself the credit for creating the holiday and control over how the holiday and its symbols were used. Her decision in 1912 to incorporate her organizing committee and to copyright the words "Mother's Day" as its trademark was an attempt to protect "her" day, but it was also part of an effort to preserve the purity of the sentiment she wanted the day to express. "Don't Kick Mother out of Mother's Day," she scolded in the 1930s as even the president of the United States used the holiday to promote an agenda beyond an unpretentious and heart-felt remembrance of one's mother. In 1934, for example, she protested Postmaster James Farley's plans to issue a special three-cent "Mother's Day" stamp featuring Whistler's *Portrait of the Artist's Mother,* blaming Hering and the War Mothers for the plan and demanding a meeting with President

Lucille Ball poses with her children after being named "Television Mother of the Year," 1954. © Bettmann / Corbis.

Roosevelt to give him a better understanding of the holiday. The Post Office issued the stamp with a vase of carnations added to the painting but without the offending words "Mother's Day." Above all, Anna objected to those who profited monetarily from the day's celebration. "Commercialism has become so blatantly a part of the activities hinging on the Day that its founder has become obsessed with it, and has devoted more of her time to fighting the alleged evil than to evangelizing the festival's tenderer meanings," observed Eugene Pharo in 1937. And, while there were many enterprises that drew her wrath, American florists came in for the lion's share of her obsession.

According to the historian Leigh Eric Schmidt, "Without the systematic, sustained campaign of commercial florists (and eventually other industries as well), Mother's Day would certainly have been a smaller observance and might well have remained a parochial event; it might even have gradually withered away like other Protestant days of the early twentieth century such as Children's Day or Temperance Sunday." The florists were quick to acclaim their role in popularizing the new holiday. As early as 1913, the trade journal *Florists' Review* blustered, "For the success of the 'day,' we are to credit ourselves, us, we, the members of the trade who know a good thing when they see it and who are sufficiently progressive to push it along—Mothers' day is ours; we made it, we made it practically unaided and alone." Jarvis created the opportunity when she made the white carnation, her mother's favorite flower, a symbol of the holiday. Florists, however, were quick to take advantage of this promise of annual revenue; unlike some other holidays, this day seemed tailor-made for their industry.

Mother's Day was not the first holiday turned into a commercial venture on a national scale. As Schmidt notes, the "commercialization of the calendar" began in the late nineteenth century as trade journals and advertising firms (both newly developed institutional supports for retail merchants) discovered the profits to be made from holiday sales. For department store window dressers, another new addition to the retail sales force, holidays provided inspiration for their creations. The greeting card industry, too, helped to make holidays an occasion for expressing sentiment by spending money. The historian William Leach calls the United States at the turn of the century a "land of desire," typified by virtually boundless consumer wants. It was an era of transition from a saving to a spending culture, a time when the individual's sense of well-being became tied to purchase and possession of material goods, and a moment when expressions of emotion like love, respect, and honor were infused with material worth. Anna Jarvis's campaign for a day to honor mothers appeared just as American retailers and American consumers were coming to terms with this new "culture of consumption."

The Society of American Florists did not create its national advertising slogan "say it with flowers" until the 1920s, but almost as soon as Jarvis began her campaign the florist trade set out to make Mother's Day their special preserve. By

1910, florists were recommending that churches, Sunday schools, and cemeteries be decorated with flowers to mark the day. Local retailers donated flowers to present to each Sunday school attendee. When the demand for white carnations created a temporary shortage, florists suggested it would be appropriate to substitute a bright flower (which quickly became a red carnation) when mother was alive and wear a white carnation to mark her passing. Trade publications advised florists to ask their town mayors to issue Mother's Day proclamations and to seek endorsements for the holiday from local newspapers (publicity tactics Anna Jarvis also employed). "Let every one boost Mother's Day—talk it up, make a fuss about it, believe in it, get enthusiastic over it." This was the advice in the *American Florist,* and local florists complied. To assist consumers in choosing a Mother's Day gift, florists by 1912 were preparing special Mother's Day bouquets. After 1910, the Florists' Telegraph Delivery Association (F.T.D.) advertised its services to children living far from home who wanted to honor mother with flowers (Leigh Schmidt reports that in the 1950s the first national television advertisement for florists was an F.T.D. advertisement for Mother's Day).

If "Advertise!" was the message sent to florists in their trade journals, these same entrepreneurs preferred to conceal the crassly commercial aspect of Mother's Day. The trade press advised florists to play to the emotions if they wanted to fully exploit the potential offered by Mother's Day. During the 1910s, Mother's Day ads began to reprint sentimental poems ("poetic propaganda") as part of the sales pitch. Although among themselves, florists claimed credit for the popularity of the holiday, they encouraged newspapers to print a "history" that attributed the celebration to one woman's efforts to assuage her grief. Through Jarvis's story, the florists hoped to stir up powerful emotions, and, as Leigh Schmidt writes, "it was precisely the profound depth of sentiment that Mother's Day evoked that made the commercial uses of the holiday possible." Florists hoped celebrants would translate the emotionalism of the day into a need to purchase flowers.

With florists in the lead, other merchants contributed to the commercialization of Mother's Day, though they appear to have been slower than the florists to see the profitability of the day. In Philadelphia where Anna Jarvis based her Mother's Day campaign, Strawbridge and Clothier ads encouraged celebrants to give small personal gifts on Mother's Day. The ads recommended a card, a box of candy, or possibly a portrait of Whistler's Mother. The Mother's Day section of the advertisement, however, was usually a minor part of an extensive full-page store promotion. From 1908 to 1918, only one Philadelphia store, Snellenberger's, suggested that Mother's Day should be celebrated by making a major purchase; in this case, the recommended gift was a Victrola. "Mother spends most of her time in the home," the store's advertisement counseled, "so for her it should be the *pleasantest* place on earth. Make it pleasant with music."

Wanamaker's department store was deeply enmeshed in promoting and commercializing Mother's Day. John Wanamaker, wealthy owner of the store, was

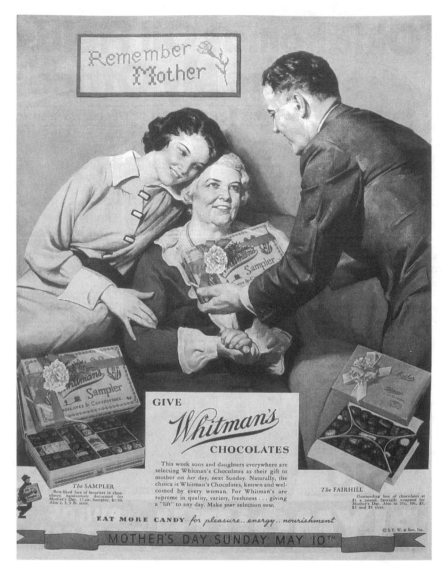

A Mother's Day advertisement from the *Saturday Evening Post,* May 9, 1936. Courtesy of the Library of Congress.

a member of Anna Jarvis's Mother's Day committee, and he was reputed to have claimed that he would rather be a founder of Mother's Day than the king of England. As a local Sunday school teacher, Wanamaker made religion an important part of his public identity. He was also a merchandizing innovator, and his store was a veritable palace of consumption, with a grand organ, a huge auditorium for special celebrations, and spectacular displays of light and color, all designed to draw customers into his kingdom. Wanamaker's was the first Philadelphia store to incorporate a Mother's Day message in its advertisements.

During the 1910s, the store held annual Mother's Day programs with music and recitations and gave away carnations to customers. John Wanamaker was a curious blend of religious sentimentalism and capitalist dynamism, and it was a combination that spelled success for the man and the holiday he promoted. On a Mother's Day promoted by Wanamaker, "celebration and consumption had been synchronized."

Anna Jarvis, the protagonist of the florists' emotional history of Mother's Day, was appalled by the commercialization of what she considered her holiday. At first, she cooperated with the florists, spoke to florists' clubs about Mother's Day, and accepted their donations, but as Mother's Day gained popularity, Jarvis became increasingly hostile to the florists' profiteering. She tried to substitute a celluloid model for the live carnations hawked by florists, and she pleaded for sons and daughters to stop giving flowers as part of their holiday ritual. Jarvis may not have used these contemporary sociological terms, but what she observed and objected to was the commodification of affection. The commemoration of mother love through Mother's Day gift-giving is a reflection of that process by which the marketplace has entered into the home and attached monetary value to domestic relations.

Jarvis's protests were to no avail. Even the churches, where Jarvis thought observances of Mother's Day rightly belonged, bought Mother's Day mementos to distribute as part of the annual celebration. Recommendations for Mother's Day gifts became a staple of store advertisements in early May. In its May 1943 issue, *Better Homes and Gardens* even offered a shopping guide titled "Gifts that Say 'We Love You, Mom.'" A letter from "The Family" illustrated the article. It asked Mom to take a "quickie" look at the list of ideas and check off the ones that would be most appreciated. Heading the list was a war bond that could be earmarked for Mom's pet after-the-war project; other suggestions included a monogrammed shower curtain, a pair of brass candlesticks, and a "flower container filled with refreshing spring posies." Gift-giving has become such a pervasive part of Mother's Day festivities that in 2005 the National Retail Federation projected that sales would exceed $11 billion.

Merchants, particularly florists, were instrumental in establishing the rituals for celebrating Mother's Day, but as the failure of attempts to establish other "commercially contrived festivals" suggests, the popular appeal of the holiday throughout the twentieth century depended on more than the merchants' sales pitch. When the greeting card industry tried to establish Friendship Day as an early August celebration, the holiday lingered from 1919 to the 1940s, but without much public enthusiasm. Candy Day, created by the National Confectioners' Association to "make the nation Candy-Conscious" also failed, and the trade journal attributed the problem to the obvious commercialism of the day; it failed to evoke the "finer sentiments" and "tender feelings" and instead smelled of a rancid search for profits. Leigh Schmidt has found that consumers thought Candy Day was a "joke." Mother's Day, in contrast, was rapidly accepted as a necessary celebration in the annual calendar.

ENDURING AND INTERNATIONAL APPEAL

What explains the popularity? To be sure, the ambivalence that marks the child's relationship with its mother is part of the appeal. At once dependent on mother for love and survival but encouraged to "individuate and separate," to become independent individuals, children have received mixed messages in the twentieth century, messages they carry into adulthood and can find difficult to reconcile. Mother's Day captures these emotions; it permits, even encourages, the expression of a child's dependency and need while at the same time it limits the expression of those emotions often thought to be ill-suited for the competitive, individualistic society that marks modern life in the United States. The positioning of the apostrophe in Mother's Day marks this holiday as one of individual remembrance and commemoration. It might be argued that with mother worship restricted to one specific day, it is that much easier to ignore for the other 364 the real needs of many American mothers for child care, wage equity, decent housing, a clean environment, and a safe neighborhood in which to raise the next generation. Were it celebrated as *Mothers'* Day, the holiday could serve as a touchstone for a national commitment to families.

Even as *Mother's* Day, the holiday has invited usage well beyond the commemoration of the bond between mother and child. Throughout the twentieth century, Mother's Day was a lightning rod for conflicts over the status and role of women in American society. It has been a symbol of gender differences and family values often associated with conservative religious congregations. It has also been used to advocate women's rights and gender equity. In 2005, the "Love Mom, Not Wal-Mart" campaign used a giant Mother's Day card as a symbol of its efforts to end gender discrimination by the superstore, with signers pledging to boycott the store when buying their Mother's Day gifts. The day devoted to mother continues to be a vehicle for politicking and for promoting particular political agendas, both liberal and conservative. The St. Louis chapter of Mothers Against Drunk Driving (M.A.D.D.), for example, sponsored a 5K walk on Mother's Day 2004 to raise money for its campaign to enforce laws against driving while under the influence. On Mother's Day celebrants have marched for peace and supported America at war—Mother's Day has served as a symbol of both patriotism and protest. And, while the holiday is compelling evidence of the commercialization of emotions, it is also tribute to an emotion that can rise above commerce. The rapid acceptance and continued popularity of the day in the United States has depended on this fluidity.

At present Mother's Day is an international as well as a national celebration. Many countries follow the custom of the United States and observe the holiday on the second Sunday in May. These nations include Australia, Brazil, Canada, China, Denmark, Germany, Italy, Japan, Taiwan, and Turkey. England and the Republic of Ireland continue to observe Mothering Sunday on the fourth Sunday in Lent. In France and Sweden Mother's Day falls on the last Sunday in May, while in Russia it takes place on November 28. In Egypt and Lebanon, it is celebrated on the first day of spring. Other nations in the Middle East including Qatar, Oman, and Saudi Arabia mark the day on May 10, as do both India and Pakistan.

Observances abroad differ from customs in the United States. In Sweden, the Red Cross sells tiny plastic flowers on Mother's Day to raise money to support vacations for mothers with many children. In France, children present mothers with a special cake resembling a bouquet. Both Spain and Portugal celebrate Mother's Day on December 8 when the large Catholic populations in these countries give thanks to the Virgin Mary along with honoring individual mothers.

The introduction of Mother's Day also followed paths unique to individual nations. During the 1920s, for example, Mother's Day became a very popular celebration in Weimar Germany where a unique constellation of postwar conditions created the opportunity to equate esteem for mothers with valorizing the German *Volk*. As had Americans, Germans found that the holiday could be molded to fit different agendas. In that country, business and conservative political groups who shared an ideology that was pro-family, antiabortion, and eugenic ran a well-organized campaign to promote Mother's Day as a national holiday. The Association of German Florists contributed to this movement, but florists were asked to minimize their visibility. German supporters of Mother's Day intended to use the holiday to promote maternity and domesticity, and they called for sex education, support for large families, and limits on women's employment. Even before they came to power in 1932, German Nazis had begun to use Mother's Day to articulate a demand for female self-sacrifice in service of the state; throughout the years of Nazi rule, German Mother's Day continued to represent mothers as "the refuge of the *Volk*, the protector of [Germany's] racial heritage."

Christian missionaries and Western business interests spread Mother's Day to Africa, Asia, Latin America, and the Middle East. In Africa, nations once colonized by the British continue to hold observances on Mothering Sunday. Christian congregations in Japan observed the holiday in 1913, and by the 1930s, it had become a popular celebration. During World War II, however, the Japanese condemned Mother's Day as a Western import and celebrations were prohibited. The holiday was resurrected after the war to console women and children who lost husbands and fathers in the conflict, and by 1950, it was well-established throughout the country, where the American occupation had a strong impact on many local customs.

Although the holiday can be found on the calendar in the Middle East, contemporary Muslim scholars differ over the appropriateness of Mother's Day observances in Islamic nations. Some regard it as blind imitation of Western, non-Islamic habits; others believe that if observed in keeping with Islamic customs, celebration of a day that honors the special place of mother in Islamic culture does not contradict the teachings of the *Quran.* The celebration of Mother's Day has aroused strong emotions in countries resisting the spread of Western cultural values, and as in the United States, the holiday has had many layers of meaning throughout the world.

In 1948, just before her death, Anna Jarvis voiced regret about Mother's Day. She was sorry, she said, that she had ever started the day; as celebrated in post-World War II America, it was not the commemoration of motherhood that she had intended. Yet, the holiday she created but never controlled is one that the majority of Americans clearly find a satisfying means for expressing a host of compelling and sometimes conflicting emotions. According to the Hallmark Company, 96 percent of American consumers take part in Mother's Day in some way. Despite her regrets, Anna Jarvis is memorialized at the Mother's Day shrine in Grafton, West Virginia, and the holiday she created is celebrated once each year, on the second Sunday in May.

FURTHER READING

Bolt, Richard A. "A New Use for Mother's Day." *American Journal of Public Health* 21 (April, 1931): 438–41.

Hausen, Karin. "Mother's Day in the Weimar Republic." In *When Biology Became Destiny: Women in Weimar and Nazi Germany,* ed. Renate Bridenthal, Atina Grossman, and Marion Kaplan, 131–52. New York: Monthly Review Press, 1984.

Johnson, James P. "How Mother Got Her Day." *American Heritage* 30 (April, 1979): 14–21.

Jones, Kathleen W. "Mother's Day: The Creation, Promotion, and Meaning of a New Holiday in the Progressive Era." *Texas Studies in Literature and Language* 22 (Summer 1980): 175–96.

Pharo, Eugene. "This Mother's Day Business." *American Mercury* 41 (May, 1937) 60–67.

Schmidt, Leigh Eric. *Consumer Rites: The Buying and Selling of American Holidays.* Princeton, N.J.: Princeton University Press, 1995.

Schmidt, Leigh Eric. "Piety, Commercialism, Activism: The Uses of Mother's Day." *Religion On-line.* www.religion-online.org/showarticle.asp?title=173.

Kathleen W. Jones

Father's Day

Close on the heels of Mother's Day came agitation for a similar holiday for fathers, in the words of Leigh Eric Scmidt in *Consumer Rites: The Buying and Selling of American Holidays* (1995), the "most obvious and extensive spin-off" of Mother's Day. And as with Mother's Day, it was the intersection of sentiment and commerce that ensured the national recognition of Father's Day. But unlike Mother's Day, the process took more than 60 years.

The notion of a Father's Day seemed a natural enough consequence of the success of Mother's Day, but while the suggestion was made in several quarters, it fell to a young woman named Sonora Dodd of Spokane, Washington to begin campaigning in 1910 for a day recognizing the role of fathers in America. Dodd's father had been a widower with six children. After witnessing his dedication and sacrifice to support his family, Dodd thought a day of official recognition for fathers as appropriate as one for mothers. She worked through local churches and the YMCA to promote such a holiday in Spokane, suggesting the third Sunday in June as an appropriate time. The idea appealed to both traditional and Progressive-era values for many of the same reasons as did Mother's Day: to celebrate and encourage strong, virtuous families. Specifically, the father's specialties were presumed to include the training of children (especially boys) and the protection of women and children.

From the start, however, Father's Day met resistance, and mostly from men. There was ambiguity about just what qualities of manhood Father's Day most honored. Dodd, with her own family history in mind, had stressed the gentle, nurturing, domestic side of fathers, while her allies in the YMCA and men's organizations espousing "muscular Christianity" emphasized the more virile characteristics—as one spokesman insisted, of "rugged, husky, stalwart" men. In a time of changing women's roles, some men saw in Father's Day a confirmation of patriarchy, but even men who supported the idea of a Father's Day were concerned about the danger of "feminizing" the day and their self-images.

While locales throughout the nation supported and experimented with Father's Day, there simply was not the same widespread enthusiasm that Mother's Day had enjoyed. Dodd had always been the most active promoter of the new holiday, but she had moved on to other concerns and careers. Even in Spokane, Father's Day was irregularly observed, and by the 1920s it was nearly dead. Mostly, Dodd's dream for Father's Day suffered from not being taken seriously *by fathers.* Men were uncomfortable with playing the role of sentimental object, traditionally a female realm, but found themselves nevertheless the reluctant targets of ritualized affection and dubious gifts. They found it preferable to scorn, ridicule, and avoid the special attentions of Father's Day. Mother's Day and (briefly) Children's Day were deemed sufficient: were there now to be holidays for every extended family member? Where, some wondered, would the nonsense stop? Even retailers, who had quickly capitalized on the commercial possibilities of Mother's Day and Valentine's Day, recognized the peculiar awkwardness of Father's Day. As a 1928 florist expressed it, "fathers haven't the same sentimental appeal that mothers have," while a greeting-card maker two years earlier had complained that "mannish-looking cards are hard to design."

As with other American holidays, Father's Day survived, and eventually flourished, through the dogged determination of commercial interests. Dodd had returned to her agitation for the holiday by the early 1930s, but while she, and retailers, strove mightily for their cause, public cynicism was largely unshaken. In part, the retailers were to blame for this; with the commercialization of holidays such as Christmas and Valentine's Day over the previous century (and, more recently, Mother's Day), there was widespread suspicion that Father's Day was merely a commercial gambit. There was something to that; certainly merchandisers wanted Father's Day to become as much of a hit as Mother's Day, especially producers of tobacco products, menswear, and haberdashers. These became more active in promoting Father's Day in the 1930s, even though by the end of the decade observance was still only spotty.

All that changed beginning in 1938, with the formation of the National Council for the Promotion of Father's Day, a trade bureau organization spearheaded by the Association of Men's Wear Retailers in New York City. Beginning with the larger cities, the goal of the council was to coordinate the efforts of retailers to make Father's Day a "merchandising event." A slow but steady growth in the number of states officially recognizing Father's Day (for which Dodd continued to work) aided the council's efforts, as did the nationwide impulse to honor American servicemen after World War II. New York's Bloomingdale's, for example, under its banner reading "Every Dad's a Hero," offered to assist patrons in celebrating "the special spirit of fatherhood." At last, coordinated marketing, the agitation of Dodd and her followers, and a resurgence of patriarchy in postwar America, combined with a greater willingness among men to accept domestic bliss as legitimately masculine, wore down lingering reservations about Father's Day. The success of the holiday, as so often the case in America, finds one measure in retail sales: by 1949 the estimated sales generated by Father's Day was $106 million. By 1975 the figure reached $1 billion, but by then Father's Day had became a national holiday, made official by Congress in 1972. Sonora Dodd, then 90 years old, had lived to see her dream come true—as had retailers everywhere.

Today, the National Retailers' Federation reports that American buyers spend an average $62 for Father's Day. According to a 2005 survey, nearly 90 percent planned to buy cards, 40 percent would buy clothing, 38 percent planned to take Dad out to dinner or brunch, 37 percent expected to purchase sporting or leisure goods, 25 percent would buy books or music CDs, 22 percent opted for home improvement or gardening needs, and 12 percent for electronics or computer accessories. Perhaps indicative of persisting masculine wariness concerning Father's Day, women planned to outspend men by more than 50 percent: $71 on average as opposed to $33. Neither is Father's Day any longer strictly the realm of the biologically defined: 56 percent of survey respondents planned to buy gifts for "father figures," including other male relatives or family friends.

MEMORIAL DAY

- [ ] Memorial Day, a federal holiday, is observed on the last Monday in May.

- [ ] It was earlier known as "Decoration Day," so named after the spontaneous act of Civil War widows strewing cut wildflowers on the graves of soldiers who died during the war.

- [ ] Memorial observations originated in the south in 1865 (later known as Confederate Memorial Day) but were quickly picked up and transported north and taken into custodianship by Union veterans and the Grand Army of the Republic.

- [ ] In 1866 Congress created an extensive system of national military cemeteries for Union war dead, including Arlington National Cemetery, providing a focal point for Decoration Day observations.

- [ ] With the failure of Reconstruction in the late 1870s African Americans began to use Decoration Day to protest continuing racism in America. For whites Decoration Day grew to become a day of national reconciliation.

- [ ] In 1889 Congress made Decoration Day a national holiday.

- [ ] In the late 1800s Native Americans were prodded into observing Decoration Day in an attempt to "Americanize" them.

- [ ] Decoration Day became more a day of recreation and leisure as the number of Civil War veterans left to rekindle the spirit of sectional sacrifice thinned in the early twentieth century, a trend accelerated by the later adoption of Armistice Day to commemorate those who fought in the Great War.

- [ ] In 1971 Memorial Day became and remained a "St. Monday"—a holiday occasion, formerly filled with meaning but now more obscure, manipulated in the calendar to create a three-day weekend, and dedicated to the proposition that Americans desire days of leisure and material consumption.

MEMORIAL DAY

Memorial Day is observed in the United States on the last Monday in May to honor the nation's war dead. The holiday emerged in the wake of the Civil War as "Decoration Day," a name that endured well into the twentieth century and that described the most common commemorative rite, a sorrowful strewing of freshly-cut flowers on the graves of soldiers who had fallen in the Civil War. The history of Memorial Day is as complicated, surprising, and paradoxical as the story of any public holiday on the American calendar. Its origins are ambiguous and its transformation dramatic, as it developed from a somber and melancholy fête into a light day of leisure and pleasure, the unofficial opening-day of summer. Memorial Day, focused largely on the mortal, patriotic service of men, has been a holiday in which women played a central role, and yet it was hardly feminist and remained profoundly conservative. Although a day originally designed to heighten memory, it has become for most Americans an occasion of blissful, escapist amusement or material consumption. Few Americans today know the origins or original purpose of Memorial Day.

ORIGINS IN RECONSTRUCTION AMERICA

The Civil War remains the greatest crisis in American history. What could be sadder, more disturbing, or call out more desperately for personal and national remembrance, than the massive number of deaths the war wrought, some 620,000 soldiers North and South? Death on such an astonishing scale was overwhelming and required some response, emotionally and psychologically, as well as socially, economically, and politically. Memorial Day emerged to perform the cultural and therapeutic work demanded by the Civil War's tragic desolation. The origins of Memorial Day are obscure. It began, not with official pronouncements, but with grassroots acts of mourning. Southern legend tells us that women of the South expressed their grief and honored their fallen husbands, sons, and brothers by strewing flowers on their graves. Late in the war, in April and May of 1865, Union soldiers in the South themselves observed this heart-felt act, and some began to imitate it, decorating the graves of their own comrades who had died far from home. The idea of Memorial Day attracted the attention of northerners when the northern abolitionist James Redpath, who was visiting Charleston, South Carolina in order to organize schools for freed slaves, led a group of African American children in May 1865 to adorn the graves of several hundred Union soldiers buried nearby.

Soon these memorial rites—particularly the decoration of graves with spring flowers—spread extensively, if separately, in the North and South. Among those solemn ceremonies, one organized by veterans in Waterloo, New York on May 5, 1866 was cited by Congress as the first Memorial Day. But certainly hundreds of others had occurred unofficially before, during, and immediately after the Waterloo commemoration. Many were organized by a new, politically powerful veterans' organization in the North, the Grand Army of the Republic (GAR), founded in 1866 and led by General John A. Logan, a radical Republican Congressman and later U.S. Senator from Illinois. On May 5, 1868, GAR commander-in-chief Logan—apparently influenced by his wife, who had seen such ceremonies on her tour of southern battlefields in the spring of 1868—issued General Order No. 11, which designated May 30 as a national Memorial Day, "for the purpose of strewing with flowers the graves of comrades who died in defense of their country during the late war of rebellion, and whose bodies lie in almost every city, village, hamlet church-yard in the land." In that year, local GAR chapters held over 100 such ceremonies, and in 1869 some 336 Memorial Day observances occurred throughout the North. Quickly this new tradition became obligatory for every post and veteran, making the failure to remember fallen comrades on the day sacrilegious if not unimaginable. New York became the first state in 1873 to make May 30 a legal holiday, followed by Rhode Island, Vermont, New Hampshire, Wisconsin, Massachusetts, and Ohio by 1881. Within another decade, every northern state had designated Memorial Day as an official holiday.

The South forwarded its own claim as inventor of Memorial Day, backed as in the North with a wealth of apocrypha. Southern women had scattered flowers over the graves of fallen Confederate (and sometimes Union) soldiers during the war. In Columbus, Georgia in 1866, a Confederate widow, Mrs. Charles J. Williams, published an appeal for southerners to designate a day "to be handed down through time as a religious custom of the South to wreathe the graves of our martyred dead with flowers." Southern states observed Decoration Day on various dates, from April in the Deep South (April 26, the date of General Joseph E. Johnson's surrender) to late May or early June in

Virginia, corresponding to the height of the local flower season. The Carolinas favored May 10, the anniversary of Thomas "Stonewall" Jackson's death. By 1916, 10 southern states had set June 3—Jefferson Davis's birthday—as their Confederate Memorial Day. If men seemed to dominate the proceedings in the North (at least as organizers if not as mourners), women took the lead in the South, forming Ladies Memorial Associations to care for graves and to disinter the remains of soldiers killed in distant locales and rebury them locally with honor. In the 1890s, southern women organized themselves into chapters of the United Daughters of the Confederacy to oversee rites of remembrance.

In 1866, Congress created an extensive system of national military cemeteries for the Union war dead. Across the Potomac River from Washington, D.C., on Robert E. Lee's former estate, Arlington National Cemetery emerged (perhaps in part as an act of retribution) as a sacred site of patriotic mourning and memory. Decoration Day at Arlington both reflected and provided a model for appropriate memorial rites for the nation. In 1868, some 5,000 attended (including former generals and future presidents Ulysses S. Grant and James Garfield), amidst the 12,000 graves of soldiers decorated with small U.S. flags. The sober event consisted of patriotic speeches, melancholy musical airs, a slow procession, hymns and prayers, a cannon salute, and the broadcast of flowers by children, orphaned by the war, over the graves of the Union dead.

In towns across the northern American landscape, similar scenes unfolded each year. Typically, in the days preceding Memorial Day, the members of the Grand Army of the Republic would construct a platform in a central place and drape it with bunting. Early on the holiday, farmers and their families arrived in their four-seated hacks. In anticipation of the day's parade, the outlanders and townspeople lined the main street, and soon the procession would appear, complete with grand marshal on horseback, colors and color guard, military band, the GAR, the fire department, and perhaps troops of Boy Scouts marching toward the cemetery, which had been decorated with flags earlier in the day. A solemn memorial ceremony at the graveyard commanded the attention of all, before the congregants moved to adorn the tombstones of their own kin with flowers. The melancholy of the mortuary rites then would give way to lighter moments of picnicking, visiting, play, and perhaps some tippling, followed by a band concert from the platform, words from the mayor, a rereading of Logan's General Order, mandating the holiday observance, a recitation of the Gettysburg Address, and a long-winded, heart-rending, and flag-waving oration. Taps and a benediction ended the affair officially, and celebrants would drift home.

Romanticized reminiscences about such rites, set in the hazy glow of yesteryear, typically suggest a unified, consensual, and patriotic world in which North and South no longer disagreed—indeed, in which the sections could hardly recall what they had been quarreling about. But the United States in the years immediately following the war was a nation still divided. General Logan's request to Congress on June 22, 1868 to make Memorial Day a national "commemoration of the gallant heroes who have sacracficed [sic] their lives in defence [sic] of the Republic," was a sectional, Union appeal. Only one side had defended "the Republic" against the other, which sought to destroy it. At a Memorial Day service at Arlington National Cemetery in 1869, although the day's orator pleaded for brotherly union between the sections, Union veterans guarded the graves of Confederate soldiers to prevent their decoration with flowers. Meanwhile southern states rejected May 30 as little more than a Yankee holiday. Southerners accused the GAR of manipulating Memorial Day for its own partisan purposes. These divisions helped to defeat a 1876 bill in the U.S. Senate that would have made May 30 a national holiday, and for a time the United States continued to have not one, but two oppositional Memorial Days, one North and another South.

But the animosity that divided North and South, which sectional Memorial Days seemed to aggravate, began to fade. Increasingly, Decoration Day became a rite of national reconciliation. Some GAR and Republican Party orators continued to waive "the bloody shirt"—stoking sectional passions with lurid recollections of war, northern sacrifices, and southern treason. And white southerners cultivated nostalgia for their Lost Cause. But Memorial Day increasingly served reunion rather than strife and spite. Joint Decoration Day ceremonies emerged by the mid-1870s, and federal troops stationed in the South joined services honoring the southern dead, where southern women scattered flowers on Union as well as Confederate graves. In the North too, as in a Memorial Day observance in Cincinnati in 1875, southern officers along with those of the North marked the day jointly with a "fraternal and charitable spirit." As early as Memorial Day 1869, the mayor of Charleston, South Carolina emphasized the similarity of the sacrifice in the North and South. Gazing over graves of both Union and Confederate soldiers, he asked, "cannot we who survive catch the inspiration which swells the chorus of these who, once estranged, are now forever glorified?"

In northern and southern towns alike, virtually indistinguishable statues arose—cast by the same foundries and sold in the same mail-order catalogs—typically depicting a common white soldier, dedicated generically to "the cause" and honoring his bravery and service to country. The "cause" and definition of "country" were unspecified, although their meaning was clear enough in context, yet such purposeful ambiguity somehow allowed the opposing causes of North and South to fade into obscurity, overshadowed by white Americans' narrowed emphasis on manly service and sacrifice. These tributes created a standardized memory locally, which ironically, on a national scale, Americans both North and South could share. "The essence of Memorial Day in relation to reconciliation was its appeal to sympathy," wrote the historian Paul H. Buck in 1937. "North and South, the sacrifice of war had led to a common meeting place, the cemetery, where strife and bitterness were hushed in death."

Left out of this reconciliation were African Americans. Such rites of reunion ignored the strife endured by blacks and the bitterness of their experience following the Civil War. Memorial Day helped to construct through celebration "a policy of historical amnesia," as the Republican Party, and northerners generally, abandoned their program of Reconstruction in the South and deserted African Americans there. After 1877, Memorial Day activities sometimes lagged in northern communities, flourishing only where local posts of Grand Army of the Republic diligently promoted them, or they assumed a less overtly political character and became more focused on individual remembrance and on leisure. Working people enjoyed a late spring holiday, filled with baseball games, horse (later bicycle) races, picnics, and ice cream festivals. In 1888, President Grover Cleveland allegedly went fishing on Memorial Day, which did not help him in his unsuccessful bid for reelection that year. Yet his angling did express a growing national mood. The GAR condemned "indulgences in public sports, pastimes and all amusements on Memorial Day," a day it still considered a solemn occasion that should inspire reverence, not revelry. Southern elites voiced similar disdain for the holiday's corruption with diversions.

Whether indulging themselves in relatively mindless pursuits of recreation, or committing themselves to a program of national and international economic development, which could not tolerate sectional divisions, white Americans willfully disregarded black contributions to the Union victory in the Civil War—some 180,000 blacks fought and suffered a 20 percent casualty rate—and neglected the current predicament and peril that faced African Americans in the South. Such neglect, of course, allowed the United States to remain a flawed republic in the wake of the Civil War, to reemerge from the devastating conflict in ways that contradicted America's founding principles, articulated in the Declaration of Independence and asserted more recently and powerfully in Lincoln's Gettysburg Address—"the proposition that all men are created equal."

A Confederate monument in Columbia, South Carolina carried an inscription, "Let their virtues plead for the just judgment of the cause in which they perished." The individual virtues or the gallantry of the Confederate dead might be acknowledged, but did that alone grant legitimacy to the southern cause? GAR members disputed southern claims of legitimacy for their cause, but most white Americans simply chose not to remember.

African Americans, however, could not forget. If white Americans ignored the issue of slavery and redefined the war "as a struggle between two ultimately compatible 'principles' of union and state sovereignty," as the art historian Kirk Savage argues, "the four years of the worst bloodshed in American history seem to be an inexplicable, Job-like test. And the local monuments that help recast the war in this light tell us in effect that neither side lost." Yet, in fact, the South lost and the North won. The war was waged for an essential purpose, which remained to be fulfilled, blacks argued. A poem published in the Kansas *State Ledger* in honor of Decoration Day in 1893 asked, for example,

Why should we praise the gray, and blue,
And honor them alike?
The one was false, the other true—
One wrong, the other right.

Frederick Douglass and other black leaders argued against oblivious reunion, and on Memorial Day they sought to link reconciliation to real southern repentance and reform. In 1871, Douglass spoke at Arlington National Cemetery on Decoration Day and addressed a great multitude, including President Grant and his cabinet. From the platform constructed near the monument honoring the "Unknown Loyal Dead," Douglass praised "those unknown heroes whose whitened bones have been piously gathered here, and whose green graves we now strew with sweet and beautiful flowers, choice emblems alike of pure hearts and brave spirits." He assured his audience, "I am no minister of malice. I would not strike the fallen. I would not repel the repentant." But if the South had fallen, was it repentant? "May my 'right hand forget her cunning and my tongue cleave to the roof of my mouth,' if I forget the difference between the parties to that terrible, protracted, and bloody conflict," the orator proclaimed, quoting Psalm 137: 5–6. Douglass prescribed a thoughtful, informed remembrance. "I say, if this war is to be forgotten, . . . in the name of all things sacred, what shall men remember?" Memorial Day should not simply honor bravery, which "marked the rebel not less than the loyal soldier," Douglass argued. "We are not here to applaud manly courage, save as it has been displayed in a noble cause. We must never forget that victory to the rebellion meant death to the republic." His praise and gratitude fell exclusively on the loyal Union dead, those who saved the nation, reunited it, and banished "the hell-black system of human bondage."

Seven years later, Frederick Douglass addressed the Grand Army of the Republic in New York City, in a Memorial Day speech on May 30, 1878. By then, Reconstruction had come to an end, without achieving its goals of equality, opportunity, and integration for African Americans. Douglass denounced southern violations of the Constitution and urged listeners to remember the justice of the Union cause. He again told his audience his purpose was not "to fan the flames of sectional animosity, to revive old issues, or to stir up strife between the races." But he insisted—in the face of the nation's absent-minded reconciliation—that "we are still afflicted by the painful sequences both of slavery and of the late rebellion." Quoting Ulysses S. Grant's famous phrase, "Let us have peace," Douglass added, "But let us have liberty, law, and justice first. Let us have the Constitution, with its thirteenth, fourteenth, and fifteenth amendments, fairly interpreted, faithfully executed, and cheerfully obeyed." "We must not be asked to say that the South was right in the rebellion, or to say the North was wrong." Douglass reiterated, there *was* a "difference between those who fought for the Union and those who fought against it, . . . between loyalty and treason." The Civil War "was a war of ideas, a battle of principles," which opposed "the old and the new, slavery and freedom, barbarism and civilization."

If the Civil War was a war of liberation, why did African Americans in the South remain oppressed, denied their rights as citizens? Douglass continued to speak out, particularly on Memorial Day. In a May 30 address at Storer College in Harper's Ferry, Virginia in 1881, Douglass went so far as to defend the radical Abolitionist John Brown, who just over 20 years earlier had led a raid on the armory there as the first step in igniting a rebellion to destroy slavery. Douglass and other African Americans saw Brown "as a hero and martyr to the cause of liberty." Increasingly, however, John Brown's zealous and violent acts on behalf of black freedom and equality in Kansas and then at Harper's Ferry were an inconvenient memory, even an embarrassment, for whites, and Douglass's words, on this and other occasions, were often lost in the ostentatious rites of reconciliation and collective amnesia that adorned Decoration Day.

REMEMBERING, AND FORGETTING

In 1889, Congress finally made Memorial Day a national holiday. That year the GAR participated in a Decoration Day ceremony at Greenwood, Louisiana. In the 1890s Arlington National Cemetery created a special section for the burial of Confederate dead, and in the next decade legislation committed the federal government to care for Confederate graves in the North. In Chicago on Memorial Day in 1895, a crowd of some 5,000 people dedicated a monument at Oak Woods Cemetery to Confederate prisoners who had died at nearby Fort Douglas. Notable Chicago citizens, including representatives of Chicago's business interests, received a distinguished delegation of former Confederate generals. They hoped reunion would promote commercial union, with investment opportunities for northern capitalists and economic development for the New South. A visiting Mississippian, General Stephen D. Lee, expressed his appreciation and his hope for the future in terms that would have struck an earlier generation, both North and South, as trivial and obscene: "We invite you to invade us again, not this time with your bayonets, but with your business." Although an orator from the black GAR, John Brown Post, representing the south side of Chicago, objected to such amnesia, the business of reconciliation was business.

In 1903, the first Confederate Memorial Day ceremony was held at Arlington National Cemetery. Ultimately, President William Howard Taft signed legislation permitting the United Daughters of the Confederacy (UDC) to erect a Confederate Memorial at Arlington. It is among the tallest monuments on this hallowed ground and includes on one side a depiction of a "faithful slave." This image of the "faithful" or "loyal slave"—which showed up in literature, history, and oratory as well as stone—did more than forget the history of African American oppression and resistance or service in the Civil War; it misrepresented the nature of slavery and the southern plantation system and served to prop up the racist myths of the postbellum "redeemed" South. Nowhere was this mythologizing work more clear than in a monument constructed in Harper's Ferry, Virginia in the early 1930s. In a strange coda to Frederick Douglass's Memorial Day address on John Brown in 1881, some 50 years later the UDC dedicated a memorial stone to one Heywood Shepherd, alleged to be a faithful slave who refused to join the raid, symbolic of those loyal slaves who stuck by their benevolent masters during the Civil War. (In fact, Shepherd was a free black railroad worker—not a slave—who happened to be in the wrong place at the wrong time and was shot in the darkness and confusion of John Brown's raid on October 16, 1859.) For white Americans, however, faithful remembrance of the war, and of black history during this period, seemed gone with the wind.

Memorial Day proved to be a profoundly conservative occasion that produced as much forgetting as remembering. Its truly memorial and liberationist content was not frequently or easily invoked, and those who did so were often ignored. Decoration Day could remain vital among African Americans, as annual observances at Beaufort, South Carolina, show. In 1897, for example, excursion trains brought celebrants from as far away as Greenville, and some 10 to 12 thousand black Carolinians filled Beaufort's streets to hail the African American regiments that fought and died for freedom and the Union. This Decoration Day commemoration continued in subsequent decades and represented a counterweight to Confederate Memorial Day as well as to the increasingly blind national one. But its impact (and the impact of black exercises elsewhere) remained local, or segregated within the African American community.

If African Americans could recall their own assistance to the Union victory in the Civil War, appreciate the courage of black troops, and implicitly (sometimes explicitly) defy mindless reconciliation through localized celebration of Memorial Day, American Indians could also highlight their own patriotism and defense of country (that is, their particular homeland if not the American nation-state) on Decoration Day. Adopting white custom in the early twentieth century, for example, Hidatsas in North Dakota celebrated the day (as they celebrated other patriotic holidays, such as the Fourth of July), gathering wild flowers when available or, if the season did not allow it, buying silk flowers to decorate their graves.

Yet Memorial Day could also be the occasion of coercive, heavy-handed indoctrination. T. J. Morgan, the United States Commissioner of Indian Affairs, in his instruction to Indian agents and superintendents of Indian schools in 1890, included Decoration Day among those holidays to be inculcated among Native students, "as a part of their education and a means of preparation and training for civilized home life and American citizenship." In the Commissioner's annual report, Morgan claimed "that both teachers and pupils entered heartily into the spirit of various occasions." Even some "adult Indians took active part, . . . and for the time being, at least, identifying themselves with the new ideas brought forward." "On a few of the reservations," Morgan noted, "Memorial Day could be as fittingly observed as elsewhere, by the decoration of graves of Indians who enlisted in the United States Army and lost their lives during the war."

At Indian boarding schools, Native American students were taught the rites of Memorial Day as lessons in Americanization. As Commissioner Morgan wrote in 1889, "The Indians are destined to become absorbed into the national life, not as Indians, but as Americans." Richard H. Pratt, the founder of Carlisle Indian School, had set this agenda with the prescription, "to kill the Indian . . . and save the man." Too often Indian policy accomplished only the former, and the cemeteries attached to boarding schools contained the mortal remains of a disturbing number of Native American children who died during the course of their Americanization. Decoration Day could be an occasion for Indian children to honor these dead as well. At Haskell Institute in Lawrence, Kansas, as elsewhere, school officials orchestrated Memorial Day rites to conform to preferred gender arrangements in their own society, requiring Indian girls to wear white dresses and designating them as the ones who would strew flowers on the Indian graves. According to the Indian Commissioner's instructions, "teachers . . . should endeavor to appeal to the highest element of manhood and womanhood in their pupils, . . . and they should carefully avoid any unnecessary reference to the fact that they are Indians."

In some instances, Decoration Day ceremonies could be cruelly colonial, forcing Native American students to adorn the graves of traditional enemies or white conquerors. After visiting the Lapwai Boarding School in Idaho in 1890, for example, the white reformer Alice Fletcher wrote a friend, "On Decoration Day we happened to see the procession of [Nez Percé] school children going to decorate the graves of the soldiers who slew their fathers in the [Chief] Joseph war." As with black Americans, Indians remembered a past at odds with the one preferred by whites; for Native American people, Memorial Day rites of reconciliation (following a different domestic conflict—the Plains Indian Wars) ignored their plight and offended their history.

Nonetheless, observance of Decoration Day among African Americans and Native Americans, at least when voluntarily adopted, suggests their efforts to cultivate ethnic or racial pride, identity, and solidarity more than to stage a public challenge to mainstream white interpretations of the past or to current social and political arrangements. American Indians have served in the U.S. military in numbers disproportionate to the size of their population, commencing in the American Revolution and continuing in virtually every war in United States history, including the Civil War (fighting for both the Union and the Confederacy). They did so for their own reasons, which varied according to the context of their own social structures, beliefs, customs, and interests. According to the Cherokee-Creek historian and Vietnam veteran Tom Holm, many Indian people have viewed military service as a family or tribal tradition. Some 75 percent of Native American Vietnam veterans volunteered or submitted to conscription for such reasons, Holm argues. In the aftermath of war, most

Native American societies honored their warriors and employed ceremonies to cleanse and reintegrate them into their peaceful communities. Native American people continue to honor military service in their own ways—even when not compelled to do so by white authorities—often employing the national Memorial Day, as well as the new holiday that appeared after World War I, Armistice Day (later Veterans Day). Since the 1920s, for example, Lakota people at the Rosebud Sioux Reservation have honored their dead, particularly veterans, on Memorial Day and Veterans Day, suggesting the significance of these solemn holidays for Native Americans. Rites such as those at Rosebud were primarily nonpolitical (or only implicitly political), designed not to critique particular wars, or to contest or promote particular policy, but to revitalize the community and its members, who had faced horror and death.

AN APOLITICAL HOLIDAY?

Groups prominent in late nineteenth- and early twentieth-century social and political reform found little ground or motivation to pursue their agendas on Decoration Day. Such was the case for women's rights advocates and labor activists, for example, no less than for those campaigning for racial justice or human rights. Labor, of course, would have its own day, and feminists similarly would look elsewhere in the calendar for politically useful moments. As Memorial Day became an occasion of national reconciliation, of a unified and conservative Americanness, it became insulated from conventional politics. As a nonpartisan festival, Memorial Day went further than depoliticizing (or rather, altering the political meaning of) the Civil War; the holiday's white supporters North and South at times seemed to demonize politics and politicians themselves, particularly the radical Republicans who had engineered Reconstruction. Meanwhile, mainstream white celebrants lionized veterans, focusing on their manly valor, heroism, and fellow feeling.

Decoration Day rites reinforced traditional gender notions and arrangements. As historian Nina Silber has shown, Memorial Day ceremonies in the North—organized largely by the Grand Army of the Republic—cultivated veterans' image of manly heroism. Union veterans affirmed their manhood through their public advocacy for the protection and support of widows and orphans, and in general women played a silent, passive, and supporting role in Decoration Day events. The adulation of women helped mark and elevate men as society's public protectors, defenders of home and hearth, where women and children found refuge. Women's sentimental floral tributes placed on men's graves recognized masculine courage, duty, and sacrifice and represented a continuation of the secondary, nurturing role played by women during the Civil War itself. As on other holiday occasions, male orators spoke and male marchers paraded while mixed audiences listened and watched approvingly. Women did not speak up or speak out; in contrast to Independence Day or even Washington's or Lincoln's birth-days, on Memorial Day one was unlikely to hear calls for woman's suffrage.

In the South, Ladies Memorial Associations dominated Decoration Day rites. Fulfilling their conventional female roles as mourners and guardians of memory, southern women reclaimed the mortal remains of their sons, hus-bands, and brothers and shed tears and flowers over their graves. Confederate Memorial Day became "the Sabbath of the South," and flowers that enveloped the cemeteries of gray soldiers emitted, according to one southern woman, an aroma "like incense burning in golden censers to the memory of the saints." Although leaders in sentimental commemoration, southern white women nonetheless remained subordinate to men, in their expressions of gratitude for male heroic efforts, in their loving embrace of returned boys in gray and their ostentatious snubs to Yankees, in their diligent efforts to relieve male anxieties and reconstruct defeated soldiers' sense of their manhood, and in expressions of a shared, racist fear of newly freed black men.

Ironically, men played a more prominent role in the various chapters of the southern Ladies Memorial Association than the name suggests; they helped in local organization, offered aid and advice, gave financial assistance, per-formed manual labor in cemetery projects, sometimes presided at meetings, and became honorary members. In the South, then, memorial projects belonged to the realm of women, but such ritual activity did little to upset the South's traditional patriarchal order. Southern white women's organizations proved uninterested in political or historical discussions, in gender realignment, or in social reform. When speeches accompanied decoration rites, the mixed audi-ences most often listened to male orators. Like their counterparts in the North, southern women embraced a politically passive, supporting role. Unlike north-ern women, however, women in the South did raise and manage the funds required to care for graves, which initially the federal government refused to support, and they presided at sentimental Memorial Day services. Their promi-nent role, however, was not motivated by any hope among southern women to redefine their roles but, instead, reflected their lack of political consequence. Because women posed no political threat, Decoration Day rites could avoid confrontation with the difficult political questions surrounding southern defeat and northern Reconstruction.

In the South as well as the North, Decoration Day was a local (and sectional) affair, even though it commemorated a national tragedy and ultimately pro-moted national reunion. Observers of Confederate Memorial Day, as we have seen, insisted on their own dates for local celebration, and southern women worked tirelessly to repatriate the remains of their dead and inter them in local cemeteries. Ladies Memorial Associations were only loosely affiliated with each other and were distinctly local institutions. Northern communities too com-memorated their dead in localized fashion, honoring common soldiers (not merely prominent officers) as never before and emphasizing the particular contributions of their own towns and villages to the Union victory. North and South nonetheless reconciled—in part through joint, intersectional Memorial Day rites that symbolized and rehearsed the national reunion. Northern, white politicians abandoned Reconstruction and removed troops from the South, returning the region to local rule. After 1877, such autonomy bred, in addition to a great deal of mischief, a more ambiguous patriotic holiday on May 30.

Increasingly drained of its sectional, partisan content, Memorial Day developed as a day of escapist leisure. The "new patriotism" of the late nineteenth century lacked a clearly-defined set of principles or programs; instead, it seemed to express an almost mindless devotion to country. On Memorial Day 1895, Oliver Wendell Holmes could declare, "The faith is true and adorable, which leads a soldier to throw away his life in obedience to a blindly accepted duty, in a cause which he little understands." Holmes characterized patriotic sacrifice as unconditional, even "senseless," if the sense or the reason behind it was best left unexamined. Such notions of history, politics, and patriotism might invite Americans to not think about the causes or the consequences of the Civil War at all, and instead devote their attention to the present, to diversionary leisure and amusement.

In the late 1880s in New York, the old Dutch carnivalesque holiday of Pinkster (Pentecost or Whitsuntide) and Barnum's Circus Day were made to coincide with Memorial Day. Elsewhere, even if Decoration Day was no circus, it was frequently a lively parade, a picnic, or an excuse for a sporting event. Beginning in 1911, Memorial Day became the traditional date of the Indianapolis 500, which remains America's oldest automobile race. As a generation of Civil War veterans died, the day transformed into an occasion for generic expressions of memory and mourning—an American Day of the Dead—with people more often visiting the graves of their deceased relatives, whether they had died in service to their country or not.

SECURING ITS PLACE IN THE AMERICAN CALENDAR

With the Spanish-American War at the end of the nineteenth century, and then World War I in the twentieth century's second decade, the United States acquired new military dead to remember and soldiers to honor. Although Americans have frequently declared, "we shall never forget," memories of recent conflicts often obscure the memories of older ones. Memorial Day exercises in Indianapolis after 1918, for example, focused attention on World War I, even though they were staged at the Civil War Soldiers and Sailors Monument, erected only in 1902. In Cleveland, the obliteration of memory was even more literal, as Cleveland's Soldiers and Sailors Monument was constructed on the very site—and required the demolition—of the city's most important previous memorial, one commemorating Oliver Hazard Perry's victory in the Battle of Lake Erie during the War of 1812. In turn, that Civil War monument, dedicated on July 4, 1894, evolved to serve new political agendas in another generation—Americanization and the commemoration of twentieth-century world wars.

Following World War I, the United States inaugurated a new memorial holiday, Armistice Day (later Veterans Day), which found a separate site in American culture—on the calendar on November 11—even though its purpose seemed to duplicate Decoration Day. Armistice Day won acceptance through the lobbying of the American Legion, the largest veterans' organization to appear in the United States after the Great War in 1919, in some ways recapitulating the previous efforts of the Grand Army of the Republic in the creation of Memorial Day. The Legion joined actively with Civil War and Spanish-American War veterans in Memorial Day rites; indeed, it even established an endowment fund to insure the decoration of American graves on foreign soil. But in addition the American Legion lobbied to create a new memorial day dedicated exclusively to those who served in World War I.

The nation's first Armistice Day observance occurred on November 11, 1919, in conformity with President Woodrow Wilson's proclamation, which emphasized peace: "A year ago our enemies laid down their arms in accordance with an armistice which rendered them impotent to renew hostilities, and gave to the world an assured opportunity to reconstruct its shattered order and to work out in peace a new and juster set of international relations." Armistice Day, for Wilson, celebrated the end of "the war to end all wars" and the new possibilities of international peace: "To us in America the reflections of Armistice Day will be filled with solemn pride in the heroism of those who died in the country's service and with gratitude for the victory, both because of the thing from which it has freed us and because of the opportunity it has given America to show her sympathy with peace and justice in the councils of nations." World War I had ended with an armistice, signed at Compiegne, France on November 11, 1918—at the eleventh hour of the eleventh day of the eleventh month—and thus American citizens were instructed to observe two minutes of silence to honor the war dead and promote the cause of peace each Armistice Day, November 11.

Yet despite its articulated purpose as a holiday to advance peace, Armistice Day quickly assumed a martial character. Its chief promoter, the American Legion, denounced pacifism and radicalism and vigorously joined efforts to destroy leftist activity in the Red Scare of 1919 and 1920. Rather quickly by the 1930s, though its annual observance continued, Armistice Day's intensity and seriousness declined, and, as with Memorial Day, celebrants turned their attention increasingly to leisure and amusement, particularly when the nation was not actually at war.

Why did Americans need another memorial day when they had one already, observed annually on May 30? Some argued they did not. Congressman

Hamilton Fish Jr., who authored legislation to create a memorial to an unknown soldier in Arlington National Cemetery in 1920, believed that Memorial Day would serve best as the occasion for the dedication ceremony. Fish and others hoped to further national unity, make Decoration Day a truly cross-sectional observance, and encourage recent veterans of World War I to adopt Memorial Day as their own. But President Warren G. Harding chose to re-inter the Unknown at Arlington on November 11, 1921 instead, giving additional support to the separate existence of Armistice Day.

Memorial Day and Armistice Day faced the same problems. As memory faded and veteran constituencies passed away, the meaning and purpose of each holiday grew vaguer. In the 1940s and 1950s new military conflicts—a second World War and the Korean War—blocked out remembrance of the first World War, just as that Great War obscured memory of the Civil War. In the twentieth century, some campaigned to broaden the mandate of Armistice Day to honor the dead who had fallen in all American wars, just as Memorial Day had become broader and less distinct, as a generic commemoration of those who died in conflicts following the Civil War. In June 1954, President Dwight D. Eisenhower signed a law that officially renamed the November 11 holiday "Veterans Day," now honoring all United States veterans living as well as deceased, and in the process perhaps better distinguishing the occasion from Memorial Day. Of course, Decoration Day (despite its articulated purpose) had earlier functioned as a day of advocacy for veterans under the auspices of the GAR. On Memorial Day in 1958, two more bodies of unknown soldiers, representing the previous two wars, were buried with honor at Arlington in the expanded Tomb of the Unknown. Maintaining the ambiguity surrounding the meaning of the two public holidays of mourning in the United States, each year the president participates in a service at the memorial, on the last Monday in May—Memorial Day—*and* at 11 o'clock on the morning of November 11, Veterans Day.

Holiday names change—from Washington's Birthday to Presidents' Day, for example, as well as from Armistice Day to Veterans Day—but that alteration does not necessarily prevent their deflation as meaningful, commemorative events in American life. Included in the 1968 Monday Holiday Bill, Veterans Day became a moveable feast and part of a three-day weekend in November, beginning in 1971. But in 1978, Congress returned Veterans Day to its original November 11 spot, in deference to veterans' organizations' complaints that such tampering had devalued the holiday. If veterans' groups were mollified, the public was unmoved. By 1974, a year after the United States' withdrawal from Vietnam, the annual Veterans Day ceremony at Arlington drew only 3,000 people. On Armistice Day in 1921, by contrast, the original dedication of the Tomb of the Unknown Soldier attracted some 100,000 people. Crowds would increase in the early 1980s at Veterans Day events, with the dedication of a new Vietnam Veterans Memorial in Washington, D.C. But Americans' fitful rapprochement with the history of their experience in Vietnam did little to invigorate Memorial Day. On Memorial Day in 2002, President George W. Bush reinstituted a lapsed practice of sending a floral wreath to adorn the Confederate Memorial in Arlington National Cemetery. No one seemed to notice.

FROM DAY OF REMEMBERING TO DAY OFF

Unlike Veterans Day, Memorial Day became and remained a "St. Monday"—a holiday occasion, formerly filled with meaning but now more obscure, manipulated in the calendar to create a three-day weekend, and dedicated to the proposition that Americans desire days of leisure and material consumption. The Monday Holiday Bill that fiddled with Veterans Day also mandated that Memorial Day would henceforth (beginning in 1971) be celebrated on the last Monday in May. While the other memorial day—Veterans Day—was removed from the three-day weekend rotation, and thus remained pure, it increasingly became just another day of the week. Memorial Day, on the other hand, retained its special status as a day off, but as an occasion of leisure rather than solemn remembrance. Foreign observers are often shocked that in the United States a fête commemorating the deaths of thousands, who gave their lives in defense of their country, is lightly observed with shopping and barbecues, while in their own countries (Israel, for example) such days are among the most somber in their calendars. Today in the United States, Memorial Day is widely greeted as the herald of summer, the day that inaugurates the summer season. Even in times of war, massive, national observations of Memorial Day or Veterans Day have become rare.

Such rites, most often and most effectively observed locally, assert a local identity and project it onto the nation. Ironically, localized rites of remembrance, in both the nineteenth-century North and South, provided a means of cultivating national reconciliation between the sections in postbellum America. Narrowing one's vision to the particular duties fulfilled by soldiers clad in both gray and blue—protection of family, home, community—and focusing on the common tragedy suffered by fellow Americans North and South, who lost sons, brothers, husbands alike, Americans could use a common rite of mourning to reimagine themselves as a single nation. In order to remember their mutual national affinity, however, Americans had to forget their animosity and the chief cause of their Civil War—the conflict over slavery and the place of African Americans in the United States (white Americans were even less conscious of Native Americans). The war between the states over the institution of slavery did not resolve the question. And Memorial Day, as a day of national reconciliation, colluded in the nation's purposeful amnesia by ignoring black contributions toward the Union victory as well as the continuing failure to achieve social, political, or economic justice for African Americans. Real remembrance and reconciliation were at odds, and the United States seemed to choose the latter over the former, opting for forgetting over historical memory and racial justice. Ultimately, as Civil War veterans died, and as new wars created new veterans and different memories, Memorial Day commemoration evolved (some would say devolved) and even spawned another memorial holiday, to serve its new constituencies, often supplying Americans simply with a day of unselfconscious leisure.

An exception to the trend, though not necessarily one that establishes a new commemorative rule, occurred during Memorial Day in 2004, with the dedication of a new National World War II Memorial on the Mall in Washington, D.C. The Jubilee of World War II, then the sixtieth anniversary of D-Day and the war's end, along with the passing of what has been called the "Greatest Generation" that fought in the war, all combined to prompt renewed remembrance of those who served and died. As in the past, a constituency proved critical in memorialization. Some 16 million Americans served in the war, and more than 400,000 died. By the 1990s and into the first decade of the twenty-first century, veterans of World War II were dying at a rate of over 1,000 per day in the United States. Veterans' organizations pressed public officials to construct a suitable memorial before this generation (by the 2000s reduced to some four million) had all passed away. The relatively noncontroversial character of the so-called Good War substantially helped this promotional work. Congress supported the proposition, and with its intervention organizers managed to defeat efforts to block construction of the memorial on the National Mall between the Washington Monument and the Lincoln Memorial. During Memorial Day weekend, on May 29, 2004, the memorial was officially dedicated by President George W. Bush, before large crowds and much fanfare.

The National World War II Memorial's opening gave new life to Memorial Day, but the emphasis on the holiday in 2004, though fitting and proper, seemed based as much on convenience and time pressure than a conscious desire to revitalize the festival. The memorial grounds had opened unofficially in April, and the dedication occurred on May 27, two days before Memorial Day that year. Moreover, the site had been dedicated previously on Veterans Day in 1995. If the memorial could have been completed by November 11, 2003, one wonders, would officials have put off the dedication ceremony until Memorial Day at all? Commemoration of D-Day—the massive landing in Normandy on June 6, 1944 that, at great cost, insured Allied victory in World War II—also augmented Memorial Day's impact in the early 2000s. In 2001, a new National D-Day Memorial was dedicated in Bedford, Virginia, a town that lost 19 of its 35 native sons who participated in the invasion. Memorial Day occurs barely a week before June 6, and the commemorative energy generated by the new memorial seemed to infuse Memorial Day as well. But for how long?

Americans will continue to visit these commemorative sites, as they do Arlington National Cemetery, but it seems unlikely that they will fully restore or sustain Memorial Day as a moment of serious, historical reflection, graced by solemn ceremonies and large, attentive crowds. On May 27, 2002, President Bush visited the Normandy American Cemetery at Colleville-Sur-Mer, France. Speaking of the American dead buried there, he declared, "The day will come when no one is left who knew them, when no visitor to this cemetery can stand before a grave remembering a face and a voice." But, he continued, "The day will never come when America forgets them." President Bush might be right, but history is not on his side, given the fate of other military contests and other veterans who are now largely forgotten, even on Memorial Day.

Nonetheless, Memorial Day will survive in the American calendar and will retain a latent power to stir up feelings of patriotism. Its very ambiguity, a legacy of its post–Civil War origins, makes it a suitable commemorative event for those committed to national reconciliation and unity, even in the face of unreconciled differences—whether related to the Civil War or Vietnam or any other divisive conflict. Memorial Day promotes toleration (or avoidance) of different interpretations of single, controversial events, particularly in its emphasis on honoring warriors rather than particular wars and in its glorification of unconditional devotion to country. It need not be the case, but Americans mostly choose to forget their past, and ironically they use Memorial Day—by definition a day dedicated to memory—to spread rather than cure the national case of amnesia.

FURTHER READING

Blight, David W. *Race and Reunion: The Civil War in American Memory.* Cambridge, Mass.: Belknap Press, 2001.

Dennis, Matthew. *Red, White, and Blue Letter Days: An American Calendar.* Ithaca, N.Y.: Cornell University Press, 2002.

Foster, Gaines. *Ghosts of the Confederacy: Defeat, the Lost Cause, and the Emergence of the New South, 1865–1913.* New York: Oxford University Press, 1987.

Litwicki, Ellen M. *America's Public Holidays, 1865–1920.* Washington, D.C.: Smithsonian Institution Press, 2000.

O'Leary, Cecilia Elizabeth. *To Die For: The Paradox of American Patriotism.* Princeton, N.J.: Princeton University Press, 1999.

Piehler, G. Kurt. *Remembering War the American Way.* Washington, D.C.: Smithsonian Institution Press, 1995.

Silber, Nina. *The Romance of Reunion: Northerners and the South, 1865–1900.* Chapel Hill: University of North Carolina Press, 1993.

Matthew Dennis

A Holiday for a Flag

One would be hard pressed to find a nation anywhere in the world that venerates its national flag to the degree that Americans do. From the time of its official adoption by Congress on June 14, 1777, Americans have been encouraged to imbue their national banner with near-religious significance. As one member of the Continental Congress later recalled, the flag was meticulously designed to embody as many symbolic associations as possible, most of which were probably lost on the soldiers engaged in the long war for independence:

> The stars of the new flag represent the constellation of States rising in the West. The idea was taken from the constellation Lyra, which in the hand of Orpheus signifies harmony. The blue in the field was taken from the edges of the Covenanters' banner in Scotland, significant of the league and covenant of the United Colonies against oppression, incidentally involving the virtues of vigilance, perseverance, and justice. The stars were in a circle, symbolizing the perpetuity of the Union—the ring, like the circling serpent of the Egyptians, signifying eternity. The thirteen stripes showed, with the stars, the number of the United Colonies, and denoted the subordination of the States of [to] the Union, as well as equality among themselves. The whole was the blending of the various flags previous to the Union flag, viz.: the red flags of the army and the white of the floating batteries. The red color, which in Roman days was the signal of defiance, denotes daring; and the white, purity.

The anniversary of the adoption of the "Stars and Stripes" attracted little or no attention for more than a century, however. As in the case of so many of the holidays described in this volume, Flag Day was an outgrowth of late-nineteenth century imperial patriotism and efforts to indoctrinate the millions of immigrants entering the United States after the Civil War, especially those of eastern and southern European origins.

B. J. Cigrand, a schoolteacher in Fredonia, Wisconsin, is generally credited with arranging the first "Flag Birthday" ceremonies on June 14, 1885 for his students to perform. Every year thereafter, Cigrand argued in newspapers and magazines for the observance of June 14 as "Flag Birthday," or "Flag Day." Cigrand's proposal found supporters in the Northeast initially, and particularly in the big cities, where patriotic pageants and exercises could reach large numbers of school children, many of them immigrants or the children of immigrants. Indeed, "Flag Day" from its inception was especially aimed at the young.

The state and city of New York can take much of the credit for Flag Day's inception, and for the ritualized Pledge that became indelibly associated with civilian display of the flag. In New York City in 1889, kindergarten teacher George Balch organized June 14 ceremonies for the children in his school. Successful and popular, his program was eventually adopted by the state's Board of Education. Flag Day received support at the highest levels of the state; for the occasion in 1894, the governor of New York ordered flags to be displayed on all public buildings, which included the public schools. Balch's school program may have been the inspiration for school ceremonies, but other teachers had considerable latitude for creativity. One New York principal turned her entire elementary school into a "theater of patriotism" each Flag Day. After a day devoted to patriotic poetry, songs, and stories, children marched onto the school's stage and, using colored streamers, transformed themselves into a "living flag." War and politics further enhanced the new flag-worship in the state; when the Spanish-American War broke out in 1898, the New York legislature ordered the state superintendent of public instruction to require the schools to begin *each day* with a salute to the flag. That same law also mandated the observance of Flag Day in the state.

Authorship of the now-familiar (and controversial) Pledge of Allegiance is credited to Francis Bellamy, minister of a church in Rome, New York. The Pledge has actually been altered several times, the most recent being in 1954, when the words "under God" were added. Bellamy reportedly wrote the Pledge for the occasion of the 400th anniversary of Columbus's discovery. Bellamy envisioned the occasion as a mass civics lesson: "Let the flag float over every school-house in the land and let the exercise be such as shall impress upon our youth the patriotic duty of citizenship." He must have been impressed with the result: on Columbus Day in 1892, the Pledge was recited by more than 12 million public school children. The transferal of the Pledge to Flag Day the next year was a simple and obvious measure.

New York may have taken the first steps, but other urban centers were not far behind. Patriotic groups gathered at the Betsy Ross House in Philadelphia in 1891, and the next year the Pennsylvania Society of Colonial Dames of America urged city authorities and citizens to display flags on June 14. The Superintendent of Public Schools of Philadelphia directed that Flag Day exercises be held on that day in Independence Square, and for the occasion the city's school children, each carrying a small flag, assembled to sing patriotic songs and listen to patriotically edifying speeches. In Illinois, citizens formed the American Flag

Day Association, with Cigrand in the lead, to promote the practice of Flag Day exercises. Chicago held its first Flag Day ceremonies in 1894, with more than 300,000 school children observing the day in the city's parks.

Together, Flag Day and the Pledge of Allegiance (the latter eventually adopted for daily recital in schools across the nation) encouraged students and teachers, and civilians generally, to create and participate in flag rituals to a level previously associated with members of the military. As Celia O'Leary maintains in *To Die For: The Paradox of American Patriotism* (1999), "the new flag rituals allowed both children and adults to become actors in the drama of nation-building." Additionally, the practices aided in the self-fashioning of immigrants into American citizens.

After 30 years of celebrations organized at the state and local levels, in 1916 President Woodrow Wilson, running for reelection on a platform of patriotic isolationism, issued a proclamation establishing Flag Day throughout the nation. But the president could not make such an arrangement permanent; it was not until August 3, 1949, as the Cold War crusade against communism intensified, that President Harry Truman signed Congress's act confirming June 14 of each year as National Flag Day.

Flag Day never became a paid holiday, however, and today Flag Day is largely ignored, as Americans go about their daily business, perhaps merely displaying the national flag more prominently. Part of the reason for this may be overexposure: over the course of the last century, the flag and the Pledge of Allegiance have become so ubiquitous that a special day to feature flag-related symbols and rituals seems redundant and superfluous. In a sense, the efforts of Cigrand and others succeeded too well.

For some, however, one cannot get too much of a good thing. In 1982, during the presidency of super-patriot Ronald Reagan, the National Flag Day Foundation was organized with the long-term goal of achieving "on each Flag Day . . . the participation of all Americans in the annual National Pause for the Pledge of Allegiance program." The Pause for the Pledge of Allegiance program, approved by Congress three years later, seeks to "provide a stage upon which all Americans, led by the President of the United States, repeat the thirty-one words that honor America." Recently, the foundation focused on a theme from the first inaugural speech of George W. Bush, that "everyone belongs," to revive its goal of a nationwide, synchronized ritual on Flag Day. Foundation spokespersons hope to "insure that everyone participates because everyone belongs." For foundation members today, as it was for B.J. Cigrand in the 1890s, patriotic ceremony is the key to being a good American, and indeed a natural outlet for all truly patriotic persons, emblematic, as the foundation expresses it, of Americans' "*need to express their allegiance to the nation and the flag, especially on Flag Day*" [italics added]. In 2005, the Republican-controlled House of Representatives passed a bill in the latest of its attempts to protect the flag from "desecration" (note the sacred connotations) with a Constitutional amendment. In the intensity of emotion elicited by "Old Glory" among many Americans, the national flag has become as much an object of worship as any religious symbol in an avowedly secular nation.

EMANCIPATION AND AFRICAN AMERICAN SLAVE FESTIVALS

- ☐ Shut out of mainstream American public festivals and holidays until after the Civil War, and even then not fully included, African Americans created and celebrated their own holidays and festivals.

- ☐ A central feature of colonial-era New England Negro Election Day festivals was the election of a black king or governor who would often wield authority within the black community, acting as arbitrator, judge, advisor, and liaison with whites.

- ☐ "Pinkster" was a slave festival that persisted into the early nineteenth century, primarily in New York State and New Jersey.

- ☐ Freedom Days started in 1808, commemorating the abolition of the trans-Atlantic slave trade by the United States, Great Britain, and Denmark, later shifting to mark abolition in New York state, then within the British Empire, and finally, abolition in the United States.

- ☐ Black Americans hoped the nation would celebrate slavery's end as an American holiday commemorating the realization of the ideal of freedom. Some whites participated in Reconstruction-era emancipation celebrations but after the 1870s white participation declined along with political interest in protecting blacks' rights.

- ☐ In Texas African Americans began celebrating June 19, or "Juneteenth," in recognition of the date in 1865 when federal troops landed in Galveston to implement the emancipation policy in that region. Made an official Texas state holiday in 1979, Juneteenth is one of the few emancipation festivals still marked in the twenty-first century.

EMANCIPATION AND AFRICAN AMERICAN SLAVE FESTIVALS

Traditions of public celebration and commemoration have long held an important place in African American history and culture, although scholars have only recently begun to explore the multiple functions they served, and the meanings they held, for black communities and activists since the eighteenth century. For much of this period, despite their consistent efforts to claim their rights as American citizens, African Americans were excluded (often forcibly) from Independence Day and other American public holidays. Blacks developed their own calendar of holidays and celebrations, even as they continued to work for their inclusion in the broader national festive culture.

NEGRO ELECTION DAY

Black Americans' first clear public role in American festive culture emerged in the eighteenth century, when free and enslaved Africans made use of public spaces in annual Negro Election Days, Pinkster celebrations, and similar events throughout much of New England, New York, and New Jersey. In these annual public celebrations, enslaved African Americans in the northeast fused European and African traditions of political and festive culture and adapted them to their own uses. Slave festivals offered opportunities for socializing, strengthened black communities, presented black leaders to the broader society, and reinforced the legitimacy of black Americans' assertive participation in American public life.

Distinctive colonial slave festivals most likely originated in impromptu social gatherings among slaves in town or brought to town by their white masters on special occasions, like the early-summer Election Week activities that were common throughout New England. Understandably wary of unregulated gatherings of their slaves, masters tried to exert their control over these festivities by providing financial sponsorship and sanction for what came to be known as Negro Election Day. Although whites maintained a degree of oversight, this holiday involved activities held primarily by and for blacks. By the middle of the eighteenth century enslaved Africans were using the festivals for their own purposes, instilling them with distinctly African forms of expression and communicating their own political meanings. Alongside the music, dancing, and general conviviality at these events, one of the central features of New England Negro Election Day festivals was the annual election of a black king or governor who would often wield considerable authority within the black community, acting as arbitrator, judge, advisor, and liaison with whites. Contenders for office vied for support with stump speeches and vigorous electioneering, partly serious and partly in mockery of white election practices. On the day of the festival the winner would be escorted through the streets of the city in an elaborate parade, usually on horseback and in resplendent attire. Negro Election Day festivities, held outdoors in the summer, attracted large numbers of whites and blacks who joined together in athletic competition, gambling, dancing, music, eating, and drinking. Enslaved blacks took advantage of the relative freedom of activity to enjoy a break from the work routine, to dress in their finest clothes, and to socialize with other blacks from around a given region with whom they might ordinarily interact in public relatively infrequently.

PINKSTER

"Pinkster" represents a variant of the slave festival that persisted into the early nineteenth century, primarily in eastern New York State and northern New Jersey. The tradition was particularly important and persistent in the Hudson River Valley and the city of Albany. Initially a Dutch religious celebration of the Pentecost brought to the American colonies in the seventeenth century, by the late eighteenth century the late spring holiday had evolved into a more secular multiethnic and multiracial affair. Most modern scholars agree that by the start of the nineteenth century, African elements of celebration—drumming, dancing, the construction of West African style thatched huts on Albany's "Pinkster Hill," the procession of an African "king"—had come to predominate. Like Negro Election Day, Pinkster provided blacks an opportunity to dominate public space, publicly express themselves in traditional African forms, and socialize with family and friends. These slave festivals also shared an expression of personal freedom at a time when most of the African American participants were enslaved. In that respect they represent important foundations for black Americans' entry into public celebrations as free people during the nineteenth century.

FREEDOM DAYS

The celebrations by free African Americans that began in the early nineteenth century all were organized around the commemoration of events that moved the race toward a more complete experience of freedom. This was a key feature that distinguished what some scholars have termed "Freedom Day" events from the earlier slave festivals, which, while they incorporated some political functions, were primarily festive celebrations. While nineteenth century Freedom Day commemorations shared many festive elements with the slave festivals, they differed in being consciously designed to commemorate important events, foster a sense of unity among black Americans, develop a sense of shared history, and agitate for social and political rights.

The first of these Freedom Days was established in 1808 to commemorate the abolition of the trans-Atlantic slave trade by the United States, Great Britain, and Denmark, which took effect on January 1 of that year. As free black communities grew and developed in northern cities after the Revolution, their leaders founded social institutions like churches, mutual aid societies, and fraternal orders, to provide support and organize community life. These leaders also recognized the importance of public rituals for establishing the collective identity of a developing community. Seeing the abolition of the Atlantic trade as an important milestone in their quest to end slavery and achieve equality, black leaders in several northern cities—especially Boston, New York, and Philadelphia—organized public commemorations to celebrate a major step toward freedom and claim their rights to use American public space.

This was particularly important because, by that time, free African Americans were increasingly being denied the basic privileges of American citizenship, including the right to participate in annual Independence Day celebrations. In fact, white celebrants were known to attack blacks who dared even to appear in public on the Fourth. In developing their own tradition of public commemoration, African Americans drew heavily upon the broader society's festive practices. But the initial celebrations of the abolition of the slave trade were far less boisterous than either white July 4 festivities or the slave festivals. Typically organized by a black benevolent or antislavery society, the primary activities involved a public procession to a black church; songs; prayers of thanksgiving; sermons, and orations emphasizing the importance of the occasion; and a private banquet in the evening. Speeches and proceedings were sometimes published as pamphlets in order to reach white and black audiences beyond those in attendance.

Considerable controversy developed among black leaders regarding black celebrants' public behavior and the relative costs and benefits of staging parades. On the one hand, parades were regular components of other American holidays and celebrations during this period, and African Americans were determined to claim their right of expression in the public sphere. However, black parades were regularly mocked in print by white commentators, or, worse yet, harassed and attacked by white mobs in the streets. Moreover, they drained a considerable amount of money from a people who were kept economically impoverished by racial oppression. The debate over parading also illustrated class divisions within black communities, as elite leaders criticized and tried to control unruly behavior by the masses, which they deemed inappropriate and damaging to the race's public image. These divisions continued into the twentieth century.

Freedom celebrations continued in a few northeastern cities into the 1820s, but with American southern slavery still deeply entrenched and rights for free blacks severely limited, these Freedom Days increasingly lacked relevance. In 1827 African Americans in communities from New England to Virginia to Ohio shifted their commemorative attention to celebrate the abolition of slavery in New York State, which became final on July 4 of that year. Celebrations were often scheduled for July 5, in order to avoid attacks by white July 4 celebrants and to protest the hypocrisy of white Americans' rhetoric of liberty. Debates over parading and threats from white mobs continued to mar these celebrations and they largely ceased by the early 1830s.

Between the 1830s and 1850s the African American Freedom Day tradition matured around the celebration of a foreign event—the 1834 British act abolishing slavery in all its colonies. August 1 became known to black and white American abolitionists as British West Indian Emancipation Day, after the nearby region of the Caribbean basin where it had the greatest impact and relevance, freeing nearly 700,000 people of African descent. West Indian Emancipation was applauded as the success of British abolitionists, and was seen as a harbinger of the eventual demise of slavery in America. Especially after 1838, when emancipation became fully enacted, American abolitionists held annual August 1 celebrations all around the Northeast and into the rapidly developing Midwest. While many African Americans participated in white-organized celebrations, blacks also organized their own events. Between 1838 and 1862 African Americans organized hundreds of West Indian Emancipation celebrations in dozens of communities across the free states and in Canada. Due to restrictive laws and the constant threat of violence, those in slave states rarely, if ever, had the opportunity to hold Freedom Day events of any kind during this period.

While they also were not immune to occasional white violence, August 1 celebrations in the North and West came to be widely known, anxiously anticipated, and heavily attended affairs in cities, towns, and villages throughout the antebellum period. This new Freedom Day featured the lighthearted and entertaining elements of the slave festivals—parades, music, dancing, games, feasting, and the like—but also the serious prayers, thanksgiving, historical orations, and political agitation that were central to free black abolitionists' goals and objectives. Whites—either sympathetic antislavery advocates or merely curious locals drawn by the festivities—also attended these events in large numbers, in some cases outnumbering black celebrants. Celebrations would generally begin in the morning, as visitors from miles around poured into town, some taking advantage of reduced rail or steamboat rates to arrive from communities 50 or 100 miles away. A parade featuring the chief marshal and his entourage, black fraternal orders, orators, literary societies, bands, and other organizations wound its way past crowded sidewalks to the speakers' platform, which might be at a church or public theater, but were more often at a nearby outdoor grove or park. Here there were sermons and orations, interspersed with poetry readings and songs. Outdoor events provided opportunities for games, refreshments, picnicking, and other leisure activities. After the conclusion of the program, the crowd dispersed for dining and more socializing. There might be an evening program as well, but often the celebrants were then left to socialize, perhaps at a formal banquet and ball that would last into the wee hours of the morning.

Black organizers of these events recognized that they needed to mobilize all facets of the black community to the abolitionist cause, and the festive elements of August 1 attracted hundreds or even thousands of African Americans from all around the region, taking advantage of the opportunity to socialize and make merry on such a scale with large numbers of other blacks. In the process they were also exposed to the sight of black leaders and organizations marching authoritatively through town, and to the powerful words of black orators, who recounted the proud history of the race from ancient Egypt through the American Revolution and the present battle against slavery. These words inspired many who could now identify themselves with a people of noble heritage, and with articulate and talented spokespersons leading the fight for freedom and equal rights. While churches, conventions, newspapers, and other institutions provided ongoing reminders of this reality, large annual public Freedom Day celebrations played an important role in reaching out to a broad audience from all social classes, many of whom were not well connected with those other institutions.

CELEBRATING EMANCIPATION

Black Americans had long awaited the moment when they might celebrate their own emancipation, rather than the act of a foreign government. When the United States finally abolished slavery in the 1860s, many of the antebellum celebratory traditions continued, but those traditions were also transformed in important ways. For one thing, the organization of Freedom Days around the single date of August 1 now had to incorporate numerous other dates marking local or national events. Of course, January 1 was widely celebrated since that was the date in 1863 that President Lincoln's Emancipation Proclamation took effect. In some regions September 22 was observed because it was on that date in 1862 that Lincoln issued his Preliminary Proclamation, which first served notice of his intention to free slaves in Confederate-held territories. Lincoln's proclamation did not affect slavery in several states that practiced slavery but did not secede from the Union. In Maryland, for example, slavery was outlawed on November 4, 1864, and black Marylanders celebrated that date for

The text of the Emancipation Proclamation decorated with a portrait of Abraham Lincoln. Courtesy of the Library of Congress.

a number of years. In many northern communities where August 1 had been celebrated for decades, African Americans continued to use that date to mark American emancipation, in part at least because it would have been impossible to maintain the outdoor celebratory festivities in northern regions in the dead of winter.

In parts of the South, various dates of local significance were deemed more appropriate than any of those mentioned above. For example, in Washington D.C. blacks celebrated on April 16 in commemoration of the date in 1862 when Congress outlawed slavery in the nation's capital. In the Confederacy, slaves learning of Lincoln's proclamation were inspired to claim their own freedom by running away, but they also realized that mere words did not immediately change their status. For that reason, many areas began to hold celebrations on the various dates when freedom became a reality in that place. In Thomaston, Georgia, celebrations were held in late May, a tradition that has continued into the twenty-first century. Blacks in the Confederate capital of Richmond, Virginia, held celebrations on April 3, to mark the date in 1865 when federal troops entered the city. In other areas blacks celebrated on April 9, often referred to as Surrender Day, marking the date of Confederate General Robert E. Lee's 1865 surrender of his army at Appomattox Courthouse. In Texas, African Americans began celebrating June 19, or "Juneteenth," in recognition of the date in 1865 when Federal troops landed in Galveston to implement the emancipation policy in that region. These and other local traditions demonstrate African Americans' awareness that the Emancipation Proclamation did not technically abolish slavery in the United States. That was only fully accomplished with the ratification of the Thirteenth Amendment to the Constitution on December 16, 1865. Interestingly, that date has never been regularly observed as part of the Freedom Day tradition.

The opportunity for southern blacks to celebrate emancipation beginning in the 1860s represents one of the most important developments in African American commemorative traditions, largely because of their sheer numbers—approximately 90 percent of African Americans lived in the South, a statistic that did not begin to change until the 1910s. As the new multiplicity of dates suggests, southern blacks were not content simply to copy the traditions of their northern counterparts but put their own distinctive stamp on the events. While much research still needs to be done in this area, it is clear that while many patterns remained fairly consistent across the nation, local and regional traditions added considerable diversity to emancipation celebrations. Celebrations, North and South, continued to draw regional attendance and feature parades, speeches, picnics, religious services, songs, balls, banquets, competitive games, and general merrymaking. But the cultural practices and customs of celebrations that had evolved under slavery were often quite different from those favored by black leaders in the North. When nearly four million slaves celebrated their freedom, they often did so in ways that many whites and northern

The famous emancipation statue in Washington, D.C. Courtesy of the Library of Congress.

blacks considered too boisterous and unruly. This, along with other factors, led to a disruption of the Freedom Day tradition in the decades after the 1870s.

In the immediate aftermath of emancipation, many African American spokespersons, with an optimism fueled by emancipation, citizenship, and the voting rights supposedly guaranteed by constitutional amendments, anticipated that blacks finally would be accepted fully as members of the American national family. African Americans finally were able to participate to a large degree in American national rituals like Independence Day and the new Decoration Day holiday, although many whites still disapproved and resisted their inclusion. Black Americans also hoped that the whole nation would join them in celebrating the end of slavery, not as a primarily "black" holiday, but as a truly American holiday commemorating the fulfillment of that most fundamental American ideal—freedom. Some whites, mainly former abolitionists, military personnel, and Republican politicians, did play a part in Reconstruction-era emancipation celebrations, but after the 1870s white participation declined along with the major political parties' interest in protecting black citizenship rights. African Americans' hopes for a national emancipation holiday followed suit. As black leaders debated among themselves over the proper form and appropriate date for celebration, they recognized that the paper promises of equality made during the early Reconstruction era would not be upheld in daily experience. They also realized that white Americans were not prepared to accept Emancipation Day as appropriate for inclusion on the national commemorative calendar.

In this context, by the late-nineteenth century some black leaders advocated discontinuing public emancipation celebrations, censuring them for wasting scarce financial resources, presenting displays of black extravagance and disorder before the white public, or being devoid of any real meaning as blacks entered a troubling era of discrimination, disfranchisement, and racial violence. Celebrations disappeared in some areas, while in others commemorations that had once been large and festive public affairs were transformed into more staid, indoor meetings limited to sermons, student oratorical contests, and selective dinners for the upper classes. At the same time, however, some communities that had not previously celebrated emancipation initiated festive commemorations around the turn of the century. Thus, even as the tradition declined, many black communities around the nation continued to celebrate emancipation on various dates with either local or national significance.

Large public emancipation celebrations enjoyed a brief resurgence during the 1910s as African Americans marked the fiftieth anniversary of slavery's demise. Between 1913 and 1915, Booker T. Washington and other black leaders tried to coordinate a series of celebrations around the country, and local leaders in New York, Philadelphia, Chicago, Richmond, and Atlantic City planned enormous events spread over several days in their respective cities. Organizers received funding from local, state, or national government sources. The events featured parades, speeches, and exhibitions, and generally were designed to demonstrate the progress the race had achieved since emancipation in the interest of attracting the attention and support of white Americans. W.E.B. Du Bois wrote and produced an elaborate pageant entitled *Star of Ethiopia* that used a cast of hundreds to present the history and progress of the race from ancient Africa to the present. First staged at the New York City semicentennial celebration, it was subsequently performed in several other cities. The large events in major cities received mixed reviews, and several were marred by financial mismanagement or conflicts among the organizers. Many smaller communities around the nation also held emancipation celebrations during this period. But, by and large, this flurry of commemorative activity surrounding the semicentennial of emancipation was short-lived, and by the 1920s large public celebrations of

African American freedom began to decline in importance for black communities in most of the United States.

SHIFTING FOCUS IN THE TWENTIETH CENTURY

During the middle decades of the twentieth century emancipation celebrations seem to have been most persistent in cities and towns in the southern states, though some northern cities also still held celebrations. Much of the shift away from commemorating emancipation during this period stemmed from a combination of factors: (1) black migration out of the South and into urban areas, and the disruption of community coherence that process engendered; (2) urban mass culture and its assortment of exciting leisure activities, which rendered the social functions of celebrations obsolete, especially in cities; (3) the emergence of black political, educational, and civil rights institutions that limited the usefulness of commemorations for filling those roles in black communities; and (4) the continuing segregation, discrimination, and violence that placed severe constraints on the experience of freedom that African Americans were supposedly celebrating. While many African Americans still saw value in annually recalling and commemorating the struggle against slavery, large public celebrations simply did not carry the same meanings or perform the same functions that they had during the nineteenth century. In those areas that did continue to hold celebrations, the observances often had lost many of their political and activist attributes and had become primarily social and festive gatherings, with food, music, ball games, and beauty pageants holding most people's attention.

Juneteenth represents one regional tradition that revived after a slight mid-century decline. Especially after the 1960s, the holiday not only renewed its vitality in Texas where it originated, but also expanded to attract national attention. As African American migration out of the South accelerated during the mid-twentieth century, many blacks from Texas and Oklahoma transplanted their observances of Juneteenth on a small scale throughout the North and West. After Juneteenth was designated as an official state holiday in Texas in 1979, national attention grew and Juneteenth celebrations began to appear in more and more locations nationwide. As of this writing, other states have established Juneteenth as an official state holiday, several national organizations are active in encouraging and facilitating the organization of local Juneteenth celebrations, and legislation has been proposed at the national level advocating the creation of an official national Juneteenth holiday.

Interestingly, there already exists an official national holiday commemorating the end of slavery in the United States, though few celebrate it, or are even aware of its existence. In 1948, President Harry S. Truman designated February 1 as National Freedom Day, in commemoration of the date in 1865

Musicians from the Crossland High School marching band are in Washington to take part in the parade to observe Emancipation Day, 2002. © AP / Wide World Photos.

when Abraham Lincoln signed the congressional joint resolution creating the Thirteenth Amendment abolishing slavery. National Freedom Day was the brainchild of Richard Robert Wright Sr., who was born a slave in the 1850s and, by the 1940s, had enjoyed a long career as a political organizer, educator and college president, and successful banker. After reinvigorating emancipation celebrations in Philadelphia during the 1930s, Wright organized the first National Freedom Day celebration in that city on February 1, 1942. He formed the National Freedom Day Association (NFDA) and campaigned vigorously among governors, senators, congressional representatives, and two presidents to establish the national holiday. Wright died in 1947, but his family and the NFDA have continued to honor the National Freedom Day holiday in Philadelphia ever since. The celebration never attracted much of a national following, although it remains an official annual national holiday.

Since the eighteenth-century slave festivals, African Americans have been consistent in asserting their rights to participate in American holiday observances and public festive cultural celebrations. Since the post–World War II Civil Rights Movement, black participation in Independence Day, Memorial Day, and other national holidays has been widespread, enthusiastic, and generally unproblematic. However, African Americans' long history of striving to be recognized as full and equal citizens of the nation has created a tension between their inherent Americanness and their distinct collective history, heritage, and experience of oppression and struggle. It makes sense that all Americans should recognize and commemorate the national significance of the end of slavery, because it indeed does fulfill the nation's professed, but long-denied, ideals of liberty and equality for all its citizens. Debates in the late twentieth century over the creation of the Martin Luther King Jr. Day holiday similarly suggest that the struggle for racial justice in America is perceived by many to be something mainly for blacks to celebrate, something at best tangential to white America's—and the nation's—interests. The absence of inclusive celebrations of National Freedom Day, and the resistance to creating a national Juneteenth holiday, indicate the continued marginalization of African Americans in American national festive and political culture.

FURTHER READING

Kachun, Mitch. *Festivals of Freedom: Memory and Meaning in African American Emancipation Celebrations, 1808–1915*. Amherst: University of Massachusetts Press, 2003.
———. "'A beacon to oppressed peoples everywhere': Major Richard R. Wright Sr., National Freedom Day, and the Rhetoric of Freedom in the 1940s." *Pennsylvania Magazine of History and Biography* 128 (2004), 279–306.
Verter, Bradford. "Interracial Festivity and Power in Antebellum New York: The Case of Pinkster," *Journal of Urban History* 28 (2002), 398–428.
White, Shane. "'It Was a Proud Day': African Americans, Festivals, and Parades in the North, 1741–1834." *Journal of American History* 81 (1994), 13–50.
Wiggins William H. Jr. *O Freedom! Afro-American Emancipation Celebrations*. Knoxville: University of Tennessee Press, 1987.

Mitch Kachun

POWWOW

The term "holiday" cannot be applied to Native American celebrations in the traditional Western sense of the word. To call powwow a reason for a holiday would have had no meaning prior to the encroachment of Europeans and white Americans on Indian America. Powwows, as they are now known, have a special significance to Plains Indians, those tribes that lived generally between the Canadian Plains and the Rio Grande, and those east of the Mississippi River and west of the Rocky Mountains. They bear names like Lakota and Dakota, Cheyenne, Arapahoe, Kiowa, and Comanche. Approximately 30 tribes resided on the plains at the time of the arrival of trappers, traders, and missionaries. Authorities today agree that the plains were the birthplace of the powwow, which began originally as a sacred ceremony, later became a celebration of war, and in the last half-century is an event celebrating purely social and cultural markers of tribal, regional, and national importance. It is only since the late nineteenth century that tribes outside the plains region began participating in their own variations of powwow through a process some call "intertribalism" or "Pan-Indianism," both terms referring to a form of cultural borrowing from tribe to tribe across vast geographic areas. The term "diffusion" is also a term used to indicate the transference of cultural traits between one tribe and another. The powwow always had been an exciting display of song, dance, and feasting sometimes including religious ceremonies and the acknowledgment of those who passed away over the year. Powwows also were a magnet for young people to escape the watchful eyes of their grandparents and seek out mates.

POWWOW

- [ ] Native Americans in the Great Plains region created the powwow.

- [ ] Beginning as a sacred ceremony and later becoming a celebration of war, over the last half-century powwow evolved to celebrate Native American social and cultural markers of tribal, regional, and national importance.

- [ ] The powwow is a display of song, dance, and feasting sometimes including religious ceremonies and the acknowledgment of those who passed away over the year.

- [ ] To call powwow a holiday would have had no meaning prior to the encroachment of Europeans and white Americans on Indian America.

- [ ] Currently powwows are frequently performed on specific days designated by the United States Congress, and to a lesser extent, on Christian holidays, particularly Christmas.

- [ ] Powwows began to assume their modern form as holidays when the federal government allowed reservations to honor Indian veterans who had served in the military.

- [ ] Practically every tribe hosts a powwow, and most are held during the summer.

- [ ] The general format of the powwow largely follows the format of a rodeo.

Today, one can find powwows from Miami to Tucson and Seattle to New York and most cities and large towns in between.

Powwows are frequently performed on specific days designated by the U.S. Congress, and to a lesser extent, on Christian holidays, particularly Christmas. There are ceremonies conducted by Pueblo Indians in New Mexico and Arizona that recognize Roman Catholic saints days, but these ceremonies are not pow-wows. They are traditional dances, many of which are related to the agricultural cycle such as planting and harvesting. Not unlike Vodoun practiced in Haiti and elsewhere in the Caribbean, the Pueblo Saints Days are difficult to separate from the Pueblo traditional religious dancing. On many occasions, after the Catholic saints are recognized in a Mass performed by a priest, the pews in the church are moved to the side, and the people perform traditional dances. This form of religious organization is frequently referred to as "syncretism"; however, since all religions, even the major religions of the world, are derived from earlier forms, "syncretism" has limited value as a concept.

It was local governments and educational institutions, both federal and religious, that imposed these holidays, mainly through schools and churches. But before these influences began to control the indigenous populations, the idea of holiday was foreign to Native Americans. Because calendars did not exist except for "winter counts"—a Plains method of indicating by pictographs on a tanned animal skin the most import event experienced by a single band over the winter months—specific days were impossible to note. This is not to say that there were not annual events, or events associated with changes in seasons such as those performed at vernal and autumnal equinoxes, or even memorial feasts of the dead, but none of these performances are remotely associated with powwow.

The particular historic reasons that gave rise to establishing particular calendar dates on reservations, and in nonreservation communities, started with an order by the U.S. government. On April 10, 1883, Secretary of the Interior and Commissioner of Indian Affairs, Henry M. Teller, moved to end what he regarded as demoralizing and barbarous customs such as holding feasts and dances, including one of the most religious of ceremonies of the Plains Indians, the Sun Dance. Other rules banned the practices of medicine men. Having more than one wife, or even accepting dowry for a wife were labeled "Indian Offenses." Indian Agents on the reservations were instructed to organize Courts of Indian Offenses, which were empowered to punish offenders with hard labor, fines, imprisonment, and, importantly, the withholding of government rations. At the time, treaties promised food, clothing, shelter, and education in exchange for living in peace with the whites. Thus, through a number of historic reasons mainly manipulated by the federal government and Christian missionaries, who feared that the Native Americans would remain savages if they were not converted to a Western way of living, holidays became an important way of life for Native Americans.

Four-year-old Bobby Morris joins hundreds of other dancers in the Prairie Island Dakota Wacipi Celebration Powwow in Minnesota, 2003. © AP / Wide World Photos.

But unknown to whites, Native Americans were not about to give up their culture and particularly their religion without a battle. Although on the surface, Native Americans had no choice but to adhere to the Indian Offenses regulations, many continued to practice their religious and secular dances outside the view of authorities. Reservations were large swaths of land and individuals and groups could take refuge in the mountains, woods, and deserts of their environment and perform without interference those dances and ceremonies handed down by their ancestors, which were critical to their cultural survival.

The relationship between powwow and holiday began with World War I and became a more intense structural component of Native American culture throughout the country as new wars emerged. Only 24 years after the last Indian massacre at Wounded Knee, where 350 Lakota men, women, and children were stripped of their weapons and shot down, Native Americans, including Lakotas, volunteered to fight for the United States in World War I. Recognizing this expression of patriotism, and the bravery of Indians in battle, the federal government allowed Indians to celebrate their own participation

A blur of feathers and color as a dancer swirls past at a powwow in Nebraska. Courtesy of Getty Images / PhotoDisc.

in military service by holding traditional dances on the reservations, particularly on July 4, and later on Memorial Day, Flag Day, and Veterans Day (originally Armistice Day). After all, there seemed to be little harm in allowing Indians to honor their veterans who returned to tell tales of France and Germany as well as properly to honor, in Indian manner, those who had been killed on the battlefield. Veterans attended the celebrations in full uniform, and flags were raised in the center of the dance area. Later, organizations such as the Veterans of Foreign Wars and American Legion were created on the reservations. Veterans in uniform carrying rifles ushered the American flag onto the dance area while traditional singers sang the praises of their brave soldiers. Surrounding the heroes were men and women dressed in their traditional costumes in the process of powwowing, and in doing so perpetuating the glorified past.

Many tribes, as a means of honoring their returning soldiers, composed "National Anthems." The Lakota people created the following song in order to honor their heroes.

Tunkašilayapi tawapaha kin
Oihankešni he najin kte lo
Iyohlate wan oyate kin k'un wicicagin kta ca
Lecamun welo

The flag of the United States
Will fly forever
Beneath it the people will flourish
That is why I do this

Interestingly, "The Star Spangled Banner" is never sung at powwows, only the local tribal "anthems." Indians always have maintained that they are patriotic, but that they essentially were fighting with the United States forces to protect *their* land. The anthem above acknowledges that the Indian people will continue to flourish under the flag of the United States, and adds "that is why I do this" meaning "that is why I am participating in this (powwow) event." Technically the United States is not directly mentioned in this song. The Lakota words *Tunkašilayapi tawapaha kin* literally mean "Grandfather's flag" because this honorific term was first applied to the president of the United States. Many tribes have their own "national anthems" used to open ceremonies, each in its own tribal language.

With the advent of World War II, Korea, Vietnam, and the Gulf War, Native Americans continued to honor their soldiers. At the same time, powwows became more commonplace throughout the plains, even when not associated with patriotic holidays. Christian and American secular holidays became the festive occasions at which dances, now known as powwows, began to proliferate in special dance arbors during the summer, and in school gymnasiums, American Legion Posts, or old traditional dance houses during winter months. Over the years, almost every Plains tribe sponsored a powwow, and during the summer when most were held, traveled from one tribe to the next in what has been described the "powwow circuit." Some powwows lasted for a day, some for several days or even a week. Some became dramatic presentations, such as the American Indian Exposition at Anadarko, Oklahoma, which drew thousands of people from several tribes as well as non-Indian spectators. Many dancers loaded their cars with camping gear, cooking equipment, and costumes, traveling the entire circuit until it was time to come home for school or work.

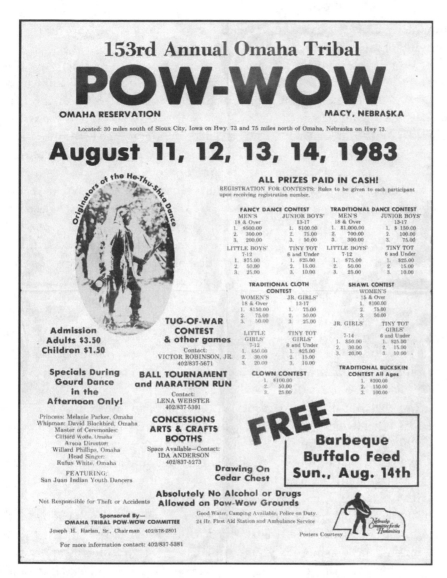

A poster advertising the 153rd Annual Omaha Tribal Pow-Wow, 1983. Courtesy of the Library of Congress.

ORIGIN OF THE POWWOW

Historically, the term "powwow" is relatively new to Native America, although the types of dance movements, songs, and costumes have existed for hundreds of years under different conditions. It is derived from *pauau,* a word from an Algonquian language family spoken mainly in the Northeast United States and adjacent Canada. It referred to a curing ceremony conducted by medicine men and attended by large numbers of people. Europeans erroneously applied *pauau* to any large gathering and thus the term was born. Ironically then, it was white men's error that gave the name to the most important Native American ceremony of the twenty-first century.

Certain tribal elements in modern America seem to have persisted over time, beginning perhaps as forms of dance that can be traced back to the mid-nineteenth century. As stated, the term is Algonquian, but the actual forms of the major singing and dancing elements date back to the Pawnee who lived in present-day Nebraska. Among the Pawnees it was a sacred ceremony called Irushka, a name referring to a particular kind of headdress made of red deer hair, in the center of which was a single eagle feather. This headdress resembled the roached mane of a horse and today is called "roach" in English. The unique form may have dated to the classic "Mohawk" type of hairdo in which all but the center strip of hair was shaven. For the Pawnee, the headdress symbolized fire; Irushka means "The fire is in me," and refers to the power of the Pawnee medicine men to cure disease and particularly, to treat burns. Another article of costume is the crow belt, or in current terms, "bustle" because of the position it is worn on the dancer's rump. Although today it is elaborately constructed mainly from eagle feathers, in the time of the Pawnee ceremony it was made from a deerskin belt to which crow feathers and a wolf's tail were attached. Significantly, the headdress and "bustle" are still two of the most important articles of costume worn in the powwow. Also significant was a ceremony in which men danced around a boiling kettle, thrusting their hands into the kettle as they passed by.

During the mid-nineteenth century, the Pawnee Irushka became popularized by other tribes. In particular, the Omaha Indians, also of Nebraska, transformed the dance from a religious ceremony into a warrior society dance. The Omaha are members of the Siouan language family along with the Ponca, Osage, Kansas, and Quapaw from the midwestern part of the country, and also with Dakota, Nakota, and Lakota people of the plains (erroneously called "Sioux"), the Crow from Montana, and others. When the Omaha adopted the dance from the Pawnee they transformed it into a dance that focused exclusively on war, and on thunder beings, supernaturals who fostered valorous acts among their warriors. They also kept the term Irushka but used their own dialect, transforming it into Hedushka (for the Omaha and Ponta), Ilonshka (for the Osage), and Helushka for the Lakota.

Despite the warlike nature of the Omaha form of the dance, a number of elements from the original Irushka were retained, namely the deer tail headdress, the crow belt, and dancing around the kettle. But where costume, paraphernalia, and rituals maintained a number of structural similarities recognizable as Pawnee, the meanings behind the symbols changed, providing new interpretations, partly sacred and partly secular, but wholly dedicated to the celebration of a warrior culture. The single feather in the headdress represented an unarmed warrior who recklessly attacks an enemy and touches him with a bow or his hand, a custom called "counting coup." The crow belt took on a new meaning also: its feathers daubed with white paint represented the dead warriors on a battlefield over whom carrion birds fly.

After the third quarter of the nineteenth century the dance and its attendant songs and ritual paraphernalia spread quickly northward and southward on the Great Plains. As each tribe received it, they gave it a new name and added local traditions to the event. The Lakota who received it from the Omaha called it the Omaha dance. The Dakota called it Grass Dance after the custom of tying bundles of grass to the dancers' belts to represent enemy scalps. The Shoshoni called it Wolf Dance, the wolf symbolizing the warrior. The central Siouan groups continued to use variants of Irushka.

A fancy dancer performs during the fifth annual Intertribal Powwow in Illinois, 1996. © AP / Wide World Photos.

It is not known precisely when the term powwow came into vogue, but it is known that the term was used widely in Oklahoma by such tribes as the Kiowa, Comanche, Apache, Caddo, Delaware, and southern Cheyenne and Arapaho. Among these people there were generally two types of powwow dancing, also called War dance. The first was the reserved "Straight Dance" of the Pawnee, Osage, Oto, southern Cheyenne, and Arapaho. The Straight Dance was believed to be the proper form of powwow dancing. Very few feathers were worn, except on the headdress, and the clothing was meticulously tailored and beaded. The second form was the "Fancy Dance," reflected in the fast and furious dancing of the Kiowa, Comanche, Ponca, and Oto. Soon however it was not so much a tribal designation but an individual choice as to what kind of powwow dancing a person chose to perform.

It was not until the middle of the 1950s that the term became popular on the Northern Plains as well. Until that time, the Lakota, for example, called this form of dancing *wacipi,* their term for dance. The reason for the widespread use of the term and the event probably stems from the end of World War II when many Native Americans returned from serving in the military. They were able to see new places and meet new people, not the least of which were other Native Americans from reservations. The exchange of ideas led to curiosity about understanding the cultures of other tribal peoples and a better understanding of their respective traditions. Powwow emerged as a significant aspect of many Indian cultures.

SINGING AND DRUMMING

In the southwest, a Navajo sings to the rhythm of his horse's hooves as he rides along though the deserts and canyon. At home, his wife sings a soft lullaby to her dozing children. In the Pueblo villages nearby, a silversmith fashions age-old designs in silver as his hammer taps out the rhythm of the song he sings. In the Florida Everglades, a group of Seminoles sings a vigorous song as they perform the Hunting Dance. In the north woods, an Ojibwa sings sacred songs as he prays to Gitche Manito, the Great Spirit. In olden days, a Lakota sang a death chant as he rode into battle. The Indian man courts his woman with a love song, cures his sick with a medicine song, and names his children with an honor song. He never ceases to sing whether happy or sad, young or old, well or ailing. From birth to death, the Indian sings.

Indians can sing without dancing, but they cannot dance without hearing an appropriate song. To the Indian people, singing is as much a part of the dance as the dancers' moccasins and bells. For every dance there is an appropriate song. No dancer can move while the singers are idle. It is the voices of the men and women that make the dancers want to dance. The dancers hear a good song, and their feet are forced to move. The singers actually control the dancers.

Indian singers and composers are respected men and women of the community. While all Indians like to sing, there are professional singers who perform at the powwows and other celebrations. Without them, no powwow could take place. The singers are paid by the powwow committee that sponsors the dance, or the people donate to them in a formal giveaway ceremony for having performed a special song for their family.

Songs are passed down from one generation to the next. But in addition to the classic songs of the elders, there are many new songs composed every spring when the powwow season is about to begin. At the annual celebrations, these new songs make their debut before the people. Some become popular enough to travel from one reservation to the next until all tribes are singing them. A new song may remain popular for several days, years, or decades.

The drum is the most popular musical instrument. Some tribes use flageolets, whistles, boraches, rattles, and even a one-string violin. But no other instrument has gained the drum's prominence. It is the instrument of choice among powwow singers. Drums come in various sizes and shapes depending on the tribes that use them. There are large dance drums that range from two to four feet in diameter. Smaller hand drums range from 6 to 18 inches in diameter. The drums may have one head or two and are normally round in shape. The heads are made from cow, goat, or deer hide stretched over a wooden or metal frame. Some singers prefer commercial bass drums that can be easily tuned to the right pitch. All Native American drums are played with single sticks, never with the bare hands. They vary in length and in choice of wood for the handle, and material for the head of the drumstick. Many modern singers prefer plastic handles cut from a fishing pole wrapped with a soft cotton tip because they are less likely to snap during the heat of a powwow song.

Although one may see a variety of individual singers playing on a small drum, all powwow songs are sung by mixed male and female groups. The men normally sit around a large drum on folding chairs, while women sit or stand behind them. At large powwows there may be 20 drum groups present, each one eagerly waiting to sing their song before relinquishing the drum to the next group. The announcer regulates the singers. When their time comes, the next group sings either one of its favorite powwow songs or may be asked to sing a special song for an honoring ceremony.

THE MODERN-DAY POWWOW

Since approximately 1900, powwow has referred to a tribal event where one tribe serves as sponsor. These powwows frequently include dances that are very specific to that tribe. Others are regarded as intertribal, hosted by an amalgamation of a few to many tribes; these powwows attract dancers from all over the country. Powwow then generally applies to an event featuring dancing, singing, costumes, feasting, giveaways, recognition of those who have passed away during the previous year, and competitions in various dance categories. Since powwows reflect characteristics of their host tribes, or intertribal committees, no one powwow is conducted in precisely the same manner. Originally the early powwows were divided into two large geographic divisions, Northern Plains and Southern Plains. Recently it has become more difficult to make this distinction as the two have begun to meld into one. This amalgamation of traits is frequently referred to as "Pan-Indianism."

It may come as a surprise to some that the general format of the powwow largely follows the format of a rodeo. The influence of one on the other is easily understandable given that the powwow and rodeo originated on the plains. Plains Indians have always been regarded as exemplary equestrians, and much of the transition from nomadic hunter and warrior came about through tribal farming and ranching programs established by the federal government. Indians not only attended rodeos but many became well-known rodeo celebrities in bronco and bull riding, roping, bulldogging, and other rodeo events.

Like the rodeo, the powwow opens with a Grand Entrance. The principal participants in both enter the area in all their splendor and circle the grounds before the spectators. When all have entered, the national anthem is played or sung and frequently a religious dignitary will utter prayers for the success of the event and safety of the participants. Among those dignitaries that enter the arena are a special class of young women representing their tribes, home towns, or states with titles such as Miss Oklahoma, Miss South Dakota, or even Miss Porcupine, or Miss Oglala, names of their home towns on the reservation. Somewhere during the pageant, these young women compete for the role of queen of the event and are celebrated for their beauty, industry, and helpfulness to the community. They frequently receive crowns and sashes identifying their particular sponsor.

What was inspired by the rodeo became ingrained in the powwow. Today, as singers start the opening songs, the Grand Entry begins. First enters the recognized chief of the tribe, carrying the local tribal flag or feathered banner, followed by a cadre of retired soldiers from the local VFW or American Legion Post carrying the American flag. Then follow the female representatives of their respective tribes known as "Royalty," of which one will be crowned as the annual Powwow Princess.

There are other references to rodeo protocol. When all the powwow participants have danced into the area, they stop in place while one group sings the National Anthem of the host tribe. After the song, the chief or a spiritual leader will give a speech welcoming everyone to the powwow and praying for good weather and good health during the length of the powwow. "Day money," a rodeo term referring to wages, is paid each day to persons helping out at a rodeo in various capacities, as well as to the singers at powwows, who also are paid on the days they perform. Finally, the idea of dance contests certainly was fostered by rodeo competitions in various events demonstrating cowboys' ranching skills.

Differences in dance styles are partly determined by the kinds of songs that are sung. Some tribes in the north were noted for singing in higher registers and their dance tempos were relatively slow. Others on the southern plains sang in lower registers and their tempos were faster. Today these distinctions are melding so that all forms of singing may be seen anywhere in the country where there are intertribal powwows.

A second distinction between types of powwows relates to the dance itself. At one time, only males danced in the center of the arbor in a free-style form, generally going clockwise or counterclockwise. Females were somewhat restricted to the outer perimeter of the dance area, dancing in place in a very restrained way. Sometime in the 1960s women began to dance in a free style in the center of the dance area, the men dancing in opposite directions. The steps of powwow are varied depending on tribe and region in terms of style, but with respect to basic steps, powwow dancing relies on alternating tap-steps with the feet, combined with head, arm, and torso movements. To these basic movements are added idiosyncratic flourishes, all of which combine to identify individuals with respect to their dexterity and showmanship.

The third form of distinguishing types of powwow is by the costume that men and women wear at the powwow. At one time it was theoretically possible to distinguish between tribes on the basis of the clothing and costumes. Today this has become nearly impossible because powwow costumes themselves have become highly stylized and these styles change somewhat year by year and are essentially determined by faddish considerations.

THE POWWOW COMMITTEE

Powwows have grown into large events, many with economic considerations. Gone are the days when a few men and women organized their community dances and relied on their neighbors to provide food for the dancers and spectators. Today, powwows require elaborate organization. Some committees may number 40 to 50 persons responsible for printing admission tickets and programs, security, construction of the dance grounds, supervising vendors, policing the camping area, sanitation, and parking, as well as for providing judges for the contests, directing special events, and cleaning up the dance grounds and making ready for next year's events.

Once the powwow is underway, all the events in the dance area are under the supervision of a director. This honor goes to a distinguished member of the tribe or community whose judgment is respected and who can make last-minute decisions and hold to them. Powwows draw thousands of people, making it necessary to have medical assistance available. Tribal or other local police are also on hand mainly for crowd control and general assistance. Like elsewhere, lost children and stalled cars are endemic to powwows and so there must be good communication channels between security officers and the committee.

The director is also chosen for his knowledge of his tribe's culture, and he may often make up special rules that apply to the powwow during his tenure.

For example, at one time dancers at the Oglala Nation Powwow began wearing a particular kind of face paint that drew criticism from many of the older generation. Faces were painted more like Hollywood or television shows portrayed Indians. During one particular powwow, the director announced that no dancer painted in such a way could hope to win any of the contests. As a result, no dancer appeared in gaudy paint. Rather they adhered to what was in keeping with traditional style.

MAJOR DANCE AND COSTUME STYLES

It is almost always impossible to predict what next year's powwow fashions are going to be. However, changes are usually based on nuance rather than the overall silhouette of the costume. Perhaps the major trend depends on new fabrics, some of them high-tech goods like Mylar, easily obtainable at dry goods stores. The kinds of fabrics to some extent will also influence color and design elements in traditional costumes, which at one time were notable for their elaborate feather work, bead work, and quill work. All these craft techniques are found among those costumes labeled "traditional" men's and women's. Sequins, tin or silver "jingles," and ready-made beaded animals, birds, and insects such as butterflies and dragonflies are easy to find in contemporary craft stores and make costume design less labor-intensive when beading or quilling large accessories such as cuffs, belts, suspenders, women's dresses, and other adornments.

What is critical to all costumes, however, is the silhouette. Although colors, designs, and materials change from year to year, the overall structure of these costumes remains fairly static. In particular, the men's headdresses—the so-called "roach" mentioned above—and the feather work known as "bustles" have remained remarkably stable, albeit with minor changes in types of feathers used. If one were to see a group of dancers in such a way that only their silhouette was discerned, the modern-day dancers would resemble very much their traditional ancestors.

Types of costumes correspond to types of songs and dances and also exhibit idiosyncratic features in accordance with the individual's sense of style. The most popular forms of these powwow dance styles and attendant costumes are:

1. Traditional Man's Style. Traditional style is associated with the plains. In Oklahoma it is typically referred to as Straight Dance style. However, in both cases the traditional style refers to an older form of a reserved dance pattern in which dancers virtually walk in time to the drum. The songs are also slower in tempo than many of the more modern songs, and the costumes, despite some change every year, are considered to be more exemplary of older forms of costume identified with Plains tribes.

    Characteristic articles of costume consist of the roach headdress with two upright eagle feathers (although some elders wear war bonnets); breech cloths, or "aprons" of cloth or buckskin; beaded or quilled belts, cuffs, armbands and moccasins in traditional designs; buckskin or cloth leggings; necklace or choker; bustles, including back bustle with trailer or "crow belt," neck and sometimes arm bustles of eagle or variegated feathers from hawk, owl, and fowl; miscellaneous articles such as bandanas, scarves, breast plates of bone or quills; or other objects of personal appeal. Dancers carry eagle wings or "straight" fans; decorated dance shields; and, rarely, weapons such as lances, bows, and war clubs. All men wear bells around their ankles, or below their knees. Some string them from their belt to their ankles.

Although many of these costumes are made with modern materials, some old-timers wear antique pieces handed down from their grandfathers. The idea of the costume is to represent what is perceived to be the old days of tipi-living and buffalo-hunting, but the art and craft of costume-making is still viable.

2. Traditional Women's Style. Like the men's style, the traditional women's costumes and movements are reflective of an earlier period. Long beaded or quilled dresses made of buckskin or cloth, with moccasins and high-top leggings are required. Women occasionally wear beaded headbands and belts made of silver or beadwork. They usually carry an eagle-wing fan or straight fan. Like the men, their dances are reserved.

3. Grass Dance Style. This style is the traditional men's style of the Northern Plains, particularly Montana and North Dakota and the Canadian provinces of Saskatchewan and western Ontario. In the 1960s it became very popular in South Dakota. Although the roach headdress remains popular, there is an absence of feathers on the remainder of the costume. Instead, dancers wear shirts and pants embroidered with ribbon work, and bands of chainette fringe and yarn applied in v-shaped patterns to shirts and pants that give a unique silhouette to the overall costume. The costume is accented by heavily beaded belts, cuffs, moccasins, and suspenders, giving the appearance of what other dancers called a "rag doll" appearance. The dancing is exaggerated, slinky, bouncy, and even "cool"; some dancers affect dark glasses as part of the their attire. This dance has remained a favorite since its inception on the lower plains and is currently danced in Oklahoma.

4. Shawl Dance Style. At the same time the Grass Dance came into the middle plains states, the Shawl Dance appeared and has become perhaps one of the most favorite dances of modern times. The costumes feature elaborately made shawls, usually from modern fabrics to which are added more traditional beaded yokes, leggings, and moccasins. Most dancers wear their hair in French braids highlighted by a single plume. Long fringe accents the flowing shawls, which are manipulated in the dance by whirling movements of the dancers as if they were horses prancing in a parade, segueing into quick spins, and subtle but bouncy footwork. Sometimes it appears that the women's feet do not touch the ground as the shawls open and close by means of dextrous arm and torso movement. It is a thrilling experience applauded by men and women alike.

5. Fancy Dance or "Feather" Dance Style. Sometimes considered the most spectacular of men's styles, its origin is on the southern plains, particularly in Oklahoma. Its popularity today is nationwide. The songs are fast and the dancing is gymnastic. It probably was the first category of dance style used for men's contests.

   The dancers wear the roach headdress with two upright eagle feathers. Of particular beauty are the matching back and neck bustles. However, the dancers are more or less stripped down for speed, wearing breechcloths or "aprons," moccasins, angora anklets and bells, beaded belts, armbands and cuffs, and necklace or choker. They frequently carry batons in each hand, which they swing as they dance. It is a very athletic dance and proponents must be in good physical condition.

6. Jingle Dress Style. This women's dance originated in Ontario, Canada and made its way into the United States via North Dakota and Montana. The name comes from the style of dress embroidery: tin jingles sewn to various parts of the dress, which provide a clinking sound as they dance. The tin jingles were originally made from snuff can lids that were bent into cones. The dance and its attendant costumes became so popular, however, that

tin jingles can now be purchased separately. Carrying a straight fan in the dance is obligatory. The dance style, compared with the other more flowing forms of powwow dancing, is rather stiff, but very precise in movement.

During the course of the powwow following the Grand Entry, all dancers, no matter what their individual styles of costume are, dance together in what is generally called "Intertribal" dancing. It is only when the contests begin that dancers wearing the same costume styles perform as a unit while others look on. When contests drag on, for whatever reason, taking up valuable dancing time for the nonparticipants, the announcer will call for intertribal dancing to take place between the contests so that all may have a chance to join in.

SPECIALS

At large gatherings, there are a number of dances called "specials," referring to specific tribal or intertribal dances that are used mainly to please the spectators (including dancers) and to provide a good show. After all, powwows have a dramatic quality about them and specials give diversion to the regular format. Perhaps the most popular is the Round Dance, in which dancers form a circle (more like an arc), and dance to special songs. Men, women, and children dance together, and frequently non-Indian visitors are invited to join in. The Round Dance is sometimes called the Welcome Dance. The Two-step or Rabbit Dance is one in which a couple dance together, again to special songs. Couples line up, one behind the other, and dance short, shuffling steps. As the announcer is quick to add, Two-steps are women's choice and there is a great deal of good humor in watching women ask men to be their partners. On the southern plains, specialty dances such as the Buffalo Dance, Snake Dance, Forty-Nine, and Stomp Dance are popular, each of them derived from tribal dances mainly of the Kiowa and Comanche.

The most spectacular is the Hoop Dance, danced by an individual male (and recently female) employing hoops made from willow or plastic, which the dancer manipulates around his body, forming designs as he dances rapidly in place. Although the most popular Hoop Dances were done in the Southwest by Pueblo Indians, the fad soon flourished across the United States. Although Pueblos danced with one to four hoops, the modern Hoop dancers use as many as 30 in their routines.

DANCE COMPETITIONS

Although dance contests have been popular among Oklahoma tribes since the turn of the twentieth century, it was not until the mid-1950s that they became popular on virtually every reservation and Indian community. Today, many of the older traditionalists, who grew up when dances were strictly for personal and social enjoyment in their own right, feel that competitions take away from the real meaning of the powwow as an expression of tribal solidarity and general "Indianness." Competitions offer money to the winners and there is a tendency for the best dancers to choose those powwows that award the largest amounts. The net result is that some of the smaller powwows see a decrease in dancers and singers who would rather travel great distances in order to be in a contest. Some have suggested eliminating them; however, dance contests have become the most important part of the powwow. The spectators demand it and the individual dancers who win often become national celebrities in Indian country. Either way, the dance contest is now such an integral part of the powwow that it is unlikely it will be discontinued.

Again, as with other features of the powwow, there are some local variations. However, generally all competitions are organized around age, gender, and dance style (hence, costume). There are usually four categories: tiny tots, both boys and girls unless there are only a few and the children participate together; teen-age boys and girls; young men and women; and senior men and women. Members of each group compete to win, place, or show in each of the dance styles. At large powwows there are so many contests in each of the competitions that they are run in two or more heats. On an average four-day weekend powwow, one can expect to see at least 48 different competitions, plus in some cases more than one heat, as well as tie breakers. Therefore, it is expected that today most powwows will be taken up by competitions.

There is also time needed to judge each of the contests. For the most part, powwow judges are former winners in the categories that they judge. Each of the dancers must register before they enter any of the contests; some may enter all three male and female competitions, in which case the dancer must change costumes to conform to the type of dance. These dancers are called "all-arounders" and some are quite adept in all three styles.

The dancers are given numbers, which are appended to their costumes during the entire powwow. Dancers are judged by their individual ability to master the style in which they are competing, to keep good time with the song, and to end precisely on the last beat of the drum. Dancers are automatically disqualified if they lose any article of costuming during the contest. This custom dates back to the early reservation, when a dancer who lost a feather was required to give away money or gifts to the man who retrieved it for him. Dancers are also required to participate in the entire powwow, not only the competitions. This is to diminish the possibility that dancers will only compete and not participate in many of the ceremonial parts of the powwow such as the Grand Entry and the closing songs. During the actual competition, the judges surround the dancers on the outer periphery of the dance area and watch each dancer closely. Clipboards in hands, they rank all of the dancers and note their numbers on a pad. At the end of the final competitions, the numbers are tallied and dancers notified. Frequently the winners perform a short solo dance after they have been handed their ribbons, trophies, and monetary rewards.

THE GIVEAWAY

The giveaway is one of the most important aspects of the powwow event. It is an old custom in which an individual or a family wishes to honor others by presenting them with cash, quilts, or even everyday household items from local stores. Giveaways are not restricted to powwows and may be seen in conjunction with births, birthdays, going away to school, graduation, or at wakes and funerals. Giveaways are likely to attract many spectators, and some are very large, requiring 10 to 20 members of a family to distribute the gifts. Usually an announcer, known for a strong, clear voice (although today sound systems are used), calls out the name of the person to be honored at the bidding of a family spokesman. The person approaches the family and receives his or her gift and then shakes hands with all of them. Customarily, a group of singers is chosen by the family to sing songs in praise of the one being honored. The family also donates money to the singers.

This custom has been around for a long time on the plains and has become an integral part of the powwow. At one time horses and treasured beadwork and quillwork were given away in great abundance. The more given away, the higher the status conferred upon those bestowing the gifts. Today, economic problems among Native Americans have curtailed giving away cherished things, such as articles of clothing and costuming, and most articles awarded today are of a practical nature such as kitchen utensils, towels, foot lockers, and plastic containers, all easily available.

Although there are the usual local and regional differences associated with giveaways, most are held during the afternoon of a powwow. When giveaways are held during the actual dance periods, singers and dancers tend to become impatient with the long speeches that frequently accompany the giveaway. The powwow, they say, is for dancing and not for too much talking!

AROUND THE DANCE GROUND

The shape of most outdoor powwow grounds is a circle covered by a donut-shaped arbor around the outer periphery to provide shade for the spectators and singers, and dancers when they are not dancing. At one end of the dance ground is an announcer's booth equipped with a sound system whose speakers are spread around the inner periphery of the shade so that everyone can clearly hear announcements and most importantly, particularly during contests, the songs. Outdoor powwows are also held in large meeting tents. At one time tribal dances were held in much smaller shades. Singers had only the strength of their collective voices to project out to the dancers and frequently singers moved from under the shade into the center of the dance groups to that they could be heard more clearly. All of this changed with the advent of the sound system; shades got larger and larger.

Originally, dances were for local people and there were very few visitors, Indian or non-Indian. The dancers and their family packed up their wagons, and later automobiles, and transported their bedding and food to the dance site. They pitched their tents and cooked their food outdoors as they had done for centuries. It was a great social event and people could visit with relatives and friends they had not seen for weeks or months. Today, many powwows are held relatively close to the dancer's home and many commute. Although campers still prepare their food at their camp sites, commuters rely on a host of vendors who surround the outer periphery of the powwow grounds where they provide a variety of food for the participants and spectators.

Although hot dogs and hamburgers, cotton candy, and soda are abundant, some local entrepreneurs provide "Indian" food. The most popular food at the powwow is "Indian tacos" made from fried bread on which is placed the toppings of (usually) beef taco. The major difference between the southwest version and Indian version is that the tortilla is replaced with fried bread. Other vendors sell t-shirts, some commemorating the present or past powwows, clothing, jewelry, artifacts, books, and almost anything of interest to a large crowd. At most powwows, vendors are required to rent the space outside the dance grounds. Part of the action of the powwow happens outside the dance grounds where spectators and hungry and thirsty dancers mill around the arbor talking to friends and stopping off at one of the many stands. Winter and indoor powwows also invite vendors who find space in auditoriums, church facilities, American Legion posts, or anywhere suitable to sell their food and wares. Vendors have become an integral part of the modern-day powwow, and success of the powwow is not only determined by the number of dancers, but the number of vendors, whose fees frequently cover a good part of expenses.

POWWOW AS HOLIDAY

Indian dancing was permitted on American holidays only after the federal government allowed it. There were no national, regional, or tribal holidays prior to those established for (mainly) white Americans. Today, Native Americans celebrate most of the holidays that other Americans do, often forming their own parades or joining those of others. They dress up in costumes and join in great feasts ranging from outdoor barbecues to massive meals for hundreds of people served Indian-style. Perhaps what makes these holidays different, including those powwows held on non-American calendar dates, is a strong feeling that Native Americans are not so much honoring the past but rather a present and future reality that views Indian cultures as indeed alive and well. Today, an exchange of tribal values manifested in song, dance, and costume styles has created an intertribal and pan-Indian validation that recognizes not only an individual's identity among his or her tribal members, but a stronger kinship among all American Indians.

FURTHER READING

Callahan, Alice Anne. *The Osage Ceremonial Dance In-Lon-Schka.* Norman: University of Oklahoma Press. 1990.

Nettl, Bruno. *Blackfoot Musical Thought: Comparative Perspective.* Champaign: University of Illinois Press, 1989.

Powers, William K. "Plains Indian Music and Dance." In *Anthropology on the Great Plains,* ed. W. Raymond Wood and Margot Liberty. Lincoln: University of Nebraska Press, 1980.

———. *War Dance: Plains Indian Musical Performance.* Tucson: University of Arizona Press, 1990.

William K. Powers

GAY PRIDE DAY

Since the 1970s, annual celebrations of "Gay Pride" have been a major feature of community life for gay, lesbian, bisexual, and transgender people in the United States. These festivities usually take place on a weekend in June, near the anniversary of the 1969 Stonewall Riots, and in many cities they feature a parade through city streets. Because many gay people spend some or all of their time living "in the closet," these events afford a degree of openness and visibility that helps people come to terms with their gay identities and to surround themselves with other gay people. For some gays and lesbians who identify strongly with urban gay communities, these celebrations involve their closest friends and family members; for others who spend less of their time with other gay and lesbian people, gay pride celebrations represent a time during the year when they can assert and celebrate this aspect of their identity. Pride celebrations began in the nation's largest cities, where gays and lesbians have their greatest concentration of political power. In the gay "meccas" of New York and San Francisco, gay pride celebrations are today major events attracting thousands of tourists. In recent years, parades, rallies, and other celebrations of gay pride have spread to smaller cities, representing the growing acceptance of openly gay people in American society.

IMPACT OF THE STONEWALL RIOTS

The Stonewall Riots constituted a pivotal moment that galvanized gays and lesbians to confront and resist the terms of their oppression. The incident began

GAY PRIDE DAY

- [ ] Gay Pride festivities usually take place on a weekend near the June 27, 1969 anniversary of the Stonewall Riots, and many celebrations feature a parade through city streets.

- [ ] New York City and San Francisco host the largest Gay Pride festivals, but the event has spread to many smaller cities.

- [ ] Gay Pride Day emerged as part of the wider Gay Liberation, or Gay Rights, movement during the early 1970s.

- [ ] Event organizers have gone from battling with police and city officials for approval to winning Fortune 500 sponsorships over the past 35 years.

- [ ] An estimated 2,000–5,000 people participated in New York City's first parade in 1970 while an estimated 500,000 marched in the city's 2005 parade.

A participant in the Brazilian contingent of New York's 2005
Gay Pride Parade marches down Fifth Avenue in New York.
© AP / Wide World Photos.

around 1:00 A.M. on the morning of Saturday, June 28, 1969, when four plain-
clothes New York City police officers arrived at a popular, crowded Greenwich
Village gay bar known as the Stonewall Inn. In fact, it was the second time in
a week that the police had raided this particular bar. Like many gay bars, the
Stonewall was controlled by the Mafia, who alone could take the significant
legal and financial risks involved. The mob recouped their investment by over-
charging gay customers, who had few other options for meeting each other,
often serving them watered-down drinks. Such police raids were a routine part

of gay life in this era, when many states and cities had laws on the books that made it illegal to serve a drink to a homosexual or for gay people to congregate freely in bars. For many gays and lesbians, these raids posed not only the risk of arrest but also the risk of disclosure of their homosexuality to their employers, neighbors, and family members.

This particular raid was unusual, in that it was conducted on a busy weekend night, late in the evening, rather than at a less busy time. Tensions flared as the police began arresting the bar's patrons. By most accounts, the riot was initiated by "street queens," young, highly effeminate men who wore makeup, dressed flamboyantly, and eked out highly marginal existences and spent a great deal of their time in the world of gay nightlife. Under assault by growing numbers of the Stonewall Inn's patrons, the police who led the raid eventually sought refuge inside the bar itself. Bar patrons and onlookers barricaded the frightened police inside, thereby reversing the usual relations of power in such raids. Although the police leading the raid called in the force's tactical riot squad, this elite unit was not familiar with the narrow, jumbled streets of New York's West Village, which made it difficult for them to control the crowd in front of the bar. The following night, as word of the events spread and additional police were dispatched to the area, there was again conflict between police and gays and lesbians. There were several more nights of sporadic disturbances in the area, and then the riot flared up again on Wednesday night, after a controversial account of the incident appeared in the *Village Voice*, whose offices were located down the street from the bar.

The concept of celebrating gay pride developed in the aftermath of the Stonewall riots, as a radical movement for "gay liberation" gained steam. This movement was led primarily by students and young people, who often repudiated the more reformist strategies of an older generation of gays and lesbians who called themselves "homophile" activists. Stopping police harassment of gay and lesbian gathering places was among the top priorities of this new movement, which drew on the energy of the Black Power movement and its extensive critique of aggressive police practices in urban African American neighborhoods. In New York, gay activists repeatedly pressured the mayor and other city officials, through both formal and informal channels, to stop police raids on gay and lesbian bars as well as the "entrapment" of gay men cruising for sex in parks and public toilets. These efforts eventually achieved a remarkable degree of success. Many big-city police departments that had previously banned gay people from serving in their ranks had, within a few years, hired gay and lesbian officers and created official liaisons to the gay community.

If changing police practices formed one pillar of the nascent strategy of gay liberation, another was combating the invisibility that the culture of the "closet" had created. Gay pride parades and similar events, in this context, constituted a remarkably effective challenge to the specific experiences of harassment, discretion, and concealment that characterized gay life in the late-twentieth-century United States, and the style of this challenge has proven popular in many other parts of the world as well. In the 1950s and 1960s, being openly gay was uncommon among middle-class Americans. Many of those who regularly appeared as visible symbols of gay life were drag queens, and they often suffered profound economic consequences. Yet, paradoxically, the radical transformation of gay political culture succeeded in part because it drew upon and renovated familiar forms of both urban spatial politics and queer spectacle.

After emerging rather suddenly in the early-1970s United States, Gay, Lesbian, Bisexual, and Transgender (GLBT) pride parades gradually became highly elaborate affairs, requiring year-round logistical planning by nonprofit organizations. By the 1990s, parades increasingly won sponsorship by major corporations, who increasingly targeted what they understood to be a lucrative consumer market. By the first decade of the new century, pride celebrations had occurred from Manila to Cape Town and from Topeka to Budapest. An international organization of pride celebration coordinators from various cities, called InterPride, has also begun to sponsor more infrequent gatherings, held every five years, called World Pride; the first such event was held in Rome in 2000.

INVENTING THE GAY PRIDE MARCH

Today, holding a march or parade on city streets to celebrate queer culture seems like a wholly natural aspect of modern gay politics, but to the organizers of the first such events, it seemed a far more risky and improbable proposition. The origins of the gay pride parades are obscured by their very political triumph. In many cities, they are among the largest annual public events, drawing visitors from those cities' gay hinterlands; gay pride parades constitute perhaps the most important collective ritual of gay American life. Gay pride parades were, in a sense, the crowning achievement of the new gay liberation politics of the early 1970s. The best-known slogan of the gay liberationists, "out of the closets and into the streets," reflects the central status of spatial confinement and expression to post-Stonewall gay politics.

The organizers of the first gay pride marches in the summer of 1970 faced difficulties that are barely imaginable today. That year, the Los Angeles police chief declared that granting a permit to homosexuals was tantamount to "discommoding the citizens by permitting a parade of thieves and burglars," and the police department demanded that the Gay Liberation Front post security bonds amounting to $1.25 million. That demand was dropped when the ACLU filed a lawsuit on the organizers' behalf. In New York, approximately 100 gays and lesbians signed up to be marshals and were trained in violence prevention by Quakers, since organizers expected the possibility of violence either on the part of municipal police or hostile onlookers.

Yet the greatest problem for the organizers of the first annual celebrations was not that "straights" were opposed, but that many middle-class gays were fearful of publicizing their homosexuality so overtly. Even though the first parade in 1970 was a project of New York's radical Gay Liberation Front, it took extraordinary efforts by organizers to round up people who were willing to be photographed, for an advance publicity poster, running through a Manhattan street. So deeply ingrained was the fear of disclosure among many American gays and lesbians at that time that only 15 brave souls could be found who were willing to risk not only marching in the streets during the parade itself, but also being depicted in the publicity photo.

To be sure, the fact that gay pride parades commemorate the 1969 Stonewall Riots has tended to obscure the continuities between the post-Stonewall politics of the gay liberationists and earlier forms of gay politics. The concept of the gay pride parade itself drew upon pre-Stonewall strategies of homophile activism. Thus, beginning in the mid-1960s, homophile organizations sponsored a number of public demonstrations in the United States demanding rights for homosexuals. Indeed, since 1965 an annual public demonstration had been held each July 4 at Philadelphia's Independence Hall by members of the Mattachine Society, the Janus Society, and the Daughters of Bilitis. Drawing directly on the strategies of nonviolent protest associated with the African American civil rights movement, these gay and lesbian activists hoped to demonstrate the hypocrisy of a society that proclaimed liberty yet denied rights to its gay and lesbian citizens.

After the Stonewall riots, many activists felt that a dramatic shift in gay activism had taken place and tried to push the gay and lesbian movement into a new phase of militancy. In November 1969, lesbian and gay activists at a regional homophile conference in Philadelphia made the decision to replace their annual Independence Day pickets with a commemoration of that summer's rioting in New York. As in many political conflicts of the late 1960s and early 1970s, younger, more radical gay liberation activists tended to confront and challenge the leadership of an older generation of activists who preferred to assert their right to further their cause through respectable rather than confrontational public events.

Gay pride marches, however, involved far more people and a far more elaborate type of mobilization than did the earlier homophile protests. In June, 1970, perhaps 2,000 to 5,000 attended the first Christopher Street Liberation Day Parade memorializing the annual Stonewall riots, which ended with a "gay-in" in Central Park. Many marchers were connected to the Gay Liberation Front or the Gay Activists Alliance. Placards screamed campy and political messages like "We are the Dykes Your Mother Warned You About" and "Better Blatant Than Latent." and chants included "What do we want? Gay Power! When do we want it? Now!"; "Say it loud: Gay is proud!"; and, famously, "Out of the closets and into the streets!" Participants recalled believing that there were many gays and lesbians among the spectators, who might perhaps take courage from watching the parade and be willing to march openly the following year. The massive "gay-in" in Central Park gave birth to a tradition of combining political protests with parties in city streets and parks.

By the late 1970s, most gay pride parades took the form of festive events including motorized floats and were annual scheduled affairs organized under the banner of "pride." But that model took some time to become the prevalent type of celebration. In San Francisco, for cxample, the 1973 "Gay Freedom Day Parade" competed with a rival "Festival of Gay Liberation"; to prevent such problems in the future, a nonprofit Pride Foundation was established later in the year to coordinate the city's annual events. In Seattle, the anniversary of Stonewall was celebrated with music festivals, picnics, and rallies from 1973 to 1976; in 1977, participants there marched through city streets for the first time.

In the late 1970s, advocates for gay and lesbian rights were given an impetus by the first major backlash against local gay rights legislation, in the form of the singer Anita Bryant's "Save Our Children" campaign in Dade County, Florida. That campaign, an antigay ballot initiative in California, and the assassination of Harvey Milk, the first openly gay member of San Francisco's Board of Supervisors, all gave momentum to the young movement. In 1979, the first major gay and lesbian march on Washington drew 100,000 marchers, and in its aftermath new organizations for GLBT people of color were formed.

San Francisco Supervisor Harvey Milk is seen in San Francisco's seventh annual Gay Freedom Day Parade, 1978. © AP / Wide World Photos.

VISIBILITY AND GAY LIBERATION POLITICS

These early marches were rooted in a new political strategy that emphasized the issue of *visibility.* "The best advertisement for Gay Liberation," declared one writer in a gay liberation newspaper in 1971, "is two gay lovers holding hands walking down the street." Achieving visibility became an important political end for post-Stonewall gay liberationists because, in their own political analysis, their *invisibility* was the main obstacle to progress in efforts to organize a political movement. The notion that one had a political obligation to disclose one's homosexuality publicly—that is, to "come out of the closet"—was, as many scholars have noted, a historically specific development of the late 1960s and early 1970s. Yet gay liberationists insisted not only that gays had an obligation to come out, but that they should assert "the right to be gay, anytime, anyplace," as one manifesto put it.

The idea that people had the right to be visibly gay in public challenged deeply entrenched forms of spatial power that were specific to mid-twentieth century American cities. If the rioters at the Stonewall Inn in June 1969 were claiming a right to socialize in commercial spaces (which had long been the most important institutions of both gay and lesbian life), the marchers of the 1970s and beyond made a related, but distinct, spatial claim by asserting their right to be gay in the streets. Gay men in this period were routinely entrapped by police officers in public places and arrested for solicitation, and gays, lesbians and others who transgressed against gender norms in public were subject to harassment and violence.

Accounts of the earliest gay pride parades testify that they held a special significance for gay people because they were so fundamentally visible and public. Coming out posed tremendous risks for gay people: "You had to be very outrageous or very radical to come out back then," one gay man recalls. "It was a death-defying act, it really was." Above all, coming out to one's entire circle of friends and acquaintances likely entailed giving up the ability to manage meticulously "who knew" and who didn't. Those who came out were irreversibly marked as homosexuals, and in many spheres of life such marking invited serious consequences. Gay activists believed that gay pride parades would challenge the dominant image of gay people among straight people as guilt-ridden and mentally unstable: "The fact that homosexuals are marching in the streets in large numbers, unafraid and unashamed, forces heterosexuals to re-evaluate their attitudes," one writer claimed in 1972.

For politically active gays and lesbians in the early 1970s, the parade was politically important not only for gay participants but perhaps even more for gay *non*participants. The activist Don Jackson, who helped plan and promote the first "Christopher Street West" parade in that city in 1972, claimed that "most of all, the parade is for closet queens." He wrote in the city's major important gay newspaper, "The reaction of many closet queens on seeing the parade on TV or reading about it, is to conclude that if my brothers and sisters are out unashamedly marching in the streets and getting away with it, so can I. One small town super-closet case attended the L.A. parade last year. Afterwards he said, 'I'll be damned if I'll live a lie, pretending to be something I'm not anymore. If my employer and friends don't like me the way I am, they can shove it.'" He also claimed that publicity and news accounts of the San Francisco parade would be helpful for gay teenagers, "especially in the small towns," with little access to an urban gay culture that was carefully hidden from view.

URBAN CULTURE AND GAY IDENTITY

For all its revolutionary aspects, the idea of the gay pride parade seemed politically plausible, and remains politically effective, partly because it was in some sense very conventional. In ways that its organizers did not fully articulate, it constituted an effort to integrate gays and lesbians into the existing schema of American urban culture. Important and accessible frameworks for the inclusion of ethnic minorities in urban politics already existed, and gay activists drew on these models. Ethnic parades and street festivals tied to the religious and cultural calendars of Americans of Italian, Irish, Puerto Rican, Greek, Russian, and Caribbean descent had long been part of American urban culture. Indeed, such festivities have constituted a critical way in which people of various backgrounds have asserted their right to belong in a diverse society. It was in part precisely by deploying the post–World War II politics of the urban "melting pot," and by analogizing themselves to an ethnic minority group pursuing full citizenship, that gays and lesbians achieved their stated aim of increasing their visibility.

The emergence of gay pride parades, then, is historically linked to the broader history of cities. White ethnic groups were, in growing numbers, abandoning the cities by the early 1970s, but young gays and lesbians were flocking to the cities at that very time. The rise of gay politics within American urban politics in the 1970s reflects, in an important sense, one way in which some gays and lesbians who identified strongly with the nascent gay liberation movement began to diverge from the broad pattern of white suburbanization. They tended, that is, to live separately from their biological families, and they maintained a preference for urban living when nongay whites were choosing to move elsewhere. Moreover, because relatively few openly gay people were then raising children, they did not, for the most part, have an immediate personal stake in conflicts over public school integration and other issues that divided urban political constituencies along racial lines in the 1960s and 1970s.

Gay pride parades also drew explicitly, and crucially, on gay and lesbian subcultural traditions of spectacle and camp. Spatialized forms of queer spectacle were already highly developed by the early 1970s, including outrageous costuming and theatricality, gender transgression, and carnivalesque erotic sociability;

gay pride parades interacted with these traditions by expanding the scale upon which they could operate as political strategies. In many cities, Halloween had long been a holiday within gay communities because police typically did not arrest people for wearing cross-gender clothing on that evening. Even after San Francisco held its first gay pride parade, the *San Francisco Chronicle* noted that "Halloween is the gay Mardi Gras, the night when hundreds of homosexuals come out of the closet to play transvestite," and Halloween remains a major holiday and cultural event today in San Francisco's best-known gay district, the Castro. In short, in spite of the tendency of the "gay liberation" generation of the 1970s to represent itself as the first generation of lesbian and gay people ever to develop themselves into a political force, pride parades succeeded in part because they fused conventional American ethnic and gay political traditions. The gay pride parade in effect relocated, in city streets, certain subcultural forms that had long been deeply entwined with queers' efforts to claim spatial "agency," even when they were largely confined, at least among middle-class gays and lesbians, to bars, nightclubs, and apartment parties.

THE AIDS CRISIS

In the 1980s, many pride marches and parades became politically charged once again, as the AIDS crisis struck the nation's urban gay communities. With tens of thousands of gay men sick and dying from the virus, radical activists formed ACT UP, which staged numerous, highly disruptive public protests, modeled after the media "zaps" pioneered by the Gay Activists Alliance in the early 1970s. The second March on Washington, held in 1987, attracted a crowd of about half a million. It featured the first public display of the NAMES Memorial AIDS Quilt on the National Mall, which later traveled to various parts of the country and became an unusually visible and accessible symbol of AIDS activism. In addition, the march witnessed the arrest of over 800 demonstrators outside the U.S. Supreme Court, which had upheld state sodomy laws the previous year in *Bowers v. Hardwick.*

COMMERCIALIZATION AND THE POLITICS OF ASSIMILATION

Numerous controversies in the history of gay pride parades can be understood as arising precisely because parades brought the gay world into the full view of the heterosexual majority—and thus made visible aspects of gay community life that some gays and lesbians thought would be better concealed. In large part, these controversies have revolved around drag queens, camp culture, and varieties of transgender experience and performance. The increasing visibility of queer Americans in the late twentieth century led to vivid encounters

The AIDS quilt is displayed at the National Mall in Washington, D.C. Courtesy of Corbis.

between gay men and religious conservative activists, who formed a growing backlash against gay rights and other changes in the late twentieth century that they associated with moral decay.

According to Martin Duberman, parade organizer Craig Rodwell insisted that the first Christopher Street Liberation Day Parade, held in 1970, be "a grass-roots project uncontaminated by any connection to commercial interests"; the parade's costs totaled about $1,000. Today, by constrast, New York's parade receives "platinum" corporate sponsorship from Bud Light, Bacardi Limon, and a few other donors, and lesser levels of sponsorship from a host of airlines, gym and fitness chains, media outlets and cable channels, Web sites, banks, and condom and lubricant manufacturers, as well as several "circuit parties" (themselves annually scheduled, hedonistic parties for well-heeled, jet-setting gay men). In addition, New York's pride parade was altered in recent years so that it reaches an endpoint not in its original destination of Central Park, but in the West Village—a historic district and the site of the Stonewall riots, but also a commercial area, where numerous bar and nightclub owners today charge hefty fees for entrance to post-parade parties. The pride organization itself, Heritage of Pride, Inc., sponsors a private party in public parkland along the Hudson River, with ticket prices ranging from $40 to $120. Parade sponsors defend these actions, arguing rightly that in an age when many municipal budgets face severe strains, corporate sponsorship is the only way to recoup the enormous logistical and material costs of assembling such a complex and massive public event.

Gay pride parades were already undergoing expansion and commercialization in their early years. At the time, however, radical activists complained not that there was too much business involvement, but too little, and within their moral economy business involvement was both necessary *and* desirable. Indeed, even *before* San Francisco's first parade was held, the chairpersons of the city's pride parade committee took it upon themselves to "absolutely disavow" a leaflet distributed by certain Gay Activists Alliance radicals, which seemed to constitute an "attempt to boycott, picket, or coerce into submission any Gay business in order to compel their support for the parade." Yet the parade organizers added this caveat to their repudiation of gay consumer power: "(We are not so choosy about straight businesses; they have had our money for years, a little return is not too much to ask)."

Increasing commercialization was closely linked to the expansion of the scale of the parades themselves. In 1970, perhaps 2,000 to 5,000 attended the first Christopher Street Liberation Day Parade. San Francisco's parade, initially limited to the downtown district, was altered in 1976 so that it progressed through the Polk Street gay commercial district and ended in the Castro, home to a growing number of gay businesses. Two years later, in 1978, a quarter of a million people attended the parade, the largest attendance yet seen at any gay or lesbian event in the world. In Seattle, a group of gay business owners, the Greater Seattle Business Association (GSBA), sought in March 1982 to gain control over the annual march's planning and content, to change its name from a "march" to a "parade," and to move it from downtown Seattle to the growing gay commercial district. Although the GSBA declared it would pay for the parade's costs, it also sought to charge fees to groups seeking to join, and many member businesses expected to reap increased profits from the event's relocation.

The institution of corporate sponsorship reflects the disinvestment of public funds from America's major cities. Yet it also requires businesses to adopt nondiscrimination policies and offer domestic partner benefits to their gay and lesbian employees in order to target gay consumers, and many sponsors also donate funds to queer health and arts organizations. To be sure, corporate advertising often facilitates the belief that homosexuals are elite consumers, uniformly members of the professional class and responsible for the gentrification of urban neighborhoods. Recently economists have begun to challenge this stereotype with the first careful studies of the economic lives of gay and lesbian Americans. Yet the gay press has an incentive for maintaining the myth.

Even as they have been commercialized, gay pride parades have continued to be lively, vital celebrations, riven by controversy and protest from grass-roots radical groups such as ACT UP (in the 1980s), Queer Nation (in the 1990s), and Gay Shame (today). "Dyke marches" are today held in many large cities without a permit on the day before the pride parade, and in many cities Black Pride and other events celebrating queers of color have been added to the calendar.

FURTHER READING

Carter, David. *Stonewall: The Riots that Sparked the Gay Revolution.* New York: St. Martins, 2004.

Duberman, Martin. *Stonewall.* New York: Dutton, 1993.

Stein, Mark. *City of Sisterly and Brotherly Loves: Lesbian and Gay Philadelphia, 1945–1972.* Chicago: University of Chicago Press, 2000.

Teal, Donn. *The Gay Militants.* New York: Stein and Day, 1971.

Timothy Stewart-Winter